THE ALEXIAD

THE ALEXIAD

OF THE PRINCESS
ANNA COMNENA

*BEING THE HISTORY OF
THE REIGN OF HER FATHER,
ALEXIUS I, EMPEROR OF THE ROMANS,
1081–1118 A.D.*

TRANSLATED BY

ELIZABETH A. S. DAWES

LONDON
ROUTLEDGE & KEGAN PAUL LTD
1967

First published in Great Britain 1928
by Kegan Paul, Trench Trubner & Co. Ltd

Reissued 1967
by Routledge & Kegan Paul Ltd
Broadway House, 68-74 Carter Lane, EC4

Printed in Great Britain
by the Alden Press (Oxford) Ltd

CONTENTS

INTRODUCTION

THE "Alexiad" of Anna Comnena has long been used as a source of information by historians of the Byzantine Empire and by writers on the First Crusade, and numerous extracts from it have been quoted and translated, yet a complete English translation of it has not been published before.

It was to supply what appeared to me a regrettable omission that I attempted to fill the gap and, as I proceeded with the work, I became more and more interested, for the book gives a picture of wonderful mental and physical energy in the person of its hero, the Emperor Alexius, and helps us to realize the enormous difficulties which confronted a Byzantine Emperor at this period.

Readers of Sir Walter Scott's *Count Robert of Paris* may also be glad to have a full translation of a work to which he so often alludes.

The present translation is not a free adaptation of the original but is as literal as a translation can well be ; hence there is much repetition of words and phrases, for I have striven to reproduce Anna's style as far as possible.

The text on which I have based my version is that of Aug. Reifferscheid in the Teubner edition of 1884.

The proper names (with the exception of those which have acquired a definite English form) I have in most cases transiterated exactly and then added in a footnote the spelling of them as found in Bury's edition of Gibbon, e.g. Apelchasem = Abul-kassim.

I have dispensed with an historical introduction in view of the fact that the Oxford University Press is shortly publishing a book by Mrs. Georgina Buckler, Ph.D., entitled *Anna Comnena : a Study*, which deals exhaustively with the chief points of interest raised by the Alexiad.

In conclusion, I wish to acknowledge my deep indebtedness to Professor F. H. Marshall, for he looked over my work in manuscript, and gave me many valuable suggestions and kind help in the elucidation of difficulties. And I must also express my grateful thanks to my sister, Mary C. Dawes, M.A., for her patient help in the revision and in the perusal of the proof-sheets.

ELIZABETH A. S. DAWES.

THE ALEXIAD

PREFACE

I

TIME in its irresistible and ceaseless flow carries along on its flood all created things, and drowns them in the depths of obscurity, no matter if they be quite unworthy of mention, or most noteworthy and important, and thus, as the tragedian says, " he brings from the darkness all things to the birth, and all things born envelops in the night."

But the tale of history forms a very strong bulwark against the stream of time, and to some extent checks its irresistible flow, and, of all things done in it, as many as history has taken over, it secures and binds together, and does not allow them to slip away into the abyss of oblivion.

Now, I recognized this fact. I, Anna, the daughter of two royal personages, Alexius and Irene, born and bred in the purple. I was not ignorant of letters, for I carried my study of Greek to the highest pitch, and was also not unpractised in rhetoric ; I perused the works of Aristotle and the dialogues of Plato carefully, and enriched my mind by the "quaternion" of learning. (I must let this out and it is not bragging to state what nature and my zeal for learning have given me, and the gifts which God apportioned to me at birth and time has contributed).

However, to resume—I intend in this writing of mine to recount the deeds done by my father for they should certainly not be lost in silence, or swept away, as it were, on the current of time into the sea of forgetfulness, and I shall recount not only his achievements as Emperor, but also the services he rendered to various Emperors before he himself received the sceptre.

II These deeds I am going to relate, not in order to shew off my proficiency in letters, but that matters of such importance should not be left unattested for future generations. For even the greatest of deeds, if not haply preserved in written words and handed down to remembrance, become extinguished in the obscurity of silence.

Now, my father, as the actual facts prove, knew both how to command and how to obey the rulers within reasonable limits. And though I have chosen to narrate his doings, yet I fear that the tongues of suspicion and detraction will whisper that writing my father's history is only self-laudation, and that the historical facts, and any praise I bestow on them, are mere falsehoods and empty panegyric. Again, on the other hand, if he himself were to supply the materials, and facts themselves force me to censure some of his actions, not because of him, but from the very nature of the deed, I dread the scoffers who will cast Noah's son, Ham, in my teeth, for they look at everything askew, and owing to their malice and envy, do not discern clearly what is right, but will " blame the blameless " as Homer says. But he who undertakes the " rôle " of an historian must sink his personal likes and dislikes, and often award the highest praise to his enemies when their actions demand it, and often, too, blame his nearest relations if their errors require it. He must never shirk either blaming his friends or praising his enemies. I should counsel both parties, those attacked by us and our partisans alike, to take comfort from the fact that I have sought the evidence of the actual deeds themselves, and the testimony of those who have seen the actions, and the men and their actions—the fathers of some of the men now living, and the grandfathers of others were actual eye-witnesses.

III   The reason which finally determined me to write my father's history was the following. My lawful husband was the Cæsar Nicephorus, a scion of the clan of the Bryennii, a man who far outshone his contemporaries by his surpassing beauty, his superior intelligence, and his accurate speech. To look at him, or to listen to him, was a pure delight. But I must not let my tale wander from its path, so for the present let us keep to the main story. My husband, as I said, was most remarkable in every way ; he accompanied my brother John, the Emperor, on several other expeditions against the barbarians . . . as well as on the one against . . . who held the city of Antioch. As Nicephorus could not abide neglecting his literary work, he wrote several excellent monographs even during times of stress and trouble. But his task of predilection was that enjoyed by the Queen, to wit, a compilation of the history of the reign of Alexius, Emperor of the Romans, and my father, and to set out the doings of his reign in books whenever opportunity granted him a short respite from strife and warfare, and the chance of turning his mind to his history, and literary studies. Moreover, he approached this subject from an earlier period (for in this detail too he obeyed the will of our mistress), and starting from Diogenes,[1] Emperor of the Romans, he worked down to the man about whom he had himself purposed to write.

At the accession of Diogenes my father had just entered upon his brilliant youth, and before this was not even a full-grown boy, and had done nothing worthy of recording, unless, forsooth, the deeds of his childhood were made the theme of a panegyric.

Such then was the Cæsar's intention as his own writing shews ; but his hopes were not fulfilled, and he did not complete his history. He brought it down to the Emperor Nicephorus (III) Botaniates, and opportunity forbade his carrying it further, thus causing loss to the events he meant to describe, and depriving his readers of a great pleasure. For this reason, I myself undertook to chronicle my father's doings, that the coming generations should not overlook deeds of such importance.

Now, the harmonious structure and great charm of the Cæsar's writings are well-known to all who have chanced to take a look at his books. However, as I have already mentioned, when he had got as far as my father's reign, and sketched out a draft of it, and brought it back to us half-finished from abroad, he also, alas ! brought back with him a fatal disease. This was induced, maybe, by the endless discomfort of a soldier's life, or by his over-many expeditions, or again, from his overwhelming anxiety about us, for worrying was innate in him, and his troubles were incessant. In addition to these causes, the varieties and severities of climate experienced, all contributed to mix the fatal draught for him. For he started hence on an expedition against the Syrians and Cilicians when seriously out of health ; from Syria he went on ill to the Cilicians, from them to the Pamphylians, from the Pamphylians to the Lydians, and Lydia sent him on to Bithynia, who finally returned him to us and to the Queen of cities suffering from an internal tumour caused by his incessant sufferings. Yet, ill as he was, he was anxious to tell the tragic story of his adventures, but was unable to do so, partly because of his disease, and partly because

[1]Romanus IV Diogenes.

we forbade it through fear that the effort of talking might cause the tumour to burst.

IV Having written so far, dizziness overwhelms my soul, and tears blind my eyes. Oh ! what a counsellor the Roman Empire has lost ! Oh, for his accurate understanding of affairs, all of which he had gained from experience ! And his knowledge of literature, and his varied acquaintance with both native and foreign learning ! Think, too, of the grace of his figure and beauty of face, which would have befitted not only a king, as the saying goes, but even a more powerful, nay, a divine person !

To turn to myself—I have been conversant with dangers ever since my birth " in the purple," so to say ; and fortune has certainly not been kind to me, unless you were to count it a smile of kind fortune to have given me " emperors " as parents, and allowing me to be born " in the purple room," for all the rest of my life has been one long series of storms and revolutions. Orpheus, indeed, could move stones, trees, and all inanimate nature, by his singing ; Timotheus, too, the flute-player, by piping an " orthian " tune to Alexander, incited the Macedonian thereby to snatch up his arms and sword ; but the tale of my woes would not cause a movement in place, nor rouse men to arms and war, but they would move the hearer to tears, and compel sympathy from animate, and even inanimate, nature. Verily, my grief for my Cæsar and his unexpected death have touched my inmost soul, and the wound has pierced to the profoundest depths of my being. All previous misfortunes compared with this insatiable calamity I count literally as a single small drop compared with this Atlantic Ocean, this turbulent Adriatic Sea of trouble : they were, methinks, but preludes to this, mere smoke and heat to forewarn me of this fiery furnace and indescribable blaze ; the small daily sparks foretold this terrible conflagration. Oh ! thou fire which, though unfed, dost reduce my heart to ashes ! Thou burnest and art ever kept alight in secret, yet dost not consume. Though thou scorchest my heart thou givest me the outward semblance of being unburnt, though thy fingers of fire have gripped me even to the marrow of my bones, and to the dividing of my soul ! However, I see that I have let my feelings carry me away from my subject, but the mention of my Cæsar and my grief for him have instilled devastating sorrow into me.

Now I will wipe away my tears and recover myself from my sorrow and continue my task, and thus in the words of the tragedian : " I shall have double cause for tears, as a woman who in misfortune remembers former misfortune." To have as my object the publication of the life of so great and virtuous a King will be a reminder of his wondrous achievements, and these force me to shed warm tears, and the whole world will weep with me. For to recall him, and make his reign known, will be a subject of lamentation to me, but will also serve to remind others of the loss they have sustained.

Now I must begin my father's history at some definite point, and the best point will be that from which my narrative can be absolutely clear and based on fact.

PREFACE

BOOK I

I

THE Emperor Alexius, who was also my father, had been of great service to the Roman Empire even before he reached the throne, for he started campaigning as early as during the reign of Romanus Diogenes. Amongst his contemporaries he shewed himself remarkable, and a great lover of danger. In his fourteenth year he was anxious to join the Emperor Diogenes on the extremely arduous campaign he was conducting against the Persians, and by this very longing he declared his animosity against the barbarians, and shewed that, if he ever should come to blows with them, he would make his sword drunk with their blood ; of such a warlike temper was the boy. However, on that occasion the Emperor Diogenes did not allow him to accompany him, as a heavy sorrow had befallen Alexius' mother, for she was then mourning the death of her firstborn son, Manuel, a man who had done great and admirable deeds for his country. In order that she might not be quite inconsolable, for she did not yet know where she had buried the elder of her sons, and if she sent the younger to the war, she would be afraid of something untoward happening to the lad, and might not even know in what part of the world he fell, for these reasons he compelled the boy Alexius to return to his mother. So on that occasion he was indeed parted from his fellow-soldiers, though sorely against his will, but the future opened out to him countless opportunities for valiant deeds ; for under the Emperor Michael Ducas, after the deposition of the Emperor Diogenes, he shewed of what mettle he was made in his war against Ursel.

Now this man was a Frank by birth who had been enrolled in the Roman Army, reached a high pitch of prosperity, and after gathering a band, or rather quite a considerable army, of men from his own country, and also of other races, he immediately became a formidable tyrant. For when the hegemony of the Romans had received several checks, and

7

the luck of the Turks was in the ascendancy, and the Romans
had been driven back like dust shaken from their feet, at that
moment this man too attacked the Empire. Apart from his
tyrannical nature, what more especially incited him to openly
establishing his tyranny just then was the depressed state of
the imperial affairs, and he laid waste nearly all the Eastern
provinces.

Although many were entrusted with the war against
him, men of high reputation for bravery and of very great
knowledge of war and fighting, yet he openly baffled even
their long experience. For sometimes he would take the
offensive himself and rout his opponents by his meteor-like
attacks, and at others he obtained help from the Turks, and
was quite irresistible in his onrushes, so that he actually
overpowered some of the most powerful chieftains, and
utterly confounded their phalanxes. At that time, my father
Alexius was under his brother, and openly served as lieutenant
under this man, who was invested with the command of all
the armies, both of the East and the West.

Then, just when the affairs of the Romans were in this
critical condition, with this barbarian rushing upon everything like a thunderbolt, my brilliant father Alexius was
thought of as the one man able to resist him, and appointed
absolute commander by the Emperor Michael. Accordingly
he summoned up all his shrewdness and the experience he
had gained as general and soldier, and that too, by the way,
he had not had much time to gather. (But thanks to his
exceeding love of industry and ever alert intellect, the picked
men among the Romans considered him to have reached the
acme of military experience, and regarded him as that famous
Roman Æmilius, or Scipio, or Hannibal the Carthaginian,
for he was quite young, and had still " the first down on his
cheeks " as the saying goes). This young man captured
Ursel as he rushed with might against the Romans, and restored the affairs of the East within the space of a few days ;
for he was quick at discovering what was expedient, and still
quicker in executing it. The manner of his capturing Ursel
is told at length by the Cæsar in the second book of his history
of his own times ; but I will relate it too in as far as it concerns
my history.

II The barbarian Tutach had just then come down with
a considerable army from the depths of the East to ravage
the Roman territory. Ursel was often hard pressed by the
general, and losing one fortress after another in spite of his

large army and his men being excellently and generously
equipped, because in ingenuity he was far surpassed by my
father Alexius, and he therefore determined to seek refuge
for a time with Tutach.

Finally, in absolute despair, he arranged a meeting with
Tutach, offered him friendship, and earnestly solicited him
to form an alliance. However, the general Alexius met this
by a counter-stratagem, and was the quicker in winning over
the barbarian, and attracting him to his side by words and
gifts and every means and device. For he was inventive
beyond ordinary men, and could find a way out of the most
impossible situations. Certainly the most effective of
his methods for conciliating Tutach was, speaking broadly, a
kind of offering the right hand of friendship ; his words were
these :—" The two, your Sultan and my Emperor, are friends !
This barbarian Ursel is lifting his hand against both, and he
is a most dangerous foe to both, for he keeps on attacking
the latter, and is always stealing away a bit here and there
from the Roman Empire, and, on the other hand, he is
robbing Persia of parts of Persia which might have been
preserved to her. In all this he uses great art, for at present
he is overshadowing me by your help, and then later, at a
propitious moment, he will leave me when he thinks himself
secure, and turn round again and attack you. So if you will
listen to me, you should, when Ursel next comes to you,
seize him with superior numbers and send him captive to us.
If you do this," he continued, " you will gain three things :—
firstly, such a sum of money as no one ever gained before ;
secondly, you will win in addition the goodwill of the Emperor ;
and as a result you will quickly reach the acme of prosperity ;
and thirdly, your Sultan will be greatly pleased at the removal
of so formidable a foe, who practised violence against Romans
and Turks alike." This was the tenor of the despatch sent
to the afore-mentioned Tutach by my father, at that time
Commander-in-Chief of the Roman Army. Together with it
he also sent some members of the noblest families as hostages ;
and at an agreed moment and for a sum of money, he persuaded
Tutach's barbarian followers to seize Ursel ; and this they did
quickly, and after his capture he was forwarded to the General
at Amaseia.

But in the meantime the money was slow to come in, for
Alexius himself had no fund wherewith to pay it off, and the
sums due from the Emperor did not arrive, consequently,
it did not only " journey at slow speed," as the tragedian

says, but it did not come at all! Tutach's followers meanwhile were insistent in their demands for the money promised
or for the surrender of the man they had sold and said that he
should be allowed to return to the place where he had been
seized ; and my father had no means of paying the purchase-
price. After spending a whole night in the greatest perplexity,
he decided to borrow the sum from the inhabitants of Amaseia.
At the break of day, though it was a hard task, he summoned
them all, especially the most influential and the richest men,
and fixing his eyes on them chiefly, he said : " You all know
how this barbarian has treated all the cities of the Armenian
theme, how many villages he has sacked, upon how many
persons he has inflicted intolerable atrocities, and how much
money he has stolen from you. But now the moment has
come for freeing yourselves from his ill-treatment if you wish.
Accordingly we must not let him slip, for you see, I suppose,
that, by the will of God above all and by our own energy, this
barbarian is now our prisoner. But Tutach, his captor, is
asking us for payment, and we are utterly penniless, for we
are in a foreign country, have been fighting against the barbarian for a considerable time, and have spent all our income.
If the Emperor had not been so far off, or the barbarian
had granted us respite, I should have endeavoured to have
the money fetched from the capital ; but since, as you yourselves know, nothing of this is practicable, it is you who must
contribute this money, and whatever you subscribe, shall be
repaid you from the Emperor at my hands." No sooner had
he said this than he was hooted and his words excited a terrible
uproar, for the Amaseians were moved to rebellion. Certain
evilly-disposed and daring fellows who were clever agitators
stirred up this tumult.

A great confusion thereupon arose, for one part insisted
that Ursel should be kept prisoner, and stirred up the multitude
to lay hold of him, while the other party made a great noise
(as is ever the case with a mixed rabble), and wished to seize
Ursel, and free him from his chains. The General, seeing
so large a mob raging, recognized that his affairs were indeed
in a parlous state, yet he was in no wise cast down, but taking
courage, quieted the multitude with his hand. After a long
time and with difficulty he silenced them, and addressing the
mob, he said : " I marvel, men of Amaseia, that you are so
utterly blind to the machinations of these men who deceive
you, and purchase their own safety with your blood, and
continually cause you some hurt. For of what benefit is

Ursel's tyranny to you, unless you count murders and mutila-
tions and the maiming of limbs as such ? Now these men, the
authors of your calamities, have kept their own fortunes
intact by paying court to the barbarian on the one hand,
and on the other they have received a glut of gifts from the
Emperor by representing to him that they had not surrendered
you and the town to the barbarian ; and that too though
they have never yet taken any account of you. For this
reason they wish to support Ursel's tyranny, so that by
fawning upon him with good wishes they may preserve their
own skins intact, and also demand honours and emoluments
from the Emperor. Should, however, any revolt occur,
they will again keep themselves out of the business, and
kindle the Emperor's wrath against you. But if you will
follow my advice, you will bid these stirrers-up of sedition
now go hang. Return quietly to your respective homes,
reflect on my proposition, and thus you will recognize who is
counselling you to your best advantage."

III On hearing these words, they changed their minds as
quickly as " heads become tails," and went home. But the
General, well aware that a crowd is wont to change its mind
in a twinkling, especially if urged on by malicious men,
feared that during the night they might come upon him with
fell intent, fetch out Ursel from prison, release him from his
bonds, and let him go. As his forces were insufficient to
resist such an attack, he devised the following Palamedian
plan : he pretended to have Ursel apparently blinded.
Ursel was laid flat on the ground, the executioner applied
the iron, while the victim howled and groaned like a lion
roaring ; but all this was only a feint of depriving him of
his sight, for he who apparently was being blinded had been
ordered to shout and shriek, and he who seemingly was
gouging out the eyes, to stare harshly at his prisoner on the
ground, and do everything savagely, and yet only to act the
blinding. And so Ursel was blinded, yet not blinded, and the
rabble clapped their hands, and the blinding of Ursel was
buzzed about everywhere. This bit of play-acting persuaded
the whole multitude, natives and foreigners alike, to swarm
in like bees to pay their contributions. For the whole point
of Alexius' device was that those who were disinclined to
give money, and plotted to rescue Ursel from Alexius' my
father's hands, should be foiled in their expectations, as he
had now made their plot futile ; and, in consequence, failing
in their plan of the previous day, would adopt his plan,

making him their friend, and averting the Emperor's wrath. Thus the admirable commander, having got Ursel into his power, kept him like a lion in a cage, with bandages still over his eyes as symbol of his supposed blinding. Even so, he was not satisfied with what had been accomplished, nor did he relax over the rest of the business, as if he had gained sufficient glory, but he annexed several more cities and fortresses, and placed under the protection of the Emperor those which had fared badly during Ursel's régime. Then he turned his horse's head, and rode straight to the Royal City. But when he had reached his grandfather's city he allowed himself and the whole army a short rest from their many labours, and after that he manifested as marvellous a deed as Heracles did in the rescue of Admetus' wife, Alcestis.

For a certain Docianus, nephew of the former Emperor, Isaac Comnenus, and cousin of this Alexius (a man too of good standing, both by birth and worth), seeing Ursel bearing the marks of blinding, and led by the hand, heaved a deep sigh, burst into tears over him, and denounced the General's cruelty. Yea, he heaped blame upon him, and upbraided him for taking the sight of such a noble fellow and a downright hero, whom he ought to have left unpunished. To this Alexius answered at the time, " My dear friend, wait a bit, and you shall hear the reasons for his blinding " ; and in a little he took him and Ursel into a small room, uncovered the latter's face, and shewed him Ursel's eyes gleaming fierily. At this sight, Docianus was struck dumb with amazement, and did not know what to make of this miracle. He repeatedly applied his hands to Ursel's eyes, in case what he had seen was only a dream perchance, or a magic portent, or some other new invention of the kind ; but when he grasped the kindness his cousin had shewn to the man, and the artfulness combined with the kindness, he was overjoyed, and embraced and kissed him repeatedly, changing his wonder into joy. And the Emperor Michael, and his suite, and indeed everybody, felt just the same about it.

IV Afterwards, the Emperor Nicephorus (Botaniates) who had now obtained the throne, sent him away again—to the West this time, against Nicephorus Bryennius, who was upsetting the whole of the West by putting the crown on his own head, and proclaiming himself Emperor of the Romans. For scarcely had Michael Ducas been deposed, and adopted the high-priestly alb and humeral in place of the imperial diadem and cloak, than Botaniates took his place on the imperial throne, married the princess Maria (as I will relate more circumstantially further on), and undertook the management of the Kingdom.   But Nicephorus Bryennius, on the other hand, who had been appointed Duke of Dyrrachium in the time of the Emperor Michael, had designs on the throne even before Nicephorus became Emperor, and meditated a revolt against Michael. The " why " and "wherefore " of this I need not relate, as his revolt has previously been recounted in the Cæsar's history. And yet it is absolutely necessary for me to narrate briefly how he used Dyrrachium as a jumping-off place for over-running all the Western provinces, how he brought them under his sway, and also the manner of his capture. But anyone who wishes for details of this revolt we refer to the Cæsar. Bryennius was a very clever warrior, as well as of most illustrious descent, conspicuous by height of stature, and beauty of face, and preeminent among his fellows by the weightiness of his judgment, and the strength of his arms. He was, indeed, a man fit for kingship, and his persuasive powers, and his skill in conversation, were such as to draw all to him even at first sight ; consequently, by unanimous consent both of soldiers and civilians, he was accorded the first place and deemed worthy to rule over both the Eastern and Western dominions.   On his approaching any town, it would receive him with suppliant hands, and send him on to the next with acclaim.   Not only Botaniates was disturbed by this news, but it also created a ferment in the home-army, and reduced the whole kingdom to despair ; and, consequently, it was decided to dispatch my father, Alexius Comnenus, lately elected " Domestic of the Schools," against Bryennius with all available forces. In these regions the fortunes of the Roman Empire had sunk to their lowest ebb.   For the armies of the East were dispersed in all directions, because the Turks had over-spread, and gained command of, nearly all the countries between the Euxine Sea and the Hellespont, and the Ægean and Syrian Seas, and the various bays, especially those which wash Pamphylia, Cilicia, and empty themselves into the Egyptian Sea. Such was the position of the Eastern armies, whilst in the West, so many legions had flocked to Bryennius' standard that the Roman Empire was left with quite a small and inadequate army.   There still remained to her a few " Immortals " who had only recently grasped spear and sword, and a few soldiers from Coma, and a Celtic regiment, that had shrunk to a small number of men. These were given to Alexius, my father, and at the same time allied troops were called for from the Turks, and the Emperor's Council ordered Alexius to start and engage in battle with Bryennius, for he relied not so much on the army accompanying him as on the man's ingenuity and cleverness in military matters. Alexius did not wait for the allies as he heard that the enemy was pushing on fast, but armed himself and his army, marched out from the Royal City, and passing through Thrace, pitched his camp without palisades or trenches near the river Halmyrus. For learning that Bryennius was bivouacking in the plains of the Cedoctus, he determined to interpose a considerable distance between his own and the enemy's armies. For he was not able to face Bryennius, for fear that the state of his forces might be detected, and the enemy have an opportunity of observing of what numbers his army consisted. Because he was on the point of fighting with inexperienced against experienced warriors, and with few against many, he abandoned the idea of making a bold and open attack, and intended to win a victory by stealth.

V   Since our story has now placed these two in opposition, Bryennius and my father, Alexius Comnenus, both brave men (for neither was a whit behind the other in courage, nor did the experience of the one surpass that of the other), it is worth our while to place them in their lines and hostile array, and thence to view the fortune of war. They certainly were both handsome and brave men, and were their bravery and experience weighed, the balance would stand level; but we must try to understand how fortune inclined it to one side. Bryennius, in addition to his confidence in his forces, was protected by their experience and orderliness, whereas Alexius, on the other hand, centred but few, and those very meagre, hopes on his army, but as counter-defence, could rely on the strength of his scientific knowledge and his strategic devices.

Now when they were aware of each other, and the right moment for battle had come, Bryennius, on being informed that Alexius Comnenus had cut off his approaches and was encamped near Calaura, drew up his troops in the following order and marched against him. He posted the main army on the right and left wings, and gave the command of the right to his brother John; the men in this wing numbered 5,000, and were Italians, and those belonging to the detachment of the famous Maniaces, as well as some horse-soldiers from Thessaly, and a detachment, of no mean birth, of the

" Hetaireia." The other, the left wing, was led by Catacalon
Tarchaniotes, and was composed of fully-armed Macedonians
and Thracians, numbering in all about 3,000. Bryennius
himself held the centre of the phalanx, consisting of Macedonians and Thracians, and the picked men of the whole
nobility. All the Thessalians were on horseback (*or* they were
all mounted on Thessalian horses), and what with their iron
cuirasses and helmets on their heads gleaming brightly, the
horses pricking up their ears, and the shields clashing together,
such a brilliant light falling from their persons and their
helmets caused terror. Bryennius too, circling amidst them
like an Ares or Giant, overtopping all the others head and
shoulders by an ell, was a sheer wonder, and object of dread
to the onlookers. Outside this regular army at about two
stades' distance were some allied Scythians, distinguished
by barbaric weapons. And the order given was that when
the enemy came in sight and the trumpet sounded the attack,
the Scythians should at once fall upon them from the rear,
and distress the enemy by thick and continuous showers
of darts, whilst the rest should form in very close order, and
attack with all their might. That was how one general
disposed his men. My father, Alexius Comnenus, on his
side, after examining the lie of the land, placed half his men
in some hollows, and the rest front to front with Bryennius.
When both sections, both the hidden and the invisible, were
in battle array, he aroused the bravery of them individually
by winged words, and enjoined upon the division lying in
ambush to attack suddenly, and dash with the greatest
possible force and violence against the right wing of the
enemy, as soon as they perceived they were to the rear of
them. The so-called " Immortals," and some of the Celtic
troops he reserved for himself, and took command of them
in person. He appointed Catacalon leader of the troops
from Coma and the Turkish forces, and bade him pay special
attention to the Scythians and to counter their incursions.
Such then were the dispositions of the armies. Now, when
Bryennius' army had come near the hollows, then, immediately
on my father, Alexius, giving the signal, the men in ambush
jumped out on them with wild yells and war-cries, and by the
suddenness of their onslaught, each striking and killing
those whom he chanced to meet, they threw the enemy into
a panic, and compelled them to flight. But John Bryennius,
the own brother of the general, mindful hereupon of his
" impetuous strength " and courage, turned his horse with his

curb, and cutting down at a blow the "Immortal" coming at him, stayed the discomfited phalanx, rallied the men, and drove the enemy off. The "Immortals," in their turn, began to flee headlong in some disorder, and many were cut down by the soldiers who were ever behind them.

Then, my father, hurling himself into the midst of the foe, by his valiant struggles did indeed discomfit just that part in which he happened to be, for he struck anyone who approached him, and laid him low at a blow, but he also hoped that some of his soldiers were following with him and protecting him, and so he kept on fighting desperately. But when he saw that his phalanx was by this time utterly broken, and fleeing in all directions, he collected the more courageous souls (who were six in all), and advised them to draw their swords, rush at Bryennius remorselessly, when they got near him, and then, if need be, to die with him. However, a certain Theodotus, a private, who had been my father's servant from childhood, dissuaded him from this plan, characterizing such an attempt as mere foolhardiness. So Alexius turned in the opposite direction, and decided to retire to a short distance from Bryennius' army; then he collected the men personally known to him from the dispersed soldiery, re-organized them, and returned to the work. But before my father could withdraw secretly from the mêlée, the Scythians with many yells and shouts began to harass the men from Coma under Catacalon; and as they had little difficulty in beating these too, and driving them to flight, they turned their minds to looting, and went off on their own devices, for such is the Scythian nation. Before they have even entirely routed their adversary, or consolidated their gain, they spoil their victory by looting. For all the slaves and camp followers who formed the rear of Bryennius' army had pressed forward into the ranks from fear of being killed by the Scythians; and as this crowd was continually augmented by others who had escaped from the hands of the Scythians, no small confusion arose in the ranks, and the standards became commingled. In the meanwhile, my father Alexius, as we said before, was cut off and moving about within Bryennius' army, when he saw one of the royal grooms leading a horse of Bryennius', decked with a purple cloth, and gilt bosses; and moreover, the men holding the large swords which customarily accompany the Emperor were running close beside it. On seeing this he covered his face with his vizor which depended from the rim of his helmet, and rushing with violence against these men with his six soldiers (whom the story has already mentioned), he not only knocked down the groom, but also seized the royal horse, and together with it carried off the swords, and then escaped unnoticed from the army. Arrived in a safe spot he started off the gilt-bedight horse, and the swords which are usually carried either side of the Emperor, and a herald with a very loud voice, bidding him run through the whole army crying out "Bryennius has fallen!" This action brought back to the battle from all quarters many of the scattered soldiers belonging to the army of the Great Domestic of the Schools (to wit, my father), and others it encouraged to carry on. They stood still, where each happened to be, and having turned their eyes behind them were astonished at the unexpected sight. And you might have witnessed a strange sight in their case! for the heads of the horses were pointing forwards, whilst their own faces were turned backwards, and they neither moved forwards, nor did they wish to turn their bridles, but were quite aghast, and at their wits' ends to understand what had occurred. As for the Scythians, they were dreaming of going home, and had no intention of further pursuit. As they were now far away from both armies, they wandered vaguely about where they were with their booty. The proclamation that Bryennius had been taken, and overwhelmed, put courage into the whilom cowards and fugitives, and the announcement gained credibility from the fact that the horse was shewn everywhere with its royal accoutrements, and the large swords all but cried aloud that Bryennius, who should be protected by them, had become the possession of the enemy.

VI Then fortune, too, contributed the following incident to Alexius' success. A detachment of the Turkish allies happened upon Alexius, the Great Domestic, and on hearing that he had restored the battle, and asking where the enemy was, they accompanied him, my father, to a little hill, and when my father pointed out the army, they looked down upon it from an observation tower, as it were. And this was the appearance of Bryennius' army ; the men were all mixed up anyhow, the lines had not yet been re-formed, and, as if they had already carried off the victory, they were acting carelessly and thought themselves out of danger. And they had slackened off chiefly because after the initial rout of our men, my father's contingent of Franks had gone over to Bryennius. For when the Franks dismounted from their horses and offered their right hands to Bryennius, according to their ancestral custom in giving pledges, men came running up towards them from all sides to see what was happening. For like a trumpet-blast the rumour had resounded throughout the army that the Franks had joined them and deserted their Commander-in-Chief, Alexius. The officers with my father, and the newly-arrived Turks, duly noted this state of confusion, and as a result they divided their forces into three parties and ordered two to remain in ambush somewhere on the spot, and the third they commanded to advance against the foe. The whole of this plan was due to Alexius.

The Turks did not attack all together, drawn up regularly into phalanx, but separately and in small groups, standing some distance apart from each other ; then he ordered each squadron to attack, charging the enemy with their horses, and to let loose heavy showers of darts. Following upon the Turks came my father Alexius, the author of this strategy, with as many of his scattered men as the occasion warranted. Next, one of the " Immortals " with Alexius, a hot-headed, venturesome fellow, spurred on his horse, and out-riding the others, dashed at full gallop straight at Bryennius, and thrust his spear with great violence against the latter's breast. Bryennius for his part whipped out his sword quickly from its sheath, and before the spear could be driven home, he cut it in two, and struck his adversary on the collar bone, and bringing down the blow with the whole power of his arm, cut away the man's whole arm, breastplate included.

The Turks, too, one group following up another, overshadowed the army with their showers of darts. Bryennius' men were naturally taken aback by the sudden attack, yet they collected themselves, formed themselves into line, and sustained the shock of the battle, mutually exhorting each other to play the man. The Turks, however, and my father, held their ground for a short time against the enemy, and then planned to retire in regular order to a little distance, in order to lure on the enemy, and draw them by guile to the ambuscade. When they had reached the first ambush, they wheeled round, and met the enemy face to face. Forthwith, at a given signal, those in ambush rode through them like swarms of wasps, from various directions, and with their loud warcries, and shouts, and incessant shooting, not only filled the ears of Bryennius' men with a terrible din, but also utterly obscured their sight by showering arrows upon them from all sides. Hereupon, as the army of Bryennius could no longer put up any resistance (for by now all, both men and horses, were sorely wounded), they turned their standard to retreat, and offered their backs as a target to their foes. But Bryennius himself, although very weary from fighting, shewed his courage and mettle. For at one minute, he would turn to right or left to strike a pursuer, and at the next, carefully and cleverly arrange the details of the retreat. He was assisted by his brother on the one side, and his son on the other, and by their heroic defence on that occasion they seemed to the enemy miraculous.

As Bryennius' horse was now very weary, and unable either to flee or pursue (in fact, it was pretty well at death's door from continuous coursing), he halted it, and, like some brave athlete, stood ready for the grip, and called a challenge to two highborn Turks. One of these struck at him with his spear, but was not quick enough to give him a heavy blow before receiving a heavier one himself from Bryennius' right hand. For Bryennius with his sword succeeded in cutting off the man's hand, which rolled to the ground, spear and all. The second man leapt off his own horse, and like a panther, darted on to that of Bryennius, and planted himself on its flank, and clung tightly to it, and tried to get on its back. Bryennius kept twisting round like an animal in his endeavours to stab him with his sword. However, he did not succeed, for the Turk behind his back escaped all the blows by bending aside. Therefore, when his right hand was exhausted from only encountering emptiness, and the athlete's strength gave out, he surrendered there and then to the whole body of the enemy. So the soldiers seized him, and with a feeling of having won great glory, led him away to Alexius Comnenus, who happened to be standing not far from the spot where Bryennius was captured, and was busy drawing up his own men, and the Turks, into line, and inciting them to battle. News of Bryennius' capture had already been brought by heralds, and then the man himself was placed before the General, and a terrifying object he certainly was, both when fighting, and when captured. And now, having secured Bryennius in this manner, Alexius Comnenus sent him away as the prize of his spear to the Emperor Botaniates, without doing any injury whatsoever to his eyes. For it was not the nature of Alexius to proceed to extremities against his opponents after their capture as he considered that being captured was in itself sufficient punishment, but after their capture he treated them with clemency, friendliness and

generosity. This clemency he now displayed towards
Bryennius, for after his capture he accompanied him a fair
distance, and when they reached the place called . . . he
said to him (for he was anxious to relieve the man's despondency and restore hope in him) : " Let us get off our
horses and sit down and rest awhile." But Bryennius, in
fear of his life, resembled a maniac, and was by no means in
need of rest, for how should a man be who has lost all hope of
life ? And yet he immediately complied with the General's
wish, for a slave readily submits to every command, more
especially if he is a prisoner of war. When the two leaders
had dismounted, Alexius at once lay down on some green
grass, as if on a couch, while Bryennius sat further off, and
rested his head on the roots of a tall oak. My father slept,
but " gentle sleep," as it is called in sweet poetry, did not
visit the other.

But lying there he raised his eyes and saw the sword
hanging from the branches, and as he did not see anybody
about just then, he shook off his despondency, conceived a
daring plan and plotted to kill my father. And the thought
would quickly have been translated into action, had not some
divine power from on high prevented him, which appeased the
fierce emotions of his mind, and forced him to look kindly
at the General. I have often heard the latter tell this tale.
Whoever likes may learn from this how God was guarding the
Comnenus, like a precious object, for a greater dignity,
intending by means of him to restore the fortune of the
Romans. If later on undesirable things happened to
Bryennius, the blame must be laid on certain of the Emperor's
courtiers ; my father was blameless. Such then was the end
of Bryennius' rebellion.

VII But Alexius, the Great Domestic, who was also my
father, was not destined to rest in quiet, but to proceed from
one struggle to another. On his return, Borilus, a barbarian,
and confidant of Botaniates, went out from the city to meet
my father, the Great Domestic, and taking over Bryennius
from him he did to him that which he did. He also brought
an order from the Emperor to my father to proceed against
Basilacius, who in his turn had now assumed the diadem,
and exactly as Bryennius had done, was making the West
seethe with unrest. Now, this man Basilacius, was one of
the most conspicuous for bravery, courage, daring, and bodily
strength, and as he possessed, moreover, a domineering
spirit, he took to himself all the most exalted offices, and as

for honours, he plotted for some and demanded others. And after Bryennius' overthrow, this man became, as it were, his successor, and arrogated to himself the whole business of the tyranny. Starting from Epidamnus (the metropolis of Illyria), he pushed on to the chief city of Thessaly, having subdued all the country on his way, and voted and acclaimed himself Emperor, and Bryennius' roving army following him whithersoever he wished. Besides other admirable qualities, this man had that fine physique, strength of arm, and dignified appearance by which rustics and soldiers are most attracted. For they do not look through to the soul, nor have a keen eye for virtue, but they stop at the outward excellencies of the body, and admire daring, and strength, speed in running, and size, and consider these as fit qualifications for the purple robe and diadem.

Now he had these qualities in no mean measure, as well as a manly, invincible soul ; in short, this Basilacius was kingly both in mind and appearance. He had a voice like thunder, of a nature to strike fear into a whole army, and his shout was enough to quell the courage of the boldest. Further, his eloquence was irresistible, whether he tried to excite the soldiers to battle or check them in flight.

With all these natural advantages and an unconquerable army under his command, the man started on his campaign, and seized the city of the Thessalians, as we have said. My father, Alexius Comnenus, made his counter-preparations as if for a battle with the mighty Typho, or the hundred-handed Giant, and girt himself for the fray with an antagonist worthy of his steel, by summoning all his strategic knowledge and courageous spirit. And before he had shaken off the dust of his late contest, or washed the gore from his sword and hands, he marched out, his spirit all aflame, like a grim lion against this long-tusked boar, Basilacius. Soon he reached the river Bardarius[1] (for that is its local name), which comes down from the mountains near Mysia, and after flowing through many intervening districts, and dividing the country round Berœa and Thessalonica into East and West, it empties itself into our so-called South sea.

What happens in every large river is this : when a considerable embankment has been raised by the deposit they bring down, then they flow to a lower level, and forsaking as it were their first bed, leave it quite dry and bereft of water, and fill the new bed they now traverse with rushing streams.

[1] R. Vardar.

Between two such channels of the Bardarius, one the old gully, the other the newly-formed passage, lay a piece of ground, and when that clever strategist, Alexius, my father, saw it, he pitched his camp there, since the two channels were not more than three stades distant from one another. The running river he considered, would be a bulwark on the one side, and the old river-bed, which had become a deep ravine from the river's strong current, he utilized as a natural trench. The men were immediately put under orders to rest by day, and strengthen themselves with sleep, and to give their horses a good feed; for as soon as night fell, they would have to watch, and expect a surprise attack by the enemy. My father made these arrangements, I believe, because he foresaw danger from the enemy that evening. He quite expected them to attack him, for either his long experience made him guess this, or he had other reasons for his conjecture. This presentiment had come to him suddenly, nor did he only foresee and then neglect the necessary precautions. No, but he left the camp with his forces and their weapons, horses, and everything needful for battle, and left it with lights shining everywhere and entrusted the camp, with the supplies of food and other equipment he carried with him, to his body-servant " Little John," a former monk. He himself drew off to a good distance with his troops ready armed, and sat down to await the course of events. This was cunningly planned so that Basilacius, when he saw camp fires burning on all sides, and my father's tent illuminated with lamps, should imagine that he was resting inside, and that it would, consequently, be an easy matter to capture him and get him into his power.

VIII   As we have already hinted, this presentiment of my father's was not unfounded. For Basilacius came down suddenly upon the army he thought to find with cavalry and infantry (10,000 men in all); there he found the men's quarters lighted up everywhere, and when he saw the General's tent gleaming, he rushed into it with a tremendous, hair-raising shout. But as the man he expected to find was nowhere to be seen, and no soldier or officer turned up anywhere, only a few insignificant camp servants, he shouted still more loudly, and cried out, " Where in the world is the Stammerer? " thus in his words too jeering at the Great Domestic. For, except in one respect, this Alexius, my father, had a very clear utterance, and no one was a better natural orator than he in his arguments and demonstrations, but only over the letter " r " his tongue lisped slightly, and stammered a little, although his enunciation of all the other letters was quite unimpeded. Shouting such insults, Basilacius continued his search, and turned over everything, boxes, couches, furniture, and even my father's bed, to see whether perchance he was hidden anywhere. And he frequently looked at " Little John," the monk so called. Alexius' mother had carefully arranged that he should have one of the better-born monks to share his tent in all his campaigns, and her kindly son had yielded to his mother's wish, not only whilst a child, but even after he had joined the ranks of youths ; nay, indeed, until he took to himself a wife. Basilacius searched through the whole tent, and, as Aristophanes would say, did not stop " groping about in darkness," while asking Little John a stream of questions about the Domestic. On John's asserting that Alexius had gone out with his whole army some time ago, he recognized that he had been grossly tricked, and in utter despair, and with much noise and shouting, he yelled out : " Fellow soldiers, we have been deceived, the enemy is outside." Hardly had he said this, as they were going out of the camp, than my father, Alexius Comnenus, was on them, for he had hurriedly galloped on ahead of the army with a few attendants. He noticed a man trying to bring the heavy infantry into battle-array— and, by the way, the majority of Basilacius' soldiers had betaken themselves to looting and plunder (this too was an old device of my father's), and before they could be re-assembled and drawn up in line, the Great Domestic loomed before them as a sudden danger. He, as I have said, saw someone drawing up the phalanxes, and judging either from his size, or from the brilliance of his armour (for his armour gleamed in the light of the stars) that he must be Basilacius, dashed swiftly up to him, and struck at his hand, and the hand, with the sword it held, fell to the ground—an incident which greatly upset the phalanx. But after all it was not Basilacius himself, but a very brave man of his suite who was not a tittle inferior in courage to Basilacius. Then Alexius with a heavy hand began a wild attack on them ; he shot with arrows, inflicted wounds with his spear, uttered war-cries, confounded them in the darkness. He used the place, the time, everything, as a means to victory, and availed himself of them with unperturbed mind and unshaken judgment, and though men of both armies were fleeing in various directions, he discerned, in every case, whether he were friend or

foe. Then, too, a certain Cappadocian, called Goules, a
faithful servant of my father's, a hard-hitter, of ungovernable
fury in battle, saw Basilacius, and making sure that it was he,
struck him on his helmet.   But he suffered the fate of Menelaus, when fighting against Paris ; for his sword "shattered
into 3 or 4 pieces," fell from his hand, and only the hilt
remained in his grip. The General seeing this straightway
mocked at him for not holding his sword tight, and called
him a coward, but when the soldier shewed him the hilt of
his sword which he still grasped, he became less abusive.
Another man, a Macedonian, Peter by name, but nicknamed
Tornicius, fell among the enemy and slew a number.   The
phalanx followed its leader though in ignorance of what was
being done ; for as the struggle was carried on in the dark,
not all were able to grasp the course of events.   Comnenus
would attack that part of the phalanx which was still intact,
and strike down all adversaries, and in a moment be back
with his own men, urging them to break up that portion
of Basilacius' phalanx which still held its ground, and sending
messages to the rear to bid them not to be so slow, but to
follow him, and overtake him more quickly.   During this
time, a Frank, belonging to the Domestic's troops, and,
to make a long story short, a brave soldier, instinct with the
spirit of Ares, noticed my father coming out from the enemy's
centre, bare sword in hand, all smoking with blood, and
took him for one of the enemy.   In a trice he fell upon him,
knocked him on the chest with his spear, and was within
an ace of hurling the General off his horse, had the General
not seated himself more firmly, and addressed the soldier
by name, and threatened to cut off his head with his sword.
However, the Frank, by pleading his want of recognition,
and the confusion consequent upon a night-battle, was allowed
to remain among the living !

IX   Such then were the deeds of the Domestic and a few
followers during that night.   As soon as dawn smiled upon the
earth, and the sun peeped over the horizon, Basilacius'
officers endeavoured with all their might to drive together
their men who had abandoned the battle and been busy about
the spoil.   The Great Domestic also re-formed his own lines,
and then marched straight against Basilacius.   Some of the
Domestic's troops saw stragglers from Basilacius' army in
the distance, so rode down upon them, routed them, and
brought some back to him alive.   Basilacius' brother, Manuel,
mounted a hillock, and from there encouraged his army by

shouting loudly, " To-day the day and the victory are to
Basilacius ! " A certain Basileios, nicknamed Curticius, an
intimate friend of Nicephorus Bryennius (whose story we
have told), and very active in war, ran from Comnenus'
battle-line up towards this hillock. Basilacius Manuel drew
his sword, and at full speed galloped down upon him ; but
Curticius, instead of taking his sword, snatched the staff
hanging from his saddle-cloth, struck Manuel on the head
with it, knocked him off his horse, and dragging him bound
behind him, brought him to my father as if he were a bit
of the spoils. In the meantime, when the remnants of
Basilacius' army saw Comnenus advance with his own
divisions, they resisted him for a little, and then took to
flight. And so Basilacius fled, and Alexius Comnenus
pursued him. When they reached Thessalonica, the Thessalonians at once received Basilacius, but straightway barred
the gates before the General. But not even then did Alexius
relax, nor did he take off his breastplate, or lay aside his
helmet, or ungird his shield from his shoulders, or cast aside
his sword, but he encamped, and threatened to besiege the
city forthwith, and then sack it. As he wished, however,
to save Basilacius, he sent his monk-companion, " Little
John " (a man renowned for his integrity) to him with a
proposal for peace, and promised that Basilacius should
suffer no ill-treatment if he gave securities, and surrendered
himself and the city. Basilacius, however, was inflexible,
but the Thessalonians, through fear of their city being taken
and destroyed, granted Comnenus ingress. But Basilacius,
when he saw what was being done by the multitude, betook
himself to the Acropolis and leapt from one spot to another.
Even in these extremities his fighting spirit did not forsake
him, although the Domestic gave his word that he should
not be barbarously treated ; but in difficulties and dangers
Basilacius ever shewed himself a man indeed. He would
not abate his courage and brave attitude in the slightest,
until at last the inhabitants and custodians of the Acropolis
drove him out of it against his will, took him by force, and
handed him over to the Great Domestic. Alexius at once
sent news of his capture to the Emperor, but stayed on himself a little longer in Thessalonica to arrange things there,
and then returned to Constantinople in triumph. Between
Philippi and Amphipolis he met messengers from the Emperor
who handed him written orders about Basilacius. They
took the latter in charge, led him to a village called Chlem-

pina, and near the spring in it put out his eyes : hence the
spring is to this day called " the spring of Basilacius." This
was the third " Labour " accomplished by the great Alexius
before he became Emperor, and he might rightly be styled
a second Heracles. For you would not be wide of the mark
in calling this fellow Basilacius the Erymanthian boar, and
my most noble father Alexius, a modern Heracles. Such,
then, were the successes and achievements of Alexius before
he ascended the throne, and as reward for them all he received
from the Emperor the rank of " Sebastos," and was proclaimed " Sebastos " in public assembly.

X It seems to me that if a body is sickly, the sickliness
is often aggravated by external causes, but that occasionally,
too, the causes of our illnesses spring up of themselves, although we are apt to blame the inequalities of the climate,
indiscretion in diet, or perhaps, too, the humours of our
animal juices, as the cause of our fevers. Similarly, like
these physical ailments, I fancy the weakness of the Romans
at that time was partly the cause of these deadly plagues :
I mean the various men before mentioned, the Ursels, the
Basilacii, and all the crowd of pretenders, but partly, too,
it was Fate that introduced other aspirants to the throne
from abroad, and foisted them on the Empire like an irremediable sore and incurable disease. To this latter class belonged
that braggart Robert, so famed for his tyrannical disposition.
Normandy indeed begot him, but he was nursed and reared
by consummate Wickedness. The Roman Empire really
brought this formidable foe upon herself by affording a pretext for all the wars he waged against us in proposing a marriage
with a foreign, barbaric race, quite unsuitable to us ; or
rather it was the carelessness of the reigning Emperor, Michael,
who united our family with the Ducas. Let no one be angry
with me if I sometimes censure one of my blood-relations
(for I am allied by blood to the Ducas on my mother's side),
for I have determined to write the truth before all things,
and, as far as this man is concerned, I have voiced the general
censures. For this same Emperor, Michael Ducas, betrothed his own son, Constantine, to this barbarian's daughter,
and from that arose all the hostilities. Now, we shall give
an account of this prince Constantine in due course ; also of
his nuptial contract, in other words this barbaric alliance,
and also of his appearance, and beauty, and size, and physical
and mental characteristics. At that point I shall also briefly
deplore my own misfortunes after I have told the tale of this

alliance, and the defeat of the whole barbarian force, and the death of these pretenders from Normandy, who had been reared against the Roman Empire by Michael's want of prudence. But first I must retrace my steps a little, and speak of this man Robert, and give details of his descent and career, and relate to what a pitch of power the turn of affairs had brought him, or to put it more reverentially, how far Providence had allowed him to rise by shewing indulgence to his mischievous desires and machinations.

This Robert was Norman by descent, of insignificant origin, in temper tyrannical, in mind most cunning, brave in action, very clever in attacking the wealth and substance of magnates, most obstinate in achievement, for he did not allow any obstacle to prevent his executing his desire. His stature was so lofty that he surpassed even the tallest, his complexion was ruddy, his hair flaxen, his shoulders were broad, his eyes all but emitted sparks of fire, and in frame he was well-built where nature required breadth, and was neatly and gracefully formed where less width was necessary. So from tip to toe this man was well-proportioned, as I have repeatedly heard many say. Now, Homer says of Achilles that when he shouted, his voice gave his hearers the impression of a multitude in an uproar, but this man's cry is is said to have put thousands to flight. Thus equipped by fortune, physique and character, he was naturally indomitable, and subordinate to nobody in the world. Powerful natures are ever like this, people say, even though they be of somewhat obscure descent.

XI   Such then was the man, and as he would not endure any control, he departed from Normandy with only five followers on horseback, and thirty on foot all told. After leaving his native land, he roamed amid the mountain-ridges, caves, and hills of Lombardy, as the chief of a robber-band, and by attacks on travellers acquired horses, and also other possessions and weapons. Thus the prelude of this man's life was marked by much bloodshed and many murders. While lingering in those parts of Lombardy, he came under the notice of Gulielmus Mascabeles, who was then ruler over the greater part of the territory adjacent to Lombardy, and as he drew a rich annual income from these lands, he furnished himself with a good body of troops and became a powerful prince. He informed himself of the manner of man, physical and mentally, that Robert was, and then with a wonderful lack of foresight, attached him to himself,

and betrothed one of his daughters to him. The marriage
was completed, and though Gulielmus admired Robert for
his strength and experience in warfare, yet his affairs did not
prosper as he had hoped. He had even given him a city as
a kind of wedding-gift, and lavished various other marks of
kindness upon him. However, Robert grew disaffected, and
meditated rebellion. At first he played the friend and
gradually increased his forces until he had trebled his cavalry
and doubled his infantry. And thereafter the cloak of
friendliness slipped off, and little by little his evil disposition
was laid bare. Daily he would give, or pick up, some pretext
for a quarrel, and continuously adopted courses of a kind
that are wont to engender disputes, and then fighting and
wars. Since the aforesaid Gulielmus Mascabeles far surpassed
him in wealth and influence, Robert renounced all idea of
meeting him openly in battle, and concocted a wicked plot
instead. For, while professing friendship and feigning
repentance, he was secretly preparing a terrible scheme,
which was hard to detect, in order to capture all Mascabeles'
towns, and make himself master of all his possessions. As a
start he opened negotiations for peace, and sent an embassy
to ask Gulielmus to come in person to a conference. Gulielmus
welcomed peace with Robert, because he was extremely fond
of his daughter, and fixed a meeting for the morrow; and
Robert indicated the place where they would meet for discussion, and arranging a truce with each other. In this
place were two peaked hills rising from the plain to equal
height, and standing diametrically opposite each other; the
intervening ground was swampy, and over-grown with all
manner of trees and bushes. On this ground that crafty
Robert planted an ambuscade of four very brave armed men,
and adjured them to keep careful watch all round, and as
soon as they saw him at grips with Gulielmus, to run up against
the latter without an instant's delay. After these preliminary preparations, Robert, the arch-schemer, forsook the
hill which he had designated beforehand for the conference
with Mascabeles, and appropriated, so to say, the second
hill, and taking fifteen horsemen and about fifty-six foot-
soldiers up with him, posted them there, and then disclosed
his whole plot to the more important among them. He also
commanded one to hold his armour ready for him to put on
quickly, namely, his helmet, shield, and short sword; to the
four men in ambush he had given injunctions to rush very
quickly to his aid directly they saw Mascabeles at grips with

him. On the appointed day Gulielmus was coming to the
hill to the spot which Robert had indicated to him beforehand, with the intention of completing a treaty ; when
Robert saw him drawing near, he met him on horseback,
and embraced and welcomed him right heartily. So they
both halted on the slope, a little distance from the summit
of the hill, talking of what they meant to do. The crafty
Robert wasted the time by talking of one subject after another,
and then said to Gulielmus : " Why in the world should we
tire ourselves by sitting on horseback ? Why not dismount,
and sit on the ground, and talk freely of the necessary
matters ? " Mascabeles foolishly obeyed, all unaware of
the guile, and the danger into which he was being led, and
when he saw Robert get off his horse, he dismounted too,
and resting his elbow on the ground, started the discussion
afresh. Robert now professed fealty to Mascabeles for the
future, and called him his faithful benefactor and lord.
Hereupon, Mascabeles' men, seeing that the leaders had
dismounted, and apparently started an argument afresh,
dismounted too ; or rather some did, and tied their reins to
the branches, and lay down and rested in the shade cast by
the horses and the trees, while the others rode home. For
they were all tired from the warmth and want of food and
drink (for it was the summer season when the sun casts its
rays vertically, and the heat had become unbearable). So
much then for these ; but Robert, the sly fox, had arranged
all this beforehand, and now suddenly throws himself on
Mascabeles, drops his kindly expression for a furious one,
and attacks him with murderous intent. And gripping, he
was gripped in return, and dragged, and was dragged, and
together they went rolling down the hill. When the four
men waiting in ambush saw this, they jumped out of the marsh,
ran at Gulielmus, bound him, and then ran back as if to join
Robert's horsemen stationed on the other hill, but they were
already galloping down the slope towards them, and behind
came Gulielmus' men in hot pursuit. Robert for his part
jumped on his horse, quickly donned his helmet, seized his
spear, and brandished it fiercely and sheltering himself behind
his shield, turned round, and struck one of Gulielmus' men
such a blow with his spear that he yielded up his life on the
spot. In the meantime, he held back the rush of his father-
in-law's cavalry, and checked the relief they were bringing
(because when they saw Robert's horsemen coming down
upon them from above with the position all in their favour,

they immediately turned their backs). After Robert had in this wise stopped the onrush of Gulielmus' horsemen, Mascabeles was taken bound and a prisoner of war to the very fortress which he had given as wedding-gift to Robert at the time he betrothed his daughter to him. And so it came about that the city had its own master as " prisoner " within it, and hence probably it got its name of " prison-house." And it will not be amiss if I enlarge on Robert's cruelty. For when he had once got Mascabeles in his power, he first had all his teeth pulled out, and demanded for each of them a stupendous weight of money, and enquired where this money was stored. He did not leave off drawing them until he had taken all, for both teeth and money gave out simultaneously, and then Robert cast his eyes upon Gulielmus' eyes, and grudging him his sight, deprived him of his eyes.

XII Having thus become master of all Mascabeles' possessions, he after that grew daily in power, and becoming ever more despotic, piled cities upon cities, and money upon money. In a short time he had risen to ducal eminence, and was nominated Duke of all Lombardy, and from that moment everybody's envy was excited against him. But Robert, being a man with his wits very much about him, now used flattery against his adversaries and now gifts, and so quelled uprisings among the populace, and by his ingenuity repressed the envy of the nobility against him, and thus, by these means, and by occasional recourse to arms, he annexed the whole realm of Lombardy, and the neighbouring country. But this Robert was for ever aspiring at further increase of power, and because he had visions of the Roman Empire, he alleged as pretext his connection with the Emperor Michael, as I have said, and fanned up the war against the Romans. For we have already stated that the Emperor Michael for some inexplicable reason betrothed this despot's daughter (Helen by name) to his son, Constantine. Now that I am mentioning this youth again, I am convulsed in spirit, and confounded in reason : however, I will cut short my story about him, and reserve it for the right time. Yet one thing I cannot forbear saying, even though it is out of place here, and that is that the youth was a living statue, a " chef d'œuvre," so to say, of God's hands. If any one merely looked at him, he would say that he was a descendant of the Golden Age fabled by the Greeks ; so indescribably beautiful was he. And when I call to mind this boy after so many years I am filled with sorrow ; yet I restrain my tears, and husband

them for " more fitting places," for I do not wish to confuse
this history by mingling monodies on my sufferings with
historical narration. To resume, this youth (whom we have
mentioned here and elsewhere), my predecessor, born before I
had seen the light of day, a clean, undefiled boy, had become
a suitor for Helen, Robert's daughter, and the written
contracts had been drawn up for the marriage, though they
were not executed, only promised, as the youth was still of
immature age ; and the contracts were annulled directly
the Emperor Nicephorus Botaniates ascended the throne.
But I have wandered from the point, and will now return
to the point whence I wandered! That man Robert, who
from a most inconspicuous beginning had grown most conspicuous, and amassed great power, now desired eagerly
to become Roman Emperor, and with this object, sought
plausible pretexts for ill-will and war against the Romans.
And there are two different tales about this. One story which
is bruited about, and reached our ears too, is that a certain
monk, named Raictor, impersonated the Emperor Michael,
and had gone over to Robert, and poured out his tale of woe
to him, his marriage-connection. Michael had seized the
Roman sceptre after Diogenes, and adorned the throne for a
short time, then he was deprived of his throne by the rebel
Botaniates, and embraced the monastic life, and was later
invested with the alb and mitre and add, if you like, the
humeral of an archbishop. The Cæsar John, his paternal
uncle, had advised this for he knew the lightheadedness of
the reigning Emperor, and feared the worst for Michael. It
was this Michael whom the aforementioned monk, Raictor,
impersonated, or if I may call him so, " Rectes," which implies
what he was, the most audacious " fabricator " of all time.
He approached Robert on the plea of being his marriage-
kinsman, and recited to him the tragic tale of his wrongs,
how he had been driven from the imperial throne, and reduced
to his present state, which Robert could see for himself, and
for all these reasons, he invoked the barbarian's aid. For
Helen, Robert's beautiful daughter, and his own daughter-in-
law, had been left destitute, he said, and openly bereft of her
betrothed, as his son Constantine, and his wife, the Princess
Mary, although very unwillingly, had been compelled by force
to join Botaniates' party.

By these words he inflamed the barbarian's mind, and
armed him with a motive for a war against the Romans.
A story of this sort reached my ears, and I must own I am not

surprised that some persons of most ignoble birth impersonate those of noble and honourable race. But on other authority a far more plausible story re-echoes in my mind, and this story avers that no monk impersonated Michael, and that no such event stirred Robert to war against the Romans, but that the versatile barbarian himself easily invented the whole thing. The story runs thus, the arch-villain Robert, who was hatching war against the Romans, and had been making his preparations for some time, was kept in check by the nobles of highest rank in his suite, and also by his own wife, Gaïta, on the ground that the war would be unjust and waged against Christians; indeed he was prevented several times when he was anxious to start. But he was determined to procure a specious pretext for war, and therefore sent some men to Cotrone and entrusted them with the secret of his plot, and gave them the following directions. If they could find any monk willing to cross from there to Italy to worship at the shrine of the chief apostles, the patron saints of Rome, and if he did not betray his low origin too openly in his appearance, they were to welcome him and make a friend of him, and bring him back with them. When they discovered the aforementioned Raictor, a versatile fellow without his equal for knavery, they signified the fact to Robert who was waiting at Salernum,[1] by a letter to this effect : " Your kinsman Michael, who has been expelled from his kingdom has arrived here to solicit your assistance." For Robert had ordered them to write the letter to him in those words. Directly he received the letter, he read it privately to his wife, and then in an assembly of all the Counts he showed it to them too, and swore they could no longer keep him back, as he had now got hold of a really just excuse for war. As they all immediately fell in with Robert's desire, he brought the man over, and entered into association with him. Thereupon he worked up the whole drama, and put it in its proper stage-setting, pretending that that monk was the Emperor Michael, that he had been deprived of his throne, and despoiled of his wife and son and all his possessions by the usurper Botaniates, and that against all law and justice he had been clothed in a monk's garb instead of a fillet and crown, and " Now," he concluded, " he has come as suppliant to us." Robert used to harangue the people like this, and professed that because of their kinship he must restore the kingdom to him. Daily he

1 Salerno.

shewed honour to the monk, as if he were the Emperor
Michael, giving him the best place at table, a higher seat,
and excessive respect. In various ingenious ways also
Robert caught the ear of the public; one day he would
commiserate himself on the sad fate of his daughter; on
another he did not like, out of consideration for his marriage-
kinsman, to speak of the evil days on which the latter had
fallen; and on yet another he incited and stirred up the
ignorant masses round him to war by artfully promising
them heaps of gold which he said he would give them from
the Imperial treasury. Thus he led all by the nose, and drew
all, rich and poor alike, out of Lombardy, or rather he dragged
the whole of Lombardy with him, and occupied Salernum,
the mother city of Amalfi. Here he made good settlements
for his other daughters, and then began his preparations for
the war. He had two daughters with him, whilst the third,
ill-fated from the day of her betrothal, was confined in the
imperial city; for her young betrothed, being still immature,
shrank from this alliance at the very outset, as children do
from bogeys. Of the two others, he pledged one to Raymond,
son of the Count Barcinon, and the second he married to
Eubulus[1], another very illustrious Count. In these alliances,
as in all else, Robert did not fail to have an eye to his own
advantage; but from all sources he had piled up and welded
together influence for himself, from his race, his rule, his
rights of kin, in a word, from innumerable devices of which
nobody else would even think.

XIII Meanwhile, an event occurred which is worth
relating, as it, too, contributed to this man's reputation and
good fortune. For I hold that the fact that all the rulers
of the West were prevented from attacking him, tended very
materially to the barbarian's successful progress. Fate
worked for him on all sides, raised him to kingly power, and
accomplished everything helpful to him. Now it happened
that the Pope[2] of Rome had a difference with Henry,[3] King of
Germany, and, therefore, wished to draw Robert into an
alliance, as the latter had already become very notable and
attained to great dominion. (The Pope is a very high
dignitary, and is protected by troops of various nationalities.)
The dispute between the King and the Pope was this: the
latter accused Henry of not bestowing livings as free gifts,
but selling them for money, and occasionally entrusting
archbishoprics to unworthy recipients, and he also brought

---

[1] —Ebal. [2] Gregory VII. [3] Henry IV.

further charges of a similar nature against him. The King of Germany on his side indicted the Pope of usurpation, as he had seized the apostolic chair without his consent. Moreover, he had the effrontery to utter reckless threats against the Pope, saying that if he did not resign his self-elected office, he should be expelled from it with contumely. When these words reached the Pope's ears, he vented his rage upon Henry's ambassadors; first he tortured them inhumanly, then clipped their hair with scissors, and sheared their beards with a razor, and finally committed a most indecent outrage upon them, which transcended even the insolence of barbarians, and so sent them away. My womanly and princely dignity forbids my naming the outrage inflicted on them, for it was not only unworthy a high priest, but of anyone who bears the name of a Christian. I abhor this barbarian's idea, and more still the deed, and I should have defiled both my pen and my paper had I described it explicitly. But as a display of barbaric insolence, and a proof that time in its flow produces men with shameless morals, ripe for any wickedness, this alone will suffice, if I say, that I could not bear to disclose or relate even the tiniest word about what he did. And this was the work of a high priest. Oh, justice! The deed of the supreme high priest! nay, of one who claimed to be the president of the whole world, as indeed the Latins assert and believe, but this, too, is a bit of their boasting. For when the imperial seat was transferred from Rome hither to our native Queen of Cities, and the senate, and the whole administration, there was also transferred the arch-hieratical primacy. And the Emperors from the very beginning have given the supreme right to the episcopacy of Constantinople, and the Council of Chalcedon emphatically raised the Bishop of Constantinople to the highest position, and placed all the dioceses of the inhabited world under his jurisdiction. There can be no doubt that the insult done to the ambassadors was aimed at the king who sent them; not only because he scourged them, but also because he was the first to invent this new kind of outrage. For by his actions, the Pope suggested, I think, that the power of the King was despicable, and by this horrible outrage on his ambassadors that he, a demi-god, as it were, was treating with a demi-ass! The Pope consequently, by wreaking his insolence on the ambassadors, and sending them back to the King in the state I have mentioned, provoked a very great war. To prevent the King's becoming too insupportable by an alliance with Robert, he anticipated him in sending offers of peace to Robert, though before this he had not been friendly towards him. Hearing that Duke Robert had occupied Salernum, he started from Rome, and came to Beneventum, and after some inter-communication through ambassadors, they also had a personal interview in the following way. The Pope set out from Beneventum with his household troops, and Robert from Salernum with an army, and when the armies were at a convenient distance, each left his own men and advanced alone. The two then met, gave and took pledges and oaths, and then returned. The oaths were that the Pope would invest Robert with the dignity of king, and give him help against the Romans if the need should arise, whilst the Duke swore a counter-oath to assist the Pope whenever the latter called upon him. But truly these oaths taken by both of them were worthless. For the Pope was furiously incensed against the King, and in a hurry to begin war against him, whereas Duke Robert had his eyes fixed on the Roman Empire, and was gnashing his teeth, and whetting his anger like a wild boar. So these oaths amounted to no more than words. And the pledges these barbarians gave to each other one day, they violated the next. After the meeting, Robert turned his bridle and hurried to Salernum. And that Pope (whom I can only call " abominable " when I recall his in-human outrages on the ambassadors), the Pope clad in spiritual grace and evangelic peace, started out for civil war with all his energy and might ; yes, he, the man of peace, and the disciple of the Man of Peace ! For he immediately summoned the Saxons and their Counts Lantulphus[1], and Velcus[2], and besides other enticements held out to them, he promised to make them kings of all the West, and thus won them over to his side. You see how ever-ready a hand the Pope had for laying hands on the heads of kings, unheeding St. Paul's advice " Lay hands hastily on no man," for he bound the kingly fillet on the Duke of Lombardy's head, and crowned these two Saxons. When either side (to wit, Henry, King of Germany, and the Pope) had brought up their armies, and set them in battle array, directly the horn had sounded the attack, the lines dashed together, and there was fanned up by either side a great and long-continued battle. So many deeds of valour were done by both parties, and such was the endurance shewn by men already wounded by spear and arrow, that in a short time the whole plain was submerged

[1] Ludolf.   [2] Welf.

in a sea of blood which flowed from the dying, and the survivors fought on, as if sailing on the abundant gore. In some
places the soldiers got entangled by the dead bodies, and fell
over, and were drowned in the river of blood. For if, as it
is said, more than 30,000 men fell in that battle, what a stream
of blood was poured forth, and how large a portion of the
earth was defiled with gore ! Both sides were, if I may so put
it, of equal stature in the battle as long as Lantulphus directed
the combat. But when he received a mortal wound, and
straightway gave up the ghost, the Pope's lines gave way,
and turned their backs to the enemy, and in their flight
many were killed or wounded.

Henry rushed wildly after them, being all the more heartened in the pursuit because he had learnt that Lantulphus
had fallen and become the prize of the enemy. By and by
he desisted from the chase, and bade his army take a rest.
Later on he got his army ready again, and hastened to Rome
to besiege it. Hereupon, the Pope recalled the agreement
and pledges Robert had given him, and sent an embassy to
ask his help. At the same time, Henry, too, when he was
starting on his march against the ancient city of Rome
sent to ask his alliance. But Robert thought both of them
silly for making such a request, and sent a verbal answer of
some kind to the King, but to the Pope he indited a letter.
His letter ran as follows : " Duke Robert to the great High-
priest and his Overlord in God. I heard a talk of the attack
made upon thee by thy enemies, but did not attach much real
importance to the rumour as I knew that none would dare to
raise his hand against thee. For what man in his senses
would assail so great a father ? As for me, I would have
thee know that I am arming myself for a most serious war
against a most formidable nation. For my campaign is
against the Romans, who have filled every land and sea
with their trophies. But to thee I acknowledge fidelity
from the depths of my soul, and when need arises, I will
prove it." And thus he dismissed the ambassadors of both
those who had sought his help, the one with this letter, and
the other with plausible excuses.

XIV But we must not omit what he did in Lombardy
before he arrived in Valona with his army. He was at all
times a man of tyrannical and very sharp temper, and now he
imitated the madness of Herod. Not being satisfied with the
soldiers who had followed his fortune from the beginning,
and were experienced in war, he recruited and equipped a new

army, without any distinction of age. But he collected all, under age and over age, from all over Lombardy and Apulia, and pressed them into his service. There you could see children and boys, and pitiable old men, who had never, even in their dreams, seen a weapon ; but were now clad in breastplates, carrying shields and drawing their bows most unskilfully and clumsily, and usually falling on their faces when ordered to march. These requisitions were naturally the cause of unending trouble throughout the country of Lombardy ; everywhere were heard the lamentations of men and the weeping of women who shared the misfortunes of their kinsfolk. One would be mourning for her husband, who was over-age for service ; another for her untried son ; a third for her brother, who was a farmer or engaged in business. This behaviour of Robert's was, as I have said, a counterpart of Herod's madness, or even worse, for the latter only vented his rage on babes, whilst Robert did so against boys and old men. Yet, in spite of his recruits being absolutely unpractised, Robert drilled them daily, and brought them into good discipline.

He did all this in Salernum, before he came to Hydruntum.[1] To that town he had sent on a very efficient army, to wait for him until he had settled everything in Lombardy, and given fitting answers to the ambassadors. He dispatched a further note to the Pope, however, saying that he had enjoined upon Roger, his son (whom he had appointed ruler of the whole of Apulia, in conjunction with his brother Boritylas), to waste no time in going with a formidable troop to the help of the Roman See against King Henry as soon as the Pope summoned him. But Bohemond, his younger son, he sent ahead with a powerful army to our territory to leap upon the country round Valona (or Aulon). Now, Bohemond took after his father in all things, in audacity, bodily strength, bravery, and untamable temper ; for he was of exactly the same stamp as his father, and a living model of the latter's character. Immediately on arrival, he fell like a thunderbolt, with threats and irresistible dash upon Canina, Hiericho, and Valona, and seized them, and as he fought his way on, he would ever devastate and set fire to the surrounding districts. He was, in very truth, like the pungent smoke which precedes a fire, and a prelude of attack before the actual attack. These two, father and son, might rightly be termed " the caterpillar and the locust " ; for whatever escaped Robert, that

---

[1] Otranto.

his son Bohemond took to him and devoured. However, do not let us cross to Valona with Robert yet, but examine first what he did on the opposite continent.

XV Leaving Salernum, he came to Hydruntum, and there spent a few days waiting for his wife, Gaïta (for she too accompanied her husband, and when dressed in full armour the woman was a fearsome sight). After he had embraced her on arrival, he set off again with his whole army, and took possession of Brindisi, the seaport which has the best harbour in the whole of Iapygia. After swooping down on this town he stayed there, eagerly awaiting the gathering together of his whole army, and of all his ships, transports and long ships of war alike ; for he intended to sail for the opposite coast from this port. At the same time, he was also eagerly watching for an answer from the reigning monarch, Botaniates, who had seized the sceptre from the Emperor Michael Ducas ; for while still at Salernum, Robert had sent one of the nobles in his cortège, Raoul by name, as ambassador to him. He had charged him with certain remonstrances to Botaniates, and apparently specious reasons for the impending war. These were that Botaniates had separated his daughter from her betrothed, Prince Constantine (to whom she was affianced, as I have stated above), and taken the crown from Constantine; therefore, he himself was getting ready for war because Botaniates had committed an injustice. And, moreover, he had sent some presents and letters promising his friendship to the Great Domestic and Commander of the Armies of the West (and this was my father, Alexius). Whilst awaiting these answers he kept quiet at Brindisi ; but before the troops had all been collected there, or the greater part of the ships launched, Raoul returned from Byzantium. He brought no answer to Robert's denunciations, and this fanned the flames of the barbarian's anger afresh. But he was even more incensed by Raoul's laying before him arguments to dissuade him from the war against the Romans. The first was that the monk in his train was a deceiver, and cheat, and only impersonating the Emperor Michael, and that the whole story about him was a pure fabrication. For he told how he had seen Michael in the royal city after his deposition from the throne clad in a grey habit, and living in a monastery, as he had made it his special business to see the deposed king with his own eyes. Secondly, he gave news of the events which had occurred during his return journey—namely, that my father had grasped the sceptre (as I will recount later), driven

Botaniates out of the kingdom, sent for Ducas' son, Constantine, the most distinguished of all men living, and had
again given him a share in the government. Raoul had
heard this on his way, and brought it forward in the hope of
persuading Robert to relinquish his military preparations.
" For with what justice," he said, " can we go to war with
Alexius, when it was Botaniates who was the author of the
wrong done you, and who deprived your daughter Helen
of the Roman throne ? Wrongs done to us by one set of
men should not make us wage war upon others who have
never offended against justice. And if your war has no
just basis, then all will be lost, ships, equipment, men, in
fine, all your military preparations." These words exasper-
ated Robert still further ; he went quite mad, and nearly
did Raoul personal violence. On the other hand, that
fictitious Ducas, and pseudo-emperor Michael (whom we have
called " Raictor "), waxed most indignant and angry, and
did not know how to contain his wrath when it was so clearly
proved that he was not the Emperor Ducas, but merely a
fictitious king. The tyrant Robert had yet another cause
for his fury against Raoul, for Raoul's brother Roger had
deserted to the Romans, and had given them detailed information of the military preparations that were being made against
them, so he burned to do Raoul some harm, and threatened
him with instant death. Raoul, however, who was not
at all slow to take flight, escaped to Bohemond, as being the
nearest refuge. Raictor vented the most abominable threats
against Raoul's brother, the deserter. With loud cries, and
beatings of his thigh with his right hand, he implored Robert,
saying, " One thing only I beg of you—if ever I recover the
crown, and am restored to the throne, hand over Roger to
me, and then, if I do not condemn him to the most miserable
death, and crucify him in the middle of the city, then may
God do so to me, and more also ! " But as I write I have to
laugh at the thought of these men's folly and infatuation, and
especially at their mutual boastfulness. Robert, for his
part, had as ostensible reason this pretender, whom he had
used as a decoy, and presentment of the Emperor, his marriage-
kinsman. He showed him in all the cities he visited, and
roused all he could possibly persuade to rebellion, purposing,
if the haphazards of war ended in success for himself, to
knock the monk on the head, and cast him out with scorn ;
for when the hunt is over, the decoy, too, is thrown to the
dogs. Raictor, on his side, nourished himself on vain hopes

that some day he would attain great power ; for such things often happen quite unexpectedly. In that case he would lay hold of the sceptre with firm hand, taking it for granted that the Roman people, and the army, would never call the barbarian Robert to the throne. In the meantime, he would use Robert as an instrument for the completion of the whole fabric of his intrigue. When I think of all this, a smile rises to my lips as I wield my pen by the light of my lamp.

XVI Robert now collected all his forces at Brindisi, both ships and soldiers ; the ships numbered 150, and the soldiers, when all ranks were counted together, came to 30,000 ; and each ship could transport 200 men with their armour and horses. The soldiers were fully equipped in this way, because the enemies they would meet on landing would probably be fully-armed horsemen. Robert intended crossing to Epidamnus, which we must call " Dyrrachium,"[1] according to the present fashion. He had, indeed, thought of crossing from Hydruntum to Nicopolis, and seizing Naupactus and the adjacent country, and all the fortresses round about it. But as the stretch of sea between these two towns was far wider than between Brindisi and Dyrrachium, he chose the latter in preference to the former, not only because he preferred the quicker passage, but also to secure a calm one for the fleet. For the season was stormy, and as the sun was turning to the southern hemisphere, and approaching Capricorn, the days were growing shorter. Therefore, to prevent the fleet's setting out from Hydruntum at daybreak and sailing all night, and perhaps meeting heavy seas, he determined to proceed from Brindisi to Dyrrachium with all sails set. As the Adriatic Sea contracts here, the length of the passage was curtailed. He did not after all leave even his son Roger behind, as he had first planned when he appointed him Count of Apulia, but changed his mind for some inexplicable reason, and took him with him too. During his crossing to Dyrrachium, the force which he had detached gained possession of the very strongly fortified town of Corfu, and certain other of our forts. After receiving hostages from Lombardy, and Apulia, and raising taxes and contributions in money from the whole country, Robert hoped to land at Dyrrachium. Duke of all Illyricum at that time was George Monomachatus, who had been appointed by the Emperor Botaniates. Once, indeed, he had refused this

[1] Durazzo.

mission, and he was by no means easily persuaded to take up this branch of service, but he finally went because two of the Emperor's barbarian servants (Borilus and Germanus, Scythians by extraction) bore a grudge against him. These men were ever inventing scandalous charges against him, and denouncing him to the Emperor, for they strung together whatever tales entered their heads, and inflamed his anger against him to such a pitch that, turning to the Queen Maria, he actually said, " I suspect this Monomachatus of being an enemy to the Roman Empire."

John, one of the Alani, and a devoted friend of Monomachatus, heard this, and as he was aware of the Scythians' spiteful and frequent accusations against him, he went to Monomachatus, and repeated to him both the Emperor's words and those of the Scythians, and advised him to consult his own interests. Thereupon, Monomachatus, a prudent man, approached the Emperor, and after appeasing him with skilful flattery, eagerly accepted the post at Dyrrachium. So, having taken leave of the Emperor previous to his departure for Epidamnus, and receiving his orders about the Duchy in writing (and those Scythians, Borilus and Germanus, did their best to expedite the matter), he quitted the royal city on the morrow for his destination, Epidamnus and the country of Illyricum. But he met my father Alexius near the so-called Pege ; here a church has been built in honour of my mistress, the Virgin-mother of our Lord, which is famous among the churches of Byzantium. They saw each other there, and Monomachatus at once began an impassioned speech to the Great Domestic. He told him that he was being exiled because of their mutual friendship, and because of the envy of the Scythians, Borilus and Germanus. This covetous couple, he said, had turned the wheel, so to say, of their universal maliciousness against him in full revolution ; and were now banishing him from his friends, and this beloved city, for seemingly good reasons. Thus he told his tale of woe in detail, and all the false information given about him to the Emperor, and all he had endured at the hands of these servants ; and the Domestic of the West deigned to console him as much as possible, and verily he was well-fitted to relieve a soul bowed down with troubles. And saying finally that assuredly God would avenge these insults, and with a reminder to him never to forget their friendship, they parted, the one bound for Dyrrachium, and the other to enter the imperial city. When Monomachatus reached Dyrrachium he heard two pieces of news ; firstly, the tyrant Robert's military preparations, and, secondly, the revolt of Alexius ; so he carefully weighed what his own conduct should be. Ostensibly he displayed hostility to both, but he had really a deeper plan than that of open warfare. For the Great Domestic had informed him by letter of the late occurrences, namely, that he had been threatened with the loss of his eyes, and that, in consequence of this threat, and of the tyrannous act that was being practised, he had taken measures against his enemies. He called upon Monomachatus to rise in rebellion also on behalf of his friend, and to collect money wherever he could, and send it to him. " For," he wrote, " we are in need of money, and without money, nothing of what should be done, can be done." However, Mono-machatus did not send money, but spoke kindly to the am-bassadors, and instead of money, entrusted them with a letter conceived in this strain—he still preserved his old friendship for Alexius, and promised to retain it in the future ; and, with regard to the money he ordered, he (Monomachatus) longed to send him as much as he wanted. " But," he wrote, " a point of justice restrains me. For I received this appointment from the Emperor Botaniates, and I swore the oath of fealty to him. Therefore, I should not appear, even in your eyes, a loyal subject as far as Emperors are concerned, were I at once to comply with your request. But if divine providence allots the imperial throne to you, then as I have been your friend from the beginning, so after this event I shall be your most faithful servant." This excuse Monomachatus made to my father, and tried to con-ciliate him (I mean my father) and Botaniates, simultaneously, but he also sent a much plainer message to the barbarian Robert, and then broke forth into open rebellion, and for this I must condemn him severely. But perhaps this kind of unstable conduct, ever changing with the changes in the government, is but natural ; and all such men are prejudicial to the public weal, but steer a safe course for themselves, for they study nothing but their own personal interests, and even so they generally fail.

Behold, my steed has run off the high road of my history, but although he is out of hand, I must bring him back to our former road. Robert, indeed, had ever been wildly impatient to cross into our country, and was ever dreaming of Dyrrachium, but now, on receipt of Monomachatus' message, his ardour burst all restraint, and he pushed on the naval expedition with all his might and main, and hurried up the soldiers, and whipped up their courage by stimulating addresses. Monomachatus, having set things in trim in this direction, now began constructing a second place of refuge for himself in another place. For he won over Bodinus and Michaelas, the Ex-archs of Dalmatia by his letters, and influenced their decisions by opportune gifts; thus opening secretly, as it were, various doors for himself. For he reasoned that if he were to fail with Robert and Alexius, and be rejected by both of them, then he would turn deserter, and go straight to Bodinus and Michaelas in Dalmatia. For, supposing that Robert and Alexius declared themselves his enemies, he placed his remaining hopes on Michaelas and Bodinus, and arranged to flee to them, should the feelings of Robert and Alexius be plainly adverse to him. But here we will let these matters rest. It is high time I should turn to my father's reign, and relate how and why he became ruler. I do not intend to narrate his life before he became ruler, but all his successes and failures as Emperor; if we shall occasionally find him unsuccessful in the course of the long stretch we are to traverse, I should not spare him for being my father if anything he did struck me as not well done; nor shall I gloss over his successes to avoid the under-current of suspicion that it is a daughter writing about her father, for in either case I should be wronging truth. This, then, is my aim, as I have repeatedly stated already, and the subject I have chosen is the Emperor, my father. We will leave Robert in the spot to which our history has brought him, and now consider the Emperor's doings. We shall reserve the wars and battles against Robert for a later book.

BOOK II

I

WE must refer the reader who wishes to know the place
and lineage from which Alexius sprang, to my Cæsar's
history, and thence he can also extract information
about the Emperor Nicephorus Botaniates.

Now Manuel was the elder brother of Isaac and Alexius
and in fact, the first-begotten of all the children descended
through John Comnenus from my paternal grandfather.
He was general in sole command over the whole of Asia to
which the former emperor, Romanus Diogenes, had appointed
him, whereas the principality of Antioch had elected Isaac
by lot as their Duke ; these two had fought in many wars
and battles, and many trophies too they had erected over their
opponents. And after these my father Alexius was promoted
to be General-in-Chief, and dispatched against Ursel by
Michael Ducas, the reigning emperor.

Later on the Emperor Nicephorus also observed his
expertness in warfare and heard how, while serving under
his brother Isaac in the East, he had taken part in many
contests and proved himself valiant beyond his years, and
when he considered the manner in which Alexius had worsted
Ursel, he made just as conspicuous a favourite of him as he
did of Isaac. He took the two brothers to his heart and
looked upon them with joy, sometimes even inviting them to
share his table. This enkindled the envy of others against
them and most especially that of the two aforementioned
Slavonic barbarians, Borilus and Germanus. For seeing the
Emperor's goodwill towards the brothers and that the latter
remained unharmed by the darts that malice hurled at them,
they were consumed with wrath. As the Emperor saw that
Alexius, although his beard was as yet scarce grown, was held
in high repute by all, he appointed him absolute General of
the West and honoured him with the rank of Proedros. Of
all the trophies which he set up throughout the West also
and of the various rebels he conquered and brought as captives

44

to the Emperor sufficient has been said already. But these doings did not please those two slaves but rather fanned the flames of their envy: They went about growling and purposing evil against them in their hearts, and told the King many tales in confidence and others in public or suborned others to tell him, for their desire was, no matter by what means, to get these brothers out of the way. In this distressing situation the Comneni judged it prudent to cultivate the officers of the women's apartments and through them to win in still greater measure the Queen's affection. For the brothers were charming men and able with their varied wiles to soften even a heart of stone. Isaac could do this the more easily as the Queen some time before had chosen him to marry her own cousin; he was a perfect gentleman both in word and deed and most like my own father. But since his own affairs had prospered so well, he took much thought for his brother Alexius, and as the latter had formerly helped him with all his power in arranging his marriage, so he in his turn now desired to see Alexius stand high in the Queen's favour. It is said that the friends Orestes and Pylades had such a deep love for each other that in time of battle either would be quite indifferent to his own foes but would ward off those who attacked his friend, and either would offer his own breast to receive the darts thrown at the other. Exactly the same phenomenon could be witnessed in the case of these two. For either brother tried to anticipate the other's dangers ; and whatever prizes and honours one gained, in short the good fortune of the one, the other considered his own, and vice versa, such close affection bound them to each other. By the help of heaven, Isaac's interests had been thus secured ; and after no long interval the officials of the women's apartments lent a willing ear to Isaac's suggestion that the queen should adopt Alexius. The Queen listened to them ; and the two brothers came to the palace on an appointed day, and then she adopted Alexius according to the ritual prescribed from of old for such cases. Thus for the future the Great Domestic of the Western armies was relieved of a great anxiety. Thenceforth they both visited the palace very often and after paying their respects to the Emperor and staying with him a little they went in to the Queen. All this still further inflamed the envy of others against them, as the Comneni were often assured, and consequently they lived in fear of being caught in their enemies' snares. As they had no protector, they cast about for a means by which,

with God's help, they might ensure safety for themselves.
After revolving many plans with their mother and examining
various schemes at various times they discovered one path
which as far as man can judge, might lead to safety. This
was to approach the Queen when some plausible reason offered,
and tell her their secret. Yet they kept their plan under water
and did not reveal their whole design to anyone, but like
fishermen they were careful not to frighten away their prey.
They intended, indeed, to run away but had been afraid to
tell the Queen this, lest she might disclose their intentions to
the emperor prematurely in her anxiety for the two parties,
to wit, her husband and the brothers. After having settled
on this plan, they turned their attention elsewhere for they
were adepts in making full use of any opportunities that might
occur.

II The Emperor was now too old to have expectations
of a son and as he dreaded the inevitable stroke of death,
he began to consider the question of his successor. At that
time there was at court a certain Synadenus of Eastern origin
and illustrious descent, fair of face, of profound intellect, courageous in battle, verging on young manhood, and above all akin
to the emperor by race. In preference to all others the Emperor
thought of leaving him as successor to the Empire, giving him
the kingdom as his ancestral portion so to speak, and in this
he was ill-advised. For he would have ensured perfect safety
and also regarded justice by bequeathing the imperial power
to the Queen's son, Constantine, as the portion rightly accruing
to him, as it were, through his grandfather and father, and
this would have increased the Queen's confidence in him and
gained her goodwill However, the old man failed to see that
he was arranging matters in a way which was not only unjust
but also disastrous, and was begetting troubles for himself.
The Queen heard whispers of this and was very sad as she
foresaw danger to her son ; but though she was despondent
she did not openly voice her grief to anyone. This did not
escape the notice of the Comneni, and they determined, if
they could find the opportunity they sought, to approach
the Queen. Their mother furnished Isaac with a pretext
for a conversation with the Queen, and his brother Alexius
went with him. When they were admitted to the Queen
Isaac said : "Lady, we do not behold you in the same health
as heretofore, but you seem worried and obsessed by unbearable thoughts and without the courage to reveal your
secret to anybody." However, she would not speak out for

some time, but sighing deeply replied : " It is not right to
question those who live away from home, for that in itself
is sufficient source of grief to them. But as for myself,
alas ! what sorrows have come upon me, one after the other,
and how many more methinks are in store for me shortly."
The brothers stood aloof and added no more words, but with
eyes cast down and both hands covered, stood a minute
plunged in thought and then made their usual obeisance and
departed home in deep distress. The next day they came
again to talk to her, and seeing that she looked at them more
cheerfully than the day before, they both went close up to
her and said : " You are our mistress and we are your most
devoted slaves, ready to die, if need be, for our Queen. And
do not let any consideration unnerve you and lead you to
indecision." Upon these words they gave the Queen an oath
and after freeing themselves from all suspicion they easily
guessed her secret, for they were sharp-witted, shrewd, and
expert in divining from a few words a man's deeply hidden
and hitherto unexpressed opinion. Straightway they associated themselves still more closely with the Queen and making
their goodwill clear to her by many proofs they promised
they would bravely assist her in any undertaking to which
she summoned them. " Rejoice with them that rejoice and
weep with them that weep," that is indeed the apostolic
injunction, and this they willingly observed. They asked
the Queen to count them as her countrymen and intimates
as they were sprung from the same stock as she was ; and one
thing more they urged—that she should not hesitate to
divulge it to them immediately if either she, or the Emperor,
got wind of a plot being formed against them by their rivals,
and thus save them from unconsciously falling into their
enemies' snares. This favour they asked and begged her be
of good cheer, saying that with God's help they would gladly
bring adequate help and as far as depended on them, her son
Constantine should not be ousted from the empire. And they
insisted too in ratifying their agreement by oaths, for there
was no time to lose because of their jealous opponents. So
the brothers were relieved of a great anxiety and recovered
their spirits and from now on showed a cheerful countenance
in their conversations with the Emperor. They were both,
but Alexius more especially, practised in concealing a secret
intention and a deeply laid plan by external pretences. But
as the burning envy of others was now growing into a mighty
fire, and nothing of what was said against them to the Emperor

was any longer concealed from them owing to the agreement (with the Queen), they recognized that those two all-influential slaves were scheming to get them out of the way ; consequently they no longer went together to the palace as had been their custom, but singly, on alternate days. This was a wise and Palamedean precaution to prevent their both perhaps falling into the barbarians' snares at the same time, for if only one were caught by the intrigues of those all-powerful Scythians, the other could escape. Such then was their precaution. However, matters turned out for the brothers very differently from what they had feared, for they anticipated their rivals in the race for power, as my story, starting from this point, will show very clearly.

III About this time the city of Cyzicus was taken by the Turks; directly the Emperor learnt of the capture of the city, he sent for Alexius Comnenus. Now it chanced that on that day Isaac had come, and when he saw his brother entering the palace contrary to their agreement, he went up to him and asked the reason for his coming. Alexius immediately told him the reason, saying : " Because the Emperor has sent for me." So they went in together and made the customary obeisance, and as it was nearly the hour for lunch the Emperor told them to stay for a little and then commanded them to sit down at table with him. And they were separated, for one sat on the right side of the table, and the other on the left, opposite each other. In a few minutes they looked intently at the attendants standing about and saw they were whispering with gloomy countenances. Then they feared lest the two slaves were meditating a sudden attack on them and that danger was nigh at hand, so they looked stealthily at each other and knew not what to do. Long before this they had won over all those in attendance on the Emperor by soft words, and paying court to them with divers forms of greetings ; and by shaking hands with him they had even coaxed the head-cook into looking at them with a friendly eye. To this head-cook there came now one of Isaac Comnenus' servants and said : " Tell my master of the fall of Cyzicus ! for a letter has come from there with this news." Then the cook carried in the meat to the table and at the same time informed Isaac in a low voice of what he had heard from the servant. Isaac in turn by moving his lips slightly, notified the message to Alexius ; and Alexius, who had very keen intuition and was quicker than fire, at once grasped what he had said, and they both recovered from the anxiety

which had held them. And pulling themselves together
they considered how they might answer readily if anyone
asked them about it and also give the right advice to the
Emperor if he consulted them. While they were busy with
these reflections the Emperor looked at them, taking for
granted they did not know about Cyzicus, and told them of
its capture. Then they roused the Emperor's depressed spirits
(for they were ready to minister to his soul which was agitated
by the sack of his cities) and heartened him up with fair
hopes by assuring him that the city could be recovered easily.
" The one thing needful," they said, " is that your Majesty
should be safe ; and as for the captors of the city they shall
render sevenfold into your bosom that which they have
taken." Then indeed the Emperor was delighted with them
and dismissing them from the feast, spent the rest of the day
free from care. Henceforward the Comneni made it their
business to visit the palace and pay court to the men about
the emperor even more assiduously ; for they did not wish to
give their adversaries the slightest handle, nor to afford
them any pretext whatever for hatred, but on the contrary
to win all over to liking them and being on their side both in
thought and speech. They also exerted themselves to win
over the Empress Maria more completely and to convince
her that they only lived and breathed for her. Isaac for his
part with the excuse of his marriage to her cousin, used his
freedom of access to the utmost, whilst Alexius, my father,
alleging his nearness of kin but still more his adoption, as a
brilliant reason, visited the Queen, without arousing anybody's
suspicion and threw a veil over the envy of his ill-wishers.
But he was well aware of the fierce resentment of those barbarian slaves and also of the Emperor's extreme lightheadedness. So they naturally took thought how not to fall from his
good favour, as, in that case, they might become a prey to
their enemies. For light-headed dispositions are ever
unstable and like the Euripus, they drift, as it were, on ever-
changing currents.

IV When the slaves saw that matters were not pro-
gressing along the lines they wished and that the destruction
of such men was not an easy job as the Emperor's goodwill
towards them augmented daily, they broached many plans
and as often rejected them and finally settled on another
course. And what was it ?—it was to send for them one
night without the ruler's knowledge and to put them out of
the way by trumping up some false charge and boring out

their eyes. The Comneni heard of this. As they recognized that danger was very near they decided after much internal conflict that their only hope of safety lay in rebellion and that they were driven to it by dire necessity. For what sense was there in waiting for the red-hot iron to be applied which would quench the light of their eyes for ever ? Therefore they kept this decision deep down in their minds. Soon after this Alexius (who was at that time Domestic of the Western Empire) was ordered to call up to the city a certain division of the army to be prepared for marching against the Hagarenes who had sacked the city of Cyzicus. Seizing this reasonable opportunity, he summoned by letter those officers in the army who were well disposed to himself and their respective troops. These were all mobilized and hurried up to the metropolis. In the meantime somebody at the suggestion of that fellow, Borilus, one of the slaves, asked the Emperor whether it was by his wish that the Great Domestic was introducing all the forces into the city. The Emperor at once sent for Alexius and asked him whether this report was true ; to which Alexius immediately answered that part of the army was coming in by his, the Emperor's, orders, and as for the whole of it being assembled there from all parts he parried the question plausibly. " The army you see," he said, " has been scattered in all directions, and now the various regiments which have received the signal are coming up from their different stations. And those who see them streaming in from various quarters of the Roman dominions, think the whole army is being assembled as if by agreement and are misled by mere appearance." Although Borilus had many objections to make to this speech, yet even so Alexius prevailed and was acquitted by the votes of all. Germanus who was simpler-minded, did not run down Alexius much. As the Emperor's soul was not perturbed even by these allegations against the Domestic, the slaves seized the opportunity and set about preparing an ambush for the Comneni. Now slaves are anyhow by nature hostile to their masters, but when they cannot injure their masters, they turn their power against their fellow-servants, and become quite insupportable. Of this type of character and spirit Alexius had experience in the case of these slaves I am speaking of. For they did not bear resentment against the Comneni from love of the Emperor, but Borilus even aimed at the throne, some said, and as Germanus was his partner in the plot, he helped him prepare the ambush carefully. And they discussed their

plans together and imagined that the affair would turn out
to their satisfaction ; and now they began to speak openly
of that which hitherto they had only mentioned below their
breath. And thus a certain man overheard their talk, an
Alanian by descent, " magister " in rank, who had long been
attached to the emperor and counted among his intimates.
Consequently the Magister stole out during the middle watch
of the night and ran to the Comneni to report everything to
the Great Domestic. Some have it that the Empress was not
altogether ignorant of the Magister's visit to the Comneni.
Alexius took him into his mother and brother ; and after
giving ear to his abominable news, they judged it necessary
to execute the plan they had kept secret so long, and with
God's help to compass their own safety. When, after the
morrow, the Domestic had heard that the army had occupied
Tzouroulus (this is a little town lying Thrace-wards) he went in
the first watch of the night to Pacurianus and related everything to him—this man was " small indeed in stature, but a
mighty warrior," as the poet says, and descended from a
noble Armenian family. To him Alexius related the slaves'
anger and envy, and their long manœuvres against them and
their immediate intention of blinding them. " But," he
continued, " we cannot suffer these things as if we were
captives, but we will die, if need be, after fighting bravely ;
for this is the prerogative of high-souled men." Pacurianus
listened to it all and seeing that such circumstances admitted
of no delay, but that some drastic step must be taken at once,
said, " If when to-morrow's dawn breaks, you leave this city
I will follow you and fight willingly on your side. But if you
put it off to the next day, then be assured that without the
slightest delay I shall go straight to the Emperor and denounce
you and your followers." To which Alexius replied, " As I
see that you really care for my safety, which is undoubtedly
the work of God, I shall not reject your counsel, only let us
mutually secure ourselves by oath." Thereupon they exchanged assurances with oaths to the effect that if Providence
raised Alexius to the Imperial throne, he should raise Pacurianus to the rank of Domestic which he himself held in the
meantime.

Taking leave of Pacurianus he hurried thence to another
man, also " full of warlike frenzy," namely Hubertopoulus,
told him of his own intentions and put before him the reason
why he had decided to escape, and invited him to join him.
Hubertopoulus immediately agreed, and added, " You will

always find me courageous, but more especially so when I am braving danger on your behalf." The reason above all others why these men were devoted to Alexius was that he outshone others in courage and intelligence ; but they also loved him because he was exceptionally generous and very ready to give, although he had not a great abundance of money. For he was not of those who plunder and open their mouths wide for riches. True liberality is not as a rule judged by the quantity of money supplied, but is weighed by the spirit of the giver. In some cases a man of few possessions who pays in proportion to his income, may justly be termed " liberal," whereas another who has much wealth and hides it in a hole in the earth, or does not give to the needy in proportion to his wealth, would rightly be styled " a second Crœsus," or " a Midas mad for gold," or " niggardly and penurious " or a " cummin-splitter " ! That Alexius was graced with all the virtues, the men I have mentioned had known for a long time already, and for these reasons they eagerly desired his elevation to the throne. After exchanging oaths with this officer too, Alexius set off home at a run and told his people everything. It was the night of Quinquagesima Sunday (or the " Cheese-eating " Sunday) when my father made these arrangements ; and on the following day at early dawn he had already left the city with his partisans. Hence it was that the populace, who approved of Alexius' spirit and shrewdness, wove a little song to him about these occurrences, composed in their own popular dialect, and it very cleverly strikes up the prelude of the affair and accentuates his prescience of the plot against him and his consequent actions. In its original words the song ran thus :

" τὸ σάββατον τῆς τυρινῆς χαρεῖς 'Αλέξιε ἐνόησές το
κἀι τὴν δευτέραν τὸ πρωῒ ὗπα καλῶς γεράκιν μου."

The meaning of that popular song is roughly this, " On the Saturday named after cheese, bravo to you for your shrewdness, Alexius ! But on the Monday after the Sunday you flew away like a high-flying hawk, out of the nets of the barbarians."

V   Anna Dalassena, the mother of the Comneni, had lately managed to affiance the grandson of Botaniates to the daughter of Manuel, her eldest son ; and now through fear of his tutor hearing of the scheme and divulging it to the emperor she formed a very good plan. It was this, she ordered her whole household to assemble that evening for the purpose, presumably, of making her devotions in the churches of God—for it was her habit to visit the sanctuaries frequently. This was done. All were present according to custom and they brought out the horses from the stables and pretended to be carefully spreading such saddle-cloths on them as befitted the women.

Botaniates' grandson and his tutor were asleep meanwhile, for a separate house had been appointed to them. About the first watch the Comneni who were now quite ready to arm themselves and ride away from the imperial city, locked the gates and gave their mother the keys, and they also noiselessly closed the gates of the house in which her niece's betrothed, Botaniates, was sleeping, though they did not bring the two leaves quite close together and fasten them perfectly for fear they should creak and this noise wake the boy. In these doings the greater part of the night had passed.

Before the first cock-crow they opened the gates, and taking their mothers, sisters, wives and children with them, they all walked together to the Forum of Constantine ; on arrival there the Comneni took leave of the women and hastened off very quickly to the palace of Blachernæ, whilst the latter ran to the Church of the Divine Wisdom. In the meantime Botaniates' tutor had awakened and guessing what had happened, went after them, torch in hand, and caught them up shortly before they reached the precincts of The 40 Saints. On catching sight of him, Dalassena, the mother of those two noble sons, said to him, " Somebody has denounced us to the emperor, I hear. I will therefore make a round of the churches, and use their help as much as I can ; and at dawn of day I shall go from them to the palace. So do you go there now and directly the porters open the gates, apprise them of our coming." And he straightway went off to do as he was bid. Then the women arrived at the precincts of Bishop Nicholas (which has retained its name of " The Sanctuary " to this day), this stands near the large church and was founded long ago for the protection of those being taken for crimes, as being a part of the large precinct, and was purposely constructed by our ancestors so that if anyone who had been convicted of a crime managed to take refuge there, he was released from the penalty of the law. For the old Emperors and Cæsars shewed great consideration for their subjects. But the watchman of this church did not unbolt the doors for the women quickly, but asked, " Who they were and whence they came," whereupon one of the women's attendants said, " They are women from the East, who have spent all their means, and are hastening to pay their acts of devotion so as to be free to return home." Then the man immediately unbolted the doors and gave them admission. At the morrow's assembly of the Senate, the Emperor, who had learnt of the brothers' doings, spoke as was to be expected and inveighed severely against the Domestic. And afterwards he sent two men, Straboromanus and Euphemianus by name, to fetch the women to the palace. But Dalassena said to them : " Give the Emperor this message : ' My sons are the faithful servants of your imperial Majesty and have willingly served you at all times, sparing neither their lives nor their bodies, and have always been the first to risk everything for your empire. But the jealousy felt by others who could not endure your Majesty's kindness and solicitude for them, caused them to stand in great and hourly peril ; and when finally their enemies decided to blind them, they got wind of it, and as they could not endure such undeserved peril they left the city, not as rebels but as your trusty servants, firstly, in order to escape this imminent danger and secondly, to inform your Majesty of the plotting against them and to implore help from your Majesty.' " But the messengers urgently pressed her to come with them, until the woman grew indignant and said, " Allow me to enter God's church and pay my devotions to Him. For it is ridiculous to come as far as the entrance and not go in and implore the mediation of Our Immaculate Mistress, the Mother of God, both for the cause of God and the life of the Emperor." Then the ambassadors respecting her reasonable request, allowed her to enter. She advanced slowly as a woman worn out with age or grief would, or rather she simulated fatigue, and when she had almost reached the very entrance of the Sanctuary, she made two genuflexions and at the third collapsed on the ground, and clinging to the Royal Doors cried out : " Unless my hands are cut off, I shall not leave these holy precincts, until I receive the Emperor's cross as pledge of my safety." Hereupon Straboromanus pulled out the cross he carried in his bosom and gave it to her, but she replied, " I am not asking for assurance from you, but from the Emperor himself I demand the security I have mentioned. And I will certainly not accept a cross sent to me if it is of minute size, but it must be of respectable size." (This she required in order that the pledge given to her might be clearly seen ; for if the promise were made over a small

cross, most of the onlookers would probably not have observed
its ratification.) " It is that man's verdict and mercy I require.
Begone, take him my message ! " And next her daughter-in-
law, the wife of Isaac (who had managed to slip into the
church at the time of the opening of the gates for the early
hymn) drew aside the veil covering her face and said to them,
" Well, she for her part may go, if she likes ; but we will
not leave this church without assurances, even though death
lay before us." Then the man seeing the stubbornness of
the women and realizing that they were growing bolder
towards them than at first, and fearing some tumult might
arise, went away and told the whole tale to the emperor.
And he, being kindly by nature and touched by the woman's
words, sent her the cross she asked for and gave her full
immunity. And when she had come out of the church he
ordered her with her daughters and daughters-in-law to be
confined in the convent of the Petrii which is situated close to
the Sidera.[1] The emperor also had her marriage-relation, the
wife of the emperor John (who held the rank of Protovest-
iaria), fetched from the sanctuary in Blachernæ, which had
been founded in honour of our mistress, the Mother of God,
and consigned her as well to the convent of the Petrii, and gave
orders that their stores of wine and corn and all their private
possessions should be preserved intact. Every morning then,
the two women went to the guards and enquired whether
they had any news of their sons ; and the soldiers dealt
fairly frankly with them and told all they had heard. But
the " Mistress of the Wardrobe," a woman generous in hand
and mind, desired to conciliate their guards and so told them
to take as much of their eatables as they liked for their own use ,
for the women were allowed to have all they required brought
in without let or hindrance. From that time on the guards
became more ready with their news and consequently not a
detail of all the Comneni were doing was concealed from the
women.

VI So much then for the women. Now the rebels on
their part when they had reached the gate in the circular
walls of Blachernæ, burst its lock and thus had free access
to the royal stables. And some of the horses there they left
after first slitting their hind-legs from the thigh downwards
with the sword, and of the rest they chose those which seemed
to them in the best condition, and thence betook themselves
with all speed to the monastery, somewhere near the city,
called Cosmidium. And here, if I may insert something to

[1] i.e. the Gate Sidera.

make my tale run more clearly, they found the afore-mentioned Mistress of the Wardrobe, before the Emperor sent to fetch her, as I have told. They took their leave of this woman when they were ready to ride away and they persuaded George Palæologus to take sides with them and compelled him to depart with them. For before this they had not divulged their plans to him because of a natural suspicion; for the father of this George was extremely devoted to the Emperor, and therefore revealing their project of rebellion to him would have been rather dangerous. And at first indeed, Palæologus did not show himself at all amenable, but opposed many objections and reproved them for their breach of faith to the emperor and for the fact that, as the proverb has it, they became turncoats. But when the Mistress of the Wardrobe, Palæologus' mother-in-law, insisted firmly on his joining them, under threat of dire punishment, he began to yield and his next concern was for the safety of the women, namely his wife Anna and his mother-in-law Maria, for the latter was descended from one of the first families of Bulgaria and was so attractive by reason of the beauty and grace of limbs and features that she was considered the most beautiful of all the women then living. Thus George and Alexius were not free from anxiety about her, and both felt that the women must be removed from that place, but while Alexius' party advised their being conveyed to some fortress, Palæologus suggested the sanctuary of our Lady in Blachernæ—and George's opinion prevailed. So they went off at once with these women and placed them under the care of the Holy Mother of the all-embracing Word. On their return to the place whence they started, they consulted on their best course of action, and Palæologus said, " You two must get away from here; and I will soon overtake you and bring my property with me." For as it happened he had all his movable property stored there. Without further delay therefore the Comneni started on their journey; and, after loading his property on the monks' beasts of burden, Palæologus rode after them. And he came up with them at Tzouroulus (a Thracian village) where by a lucky chance they all joined the army which had occupied it by command of the Domestic. Then thinking it right to send news of their doings to John Ducas, the ex-emperor, who was at that time living on his own property in the country of Morobundus, they dispatched a messenger to inform him of their rebellion. The man carrying the message happened to arrive at early dawn and was standing outside the gates of the farm asking for the Emperor. And his grandchild John, still quite a child, not even a boy yet, and consequently always with the Emperor, saw the man and at once ran in, woke up his grandfather who was still asleep, and told him of the rebellion. But the latter astounded by the words, gave the child a box on the ears, and advising him not to talk nonsense, sent him off. In a little while, however, he came back again, bringing the same news, and in addition the message addressed to his grandfather by the Comneni. Now this message had an excellent touch of wit in it which hinted at Alexius' doings, for it said : "We on our side have prepared a right good meal, not wanting in rich condiments, but if you on your side wish to share this banquet, you must come with all speed to partake of it." Then the Emperor sat up and propping himself on his right elbow bade them bring in the messenger, and when this man had finished his tale about the Comneni, he at once exclaimed : "Woe is me !" and clapped his hands over his eyes. And after grasping his beard for a time, as a man will when revolving matters of deep import in his mind, he settled on this one point, namely, that he too would yield to their wish. Therefore he immediately summoned his grooms and mounting his horse, rode off to join the Comneni. On the way he chanced upon a Byzantine who was carrying a heavy purse of gold and travelling to the capital, so in the words of Homer he asked him, "Who and whence art thou ?" On learning that he had collected a large sum from certain taxes and was conveying it to the treasury, he urged him to halt for the night with him, promising that at daybreak he should go off where he liked. At the other's refusing and getting angry, the Emperor insisted all the more and finally persuaded him—for he was marvellously glib of speech and quick in thought, and persuasion sat on his tongue as if he were a second Æschines or Demosthenes. So he took him with him and turned in at an inn, where he detained him by looking after him kindly in all ways, making him share his table and seeing that he could rest comfortably. But at dawn just when the sun was climbing up the eastern horizon, the Byzantine spread the cloths on the horses and was for hurrying off to ride at full speed to Byzantium. The Emperor seeing this called : "Stop and travel with us," but the other not knowing where he was going and being moreover quite in the dark about the reason which made him the object of so much solicitude, became vexed and suspicious again of the Emperor and his friendly ways. But the Emperor insisted and began pulling at him, and as the other still did not yield, he changed his manner and spoke more roughly and threatened him if he would not do as he was ordered. As the other still did not obey he ordered all the stranger's possessions to be packed with his own on his beasts and started on his journey, giving the other permission to go where he liked. Then the man abandoned his intention of going to the Palace from fear of being imprisoned if the Treasury-officials saw him come with empty hands ; again he was not anxious to return home because of the unsettled and confused state of the country resultant upon the rebellion of the Comneni which had emerged, and so against his will he followed the Emperor.

And next the following incident took place. As he was starting, the Emperor fell in with some Turks who had just crossed the river Eurus.[1] So drawing reign, he enquired whence and whither they were going, and straightway promised them much money and all kinds of rewards if they would accompany him to the Comneni—and so they consented. Later he demanded an oath from their leaders as he wished to confirm their agreement by it, and this they immediately gave after their fashion and assured him that they would most readily fight on the side of the Comneni. After this he started taking the Turks with him as well to the Comneni. The latter saw him from afar and were overjoyed at his strange booty, and they both, but especially my father Alexius, could scarcely contain themselves for delight. Alexius went to meet him and embraced and kissed him. And what followed ? At the Emperor's suggestion and suasion they set forth on the road leading to the capital. And all the men from the country-towns flocked to Alexius as volunteers and proclaimed him Emperor—the only exception were the men of Orestias who had an old grudge against him for having captured Bryennius, and therefore they adhered to the part of Botaniates. When they had reached the Athyras, they rested there for one day and then pushed on and reached Schiza (which is also a village in Thrace) and formed an entrenched camp there.

VII The whole world, agog with excitement, was eagerly looking forward to what would happen and each longed to see the man who was expected to be proclaimed Emperor. The majority certainly wished Alexius to gain that honour, but neither were Isaac's partisans idle, but as far as possible, they solicited everybody. And thus matters were apparently

[1] R. Hebrus.

at a deadlock, for half the population desired to see the elder,
and the other half desired to see the younger, brother raised
to be pilot of the imperial dignity.   Amongst the men present
at that time were several of Alexius' kinsmen, for instance,
the above-mentioned Emperor, John Ducas, a man clever in
council and swift in action (whom I also saw once for a short
time) and Michael and John, his grandsons, as well as the
husband of their sister, George Palæologus.   These helped
each other and worked hard to convert all people's opinions
to their own, and letting out every reef, as they say,
skilfully used every possible expedient for getting Alexius
proclaimed.   Consequently they won people over to agree
with them, with the result that the number of Isaac's partisans
gradually diminished.   For wherever the Emperor John was,
not a single person was able to resist him, as he was unrivalled
in the dignity of his principles, the size of his body, and his
king-like appearance.   What did the Ducases not do ?   What
did they not say ?   What good thing did they not promise
both to the leaders and the whole army, if Alexius were raised
to the Imperial eminence ?   For example they would say,
" He will requite you with very great gifts and the highest
honours in accordance with each man's merit, not in a hap-
hazard way, as the ignorant and inexperienced among leaders
do, for he has borne the title of " Military Commander " for
a long time now and " Great Domestic of the West " ; he has
shared your salt, in war he has fought nobly at your side,
be it in ambush or in close combat, never did he grudge his
body, limbs, or even his life to ensure your safety ; he has
often traversed mountains and plains with you, and learnt
the hardships of warfare ; finally, he knows you all both as a
body and individually, and being himself dear to Ares, he
above all longs for brave soldiers."   In this manner spake
the Ducases, but Alexius deemed Isaac worthy of much honour
and in all things preferred him, either owing to the charm
of brotherhood, or rather, and this must be mentioned, for
another reason.   For, as the whole army was veering to his
side and advocating his claims while it did not favour Isaac
even in the slightest, Alexius saw that strength and power
and the realization of his hopes would come from that quarter,
and so he supported his brother in his intrigues for the throne,
knowing that nothing untoward to himself would result
from so doing, provided he for his part were raised up by force,
as it were, by the whole army to the pinnacle of earthly honours
and he flattered his brother in words only and made a pretence

forsooth of yielding the power to him. After some time had
been spent in this manner, the whole soldiery were assembled
near the General's tent in a great state of excitement and each
anxious for the accomplishment of his wish. Then Isaac
rose and taking the red buskin tried to put it on to his brother's
foot ; but the latter refused several times until Isaac cried,
" Let me do it, for through you God wishes to restore the
dignity of our family." He also reminded Alexius of the
prophecy once addressed to him by a man who appeared to
them somewhere near Carpianum as they were returning home
from the palace. For they had reached that spot when a
man suddenly met them, perhaps belonging to a race higher
than mortal, but in any case gifted with very clear insight
into the future. From his appearance he seemed to be a
priest, with his bare head, grey hair and shaggy beard ; he
took hold of Alexius' leg and being on foot himself, he dragged
down Alexius, who was on horseback, by the ear and recited
to him this line of David's psalm : " In thy majesty ride
on prosperously, because of truth and meekness and righteous-
ness," and addressed him by the title " Emperor Alexius ! "
With these words which sounded like a prophecy he vanished.
And Alexius could not capture him, though he looked round
carefully in all directions in order, if possible, to catch sight
of him, and then pursued him at full speed if perchance he
might catch him and ask more in detail who he was and whence
he came. But what had been seen had completely vanished.
On their return home Isaac was very inquisitive about this
vision and asked Alexius to disclose the secret : and as he
insisted strongly, Alexius at first made a feint of refusing but
finally repeated what had been said to him in secret. Now
in discussing this openly with his brother he treated the
words and incident as a fraud and deception, but in his private
meditations upon this man in priestly garb who had appeared
to him, he likened him to the theologian, the Son of Thunder.
Therefore when Isaac saw that what the old man had prophesied was being fulfilled in deed, and expressed in words,
he insisted more vehemently and by force put the red buskin
on his brother's foot, especially because he saw the fervid
longing of all the soldiers for Alexius. After this act the
Ducases led the acclamations for they favoured this man
for many reasons and especially because their relation, Irene,
my mother, had been legally married to my father. And
simultaneously all those akin to them by blood did likewise
with a will, and the rest of the army took up the shout and

sent their voices almost to the heavens. And then was witnessed a curious phenomenon—for those who before had held opposite opinions and preferred death to failure in their desire, became in one moment of the same opinion, and that too, so decidedly, that nobody could have even suspected there had been a variance of opinion between them.

VIII While these events were taking place, a rumour spread that Melissenus had already reached the promontory of Damalis with a fair-sized army, had assumed the purple and was being acclaimed as emperor. For some time the Comneni would not believe this report, but Melissenus on learning of their doings, at once dispatched ambassadors to them, who on arrival handed over his letters to the Comneni, which ran somewhat as follows : " God has brought me safely as far as Damalis together with the army under my command. I have heard of your experiences, and the measures you have taken for your own safety after being delivered by the mercy of God from the malice of those slaves and their cruel plots against you. Now, as concerns relationship, I am already allied to you by ties of kin, thanks be to God ! and as concerns purpose, I yield to none of your blood-relations in my unalterable affection for you (let God, the Judge of all, be my witness !). It is right that we should consult together and ensure for ourselves a firm and stable position so that we may not be upset by every wind that blows, but arrange the affairs of the empire well and thus stand on a sure foundation. This we shall certainly accomplish if, after you have captured the city by the help of God, you two administer the affairs of the West and allow the kingdom of Asia to be allotted to me. I too must wear the diadem and be clad in purple, and, as is the custom with royalties, my name must be joined in proclamations with the name of that one of you who is chosen Emperor, so that acclamations may be made for us conjointly. In this wise, even though the countries and the business have been divided, yet our mind would be one and the same, and while we so continue the Empire would be administered by us both in perfect peace." The ambassadors did not then and there receive a full answer to the letter they had presented ; the next day the Comneni sent for them, and in lengthy speech pointed out to them the impracticability of Melissenus' proposals ; they further promised to let them know their decision on the matter shortly through George, called Manganes, to whose care they had entrusted the ambassadors. In spite of this business they did not by any means neglect the siege but as often as possible made skirmishing attacks upon the walls. On the following day they called the ambassadors and announced their decision to them. This was that Melissenus should be elevated to the rank of ' Cæsar,' should be adjudged the fillet and salutes and all other privileges which belong to this rank, and also that the largest town in Thessaly should be given to him. (In this town there is the magnificent church named after the great martyr Demetrius, where the myrrh which ever trickles from his venerable coffin works marvellous cures for those who approach it in faith.) The ambassadors were displeased with the terms but, since those they proposed were not accepted, and they observed also the rebel's great preparations against the city and the enormous army under him, and as they were pressed for time, they began to fear that if they captured the city, the Comneni would not grant even that which they now promised, so they asked that the conditions should be put in a Golden Bull and signed in red letters. To this Alexius, the new Emperor, consented and immediately summoned George Manganes, who served him as secretary, and ordered him to draw up this Golden Bull. But the latter deferred it for three days, always stringing together various excuses, saying once that after getting over-tired during the day he could not finish the whole letter at night, and at another time that a spark had fallen on what he had written at night and burnt it up. By making such and similar excuses and, true to his name, playing tricks, Manganes postponed writing by one means or the other. Pushing on further the Comneni quickly seized the place called Aretæ. This is a district lying close to the city and overlooking the plain, and to persons standing below and looking up to it, it looks like a hill; on the one side it slopes down to the sea, on the other to Byzantium, but on the North and West sides it is exposed to all the winds; it has perennial supplies of clear, fresh water but is so utterly devoid of bushes and trees that you would have said the hill had been laid bare by woodcutters. Because of its pleasant situation and climate the Emperor Romanus Diogenes erected some fine houses suitable for kings for short periods of rest. When the Comneni were established there, they made attempts on the wall not by means of siege-engines or machines or stone-throwing instruments, since there was not time enough for those, but with light-armed troops, far-shooters, spearmen and fully-armed soldiers.

IX Now when Botaniates saw the size of the army of the Comneni and its composition of men of all races, and that it was already approaching the gates of the city, and that Melissenus Nicephorus had reached Damalis with no less a force than theirs and was likewise a claimant for the throne, he knew not what to do, and was quite unfit to contend against two foes. For old age had chilled his spirit and made him over-fearful, though in youth he had been very brave, and now he only breathed freely as long as he was encircled by the walls, and he had already ideas of abdicating. Hence the citizens were naturally seized with alarm and unrest and thought the whole place could easily be captured from any side. The Comneni on their side thought the taking of the city would be difficult (for their forces were composed of various nationalities besides natives, and wherever there is a mixed crowd, their temper also is wont to be mixed), so Alexius, the newly-shod Emperor, seeing the city would be difficult to capture, and suspecting the unstable character of his soldiers, adopted a new plan which was by flattery and promises to suborn some of the guards of the walls, and by thus stealing, so to say, their goodwill, to capture the city. After thinking out these things all night he went into the Cæsar's tent at early morning and told him his intention and asked him to accompany him on a tour round the walls in order to investigate the defences and their guards (who were chosen from different regiments), and to determine how it would be possible to take the city. The Cæsar, however, was annoyed at this order, for he had only adopted the monastic habit very lately and naturally shrank from going near the walls for he felt he would be laughed at by the men on the walls and battlements. And so it fell out. For when he followed Alexius under compulsion, directly the men spied him from the walls they jeeringly called him " Father " and added some insulting remark. However he knitted his brows and though inwardly insulted, disregarded them but gave his full attention to the purpose in hand. For men of firm disposition can fix their mind on the matter before them and overlook external disturbances. He therefore found out which soldiers were on duty in the various towers. He learnt that in one place the " Immortals " were on guard (this is the most select regiment of the Roman army) and in another the Varangians from Thule[1] (by these I mean the

---

[1] By some interpreted as the British Isles, by others as part of Scandinavia, particularly Thyland in Jutland.

axe-bearing barbarians) and in yet another the Nemitzi[1]
(these too are a barbaric tribe who have been subjects of
the Roman Empire from of old) ; and he thereupon advised
Alexius not to make an offer to the Varangians or the Immortals.   For the latter, being indigenous, naturally cherished
a great affection for the Emperor and would sooner lose their
lives than be persuaded to adopt any treachery against him.
The Varangians, too, who carried their axes on their shoulders,
regarded their loyalty to the Emperors and their protection
of the imperial persons as a pledge and ancestral tradition,
handed down from father to son, which they keep inviolate
and will certainly not listen to even the slightest word about
treachery.   But if Alexius approached the Nemitzi he would
perhaps not be far from the mark, but be lucky enough to
gain entrance into the city through the tower where they kept
watch.

Alexius listened to these words of the Cæsar as if they came
from an oracle and at once acted upon them.   He sent one
of his men to sound the leader of the Nemitzi carefully from
the foot of the wall ; the leader looked down from above
and after a brisk interchange of questions and answers, he
soon agreed to betray the city.   So the soldier returned
bringing the message and as soon as Alexius and his companions heard this unexpected news, they were delighted
and very eagerly prepared to mount their horses.

X   At the same time the ambassadors from Melissenus
were insistently demanding the Golden Bull which had been
promised them, and Manganes was summoned to bring it.
He said that he had indeed written the letter, but protested
that the implements necessary for the royal signatures and
sealing had been lost, pen and all !   For he was a dissembler
and clever at easily forecasting the future, at picking out
what was advantageous from the past, and also accurately
diagnosing the present and skilfully arranging matters to
his own liking while he covered his doings as long as he wished.
Thus Manganes postponed the writing of the Golden Bull in
order to keep Melissenus in suspense, for he feared that if the
Bull, which bestowed upon him the rank of Cæsar, were
dispatched more hastily than was wise, Melissenus would
scorn that honour and cling at all costs to gaining the empire,
as he had informed the Comneni, and venture on a very bold
stroke.   Such then was the art and wiliness of Manganes
in postponing the writing of the Golden Bull for the Cæsar.

---

[1] = Germans.

While these things were being arranged and time was pressing
for entering into the city, the ambassadors became suspicious
of some trick, and were still more insistent in their demands
for the Golden Bull. But the Comneni said to them, " Since
we practically have the city in our hands, we are going now
to take possession of it with the help of God, so do you depart
and take this news to your lord and master." And they
added further, " If events do indeed turn out according to our
hopes, he must come to us, and then all matters will easily
be arranged in a manner agreeable both to ourselves and to
him "—this was their answer to the ambassadors. Then
they sent out George Palæologus to Gilpractus, the leader of
the Nemitzi, to find out the latter's intentions, and if he
discovered that he was ready to admit the Comneni, as he
had promised, he was to give the preconcerted signal, and
directly they saw it they would hasten their entrance, while
Gilpractus himself would quickly ascend the tower and open
the gates to them. Palæologus undertook this errand very
willingly, for he was a man eager for military exploits and the
sacking of cities, and the term " stormer of cities " which
Homer applies to Ares, would fit him exactly. Next the Comneni got ready and drew up all their heavy-armed troops
in a very clever way, and then, marching slowly, they approached the city in troops. But in the evening George
Palæologus approached the wall and receiving the signal
from Gilpractus, he went up into the tower with his
companions. Alexius meanwhile and his men were only a
short distance from the walls and after throwing up a palisade,
they encamped comfortably and remained at rest there for a
brief period of the night. During the rest of the night,
however, after posting the light-armed, they pushed on at a
marching pace—the Comneni held the centre of the line with
picked cavalry and the flower of the troops—and just at daybreak they stood outside the walls with the whole of their
army. All the soldiers were fully armed as if for battle so
that they might strike terror into the hearts of the citizens.
But when Palæologus gave them the signal from above and
opened the gates, they rushed in pell-mell, no longer with
military discipline, but just as each could, carrying their
shields, bows and spears.

Now the day was Good Friday (the day on which we
offer and feed upon our Mystical Passover) of the fourth
" Indiction " in the month of April in the year 6589.[1] And
as the whole army (which was composed of foreign and native

---

[1] i.e. of the Byzantine era = 1081 A.D.

troops and had come together from home and neighbouring countries) knew that the city had for a long time been crammed with all kinds of riches which were continually imported from other lands and seas, they entered very quickly through the Charisian Gate and scattering in all directions along the main streets, the cross-roads and the by-lanes, they spared neither houses, churches nor even the innermost sanctuaries but amassed a large amount of booty and only desisted from killing, and in every way they acted throughout with the greatest recklessness and shamelessness. Indeed the worst feature was that not even the natives themselves abstained from these deeds but apparently forgot themselves, changed their manners for the worse and did themselves exactly the same things as the barbarians.

XI On being informed of these events, Nicephorus Botaniates realized that his own situation had become exceedingly difficult as the city was being besieged on the West, and Nicephorus Melissenus was encamped at the promontory of Damalis on the East ; he did not know what to do but rather inclined to abdicate in favour of Melissenus. And when the city was already surrounded by the Comneni, he bade one of his most trusty attendants go and bring Melissenus through the fleet to the palace ; and a certain very fierce guardsman was to accompany him. But before this project could be fulfilled, the city was taken. And Palæologus, taking one of his servants with him, walked down to the sea, and finding a boat, got in at once and told the oarsman to row to the place where the fleet was usually anchored. When he was already drawing near to the other coast he saw the man sent by Botaniates to fetch Melissenus getting the fleet ready, and the guardsman was on one of the men-of-war. Recognizing the latter from afar as one of his former acquaintances, he sailed alongside the vessel, hailed him and asked the usual questions, " Whence he came and whither going " and then begged him to take him up into his ship. But the guardsman, seeing him with a shield and sword, was frightened and replied, " I would gladly have taken you, had I not noticed that you are fully armed." Hereupon Palæologus at once consented to lay aside his helmet, shield and short sword, provided only the other would pick him up. Directly the guardsman saw him taking off his weapons, he allowed him to board his own ship, and took him in his arms and embraced him effusively. But Palæologus, a man of energy, did not delay even for a moment before embarking

on his task. Running up to the prow he began asking the
rowers, " What are you doing ? and where are you going,
taking part in a business which will bring dire misfortune
to yourselves ? the city, as you see, has been taken. He
who was once the ' Great Domestic ' has been proclaimed
Emperor ; you see his soldiers and you can hear the shouts ;
and there will be no room in the palace for anybody else.
Botaniates for his part is a fine man, but then the Comneni
on theirs are far finer. Large too is the army of Botaniates,
but our army is many times larger. You ought not therefore
to betray yourselves, your wives and children, but rather
take a good look at the city, notice that the whole army is
already inside it and the standards fixed, listen to the loud
shouts of acclamation, and while the late Domestic draws
near to the palace as Emperor and is even now girding on the
royal insignia, put your ship astern and go and join him,
and thus assure him complete victory ! " The crew were
immediately convinced by his words and came over to his
opinion, whereupon the guardsman grew angry and that
warrior George Palæologus threatened to put him into chains
there and then on the deck or to throw him into the sea. Then
Palæologus at once started the cheering and the rowers
joined in, but as the guardsman was angry and refused to do
so, he had him bound to the deck and left him. After sailing
a little further, he again took up his sword and shield, and then
brought his ship to the place where the fleet lay, and soon he
had all the sailors joining in cheers for the new Emperor.
He happened, also, upon the man dispatched by Botaniates
to take over the fleet and bring Melissenus through, so he
straightway apprehended him and ordered the sailors to loose
the cables. Next he sailed away from there with the fleet
and reached the Acropolis where he led fresh shouts of acclamation. There he commanded the rowers to cease rowing and
to stand by quietly and thus prevent the landing of any who
were trying to cross from the East. Within a short time he
saw a vessel putting in to the palace, and by bidding the
rowers of his own boat row their hardest, he outstripped it.
And when he saw his own father in it, he stood up and at
once gave him the salutation due to parents. But his father
did not look at him pleasantly, nor did he call him the " dear
light of his eyes," as Odysseus of Ithaca once did on beholding
Telemachus. On that occasion there was a banquet, suitors,
a contest of strength, bows and arrows and the prudent
Penelope set as prize for the victor, and Telemachus was not

an enemy, but a son assisting his father ; but on this there
was fighting and war and the father and son were opposed
in spirit.   And each was well aware of the other's feelings,
even though their opinions had not yet been manifested in
action.   So the father called his son a "fool" and asked
him : "What have you come to do here ? " and his son
replied " As it is you who ask me, nothing ! "   To this the
other answered, " Wait a little, and if the Emperor will
follow my advice, I will let you know shortly."   The aforesaid Nicephorus Palæologus entered the palace where he
found the soldiers dispersed in all directions intent on collecting booty, and judging that they could easily be overcome,
he begged Botaniates to let him have the Varangians from
the island of Thule, in order to drive the Comneni out of the
city with their help.   But Botaniates, having once for all
despaired of his cause, pretended that he did not want civil
war.   " If perchance you will listen to me, Nicephorus,
then I pray you go to the Comneni as soon as they are in the
city and make overtures of peace to them."   And so, though
very unwillingly, he went.

XII   The Comneni on entering the city, had already
gained confidence and halted near the square of the Great
Martyr George, called Syceotes, discussing whether they
should first go and salute their mothers, according to custom,
and then proceed to the palace ; but the Cæsar, being informed
of this, sent one of his body-servants and upbraided them
severely for their dilatoriness.   So they hastened to the
house of Iberitzes where Nicephorus Palæologus overtook
them and said, "The Emperor sends you this message:
' I am already an old man and a lonely one, and possess
neither son nor brother nor any blood-relation, and if you are
willing ' (here Nicephorus addressed his speech to the newly-
made Emperor Alexius), ' do you become my adopted son.
And I will not prevent your giving whatsoever you have already
promised to your fellow-soldiers, nor will I even share your
royal power in any way ; I merely ask to retain the name of
Emperor, public acclamations and the red buskins, and
further the permission to live quietly in the palace.   The
administration of the affairs of the Empire shall be
handed over entirely to you.' "   In response the Comneni said a few words, suggestive of agreement, which
were repeated to the Cæsar who thereupon made haste to
get to them to urge them with threats to hurry to the palace.
The Comneni, who were going out, met him who was on foot,

entering the courtyard from the right and he censured them
severely. As he was entering he also caught sight of Nicephorus Palæologus who was approaching the house again
from the left and said to him, "What have you to do here ?
and for what purpose have you come, kinsman ? " to which
the other replied, "My coming will accomplish nothing,
meseems, but I come to bring the same message from the
Emperor as this morning. For the Emperor is resolute to
keep to the terms he has offered and to treat Alexius as his
son ; he proposes to invest him with full imperial power so
that he may administer the affairs of the Empire according
to his pleasure, provided he himself may merely retain the
name of Emperor and the red buskins and his purple clothing
and the right of living quietly in the palace, as he is an old
man now and needs repose." Hereupon the Cæsar with a
fierce glance and heavy scowl said, "Get away and tell the
Emperor that those offers would have been more useful
before the city was captured ; for the future ambassadorial
messages are uttered out of place. Tell him too, ' As you are
already an old man, get off the throne and take thought for
your own safety.' " That was the Cæsar's answer. Now
when Borilus learnt of the entry of the Comneni and of the
army's dispersal throughout the city, occupied with plundering and wholly intent on collecting booty, he determined to
attack them, thinking they could easily be defeated owing
to their scattered state (for the chiefs had been left alone
with their kinsmen by blood or marriage and a few foreign
soldiers). So he collected all the men who brandished their
axes on their shoulders and those who hailed from Coma,
and marching from the Forum of Constantine to the so-called
Milestone, he drew them up there in ranks with utmost pre-
cision ; so there they stood, in close order, ready for battle
and keeping quiet for the time being.

The Patriarch at that time was a truly holy man and poor,
and had practised every species of asceticism such as the
fathers of old who lived in the deserts and on the mountains
used ; he was also endowed with the divine gift of prophecy
and had at various times predicted various things in none of
which he had been wrong ; in a word, he was a model and type
to posterity. This man was perfectly well aware of all that
had befallen Botaniates, and now either by divine inspiration
or at the suggestion of the Cæsar (for this, too, was whispered,
as the Cæsar had long been his friend on account of his high
standard of virtue) he counselled the Emperor to abdicate.

" Do not begin a civil war," he said, " nor resist God's decree. Do not allow the city to be defiled with the blood of Christians, but yield to the will of God, and depart from our midst." The Emperor followed the Patriarch's advice, and fearing the army's insolence, he girt his clothes around him and went down to the great church of God, hanging his head ; and in his very disturbed state of mind, he did not notice that he was still wearing the robes of an Emperor. But Borilus turned to him and catching hold of the mantle attached to his arm by a pearl clasp, pulled it off his dress remarking with a sneer and a grin, " Such a pretty thing truly suits me better now ! " And the Emperor entered into the great church of Divine Wisdom, and stayed there for a time.

BOOK III

I

DIRECTLY the Comneni had taken possession of the palace they dispatched to the Emperor their niece's husband, Michael, who later became Logothete of the private treasure. With him went a certain Rhadinus who was then Prefect of the city, and by them the Emperor was conducted into a barque and taken a short distance to the famous Monastery of the Peribleptos where they both urged him to don the monastic habit. He, however, wished to defer this for a time, but they in their dread lest a rebellion should be manœuvred by those two slaves and the soldiers from Coma during the prevailing disorder and confusion, urgently counselled him to be tonsured, and he yielded to their persuasions and forthwith assumed the " dress of angels." Such is Fortune's way ! At one moment she exalts a man when she wishes to smile on him, and places a kingly diadem on his head, and purple shoes on his feet ; at the next she frowns upon him, and in place of diadems and purple she clothes him in black rags. And this is what happened to the Emperor Botaniates. When asked once by an acquaintance if he easily bore the change, he replied, " Abstinence from meat is the only thing that bothers me, as for the rest I care very little."

In the meantime Queen Maria with her son, Constantine (whom she had by the ex-emperor Michael Ducas) still stayed on in the palace, for she was anxious about her fair-haired Menelaus, as the poet says ; and her relationship gave her quite sufficient excuse for remaining, although there were some who, prompted by envy, suggested other reasons, and said she had anticipated matters by making one of the Comneni her son-in-law, and the other her adopted son. This consideration alone decided her to remain, and not a reason which is generally censured, nor the attractiveness and affability of the Comneni, on the contrary it was because she was in a foreign country, without kith or kin, or even a fellow-

71

countryman near her. She did not wish to quit the palace
hurriedly for fear lest some evil should befall her son unless
she first received a guarantee for his safety ; for such accidents
do occur during a change of dynasty. The child was very
beautiful and quite young, being only in his seventh year and
(I trust I may be allowed to praise my own relations when the
nature of the circumstances demands it) in the opinion of
those who saw him at that time he was unrivalled for his
sweet disposition and his childish grace in all his movements
and games, as those who were there with him afterwards
said. He was fair-haired with a milk-white complexion,
suffused in the right places with a delicate pink, like that of a
rose just bursting its sheath ; his eyes were not light, but
gleamed from under his eyebrows like those of a hawk's
under a golden hood. As a result he affected all beholders
pleasurably in one way or the other and seemed to be of
celestial, rather than earthly, beauty—in short he exactly
resembled a picture of Eros, as who beheld him might have
remarked. This was the true reason of the Queen's remaining
in the palace. Now I am by nature averse to fabricating
tales and inventing slanders, though I know this is a common
practice, especially if people are bitten by envy or malice,
nor do I lend a ready ear to popular calumnies; moreover,
in this matter I know from other sources the truth of the
matter. For from childhood, from eight years upwards, I was
brought up with the Queen, and as she conceived a warm
affection for me she confided all her secrets to me. I have
also heard many others discussing the course of events at
this time, and they differed from each other, each one interpreting them according to his own state of mind or to the degree
of good-will or hatred he bore the Queen, and thus I discovered
that they were not all of the same opinion. Likewise I have
heard her herself too narrating the occurrences, and the
panic into which she fell about her son, when Nicephorus was
deposed. Thus in my opinion and that of the real seekers
after the truth, it was only anxiety for her son which detained
the Queen in the palace for a short time then. I have said
enough about Queen Maria. My father Alexius who had now
grasped the sceptre came and dwelt in the palace, but left his
wife, fifteen years of age, with her sisters, mother and her
imperial grandfather on her father's side in the ' Lower '
palace as it was generally called from its site. And he himself with his brothers and mother and nearest male relations
moved into the ' Upper ' palace, which is also called

'Boucoleon' for the following reason. Not far from its walls a harbour had been constructed long ago of native stone and marbles, and there stood a sculptured lion seizing a bull—for he is clinging to the bull's horn, pulling his head back, and has fixed his teeth in the bull's throat. So from this statue the whole place, that is both the buildings there and the harbour itself, has been named Boucoleon.

II   And now, as I said above, many people were suspicious of the Queen's staying in the palace, and began to whisper that the present holder of the sceptre would take her in marriage. The family of Ducas, however, did not imagine any such thing (for they were not biassed by current opinion), but as they had long recognized the undisguised hatred the mother of the Comneni bore them, they lived in constant dread and suspicion of her, as I have repeatedly heard them tell. Therefore when George Palæologus arrived with the fleet and started the acclamations, those in attendance on the Comneni bent down to them from the walls, and told them to be silent, fearing they might join the name of Irene to that of Alexius and acclaim them together. At this George waxed angry and shouted up to them, " It is not for you that I undertook this heavy conflict, but just for her you mention, Irene." And straightway he bade the sailors shout for Irene as well as Alexius. These doings cast dire terror into the souls of the Ducas family and furnished the malicious with material for ribald jokes against Queen Maria. Meanwhile the Emperor Alexius, who had never had any such idea (for why should he ?), having taken over the Roman Empire, and being a man of unvarying energy, at once undertook the whole management of the affairs, and began directing everything from the centre, so to say. For he took possession of the palace at sunrise and before even shaking off the dust of combat or allowing his body any rest, he was wholly plunged in thought about military matters. His brother Isaac, whom he reverenced as a father, he made his confidant on all matters, as he did his mother, and they both assisted him in the administration of the common weal ; not but what his great and active mind would have sufficed not only for the administration of one kingdom, but several. Alexius first directed his attention to the most urgent question and spent the rest of that day and the whole of the night in anxiety about the crowd of soldiers dispersed throughout Byzantium. For these were indulging their animal passions to the full, and he was devising a means of checking their undue licence without causing a revolt, and of ensuring peace for the citizens in the future. In any case he feared the recklessness of the soldiers all the more because the army was composed of many different elements, and he wondered whether they might not even be hatching some plot against himself. And the Cæsar, John Ducas, was anxious to get rid of Queen Maria, and drive her out of the palace as quickly as possible, and thus allay people's unjust suspicions, so first he tried in divers ways to win over the Patriarch Cosmas, imploring him to be on their side and to turn a deaf ear to the suggestions of the Comneni's mother. and secondly he very sensibly advised the Queen to ask the Emperor for a letter to assure her own and her son's safety and then to leave the palace, and in this instance he used what is called the " Patroclus " excuse.[1] For once before he had succeeded in providing for her, namely, after Michael Ducas' deposition, when he had advised the latter's successor, Nicephorus Botaniates, to take her in marriage, because she came from another country and had not a crowd of kinsfolk to give the Emperor trouble, and he had told Botaniates a great deal about her family and personal beauty, and often praised her to him. And certainly she was as slender of stature as a cypress, her skin was white as snow, and though her face was not a perfect round, yet her complexion was exactly like a spring flower or a rose. And what mortal could describe the radiance of her eyes ? Her eyebrows were well-marked and red-gold, while her eyes were blue. Full many a painter's hand has successfully imitated the colours of the various flowers the seasons bring, but this queen's beauty, the radiance of her grace and the charm and sweetness of her manners surpassed all description and all art. Never did Apelles or Pheidias or any of the sculptors produce a statue so beautiful. The Gorgon's head was said to turn those who looked upon it into stone, but anyone who saw the Queen walking or met her unexpectedly, would have gaped and remained rooted to the spot, speechless, as if apparently robbed of his mind and wits. There was such harmony of limbs and features, such perfect relation of the whole to the parts and of the parts to the whole, as was never before seen in a mortal body, she was a living statue, a joy to all true lovers of the beautiful. In a word, she was an incarnation of Love come down to this terrestrial globe.

By use of the above-mentioned arguments the Cæsar soothed and appeased the Emperor's mind, although many

[1] Cf. *Iliad*, xix, 302.

advised him to marry Eudocia. Of her it was whispered
that in her desire to become " Empress " for the second
time, she wooed Botaniates with letters at the time that he
occupied Damalis and was hoping to be raised to imperial
power. Others say that she did not do this for herself, but
for her daughter Zoe Porphyrogenita ; and perhaps she
would have attained her desire, had not one of the servants,
the eunuch, Leo Cydoniates, checked her by giving her much
cogent advice. What this was it would not be right for me
to detail as I am by nature averse to slander, so I will leave
it to those who like to chronicle such things. However the
Cæsar John who had approached Botaniates on this subject
with every kind of art, finally settled the matter by persuading
him to marry the Princess Maria as I have already plainly
stated and from henceforth John was allowed much freedom
of speech in her presence. It took some days to arrange
matters, and the Comneni did not want to drive her from the
palace at once, seeing that they had received so many kindnesses at her hands during the time she was Empress, and also
because of the intimacy between them which had grown up
owing to their mutual connection. Consequently many
rumours indicative of varying dispositions were set afloat,
some interpreting the facts in one way, others in another,
according to the degree of good- or ill-will each individual
bore her, for people are wont to judge according to their
prejudices rather than according to the real facts. During
this time Alexius was crowned without his Queen by the right
hand of the Patriarch Cosmas. The latter, a reverend man full
of holiness, had been elected to succeed the saintly Patriarch
John Xiphilinus, who had died on the 2nd August of the
thirteenth Indiction in the fourth year of the reign of Michael
Ducas, the son of Constantine. The fact that the imperial
diadem had not yet been conferred on the Queen, still further
alarmed the family of Ducas, who now insisted on Queen
Irene's being crowned too. Now there was a certain monk
Eustratius, surnamed Garidas, who was building a house
near the large church of God, and from this it seems, had
gained a reputation for sanctity. He had already in former
times been a frequent visitor to the mother of the Comneni
and had predicted her son's rise to the throne. She was in
any case fond of monks, and in this instance being soothed by
flattering words, she daily showed him increasing confidence
and had begun to plan his elevation to the patriarchal seat
of the metropolis. Alleging as excuse the simple and un-

practical mind of the reigning patriarch she persuaded some friends to suggest to him the idea of resigning in the form of advice which they pretended to offer as most conducive to his welfare. But the holy man was not blind to these machinations, and finally he swore by his own name and said, " By Cosmas, unless Irene receives the crown from my hands, I shall not resign from the patriarchate." The men forthwith reported these words to the " Mistress," for thus she was generally called now by the wish of the Emperor who was devoted to his mother. And so seven days after Alexius was publicly proclaimed Emperor, his wife Irene was also crowned by the Patriarch Cosmas.

III Now the appearance of this imperial couple, Alexius and Irene, was inconceivably beautiful and absolutely inimitable. No painter striving after the archetype of beauty, would have been able to picture them nor would a sculptor be able so to compose the lifeless material. Even that well-known canon of Polycleitus would have seemed to lack the first principles of art, if anyone looked first at these " natural statues "—I mean the newly-crowned couple—and then at Polycleitus' masterpieces. Alexius indeed was not especially tall but rather broad, and yet his breadth was well proportioned to his height. When standing he did not strike the onlookers with such admiration, but if when sitting on the imperial throne, he shot forth the fierce splendour of his eyes, he seemed to be a blaze of lightning, such irresistible radiance shone from his face, nay from his whole person. He had black arched eyebrows, from beneath which his eyes darted a glance at once terrible and tender, so that from the gleam of his eyes, the radiance of his face, the dignified curve of his cheeks and the ruddy colour that suffused them, both awe and confidence were awakened. His broad shoulders, muscular arms, mighty chest, in fact his generally heroic appearance, evoked in the multitude the greatest admiration and pleasure. From his whole person emanated beauty and grace and dignity, and an unapproachable majesty. And if he entered into conversation and let loose his tongue, you would have realized from his first words that fiery eloquence dwelt on his lips. For with a flood of argument he would carry the opinions of his hearers with him, for truly he could not be surpassed in discussion or action, being as ready with his tongue as with his hand, the one for hurling the spear, the other for casting fresh spells.

On the other hand, Irene, the Empress and my mother,

was only a girl at the time for she had not yet completed her
fifteenth year. She was the little daughter of Andronicus,
the eldest son of the Cæsar, and of illustrious lineage, for she
traced her descent from the famous houses of Andronicus and
Constantine Ducas. She was just like some young, ever-
blooming plant, all her limbs and features were perfectly
symmetrical, each being broad or narrow in due proportion.
She was so charming to look at as well as listen to that eyes
and ears seemed unable to get their fill of seeing and hearing.
Her face too shone with the soft glamour of the moon, it was
not fashioned in a perfect circle like the faces of the Assyrian
women, nor again was it very long like those of the Scythians,
but it was just slightly modified from a perfect round.   And
the bloom of her cheeks was such that their rosy hue
was visible even to those who stood afar off. Her eyes
were blue, yet in spite of their gaiety, they were somewhat awe-inspiring, so that though by their gladness
and beauty they attracted the eyes of all beholders, yet
these felt constrained to close their eyes so that they
knew neither how to resist looking at her nor how to look.
Whether there ever existed such a person as the Athena
described by the poets and writers of old, I really cannot say, but the following tale I have often heard repeated,
namely that, if in those olden days a man had said that this
Empress was Athena in mortal guise or that she had glided
down from heaven in heavenly brilliance and unapproachable
splendour he would not have been far from the truth.   The
most surprising feature, seldom found in other women, was
that she abashed the audacious, but by a single glance gave
fresh courage to those abashed by fear. Her lips were
generally closed, and thus silent she resembled a living statue
of beauty, a breathing pillar of grace. She usually accompanied her words with appropriate gestures, displaying her
forearm up to the elbow, and from the shape of her hands
and fingers you would have thought they were wrought in
ivory by some artificer. The pupils of her eyes resembled a
calm sea shining with the intense blue of quiet deep water ;
the white surrounding the pupils was extraordinarily bright,
thus giving the eyes an indescribable dazzling and exquisite
beauty.   This then, was the appearance of Irene and Alexius.
My Uncle Isaac, again, was like his brother in stature, and
not very different from him in other respects, his complexion
however was paler, and his beard less thick than his brother's
especially round the jaws.   Both the brothers often indulged

in the chase if there was no great stress of business, but their chief pleasure they found in military, rather than in hunting, adventures. In an attack on an enemy, nobody ever outran Isaac, even when he was commanding a regiment, for no sooner did he see the enemy's lines than he forgot all else and hurled himself into their midst like a thunderbolt and quickly threw their men into disarray. For this reason he was captured more than once, when fighting against the Hagarenes in Asia. This characteristic of his, that in battle he would not be restrained, is the only one worthy of censure in my uncle.

IV   As it was necessary in accordance with his promise to bestow upon Melissenus Nicephorus the dignity of ' Cæsar,' and it was only right that his eldest brother Isaac should be honoured with some higher title and there was no second degree except that of ' Cæsar,' the Emperor Alexius invented a new name by compounding the names of ' Sebastos ' and ' Autocrator,' and bestowed upon his brother the title ' Sebastocrator,' making him, as it were, a second Emperor, and exalting him a step above the ' Cæsar ' who was now counted third in the acclamations, including the acclamation to the Emperor. Further he ordered that on the public festivals both the Sebastocrator and the Cæsar should wear crowns which were, however, very inferior in grandeur to the diadem he wore himself. The imperial diadem, or tiara, was like a semi-spherical close-fitting cap, and profusely adorned with pearls and jewels, some inserted and some pendent ; on either side at the temples two lappets of pearls and jewels hung down on the cheeks. This diadem is the essentially distinctive feature of the Imperial dress. But the coronets of the Sebastocrators and Cæsars are but sparingly decorated with pearls and jewels, and have no globe.

Simultaneously, Taronites who had married the Emperor's sister, was created ' Protosebastos ' and ' Protovestiaire,' and soon afterwards he was gazetted ' Panhypersebastos,' and then sat with the Cæsar. Besides these his brother Adrian was dignified with the title of most illustrious Protosebastos, and his youngest brother Nicephorus, who had been promoted to be the ' great Drungaire ' of the fleet, was now raised to the rank of the Sebasti. Now my father was the inventor of all these new honorary titles, some he made by compounding names, of which I gave an instance above, and the others by applying them to a new use. For names like ' Panhyperse-

bastos ' and ' Sebastocrator ' and similar ones he compounded,
but the dignity of ' Sebastos ' he seems to me to have applied
to a new use. For from olden times the epithet ' Sebastos ' had
been given only to the Emperors and the name ' Sebastos '
was peculiar to them, and my father was the first to bestow
it on several of lower rank. And if anyone were to reckon
the art of ruling as a science and a kind of high philosophy,
as if it were the art of all arts and the science of all sciences,
then he would certainly admire my father as a skilful scientist
and artist for having invented those new titles and functions
in the Empire. Not but what the masters of the logical
science have invented new names for the sake of clearness,
but this man Alexius, the arch-scientist of Emperors,
instituted them for the advantage of the Empire and often
made innovations both in the apportioning of duties and in
the bestowal of titles.

To return, however, to the revered Patriarch Cosmas, of
whom we were speaking—a few days after he had solemnised
the sacred rites in memory of the hierarch, John the Theologian, in the chapel in Hebdomon named after him, he
resigned his high office, after gracing it for five years and nine
months, and retired to the monastery of Callias. And after
him the aforementioned eunuch, Eustratius Garidas, was put
at the helm of the patriarchal government.

Now when his father Michael Ducas was ousted from the
throne, Queen Maria's son, Constantine Porphyrogenitus,
doffed the red buskins of his own accord and assumed ordinary
black ones, but Nicephorus Botaniates who succeeded his
father as Emperor, bade him take off the black buskins
and wear silk shoes of varied colours, as he felt some reverence
for the young man, and liked him for his beauty and his
high descent, for he grudged him indeed the splendour of
entirely red buskins, but allowed him to have a few spots of
red shewing in his woven shoes. Then after Alexius Comnenus
had been proclaimed Emperor, the Queen Maria, Constantine's
mother, in obedience to the Cæsar's suggestion, demanded
from the Emperor a written pledge, which would be inviolable
by being written in red and sealed with a gold seal, to the
effect that not only she and her son should suffer no harm,
but further that her son should be the Emperor's partner,
allowed to wear red buskins and a crown, and be acclaimed as
Emperor together with Alexius himself. Nor did she fail
in her request, for she received a Golden Bull granting all
she asked. Next they took from Constantine the woven silk

shoes he used to wear, and gave him red ones, and in the future he put his signature in red after that of Alexius to all deeds of gift and to Golden Bulls, and in processions he followed him, wearing the imperial diadem. Some persons assert that the Queen had made an agreement with the Comneni before their revolt that these privileges should be granted to her son. Matters being thus settled, she left the palace with a decent suite, to reside in the house built by the late Emperor Constantine Monomachus close to the monastery of the great martyr George (still popularly called ' Mangana '),and Isaac the Sebastocrator accompanied her.

V   Such then were the arrangements made by the Comneni for the Queen Maria. The Emperor who from infancy had received a good education and always conformed to his mother's counsels, and was imbued with a deep-seated awe of God, was now tortured with remorse for the plundering of the city, which had taken place on his occupation of it, and brought suffering upon all the inhabitants. For indeed a smooth path occasionally drives a man to some act of madness if he has never in the smallest degree come into contact with rude shocks ; but provided the man be one of the cautious and prudent-minded, when such a one has lapsed, his spirit is immediately smitten with fear of God, and overwhelmed and alarmed, and more especially so, if he has undertaken a great enterprise and risen to a proud station. For he is troubled by a dread that by acting ignorantly, audaciously and insolently he may call down the wrath of God upon himself, and be hurled from his throne and lose all he had hitherto possessed. For such was the state of Saul long ago ; when God, because of the King's presumptuousness, rent his kingdom in twain. Alexius was distraught with these reflections and vexed in soul, lest God should make him a scapegoat—for whatever crime had been committed anywhere in the city by any individual soldier—and the rabble which had surged through it at that time had been enormous—he counted as his own and reckoned that it was as if he himself had perpetrated the many deeds of shame. Thus he was wounded and sore stricken in mind ; and his Empire and power, his purple robes and diadem encrusted with jewels, and his golden dress sewn with pearls he accounted, as was only right, as of no value compared with the indescribable calamity which had overtaken the Queen of Cities. For nobody, were he to attempt it, could adequately describe the evils which at that time had overwhelmed the city.

Even the very churches and shrines and all property, both
public and private, had been ruthlessly despoiled everywhere
by everybody, one's ears were deafened by the cries and
shouts raised on all sides—in fact, an onlooker would have
said an earthquake was taking place. All these things
Alexius revolved in his mind and was consequently vexed
and harassed in spirit, and did not know how to stem the tide
of his sorrow. For he was very quick in coming to the right
appreciation of any evil deed. And although he knew that
these occurrences under which the city had been so evilly
entreated, were wrought by other men's hands and minds,
yet he was also most keenly conscious that he himself had
furnished the pretext for, and the beginning of, the calamity ;
although again the primary cause of Alexius' revolt had been
the two slaves of whom I have spoken before. But even so
he attributed the whole blame to himself, and was anxious
and desirous to heal the wound. For he felt that only after
the wound had been healed and the stain of guilt removed,
could he set his hand to the affairs of state, and successfully
direct and carry out his plans for the army and military operations. Accordingly he visited his mother, laid bare to her
his creditable remorse and asked her how he could allay and
gain relief from the anxieties which gnawed at his conscience.
She embraced her son and listened to his words with gladness.
And then with Alexius' consent she sent for Cosmas (who had
not yet resigned his seat), and some of the leaders of the
sacred synod and of the monastic body. Alexius placed
himself before these men as a condemned criminal, as a humble
suppliant, nay, more as a man arraigned before the magistrate
and momentarily expecting the verdict which the judge will
pronounce against him. He related everything, omitting no
offence, or humiliation, or deed, or reason for his actions, but
in fear and faithfulness he told everything and earnestly
besought them to cure him of his sufferings and submitted
himself to their punishments. Thereupon the priests subjected not only him but all his blood-relations, as well as the
participators in the rebellion, to the same penances,
prescribing fasting, sleeping on the ground, and the other
accompanying rites for the propitiation of God. And they all
accepted these penances and performed them zealously. Nor
would their wives allow themselves to be exempted from these
penances (for being very fond of their husbands why should
they ?) but of their own free will they put on the yoke of
penitence. In those days you could have seen the palace

full of weeping and mourning, mourning which was not reprehensible or indicative of weak minds, but commendable and a harbinger of that far greater joy which shall never cease. But the Emperor, such was his piety, went even further and wore sackcloth next to his skin underneath his imperial purple for forty days and nights. At night he lay on the ground with only his head raised on a stone and lamenting his faults as was right. After his penance was over, he resumed the management of state affairs with pure hands.

VI He really longed that his mother rather than himself should take the helm of the state, but so far he had concealed this design from her, fearing that if she became cognizant of it, she might actually leave the palace, as he knew she aimed at the higher life. Therefore in all daily business he did nothing, not even a trifling thing, without her advice, but made her the recipient and coadjutor of his plans, and gradually he stole a march upon her and made her a partner in the administration of affairs, sometimes too he would say openly that without her brain and judgment the Empire would go to pieces.

By these means he kept and bound his mother more closely to himself, but hindered and thwarted her in her desires. She however looked towards her last abode and dreamt of a convent in which she might spend the remainder of her life in pious meditation. This was her intention, and she always prayed that her wish might be granted. Although she cherished this hope in her heart and steadfastly yearned towards a higher life, yet she was, on the other hand, perhaps more devoted to her son than most women. And so she wished to help her son to breast the stormy waters of government and to steer the ship as well as possible, whether she ran with a fair wind or were tossed hither and thither by the waves ; and her desire to help was the stronger because her son had only just taken his seat in the stern and put his hand to the tiller, and had never before come in contact with a sea and waves and winds of such magnitude. By this metaphor I mean to indicate the very varied and disturbing troubles of Government. Thus her mother-love constrained her and she ruled conjointly with the Emperor, her son, and at times even took the reins alone and drove the chariot of Empire without harm or mishap. For besides being clever she had in very truth a kingly mind, capable of governing a kingdom. On the other hand, she was drawn in an opposite direction by her longing after God.

When in August of the same Indiction, Robert's crossing
into Epirus forced Alexius to leave the capital he divulged
his cherished plan, and gave effect to it, by entrusting his
mother single-handed with the imperial government and by
a Golden Bull he published his wishes to all the world. Since
it is the duty of a historian not merely to catalogue roughly
the deeds and decrees of good men, but wherever possible,
to add details about the former and to expound the latter, I
will adopt this course, and give the words of this Golden Bull,
only omitting the scribe's embellishments. It ran thus :
" Nothing is equivalent to a sympathetic and devoted mother
nor is there any stronger bulwark, be it that danger is foreseen, or any other horror apprehended. For if she decides
anything that decision will be a firm one ; if she prays, her
prayers will be a support and invincible guardians. Such a
woman my saintly mother has proved herself actually to me,
your sovereign, even from my immature years, and she has
been mistress in everything to me, and nurse and upbringer.
For though my mother herself was enrolled in the senate,
yet her love for her son was her prime course and her confidence in that son was preserved intact. One soul in two
bodies we were recognized to be, and by the grace of Christ
that bond has been kept unbroken to this day. ' Mine '
and ' thine,' those frigid words, were never spoken, and a
matter of still greater import is that her prayers, of great
frequency throughout her life, have reached the ears of the
Lord and have raised me to my present position of sovereign.
After I had taken the sceptre of empire, she could not bear to
be dissociated from my work and from interesting herself in
mine and the public weal, and now I, your sovereign, am
preparing, with the help of God, for a sortie against the
enemies of Rome, and with great care am collecting and
organizing an army, yet I deem the administration of financial
and political affairs the matter of supreme importance. And
certainly I have found what is an unassailable bulwark for
good government, that is, that the whole administration should
be entrusted to my saintly and most deeply honoured mother.
I, your sovereign, therefore decree explicitly by means of this
same Golden Bull that, in virtue of her ripe experience of
worldly matters (though she utterly despises them), whatever
decrees she gives in writing whether the matter be referred
to her by the president of the Civil Courts, or by the judges
under him, or by any of all those others who prepare registers
or demands or verdicts concerning public remissions of fines,

these decrees shall have abiding validity just as if they had been dispensed by my own serene Majesty or ordered by my own word of mouth. And whatever solutions or whatever orders, written or unwritten, reasonable or unreasonable, she shall give, provided they bear her seal—the Transfiguration and the Assumption—these shall be accounted as coming from my sovereign hand. And in the mouth of him who, for the time being, presides over the financial department, as also with regard to promotions and successions to the judgeships of the higher and lower tribunals, and with regard to dignities, magistracies and gifts of immovable property, my holy mother shall have sovereign power to do whatsoever shall seem good to her. And further if any be promoted to judgeships or succeed to minor posts, if any receive the highest, lower, or lowest orders of merit, these they shall retain for ever unchangeably. And again with regard to increase of salaries, supplements to gifts, remission of taxes, and retrenchments and curtailments, these my mother shall settle absolutely. And to put it comprehensively, nothing shall be accounted invalid, that she shall order either by letter or by word of mouth. For her words and her commands shall be considered as given by me, your sovereign, and not one of them shall be annulled, but shall remain valid and in force for the coming years. And neither immediately nor in the future shall she ever be called to give an account or to undergo an examination by anyone whatsoever, either of her ministers or by the Chancellor for the time being, whether her decrees appear reasonable or unreasonable. In fine, whatsoever shall be done under confirmation of this same Golden Bull of that no account shall ever be demanded in the future."

VII Such were the words of the Golden Bull. Men may perhaps marvel that my father, the Emperor, should have shown so much honour to his mother in it, and handed over everything to her, whilst he himself, so to speak, took his hands off the reins of Government and whilst she metaphorically drove the chariot of state, he only ran alongside and merely shared with her the title of ruler. And this in spite of his having passed the years of boyhood and being of an age when characters like his are generally obsessed with the lust of power. He did certainly himself undertake the wars against the barbarians and all the labours and difficulties connected with those, but the whole administration of affairs, the choice of civil officers and the accounts of the income and expenditure

of the Empire he entrusted to his mother. Very likely someone at this point would blame my father's management in
transferring the administration of the Empire to the woman's
apartments, but if he thoroughly understood this woman's
high-mindedness and knew what virtue and intellect and
remarkable energy she possessed, he would leave off blaming
and turn his censure into wondering praise. For my grandmother was so clever in business and so skilful in guiding a
State, and setting it in order, that she was capable of not
only administering the Roman Empire, but any other of all
the countries the sun shines upon. She was a woman of wide
experience and knew the nature of many things, how each
thing began and to what issue it would come, and which
things were destructive of certain others, and which again
would strengthen others ; she was very keen in noting what
should be done and clever in carrying it out to a sure end.
And not only was she so remarkable intellectually, but her
powers of speech too, corresponded to her intellect, for she
was really a most convincing orator, not verbose or apt to
drag out her speeches to a great length nor did the spirit of
her subject quickly fail her, but she would start happily,
and also end in the happiest way. For imperial authority
had devolved upon her when she was of a ripe age, just when
the powers of thought are at their height, and judgment has
matured, and knowledge of affairs is correspondingly at its
height, and from these management and administration
gain their force. People of this age can naturally not only
speak with more wisdom than the young, as the tragedian
says, but they can also act more expediently. In earlier days
too when she was still counted among the younger women,
it was quite wonderful how she seemed to have " an old head
on young shoulders." Anyone who had eyes to see could
have gathered from her expression the fund of virtue and
worth that lay in her. However, as I was saying, my father,
when he had taken the sceptre, reserved for himself the
contests and sweats of war at which his mother looked on,
but her he established as mistress and like a slave he would
do and say whatever she bade. The Emperor verily loved
her exceedingly, and he hung on her counsels (so fond was he
of his mother) and he made his right hand the servant of her
wishes and his sense of hearing the listener to her words, and
in every case the Emperor would agree or disagree according
as she agreed or disagreed. To put it concisely, the situation
was as follows, he indeed had the semblance of reigning but

she really reigned—moreover she drew up laws, administered and directed everything ; all her orders, written or unwritten, he confirmed by his seal or by word—and thus it may be said, he was the instrument of Empire for her, but not the Emperor. He was satisfied with everything his mother arranged and decided and not only was he very obedient as a son to his mother, but he subjected his mind to her as to a master of the science of ruling.   For he was convinced that she had reached perfection in all points and that in knowledge and comprehension of affairs she far surpassed all men of the time.

VIII   Such was the beginning of Alexius' reign, for to style him ' Emperor ' at this time would be scarcely correct, as he had handed over the supervision of the Empire to his mother.   Another person might yield here to the conventional manner of panegyric, and laud the birthplace of this wonderful mother, and trace her descent from the Dalassenian Hadrians and Charons, and then embark on the ocean of her ancestors' achievements—but as I am writing history, it is not correct to deduce her character from her descent and ancestors, but from her disposition and virtue, and from those incidents which rightly form the subject of history. To return once again to my grandmother, she was a very great honour, not only to women, but to men too, and was an ornament to the human race.   The women's quarter of the palace had been thoroughly corrupt ever since Monomachus assumed the power of Emperor, and had been disgraced by licentious ' amours ' right up to my father's accession.   This my grandmother changed for the better, and restored a commendable state of morals.   In her days you could have seen wonderful order reigning throughout the palace ; for she had stated times for sacred hymns and fixed hours for breakfast and for attending to the election of magistrates, and she herself became a rule and measure for everybody else, and the palace had somewhat the appearance of a holy monastery.   Such then was the character of this truly extraordinary and holy woman.   In sobriety of conduct she as far outshone the celebrated women of old, as the sun outshines the stars.   Again, what words could describe her compassion for the poor and her liberality to the needy ? Her home was a refuge, open to any of her kinsfolk who were in want and equally open to strangers too.   But above all she honoured priests and monks, and nobody ever saw her at table without some monks. Her character as outwardly manifested was such as to be revered by the angels, and dreaded by the very demons; even a single look from her was intolerable to incontinent men, mere wild pleasure-seekers, whereas to those of sober conduct she was both cheerful and gracious.   For she understood the due measures of solemnity and severity, so that her solemnity did not in any way appear fierce and savage, nor on the other hand her tenderness slack and unchaste.   This, methinks, is the due bound of orderliness, viz : when kindliness has been mingled with elevation of soul.   She was naturally inclined to medita-tion and was constantly evolving new plans in her mind, which were not subversive of the public weal, as some mur-mured grumblingly, but were its salvation and destined to restore the State which was now corrupt to its former sound-ness, and revive, as far as possible, the almost bankrupt finances.   Moreover, although she was very busy with public business, she never neglected the rules of conduct of the monastic life, but spent the greater part of the night in singing hymns, and became worn out with continual prayer and want of sleep ; yet at dawn, and sometimes even at the second cock-crow, she would apply herself to State business, deciding about the election of magistrates and the requests of petitioners, with Gregory Genesius acting as her secretary. If an orator had wished to take this theme as the subject for a panegyric, who is there of those of old times of either sex distinguished for virtue whom he would not have cast into the shade, lauding to the skies the subject of his pane-gyric (as is the way of panegyrists), for her actions, ideas, and conduct, as compared with others ?   But such licence is not granted to writers of history.   Wherefore if in speaking of this queen we have treated great themes somewhat too slightly, let no one impute this to us for blame, especially those who know her virtue, her majestic dignity, her quick wit on all occasions and her mental superiority.   But now let us return to the point from which we deflected somewhat to speak about the Queen.

Whilst she was directing the Empire, as we said, she did not devote the whole day to worldly cares but attended the prescribed services in the chapel of the martyr Thecla, which the Emperor Isaac Comnenus, her brother-in-law, had built for a reason I will now relate.   At the time when the chief-tains of the Dacians decided no longer to observe their treaty with the Romans and broke it treacherously, then, directly they heard of this, the Sauromatæ (anciently called Mysians) also decided not to remain quiet in their own territory.

Formerly they dwelt on the land separated from the Roman Empire by the Ister, but now they rose in a body and migrated into our territory. The reason for this migration was the irreconcilable hatred of the Dacians for their neighbours, whom they harassed with constant raids. So the Sauromatæ seized the opportunity of the Ister being frozen over and by walking over it as if it were dry land, they migrated from their country to ours, and their whole tribe was dumped down within our borders and mercilessly plundered the neighbouring towns and districts. On hearing this, the Emperor Isaac decided to go to Triaditza and as he had formerly succeeded in checking the enterprises of the eastern barbarians, so he effected this stroke too with very little trouble. He collected the whole army and started on the road thither intending to expel them from Roman territory. And when he had set his infantry in battle-array, he led an attack against them, but directly they saw him, the enemy broke up into dissentient parties. Isaac, however, thinking it unwise to trust them overmuch, attacked the strongest and bravest part of their army with a strong phalanx, and on his approaching with his men, they became panic-stricken. For they did not venture so much as to look straight at him, as if he were the Wielder of the Thunder, and when they saw the phalanx' unbroken array of shields they turned faint with fear. So they retreated a short distance and offered to meet him in battle on the third day from then, but that very same day they deserted their camps and fled. Isaac marched to the spot of their encampment and after destroying the tents and removing the booty found there, he returned in triumph. When he had got to the foot of Mount Lobitzus, a violent and most unseasonable snow-storm overtook him, for it was the 24th September, a day sacred to the memory of the martyr Thecla. The rivers at once became swollen and overflowed their banks, so that the whole plain on which the royal tent and those of the soldiers stood, looked like the sea. In a short time all their baggage had disappeared, swept away by the raging torrents, and men and beasts were numbed by the cold. Thunder rumbled in the heavens, lightning was continuous with scarcely any interval between the flashes which threatened to set all the country around on fire. The Emperor in this dilemma knew not what to do ; but during a short cessation in the storm, as he had already had a great many men carried off by the wildly rushing streams, he with a few picked men left his tent and went and stood with

them under an oak tree.   But because he heard a great noise
and rumbling which seemed to proceed from the tree itself
and the wind was rising quickly, he was afraid that the tree
might be blown down by it, and therefore moved far enough
away from the tree to ensure his not being struck by it if
it fell, and there he stood dumbfounded.   And immediately
as if at a given signal, the tree was torn up by the roots and
was seen lying along the ground; whereupon the Emperor
stood amazed at God's solicitude for him.   Tidings of a
revolt in the East were now brought to him, so he returned
to the palace.   In gratitude for his escape he had a very
beautiful chapel built in honour of the proto-martyr Thecla,
at no little cost, richly furnished and decorated with various
works of art ; there he offered sacrifices of a kind befitting
Christians for his safe delivery, and for the rest of his life
he attended divine service in it.   That was the origin of the
building of the chapel of the martyr Thecla, in which as I
have said, the empress-mother of the Emperor Alexius
regularly paid her devotions.   I myself knew this woman
for a short time and admired her, and all who are willing to
speak the truth without prejudice, know and would testify
that my words about her are not empty boasting.   Had I
preferred writing a laudatory article instead of a history,
I could have greatly lengthened my story by different tales
about her as I made plain before ; now however I must bring
my story back to its right subject.

　　IX   Alexius saw that the Empire was nearly at its last gasp,
for in the East the Turks were grievously harassing the
frontiers whilst in the West things were very bad, as Robert
was letting out every reef in his endeavour to foist that
Pseudo-Michael, who had appealed to him, upon the throne.
This was in my opinion only a pretext and it was rather the
lust for power which inflamed him and allowed him no rest ;
consequently he used Michael as a Patroclus excuse and
fanned the smouldering ashes of his ambition into a mighty
flame and began arming himself with all his might against
the Roman Empire.   He prepared ' dromones '[1] and biremes
and triremes and ' sermones ' and various kinds of freight-
ships, fitting them out from the maritime districts and
collecting as large forces as possible from the continent to
further his purpose.   Consequently the young and brave
Emperor was desperate, and did not know which way to turn
first, as each of his enemies seemed to be trying to begin war

---

[1] Light galleys.

before the other, and thus he grew sorely vexed and disturbed.
For the Roman Empire possessed only a very insufficient
army (not more than the 300 soldiers from Coma, cowardly
and inexperienced in war, besides just a few auxiliary barbarian troops, accustomed to carry their swords (?) on their
right shoulder). And further there was no large reserve of
money in the imperial treasury with which to hire allied troops
from foreign countries. For the preceding Emperors had been
very inefficient in all military and warlike matters and had
thus driven the State of Rome into very dire straits. I
myself have heard soldiers and other older men say that
never within the memory of man had any State been reduced
to such depths of misery. The Emperor's position was, as
you can judge, very difficult and he was distracted by
manifold anxieties. However, he was brave and fearless
and had acquired great experience of war, so he determined
to bring the Empire out of this heavy swell back to anchor
by quiet shores, and with the help of God to beat these enemies
who had arisen against him into empty foam, as waves are
beaten when they break on rocks. He decided that first of
all it was necessary to summon quickly all the local governors
in the East who were holding forts and cities, and making
a valiant resistance against the Turks. So he immediately
drafted letters to them all ; to Dabatenus, temporary governor
of Heraclea in Pontus and of Paphlagonia ; to Burtzes,
governor of Cappadocia and Coma, and to the other leaders.
He first set forth the occurrences which by God's providence
had raised him to the imperial throne, and saved him miraculously from imminent danger, and secondly he bade them
make provision for their respective districts to ensure their
safety and leave sufficient soldiers for this purpose, and with
the rest to present themselves at Constantinople and also
bring up as many newly-recruited men in the prime of life
as possible. Next he saw that he must take whatever steps
were possible to guard himself against Robert and to try
and deter the chieftains and counts who were flocking to the
latter's standard. About this time the messenger returned,
whom Alexius had dispatched before seizing the capital, to
ask Monomachatus for help, and to beg him to forward some
money. However the messenger only brought back letters
detailing the reasons for which forsooth (this we have already
related) Monomachatus could not help him as long as Botaniates still sat on the throne. After reading these letters Alexius
was terrified lest on hearing of Botaniates' fall from the throne,

Monomachatus should join Robert, and he became very despondent. He therefore sent for his brother-in-law, George Palæologus, and dispatched him to Dyrrachium (a city in Illyria) praying him to use every possible device for driving Monomachatus out of the town without fighting, since his forces were too small to eject him against his will, and to lay what counterplots he could to Robert's plots. He also ordered him to have the bulwarks remade in a new way with most of the nails that held the beams together left out so that if the Latins scaled them with ladders, directly they set foot on the beams, the latter, together with the men on them, would give way and be dashed to the ground below. He also wrote to the chiefs of the maritime districts and even to the islanders urging them not to lose courage nor to be careless but to watch and be sober, take measures for their protection and be on the look-out for Robert. Otherwise he might by a sudden descent upon them, make himself master of all the maritime towns, and even of the islands, and after that cause embarrassment to the Roman Empire.

X   Such then were the precautions taken by the Emperor for Illyria ; and he seemed to have firmly secured the towns which at that moment lay directly in front, or at the feet, of Robert ; nor was he unmindful of the districts which lay in his rear. Therefore he first sent a letter to Hermanus, Duke of Lombardy, next to the Pope of Rome, followed by one to Erbius,[1] the Archbishop of Capua. Nay, he went even further and wrote to the princes, and to the various chiefs of the Frankish provinces, and by offering them moderate presents and by promising great gifts and dignities he tried to incite them to war against Robert. Some of these had already abandoned their alliance with Robert and others promised to do so, if they received further inducements ! But as he knew that the King of Alamania[2] was the most powerful of them all and could do whatever he liked against Robert, he wrote to him more than once, and tried to win him over by honeyed words and promises of all sorts. And when he noticed that the King listened to persuasion and seemed likely to yield to his wishes, he sent Chœrosphactes to him with yet another letter couched in the following words :—" Most noble and most truly Christian brother, it is the fervent prayer of our Majesty that your Excellency should prosper and advance to greater power. For will it not be fitting that he, a pious sovereign, should wish you all

---

[1] =Hervæus.   [2] =Germany.

that is good and profitable now that he has learnt the piety
that dwells in you ? For your brotherly inclination and
affection towards our Empire, and the labours you have
promised to undertake against that evil-minded person, in
order to make him, the guilty miscreant, the enemy of God
and all Christians, pay due retribution for wicked plots,
proves the true right-mindedness of your soul, and fully
confirms the report of your piety. Our Majesty, prosperous
in other respects, is exceedingly disturbed and agitated by
the news about Robert. But if we are to place any trust in
God and His righteous judgments, then the downfall of this
most iniquitous man will be swift. For surely God will never
allow the scourge of sinners to fall upon His own inheritance
to such an extent. The gifts our Majesty agreed to send
to your mighty Highness, to wit the 144,000 ' nummi ' and
one hundred pieces of purple silk, are even now being sent
under the care of Constantine, our Supreme Magistrate and
Overseer of dignities, according to the arrangement made
with your most faithful and high-born Count Bulchardus.
The sum of money agreed upon and now sent consists of
coins stamped with the head of Romanus and of ancient
quality. And when your Highness has accomplished the
oath, the remaining 216,000 ' nummi ' as well as the stipend
of the twenty dignities conferred, shall be sent to your
Highness by your trusty servant Bagelardus, when you
come down into Lombardy. In what manner it behoves the
oath to be fulfilled has been explained to your Highness
already ; but Constantine, our Supreme Magistrate and
Overseer, will expound still more fully, in accordance with
our commands, each of the points we require and which
must be confirmed by you on oath. For when the conference
took place between our Majesty and the ambassadors of your
Highness, the points of greatest importance were discussed
but, as the envoys of your Highness said they had no mandate,
for this reason our Majesty suspended the oath. Wherefore
we pray that your Highness will fulfil the oath as your faithful
friend Albert assured me solemnly you would do, and as our
Majesty begs of you as a necessary corollary. The return
of your most faithful and high-born Count Bulchardus was
delayed because our Majesty wished him to see our beloved
nephew, the son of the most fortunate Sebastocrator, our
Majesty's much beloved brother, so that on his return he
might report to you the precocious intelligence of the boy
who is still of tender years ; for our Majesty considers external

and bodily graces as of secondary account, although of these too he has his full share. Your envoy will tell you this for as he was residing in the metropolis, he saw the boy, and as was right had a conversation with him. And since God has not yet blessed our Majesty with a child, this dearly beloved nephew is to us as a son, and, God willing, there is nothing to prevent our being united by ties of blood, and being kindly disposed towards each other, as becomes Christians, or even becoming each other's intimates like relations, and then in the future through mutual assistance we shall become formidable to our enemies and, with the help of God, invincible. As a token of friendship we are sending your Highness together with the other presents a gold pectoral cross inset with pearls and a gold pyx which contains relics of several saints, each of which can be recognized by the card attached to it ; a chalice of sardonyx, a crystal goblet, a radiated crown of gold[1] and some ' opobalsamum.[2] May God grant thee long life, enlarge the borders of thy power and make all those who rise against thee thy footstool. Peace be with thy Highness and may the sun of content shine upon all lands subject to thee, and may all thy enemies be brought to naught by the help of the Mighty Power above who will grant thee the victory over all, because thou dost worship His true name and art arming thy hand against His enemies."

XI These were the measures he took for the Western part of the Empire and next he prepared himself against the immediate danger that threatened ; he continued to reside in the capital, busily devising by what possible means he might resist the enemy who were almost at the very gates of the Empire. My history has already told how at this time the godless Turks were living round the Propontis[3] and Solyman, the ruler of the whole of the East, was encamped around Nicæa (where he had his ' sultanicium ' corresponding to our ' palace ') and incessantly sending out raiders to devastate all the country round Bithynia and Thynia, and they made incursions on horse and on foot even as far as the Bosporus (now called Damalis), and carried off much booty, and they all but attempted crossing the sea itself. The Byzantines saw them living fearlessly in all the little towns along the coasts and in the sacred precincts even, as nobody drove them out, for the inhabitants were absolutely panic-stricken and

---

[1] *Lit.*, ' A thunderbolt bound with gold.' Finlay translates, ' A gold ornament containing a protective charm against thunder.'
[2] Balm of Mecca.   [3] = Sea of Marmora.

did not know what steps to take. When the Emperor saw this, he hesitated between different plans, and often changed his mind and finally chose the plan which he considered the best and executed it as far as was possible. He had recently recruited soldiers from among the Romans and from Coma, from these he chose ' decurions ' and put them in command of boats with some light-armed troops who only carried their bows and a shield, and with others who according to their custom were fully armed with helmets, shields and spears. He instructed them to row along the coasts of the Propontis secretly during the night and to jump out and make an attack upon the infidels at any point where they noticed that the latter did not much outnumber themselves and then to run back quickly to their respective boats. As he knew that his men were quite inexpert in war, he told the rowers to row without making any noise, and also warned them to be on their watch against the infidels who would be in ambush in the clefts of the cliffs. After they had executed this manœuvre for several days, the barbarians did indeed gradually retire inland from the seaside districts. On being informed of this, the Emperor directed the soldiers to occupy the villages and buildings recently held by the Turks and to pass the night in them ; and at break of day when for foraging or any other reason the enemy generally came out into the country, to make a sudden massed attack upon them, and be satisfied if they gained an advantage over them, however slight it might be, and not to risk restoring confidence to the enemy by seeking for further success, but to retire at once to the shelter of their forts. In consequence the barbarians after but a brief space of time again retreated to an even greater distance. Hereupon the Emperor gained courage, had the foot-soldiers put on horses and given spears to brandish, and made many cavalry raids upon the enemy, and no longer secretly during the night but in the daylight too. And those who had hitherto been decurions were now created captains over fifty and the men who had fought the enemy on foot at night with great fear now attacked them in early morning or at noon, and with confidence entered upon brilliantly successful engagements. Thus fortune now deserted the infidels and the power of the Roman Empire which had been temporarily obscured shone forth. For Comnenus not only drove them far back from the Bosporus and the whole sea-board, but also routed them out of the whole of Bithynia, Thynia and the province of Nicomedia and reduced the sultan to making urgent overtures for peace. As Alexius was hearing from many quarters of the tremendous onset Robert was preparing and of the immense number of troops he had collected, and that he was hastening on his march to the coast of Lombardy, he gladly received the proposal of peace. For, if even the hero Heracles could not fight two men at the same time, as the proverb suggests, much less could this young ruler, who possessed neither forces nor money and had only just taken over a state already corrupt which had for a long time been gradually diminishing and had sunk practically to the lowest depths ; and all its money had been squandered without any useful result. This was the reason he felt himself compelled to agree to terms of peace after, by various methods, chasing the Turks away from Damalis and its coasts, and further buying them off with bribes. He fixed the river called Dracon as their boundary, and compelled them to promise never to cross it or make incursions into Bithynian territory.

XII In this way then affairs in the East were lulled to rest. On reaching Dyrrachium Palæologus sent off a runner with the news about Monomachatus, which was that on hearing of Palæologus' journey he had hurriedly betaken himself to Bodinus and Michaelas. For he was afraid because he had not obeyed Alexius' order but had sent back empty-handed the messenger whom the Emperor Alexius had sent with a letter asking for money before he commenced the rebellion he was meditating. In reality the Emperor did not intend to punish him further than by dismissing him from his position for the reason just given. When the Emperor learnt what Monomachatus had done, he sent him a Golden Bull granting him full immunity, and as soon as Monomachatus received it, he returned to the palace.

Robert, meanwhile, had reached Hydruntum and after delegating the rule over that town and the whole of Lombardy to his son Roger, he sailed and occupied the port of Brindisi. When he heard of Palæologus' arrival in Dyrrachium, he at once had turrets constructed on the larger vessels, built of wood and covered with hides. And he speedily had everything necessary for a siege packed on board the ships, and horses and fully-equipped cavalry he embarked on the cruisers, and with wonderful celerity he collected from all sides all the apparatus for war, for he was in a hurry to cross the sea. His plan was to surround Dyrrachium, when he reached it, with battering engines both on the land- and sea-side so as to strike dismay into the hearts of the inhabitants and also by thus hemming them in completely, to take the town by assault. Consequently when the Islanders and the dwellers along the coast by Dyrrachium heard of this plan, great confusion fell upon them. When Robert had everything completed to his liking, he loosed anchor ; the freight-ships, the triremes and monoremes were drawn up in the battle array of nautical tradition, and thus in good order he started on his voyage. Meeting with a favourable wind he struck the opposite shore at Valona and coasting along it, came up to Buthrotum.[1] There he joined forces with Bohemund who had crossed earlier, and taken Valona by storm. He now divided the whole army into two parts, with the one he meant to sail to Dyrrachium, and commanded it himself, and Bohemund he put in command of the other half with which to march to Dyrrachium over land. After he had passed Corfu and was directing his course to Dyrrachium, he was suddenly caught in a most terrible storm off the promontory called Glossa. For a heavy fall of snow and the winds rushing down from the mountains churned up the sea violently. Then the waves rose and roared and the oars of the rowers were broken off as they dipped them ; the winds tore the sails to shreds ; the yard-arms were snapped off and fell on the deck, and the boats, crews and all, sank. And yet this was in summer when the sun had already crossed the tropic of Cancer and was hastening towards the Lion, just at the season which is called the Rising of the Dog Star. They were naturally all much disturbed and agitated and quite helpless to cope with such enemies. There was a frighful tumult, for men wailed and shrieked, called upon God to save them, and prayed to be allowed to see the dry land. The storm did not lessen meanwhile, it was as if God were pouring out his wrath upon Robert's insolent and over-weening presumptuousness, and shewing him from the very start that the issue would not be successful. Some of the ships were lost, crews and all, others were dashed on the rocks and broken to pieces. The hides covering the turrets became stretched by the rain, so that the nails fell out of their holes and the weight of the hides soon dragged down the wooden turrets which in their fall swamped the ships. However, the boat which carried Robert was saved with difficulty, though sadly battered ; and some of the freight-ships with all on board were also miraculously saved. The sea threw up many of the men and quite a number of pouches and other

[1] = Butrinto.

oddments which the sailors had taken with them and scattered them over the shore. The survivors buried the dead with due rites, and consequently they became infected with the horrible stench, as it was not easy for them to bury so many quickly. Now all the provisions had been lost and probably the survivors would have died of starvation, had there not been a luxuriance of crops and fruits in the fields and gardens.

Now the moral of all this was plain to all right-minded persons, but none of these occurrences daunted Robert, for he was quite fearless and only prayed, I believe, that his life might be spared long enough to allow of his fighting against his chosen enemies. Therefore nothing of what had happened deterred Robert from the object he had set himself ; and so with the remaining troops (for some by God's almighty power had escaped from the peril) he reached Glabinitza on the seventh day. Here he stayed so that he and the other survivors from the storm at sea might recuperate, and that those he had left behind at Brindisi and others, whom he expected to come by sea from other places, might join him, as well as the troops who had started overland a short time before, the fully-equipped cavalry, infantry and the light-armed soldiers. When he had collected his whole army from land and sea, he occupied the plain of Illyria with all his troops. In his company there was a Latin, an envoy, as he said, from the Bishop of Bari to Robert, and he it was who gave me an account of all this, and assured me that he went through this whole campaign with Robert. And next, huts were put up inside the ruined walls of the city once called Epidamnus, and the soldiers lodged in them by battalions. In this city the Epirote King, Pyrrhus, dwelt when he made an alliance with the Tarentines and began his fierce struggle with the Romans in Apulia. And at that time such a frightful slaughter took place that all to the last man fell a prey to the sword, and the city was left uninhabited. But in later years, as the Greeks say, and to this the inscriptions in the town bear testimony, the city was rebuilt by Amphion and Zethus in the style that it still retains, and its name was changed to ' Dyrrachium.' These few words about this city must suffice, and here I will conclude my third book and continue the tale of Robert's doings in the next.

BOOK IV

I

THUS the Continent was now occupied by Robert, who pitched his camp in it on June 17th of the fourth Indiction with an exceedingly great number of horse- and foot-soldiers who formed a terrifying sight as well because of their equipment as from their strategic arrangement; for by this time the whole army had re-assembled from all sides. And at sea rode his fleet composed of every kind of vessel with a different set of soldiers, highly experienced in naval warfare. The inhabitants of Dyrrachium were hemmed in on either side, that is by sea and by land, and as they could see Robert's innumerable troops, which exceeded all their expectations, they were overcome with fear. However, George Palæologus, a brave man and expert in every sort of strategy, who had fought thousands of battles in the East and come out victor, was undismayed, and began fortifying the city. He built bulwarks according to the Emperor's suggestions, placed a number of stone-throwing engines on the walls, put fresh heart into the discouraged soldiers, set watchmen all along the wall, made the circuit of them himself every day and night, and exhorted the guard to keep unceasing watch. At the same time he sent the news by letter to the Emperor of Robert's incursion and his intention of besieging Dyrrachium. When the inhabitants of Dyrrachium saw the siege-engines outside and the enormous tower that had been constructed, over-topping even the walls of Dyrrachium—and encased in hides with catapults standing on the top of it—when they saw the whole circumference of the walls girt round by the army, and the allies flocking in from all directions to Robert, and the neighbouring towns being raided, and the tents increasing in number daily, then indeed dread fear fell upon them. For now they recognized Duke Robert's aim, and saw that he had occupied the plain of Illyria, not for the purpose of pillaging towns and country, collecting a large store of booty, and then returning to Apulia, as rumour had reported, but that he was really striving for the mastership of the Roman Empire, and was anxious to take Dyrrachium by storm, to start with, so to say.   So Palæologus ordered the question to be asked from the walls : ' For what purpose had Robert entered their country ? ' He replied, " In order to restore Michael, my kinsman, who was expelled from the Empire, to his former high position, to wipe out the insults heaped upon him, and generally to avenge him." To this the besieged replied : " If when we see Michael we recognize him, we will immediately do obeisance to him and hand over the city."   On hearing this Robert forthwith commanded Michael to be clad in magnificent robes and exhibited to the inhabitants of the city.   So with a magnificent procession as escort and to the music of a band and cymbals he was shown to the townsfolk.   But directly they saw him, they poured down a stream of insults upon him from the walls and swore that they certainly did not recognize him.   Robert paid no heed, however, and went on with the work he had in hand.   Whilst the men inside and outside the walls were thus bandying words with each other, a few made a sudden sortie from the city, engaged the Latins in combat, and after inflicting a slight loss upon them, re-entered Dyrrachium.

There was a great diversity of opinion about the monk who was accompanying Robert.   Some declared he was the cup-bearer of the Emperor Michael Ducas, others asseverated that he was indeed the Emperor Michael himself, the barbarian's kinsman by marriage for whose sake alone he had undertaken this great war ;   and yet another party contended that they knew positively that the whole thing was a fiction invented by Robert ;   nor, said they, had the monk come to him of his own accord. But Robert raised himself from extreme poverty and complete obscurity by physical energy and mental predominance and carved himself a kingdom by conquering all the towns and districts of Lombardy, and even of Apulia, as has been told in this history.   Very soon he coveted more, as is generally the rule with men of insatiable ambition, and decided he ought to make an attempt upon the cities scattered throughout Illyria, and then, if that venture was successful, to proceed still further.   For covetousness, whenever it grasps at Empire, does not differ at all from gangrene, which can never be arrested once it has attacked a body, until it has passed right through and vitiated it entirely.

II   The Emperor was kept informed of all these events by the letters of Palæologus—namely, that Robert crossed the sea in June (as already told) ; that, in spite of being caught in a terrible storm and shipwrecked and subjected to God's wrath, he was nothing daunted, but took Valona at first assault with the forces he had brought with him ; further, that innumerable troops from all quarters were rallying to his standard, as many as the flakes of a snowstorm in number ; and that the lighter-headed were joining Robert because they believed that the impostor Michael was really the Emperor.   Consequently Alexius was afraid and considering the magnitude of the task before him and realizing that the forces at his command were only equal to a small fraction of Robert's, he deemed it necessary to call upon the Turks in the East for help, and signified his desire to the Sultan. By promises and bribes he also solicited the aid of the Venetians (from them, it is said, the Romans had previously introduced the name " Venetian colour " in their horse-races).   Some things he promised, and others he offered to give at once, provided that they would equip their whole navy and with all speed sail to Dyrrachium with the object firstly, of protecting the city and secondly, of engaging in battle with Robert's fleet.   And if they carried out his request, and by God's help gained the victory or (as may always happen) they were defeated, even then they should receive all he had promised, just the same as if they had conquered.   And all their desires, provided only they were not injurious to the Roman Empire, should be fulfilled and confirmed by Golden Bulls.   On hearing this the Venetians signified their desires through their ambassadors and received definite promises. Thereupon they got their navy ready with every kind of ship and started for Dyrrachium in good order.   They passed safely over the high seas and reached the chapel built long ago to the Immaculate Virgin at a spot called Pallia, about eighteen stades distant from Robert's camp outside Dyrrachium.   But when from the region of Dyrrachium they had viewed Robert's fleet fitted out with every species of military instruments they lost heart for the war.   As soon as Robert knew of their arrival he sent his son Bohemund to them with the fleet to bid them ' hurrah ' for the Emperor Michael and for Robert.   However, they put off their hurrahing to the morrow.   When night fell, as they were not able to approach the shore, and there was a calm, they tied the larger vessels together with ropes and constructed a so-called " sea-harbour," and built wooden towers at their mastheads and hauled up on to them by ropes the small boats which were usually towed together at their sterns. In these they placed armed men and cut up heavy beams into pieces about a foot-and-a-half long and studded them with sharp iron nails and then awaited the approach of the Frankish fleet. At day-break Bohemund came demanding their acclamations. But when the Venetians laughed at his beard, he could not stand their ridicule, and himself led the attack against the largest of their ships and soon the rest of the fleet joined in. A fierce battle commenced and as Bohemund was fighting very savagely against them, they threw down one of the bludgeons mentioned above, and knocked a hole into the ship on which Bohemund was. As the water was sucking down the vessel and they were in danger of sinking, some of the men actually jumped out into the water and were drowned whilst the rest still continued fighting with the Venetians, and were killed. And Bohemund being in imminent danger leapt on to one of his own boats and was saved. Then the Venetians took fresh courage and carried on the battle with greater energy until at last they routed the enemy and pursued them to Robert's camp. Directly they touched the land they jumped on to it and started another battle with Robert. When Palæologus saw them he too rushed out from the citadel of Dyrrachium and fought on the side of the Venetians. After a fierce battle which surged right up to Robert's encampment, a large number of men were driven out from this and many too fell a prey to the sword. Afterwards the Venetians carried off much spoil, and returned to their ships and Palæologus re-entered the citadel. And after taking a few days' rest the Venetians sent ambassadors to the Emperor to recount these happenings. He received them with great honour, as was natural, bestowed many benefactions upon them, and then dismissed them with a large gift of money for the Doge of Venice and his subordinate magistrates.

III But Robert being of a most warlike disposition, decided not to discontinue the war, but to fight on bravely. As it was winter he was unable to launch his ships, and moreover, the Roman and Venetian fleets kept a strict guard over the straits and prevented his reinforcements and commissariat from Lombardy reaching him. Now when spring had

set in and the storms at sea had ceased, the Venetians were
the first to slip their cables and take the water against Robert,
and behind them sailed Maurix with the Roman fleet. A bitter
combat ensued hereupon and Robert's men fled, which led to
Robert's deciding to haul up his whole fleet. Then the
islanders and the towns along the coast and whoever else
had been paying tribute to Robert, took heart because of his
misadventures, and after they heard of his defeat at sea
did not readily pay the taxes he had imposed. So he resolved
to carry on the war with greater diligence and fight again
both on land and sea. But as he could not proceed to put
his plans into action, for strong winds were blowing at the time
and he feared shipwreck, he waited patiently for two months
near the harbour of Hiericho and got ready everything that he
needed for fighting again on land and sea. The Roman and
Venetian fleets guarded the straits as far as possible and
whenever the sea lent itself even slightly to the idea of sailing,
they intercepted the ships which were trying to cross from
Italy to Robert. Since it was not easily possible to collect
the necessary provisions, not even from the mainland, for
Robert's army which was encamped along the river Glycis,
as the men from Dyrrachium caught those who came out
from Robert's trenches for foraging or anything else, his
men began to suffer from hunger, and besides this the incle-
ment climate of the district did them great harm. So that in
the course of three months a total of ten thousand men are
said to have perished. The same disease also attacked
Robert's cavalry-forces and destroyed many. In the cavalry
nearly five hundred of the Counts and the most valiant picked
men were carried off by illness and famine, whilst in the lower
ranks countless horsemen perished. Now Robert's ships, as
we have said, had been hauled up into the river Glycis, this
was almost dried up by the drought, as a very hot summer
had set in after the winter and the spring, and it had scarcely
as much as water running down its bed as usual, and
therefore he hardly knew how to drag them down to the
sea again. But being of an inventive mind and a deep
thinker, he had posts fixed along either side of the river, and
connected with closely woven wattle-work, then behind
these he had large trees cut down at the root, laid flat and
sand strewn over them, so that the water was collected and
flowed all together into one spot, that is the channel formed
by the posts. Gradually the water formed pools and then
filled the whole bed of the river and reached a fair depth,

until finally it raised the ships which had hitherto been em-
bedded in the soil so that they floated on the top. Then after
this all was fair sailing and the ships were drawn down to
the sea without any difficulty.

IV When the Emperor heard what Robert had done,
he wrote immediately to Pacurianus telling him of Robert's
irresistible assault on, and capture of, Valona, and of his total
disregard of the ills which had befallen him on land and sea,
and even of that defeat which he had suffered at the first set-
off. He therefore commanded Pacurianus not to delay
but collect his forces more quickly and come and join him.
That then was his message to Pacurianus. He himself at once
set out from Constantinople in the month of August in the
fourth Indiction, leaving Isaac in the capital to carry on
the civil administration. If he heard any seditious talk
among their enemies, as would be likely, Isaac was to scatter
them, also to guard the palace and the city and try to dissipate
the women's grief. As far as his mother was concerned, she
did not require any consoling, I fancy, for she was very strong-
minded, besides being so clever in business.

Pacurianus, after reading the letter, appointed Nicholas
Branas, a brave man with great military experience, as his
lieutenant-general. He himself with his whole army and
with the flower of the nobility of the Orestias, started quickly
and hurried to join the Emperor. Immediately the latter
arrived, he arranged the whole army in order of battle, ap-
appointed the bravest men leaders of the battalions, and
told them to continue the journey in that same order where-
ever the nature of the ground permitted, so that by understanding the whole arrangement and each man knowing his
exact place, they would not become confused in the heat of
battle and would not easily or accidentally shift their place.
Constantine Opus led the Guards, Antiochus the Macedonians,
Alexander Cabasilas the Thessalians, and Taticius, at that
time ' Primicerius,'[1] the Turks of Achrida. He was extremely brave, and absolutely fearless in battle, although
he was not descended from free-born stock ; for his father,
who was a Saracen, fell into the hands of John Comnenus, my
paternal grandfather, on a foraging expedition. The leaders
of the Manichæans, who totalled two thousand eight hundred,
were Xantas and Culeon, also of the same heresy. All these
were very warlike and ever ready to spill their enemies' blood
when opportunity offered, they were moreover audacious and

[1] = Chief of the household.

insolent. Of the household troops (generally called " Vestia-ritæ ") and the Frankish regiments Panoucomites and Constantine Hubertopoulos, so called after his origin, were in command. Then after arranging his troops in this manner, he set out with all his forces against Robert. On his way he met a man coming from Dyrrachium and obtained from him a clearer account of the events there and learnt that Robert had moved up all the engines necessary for a siege and drawn them close up to the walls. George Palæologus had led a counter-attack by day and night, and then in despair had flung open the gates and commenced a fierce battle with the enemy. He had been severely wounded in various parts of the body, and most seriously by an arrow which had pierced his head near the temple. As he struggled in vain to pull it out he sent for an expert who cut off the end, I mean the tail-end which is usually furnished with feathers, and the rest of it he left sticking in the wound. Then with his head bound up as well as possible under the circumstances, he rushed back into the midst of the foe, and continued fighting without flinching until the evening. When the Emperor heard this, he realized that Palæologus was in need of immediate relief, and therefore marched on at greater speed. On reaching Thessalonica the news about Robert was fully confirmed in detail by several. He was told that Robert, ever alert, had not only set apart extra brave soldiers, but had also collected a heap of material from the plain of Dyrrachium and then pitched his camp within a dart's throw from the walls, while he had also disposed others of his troops all around on the mountains and valleys and slopes. At the same time many also spoke to him of Palæologus' untiring industry. For Palæologus had now planned to set fire to Robert's huge wooden tower, and had collected naphtha and pitch and faggots of dry wood and catapults on the walls, and was awaiting the enemy's attack. As he expected Robert the next day, he placed the wooden tower (which he had had made inside the town) in the direct route of the mighty one which would come from the outside ; then the whole night through he made tests with the beam which was hung at the top of his tower and intended to be pushed against the door of the huge tower which would be brought up ; for he wanted to see if it moved very easily and would really fall directly against the door and prevent this being readily opened. When he was satisfied that the beam moved easily and would accomplish its purpose, he confidently awaited the attack. On the follow-

ing day Robert commanded all to take arms, and about
five hundred foot and horse soldiers to place themselves in
the tower, and when this had been pushed up to the walls,
they at once tried to throw open the door at the top which
they intended to use as a draw-bridge for crossing into the
citadel. Then Palæologus from the inside drove forward the
enormous beam with the help of the large body of brave
men and the machines he had got ready, and thus rendered
Robert's tower useless, for the beam effectually prevented
the door being opened. Next the Franks who were standing
on the top of the tower were subjected to a continuous volley
of darts which they could ill bear and therefore hid themselves. Hereupon he ordered the tower to be fired, and
almost before he had spoken it went up in flames. The men
on the top threw themselves down and those below opened
the door at the foot and fled. When Palæologus saw them
fleeing he made a sortie through the postern gate with a
troop of brave soldiers in full armour and of others who
carried axes with which to cut down the tower. And herein
too he was successful, for he burnt the upper part of it and
the lower was entirely destroyed by a few blows of a stone-
cutter's tool.

V. And now, the informant continued, Robert was busily
building a second mighty wooden tower. just the same as the
other, and was getting ready battering-machines to use
against Dyrrachium ; from all this the Emperor recognized
that the besieged in Dyrrachium were in need of speedy help,
so set his troops in order and took the road to the town. When
he arrived there and had settled his troops in an entrenched
camp near the river Charzanes, he at once sent messengers
to ask Robert for what purpose he was there, and what his
object was. Then he moved on to the Chapel dedicated to
the memory of Nicholas, greatest of all Bishops, four miles
distant from Dyrrachium, and reviewed the nature of the land
in order to pick out beforehand the most suitable spot for
drawing up his phalanxes for battle. And that day was the
fifteenth of October. There was a neck of land running
out from Dalmatia to the sea and terminating in a promontory which was almost a peninsular, and on this stood
the chapel I have mentioned. The side of this neck which
looked towards Dyrrachium sloped very gradually down to
the plain and had the sea on its left, and on its right a steep,
overhanging mountain. To this spot he brought his whole
army, and after having fixed his palisades, sent for George

Palæologus. However he had had long experience of such tricks and as he deemed it inexpedient he refused to come out and explained this to the Emperor. But on the Emperor's again summoning him more urgently, he replied, " I think it would be fatal for me to leave the city while it is being besieged, and I shall not come out unless I actually see the ring from Your Majesty's finger." The ring was sent and upon seeing it Palæologus joined the Emperor with ships of war. Then the Emperor asked him all about Robert and after Palæologus had given him a clear account, he asked whether it would be well for him to venture on a battle with Robert ; but Palæologus disagreed with this proposal. And others too who had gained military experience by long service opposed it strongly. They counselled endurance and embarrassing Robert by skirmishes and not allowing any of his men to come out from their quarters to forage ; they suggested he should send orders to Bodinus and the Dalmatians and the other chiefs of the adjacent provinces to do the same, and assured him that in this way Robert could easily be worsted. But the majority of the younger officers preferred a battle, and most vehement among them were Constantine Porphyrogenitus, Nicephorus Synadenus, Nabites, leader of the Varangians, and even the two sons of the late Emperor Romanus Diogenes, Leo and Nicephorus. At this moment the envoys sent to Robert returned and brought the latter's verbal message to the Emperor which ran, " It was certainly not against Your Majesty that I took the field, but simply in order to avenge the injustice done to my kinsman by marriage. But if you desire peace with me, I too shall gladly welcome it, though only on condition that you are ready to fulfil the conditions signified to you by my ambassadors." However his requests were absolutely impossible and injurious, moreover, to the Roman Empire, although he promised that if the Emperor granted him his requests, he would consider that he held Lombardy too from his hand, and that he would give military assistance, whenever required. But his real plan was clear from the fact that he made requests as if he himself desired peace, but by making impossible ones and not obtaining them he would have recourse to arms, and thus attribute the blame for the war to the Roman Emperor.

Then after ineffectually making impossible demands, Robert convoked all the Counts and addressed them in these words, " You all know the injustice done to my kinsman by marriage by the Emperor Nicephorus Botaniates, and the

dishonour put upon my daughter Helen by her being expelled
from the Empire with him. As we could not put up with such
things we marched out against Botaniates' country to avenge
these wrongs. He however has been moved from the throne,
and we now have to do with a young Emperor, who is a brave
soldier and gifted with strategic knowledge far beyond his
years, and with such a man we cannot go to war lightly.
Now wherever there is division of command, confusion
results from the diversity of opinions. Hence it is necessary
that all the rest of us should obey one single commander who
must consult us all and not act on his own judgment heedlessly and casually ; the rest of us should openly express our
views, but at the same time be ready to follow the advice
of the elected commander. And here am I, one of you all,
ready to obey whomsoever ye agree to elect." All approved
of this proposition and declared that Robert had spoken well,
and then unanimously awarded him the first place. But he
simulated indifference and for some time refused the honour,
whereupon they insisted all the more. And finally he yielded,
as if overcome by their persuasions, though in reality he had
been aching for this all the time ; but by piling one argument
upon another and skilfully weaving a tissue of excuses, he made
it appear to those who did not penetrate his intention, that
he had been exalted against his will to the position which
really he had coveted. Then he said to them " Listen to
me, Counts and all the rest of you. We have left our own
countries and are here in a foreign land, and we shall shortly
have to fight against an Emperor who is very brave ; although
he has only recently assumed the reins of government, yet
under the previous Emperors he came out conqueror in many
wars and brought back to them the fiercest rebels as captives
of his spear, therefore we must enter upon this war with our
whole heart and soul. And if God should allot us the victory,
we shall no longer be in need of money. Consequently we
ought to set fire to all our baggage and equipment, scuttle
our ships, and then enter into battle with him, as if we had
been born in this place and intended to die here." To this all
assented.

VI Such, you see, were Robert's plans and intentions.
The Emperor's on the other hand were different, more subtle
and more clever. Both the leaders, however, kept their
troops in camp whilst meditating upon their strategy and
tactics, so that they might use their powers scientifically.
And the Emperor was planning a sudden night-attack from

both sides upon Robert's entrenchments. He commanded the whole native army to march by way of the salt-pits and attack from the rear, and he did not object to their undertaking this longer march as it would add to the unexpectedness of their attack. He himself intended to attack Robert from the front directly he ascertained that his other troops had arrived. Robert, however, left his tents standing empty, and crossing the bridge by night (on October 18th of the fifth Indiction) took possession with his whole army of the chapel built long ago to the Martyr Theodore. And there throughout the night they sought to propitiate the Deity, and also partook of the Immaculate Sacred Mysteries. In the morning he drew up his troops in order of battle and stationed himself in the centre of the line ; the wing near the sea he entrusted to Amicetas (one of the illustrious Counts, brave in thought and deed), and the other to his son Bohemund, nicknamed Saniscus. When the Emperor learnt of this, as he was clever in hitting upon the best expedient in a serious crisis, he re-adapted his plans in accordance with these happenings, and drew up his lines on the slopes by the sea. After dividing his forces, he did not interfere with the barbarians who were starting to make their attack upon Robert's camp, but detained those of them who carried double-edged axes on their shoulders, and ordered them to discard their horses and with their leader, Nabites, to march in rows at a short distance in front of the regular army; this tribe all carried shields. The rest of the army he divided into phalanxes and himself took the centre of the line, on his right and left he placed respectively the Cæsar Nicephorus Melissenus and Pacurianus, called the " Great Domestic." The space between himself and the barbarians who were walking he filled with a fairly large number of soldiers skilled in archery whom he planned to send on ahead against Robert, and so he told Nabites that when these archers wanted to ride out suddenly against the Franks and retreat again, he must immediately give them passage by withdrawing his men to either side, and then afterwards close up again and march on in close order. Having re-arranged the whole army in this manner, he himself started along the sea-coast in order to attack the Frankish army from the front. The barbarians appointed for the rear-attack, after passing through the salt-pits, made an assault upon the Frankish camp in conjunction with the garrison of Dyrrachium, who by the Emperor's command had opened their gates. As the two leaders were marching against each other, Robert ordered groups of cavalry to harass the Roman troops and thus perhaps draw away some of them. But even in this detail the Emperor did not fail, for he kept on sending large numbers of light-armed troops to oppose them. Then after a little preliminary skirmishing on either side, as Robert was leisurely following his men, and the distance between the armies was by now fairly short, some infantry and cavalry belonging to Amicetas' phalanx dashed out and attacked the extremities of Nabites' line. These however, resisted the attack very stoutly, so the others turned their backs (since they were not all picked men), threw themselves into the sea, and up to their necks in water, made their way to the Roman and Venetian ships and begged them for protection, which they did not receive. And now, as rumour relates, directly Gaïta, Robert's wife (who was riding at his side and was a second Pallas, if not an Athene) saw these soldiers running away, she looked after them fiercely and in a very powerful voice called out to them in her own language an equivalent to Homer's words, " How far will ye flee ? Stand, and quit you like men ! " And when she saw they continued to run, she grasped a long spear and at full gallop rushed after the fugitives ; and on seeing this they recovered themselves and returned to the fight. Meanwhile the axe-bearing barbarians and their leader Nabites had in their ignorance and in their ardour of battle advanced too quickly and were now a long way from the Roman lines, burning to engage battle with the equally brave Franks, for of a truth these barbarians are no less mad in battle than the Franks, and not a bit inferior to them. But they were already tired out and breathless, Robert noticed, and naturally so he thought, considering their rapid advance, their distance from their own lines and the weight of their weapons, and he ordered some of the foot to make a sudden attack on them. The barbarians having been previously wearied out, proved themselves inferior to the Franks, and thus the whole corps fell ; a few escaped and took refuge in the chapel of Michael, the ' Captain of the Host,' as many as could crowded into the chapel itself, and the rest climbed on to the roof, being likely in this way, they imagined, to ensure their safety. But the Latins started a fire and burnt them down, chapel and all. Meanwhile the rest of the Roman army fought on bravely. But Robert like a winged horseman, dashed with his forces against the Roman phalanx, drove it back and split it up into several fragments. Consequently some of his opponents

fell fighting in this battle, and others ensured their own
safety by flight. But the Emperor Alexius stood fast like
an impregnable tower, although he had lost many of his
comrades, men pre-eminent for their birth or military skill.
For instance, Constantius fell there, the son of the ex-Emperor,
Constantine Ducas, not born while his father was still a private
man, but born and reared in the purple and deemed worthy
formerly by his father of the royal fillet. There fell too
Nicephorus by name, but nicknamed Synadenus, a brave
and very handsome man who strove to surpass all in fighting
on that day. With him the aforementioned Constantius had
often spoken about marrying his sister. Nay, Nicephorus the
father of Palæologus, and other well-known men fell too,
and Zacharias received a blow in the chest which cost him
his life. Aspietes and many other picked men also perished.
The battle did not come to an end because the Emperor still
maintained his resistance, therefore three of the Latins,
one of whom was Amicetas already mentioned, the second
Peter, son of Aliphas, as he himself asserted, and a third,
not a whit inferior to these two, took long spears in their
hands and at full gallop dashed at the Emperor. Amicetas
missed the Emperor because his horse swerved a little ;
the second man's spear the Emperor thrust aside with his
sword and then bracing his arm, struck him on the collar-bone
and severed his arm from his body. Then the third aimed
straight at his face, but Alexius being of firm and steadfast
mind was not wholly dismayed, but with his quick wit grasped
in the flash of an instant the thing to do, and when he saw the
blow coming, threw himself backwards on to his horse's tail.
Thus the point of the spear only grazed the skin of his face a
little and then, hitting against the rim of the helmet, tore
the strap under the chin which held it on and knocked it
to the ground. After this the Frank rode past the man
he thought he had hurled from his horse, but the latter
quickly pulled himself up again in his saddle and sat there
calmly without having lost a single weapon. And he still
clutched his naked sword in his right hand, his face was
stained with his own blood, his head was bare, and his ruddy,
gleaming hair was streaming over his eyes and worrying him,
for his horse in its fright spurned the reins and by its jumping
about tossed his curls in disorder over his face ; however,
he pulled himself together as much as possible and carried
on his resistance to his foes. Soon however he saw the Turks
fleeing and Bodinus, too, retreating without having fought

at all.   This ally had donned armour and arranged his
army in battle-order and hovered about throughout the day
as if to succour the Emperor, if need be, according to their
mutual agreement ; but evidently he was watching, purposing to help in the attack on the Franks if he saw victory
incline to the Emperor ; or, in the contrary case, to keep
quite still and then beat a retreat.   This being his intent, as
events proved, directly he perceived that the Franks had
gained a complete victory, he rode off home without having
struck a single blow.   The Emperor, seeing this and not
finding any one to help him, turned his back upon the foe
and fled.   Thus did the Latins beat the Roman army.

VII   Robert took the Church of St. Nicolas where the
Imperial tent and all the equipment of the Roman army
were ; and sent off all the strongest men he had to pursue
the Emperor, whilst he stayed where he was, picturing to
himself the capture of the Emperor—for such ideas inflamed
his overweening pride.   And the soldiers pursued the Emperor very smartly to a place called by the natives Kake
Pleura, its situation is this—a river, named Charzanes, flows
below and over one side impends a tall cliff.   Between these the
pursuers overtook him ; some of them thrust him with their
spears on the left side (they were nine altogether) and thus
made him lean to the right.   And he certainly would have
fallen had he not managed to fix the sword, which he carried
in his right hand, in the ground and support himself upon it.
Moreover the rowel of the spur on his left foot caught in the
edge of his saddle-cloth, (often called 'Hypostroma') and made
it more difficult for the rider to move ; with his left hand
too he grasped the horse's mane and thus held on.   And he
was succoured by Divine interposition, which unexpectedly
brought him aid from his enemies themselves.   For Providence produced some more Franks on the right side who also
raised their spears at him, and thus by thrusting the tips of
their spears against his right side, they lifted the soldier
and set him upright in their midst.   And a strange sight it
was to behold.   For those on the left strove to overthrow
him whilst those on the right fixed their spears against his
right side as if opposing the others, and by spears set against
spears, they kept the Emperor upright.   When he had
settled himself more firmly in the saddle and held his horse
and also the saddle-cloth tightly between his thighs, the
horse gave a signal proof of its mettle.   (Alexius had once
received this horse and a purple saddle-cloth as a gift from

Bryennius, after he had taken him captive in battle at the time when Nicephorus Botaniates was still Emperor.)   This horse, besides being very fiery and supple in the legs, was also remarkably strong and warlike, and now to put it briefly, inspired by Divine Providence, he suddenly leapt through the air and stood on the top of the cliff, springing up lightly like a bird, or, as the myth would say, with the wings of Pegasus.

Bryennius used to call this horse Sgouritzes).[1]   Some of the barbarians' spears were hurled into the empty air as it were, and fell from their hands while others remained sticking in parts of the Emperor's clothes and, borne aloft, followed the horse.   Alexius at once cut off the clinging spears.   Not even now, when in such dire peril, was he disturbed in soul or confused in his calculations, but swiftly saw his best course and unexpectedly freed himself.   The Franks on their side stood gaping, awestruck at what they had seen, and certainly it might well cause consternation ; but when they saw Alexius riding off down another road, they recommenced their pursuit.   After showing his pursuers his back for some considerable time, he turned upon them and encountering one of them, ran his spear through his chest, and the man fell backwards to the ground.   Then the Emperor turned his horse again and held on his former way.   And so he met a number of the Franks who before had been chasing the Roman troops.   When they saw him in the distance, they formed in close order and halted, partly to wind their horses, but also because they were anxious to take him alive and carry him off as booty to Robert.   But when he saw that besides the men pursuing him there were now others in front as well, he had well-nigh despaired of safety ; nevertheless he collected himself and noticing a man amongst the foe whom from his stature and gleaming weapons he judged to be Robert, he set his horse straight at him ; and the other aimed his spear at him.   So both joined combat, and launched themselves the one against the other in the intervening space.   The Emperor first directing his hand aright, struck at his opponent with his spear, which passed right through his breast, and out at the back.   Straightway the barbarian fell to the ground and gave up the ghost on the spot, for the wound was mortal.   And next the Emperor dashed right through the middle of the company and rode away, for by slaying that one barbarian he had gained safety for himself.   As soon as the Franks saw their hero wounded and hurled to the ground, they crowded round the fallen and busied them-

[1] =a dark bay.

selves about him. And when those who had been pursuing
the Emperor saw them, they, too, dismounted, and on recognizing the dead man, began beating their breasts and wailing.
However, the man was not Robert, but one of the nobles,
second only in rank to Robert. While they were thus
occupied, the Emperor continued his flight.

VIII And truly when writing this, partly from the
nature of history and partly because of the extravagance of
the events, I forgot that it was my father's deeds that I was
describing. In my desire to make my history free from
suspicion, I often treat my father's doings in a cursory way,
neither amplifying them nor investing them with sentiment.
Would that I had been free and released from this love of
my father, in order that I might have, as it were, laid hold
upon the rich material and shown the licence of my tongue,
how much at home it is in noble deeds. But now my zeal is
hampered by my natural love, for I should not like to afford
the public a suspicion that in my eagerness to speak about
my relations I am serving them with fairy-tales ! Indeed very
often I recall my father's successes, but I could have wept
my life away in tears when recording and describing the many
ills that befell him, and it is not without private lamentation
and plaint that I quit the subject. But no elegant rhetoric
must mar this part of my history, and therefore I pass lightly
over my father's misadventures, as if I were an insensible piece
of adamant or stone. I ought really to have used them as
a form of oath, as the young man does in the Odyssey (for I
am not inferior to him who says " No, by Zeus, Agelaus,
and by my father's sufferings ") and then I should both really
be, and be called, a lover of my father. However, let my
father's woes be a subject of marvel and lamentation to me
alone, and let us proceed with our history.

Afterwards the Franks hurried back to Robert. When he
saw them coming empty-handed and heard all that had befallen them, he blamed them all severely, and picked out
one of them and threatened to scourge him, and cursed him
for a coward and a fool at war. He asked why he had not
also jumped up to the rock with his horse and either knocked
down and killed the Emperor, or else caught him and brought
him back alive, until the soldier thought the worst was in
store for him. For that was Robert—on the one hand very
courageous and adventurous, and on the other, full of bitterness ; wrath ever sat in his nostrils, and his heart was overflow-
ing with anger and fury, and towards his enemies he always felt

that he must either run his foe through with his spear, or
he exclaimed that he must get rid of himself in defiance of
the thread of destiny, as they say.   However, the soldier
at whom Robert was hurling abuse, very clearly described the
steepness and inaccessibility of the rock, and told him what
a sheer ascent the rock made, and that the cliff was so steep
and dangerous that no foot- or horse-man could possibly
climb it without Divine intervention, let alone one engaged in
battle and fighting, for even apart from fighting, it was impossible for anyone to attempt the ascent.   " If," he continued, " you disbelieve me, go and try yourself, or send
the most daring of your horsemen, and he will soon see the
impossibility.   But if anybody does really manage to climb
that rock, be it with or without wings, then I am willing to
submit to any terrible punishment and to be condemned
for cowardice."   Speaking like this amidst awe and astonishment, the barbarian appeased Robert's fury, made him
forget his anger and moved him instead to wonder.

And the Emperor rode along the windings of the surrounding mountains and the almost impassable tracks, and
after two days and nights made his way out of them and
reached Achrida.   On this journey he crossed the river
Charzanes and rested a little in the secluded valley called
Babagora, and his spirit was not broken by his defeat nor by
the other accidents of the battle nor would he give way
to the pain of the wound in his forehead ;   and though
inwardly he was consumed with sorrow for those who had
fallen in the battle, especially for the heroes who had fought
so bravely, yet, above all, his mind was wholly occupied with
the thought of Dyrrachium.   For he reflected with pain
that this town was left without a governor, as Palæologus
had been unable to re-enter it after the battle was lost.   So
he secured the safety of the inhabitants as far as possible
by entrusting the custody of the Acropolis to the chiefs of the
Venetian colonists there, and the care of the rest of the city
to Comiscortes of Albanian origin to whom he transmitted
orders by letter.

BOOK V

I

AND meanwhile Robert, entirely freed from anxiety, collected all the booty and the Imperial tent, and, with these trophies and with much exultation, settled down again in the plain which he had occupied before when besieging Dyrrachium. After a short rest he began to consider whether he ought to make another attempt on that city's walls, or postpone the siege to the following spring and for the present invest Glabinitza and Joanina and winter there, while lodging all his troops in the sequestered vales that lie above the plain of Dyrrachium. But the inhabitants of Dyrrachium (the majority of whom were colonists from Amalfi and Venice, as already stated), on hearing of the Emperor's misfortune, and the terrible carnage, and the death of so many valiant men and the departure of the fleet and Robert's intention of renewing the siege in the coming spring—on hearing all this they began individually to deliberate what action they had better take to ensure their safety and not incur such risks again. Consequently they called an assembly where they openly stated their private opinions and after discussing the vital points they thought they had found the only path, as it were, out of a pathless wood, which was to decide to listen to Robert and surrender the city to him.

One of the colonists from Amalfi still further incited them to this course, so they allowed themselves to be persuaded by his arguments, and threw open the gates and gave Robert entrance. After taking possession, he sent for the troops and dividing them according to race, enquired of each soldier individually whether he had been seriously wounded or had perhaps received a slight scratch from a sword; at the same time he found out how many and what class of men had fallen in the preceding battles. And, during the winter which was then close at hand, he intended to collect a second army of mercenaries and recruit foreign troops, and at the coming of spring to march against the Emperor with his whole army. However, Robert was not alone in formulating such plans, although he congratulated himself on being the victor and winning the trophies, for the Emperor, worsted and badly wounded, was scared, so to say, and much depressed by this intolerable defeat and the loss of so many brave soldiers—but in spite of this as he never underestimated his own powers and had not slackened in his reasoning, his whole mind was intent on the problem of retrieving this defeat in the following spring. Both these men were clever at foreseeing everything, and in grasping the essentials, and there was no strategic trick unknown to them ; they were conversant with every kind of siege, ambuscade and regular battles in the open field, swift and brave in actual fighting, and of all the leaders in the world they were the adversaries most alike in intellect and courage. The Emperor Alexius had, however, a slight advantage over Robert in that while younger he was no whit inferior to the other who was already in his prime, and used to boast that he could almost make the earth quake and throw a whole army into a panic by one single shout !

But these details can be left for a different kind of writing, and are sure to be mentioned by encomiasts. The Emperor Alexius allowed himself a short rest in Achrida, and after regaining his physical strength, went to Diabolis. Here he sought as far as possible to reinvigorate the survivors from their sufferings in the battle, and he sent for his remaining followers from all parts and told them to assemble at Thessalonica.

Now that he had made experience of Robert and the boldness of his large army, he condemned his own leaders for great negligence and cowardice (I will not add the soldiers for the majority of those who had been in the battle had had neither training nor military experience), and therefore he needed allies. But how was he to get them without money ? For there was none in the Imperial Treasury which had been depleted so thoroughly and for no useful purpose by his predecessor, Nicephorus Botaniates, that the gates of the treasure-house were not even locked now, but carelessly left open for anyone who liked to walk through them ; for all its contents had been squandered. Hence the present embarrassment of the Roman state, which was oppressed simultaneously by weakness and poverty.

At such a moment then what was the young ruler to do who had only lately put his hand to the helm ? He must either in sheer desperation throw everything overboard and resign his command, so that, being blameless, he might not be blamed for being an inexperienced and unskilful general, or else in this extremity he must gain as many allies as possible and collect from some quarter or other sufficient money to pay them ; he must also recall the scattered remnants of his army by offering bribes which would raise their hopes and cause those who were with him to stand firmly by him, and those away to become more eager to return, and then they would be able to put up a braver resistance to the Frankish hordes.   As he did not wish to do anything unworthy of, or inconsistent with, his own military knowledge and bravery, he focussed his attention on these two points—the first was to collect allies from all sides, who would easily be allured by the promise of heavy largess, and the second, to request his mother and brother to procure money somehow from somewhere, and send it to him.

II   These two could not discover any other means of procuring money, so to begin with they collected whatever silver and gold articles they possessed and sent them to the imperial mint ; but first of all the Empress, my mother, deposited the sum that remained to her of her parents' patrimony, hoping thereby to instigate others to do the same ; for she was extremely anxious for the Emperor, seeing the straits into which his affairs had fallen.   Secondly, they took from the persons who were well-affected towards the imperial family, and had voluntarily offered to advance money, as much gold and silver as each was ready to give, and sent it to be used partly for allies and partly for the Emperor himself.   But these monies were far from sufficient even for the immediate need (for some of the soldiers asked for rewards on the plea that they had fought on the Emperor's side, and others who were mercenaries kept clamouring for higher pay) ; the Emperor urgently pressed for more, and thought that the goodwill of the Romans had vanished.   His relatives were quite at a loss, and after discussing many schemes in public and in private, when they heard that Robert was again preparing for war, they turned in their despair to an examination of the ancient laws and canons dealing with the sale of Church property.   And amongst them they found that it was lawful to sell the sacred properties of the churches for the ransoming of prisoners of war (for it was well known that the Christians who remained under the domination of the barbarians in Asia, and had escaped massacre, became defiled by their intercourse with the infidels). Therefore to furnish pay for the allies and the soldiers, they considered turning into coin a few church properties which served no purpose and were amongst those which had long been lying idle and neglected, and only afforded the populace an excuse for sacrilege and impiety. When they had come to this conclusion, the Sebastocrator Isaac went up to the great House of God where he had convoked an assembly of all the clergy. The members of the Holy Synod who were fellow-councillors with the Patriarch were astounded at seeing him and asked him what brought him there. He replied, " I have come to speak to you of a matter which will be of service in this terrible crisis, and will be the means of maintaining the army." Thereupon he began reciting the Canons about " superfluous Church vessels " and after saying a good deal about them, he concluded with the words, " I am compelled to compel those whom I do not wish to compel." And by putting forward various bold arguments he seemed likely to win over the majority. But Metaxas opposed him, advanced some very specious counter-arguments and even jeered at Isaac himself. But in spite of him, Isaac's proposal was carried. This decision became the subject of a very grave scandal to the Emperors (for I do not hesitate to call Isaac " emperor " even though he did not wear the purple), which lasted not only for the moment but for a considerable time. The head of the church of Chalcedon at this time was a certain Leo, not one of the especially wise or intellectual, but of very virtuous life, though his manners were rough and disagreeable. This man tore off the silver and gold ornaments on the doors of the church in Chalcoprateia, and rushed into the assembly and spoke his mind freely without so much as a reference to the financial condition or the extant laws regarding Church property. Moreover he behaved very insolently, and in a most disorderly manner, to the Regent, and each time he visited the capital he abused the latter's forbearance and kindness. And indeed when Alexius left the city the first time to march against Robert, and the Sebastocrator Isaac, his own true brother, was collecting money from every possible source, but always with the consent of the people and in accordance with the laws and justice, Leo aroused Isaac's wrath by his shameless behaviour. At last after many defeats and then after countless successful encounters with the Franks, the Emperor, by the sanction of Heaven, returned a crowned victor, and then he learnt that a fresh swarm of enemies, I mean the Scythians, were ready to descend upon him. Consequently the raising of funds was hurried on for similar reasons as before, even while the Emperor was residing in the capital, and at that time Bishop Leo attacked the Emperor most impudently. About this time a great controversy arose about the holy images, and Leo laid down the principle that we should adore the sacred images, and not only give them relative honour. On some points he argued reasonably and in a manner befitting his station, but on others he laid down the law wrongly, whether this was to be attributed to the heat of contest and his hatred of the Emperor, or to ignorance, I cannot say. He was incapable of making a precise statement with conviction as he was absolutely untrained in the science of reasoning. By the advice of malicious persons of whom there were a number in the Government then, he grew still bolder towards the Emperors and egged on by his friends he even resorted to insults and untimely blasphemies. The Emperor besought him to change his opinion about the images and also to desist from the enmity towards him, he also promised to restore even finer vessels to the churches and to do all that was necessary to repair the loss. The Emperor himself was already acquitted of blame by the more liberal-minded of the senate whom the partisans of the Chalcedonian called " flatterers." As a result of this behaviour, Leo was condemned to deposition from office.

As he did not knuckle under and did not keep quiet at all, but again disturbed the Church meeting, coming with a considerable crowd of followers, for he was absolutely irreconcilable and incorrigible, he was condemned by a unanimous vote after the lapse of some years and a sentence of exile was pronounced against him. The city of Sozopolis on the Black Sea received him and treated him with much care and consideration by order of the Emperor, none of which he accepted because of his grudge against the latter, I suppose.

This account of him must suffice.

III When it became known that the Emperor had escaped from the battle, recruits in large numbers flocked to him, and these he had carefully trained to ride very securely, to shoot very accurately, to fight in full armour and to lay ambuscades cleverly. He had also sent ambassadors again to the King of Alamania, of these Methymnes was the leader, and in his letter he urged him not to delay any longer, but to take the troops he had at hand, and occupy Lombardy with all haste, according to his promise. In this way Robert would be fully occupied and he himself would gain a respite during which he could reassemble his army and collect foreign troops and by their help drive Robert out of Illyria. He assured the King of Alamania that he would be deeply indebted to him if he would do this, and promised him that he would fulfil the marriage-contract which he had proposed through his ambassadors.

After arranging these matters he left Pacurianus, the Great Domestic in those parts, and himself returned to the capital, for the purpose of collecting foreign troops from all sides, and to arrange other matters connected with the times and the actual circumstances. Now the Manichæans, Xantas and Culeon, with the men under them who totalled about two thousand five hundred, went off home unceremoniously, and when invited several times by the Emperor to return, they did indeed promise to come, but kept postponing their coming. But he persisted and made them written promises of gifts and honours, but even so they did not return. Whilst the Emperor was engaged in these preparations for an advance against Robert, a messenger came to tell Robert that the King of Alamania had all but arrived in Lombardy. Then Robert was in a dilemma and deliberated what would be the best thing to do. After much reflection, as he had left Roger to be ruler over his Kingdom when he crossed to Illyria, but had not yet assigned any territory to his younger son, Bohemund, he assembled all the Counts and picked men among the soldiers, and summoning also his son, Bohemund, nicknamed Saniscus, he made a public harangue and said, " You know, Counts, that when I settled to cross to Illyria I appointed my beloved first-begotten son Roger, ruler of my country. For I could not have started from there and undertaken a task of great magnitude if I had left my own country without a leader, a ready prize at the mercy of the first comer. But now that the King of Alamania has entered it with hostile intent, it is my duty to defend it as far as in me lies. For certainly the man who attacks the possessions of others, must not in any way be careless of his own. Consequently it is necessary for me to leave you, in order to look after my own country, and engage in battle with the King of Alamania. Therefore to this, my younger son, I hand over Dyrrachium, Valona and all the remaining towns and islands which I have won by my sword since my arrival. And I commend him to you and ask you to regard him as my substitute and to fight for him with all your heart and mind."

Then addressing himself to Bohemund, he said, " And you,
my very dear son, I enjoin you to treat the Counts with all
honour and ask their advice on all occasions and not to
' play the master ' by yourself, but to communicate everything to them.   Above all, take care not to neglect the
continuance of the war against the Roman Emperor, but see
that you do not relax at all now that he has suffered a severe
defeat and all but fallen a victim to the sword, and the
greater part of his army has been wiped out in the battle.
(And truth to tell," he continued, " he came near being
captured alive and only escaped from our hands after being
terribly wounded).   Therefore take care lest by gaining a
respite he should recover and resist you more bravely
than before.   For he is not one of the common herd, but
has been nurtured from childhood on wars and battles, he
has travelled over the whole of the East and the West, and
how many rebels he hunted down and brought back captive
to the preceding emperors, you can learn yourself from many
informants.   Therefore if you lose heart at all and do not
march against him with firm resolve, you will lose all that I
personally have won by great effort, and you yourself will
undoubtedly reap the fruits of your own laziness.   And
now I am leaving immediately to drive the King of Alamania
out of our country and thus firmly establish my son Roger
in the dominion I gave him."   After thus bidding his son
farewell, Robert embarked on board a monoreme and reached
the opposite coast of Lombardy, and from there hurried on
to Salernum, which had formerly been appointed the residence
for those who attained ducal rank.   He stayed there until he
had collected a large force and as many mercenary troops
from surrounding countries as possible.   Meanwhile the King
of Alamania in accordance with his promise to the Emperor,
was already hastening to take possession of Lombardy.
Robert on hearing this news hurried to Rome to join his
army with the Pope's and to deter the King of Alamania
from carrying out his intention.   As the Pope was not at all
unwilling, they both set out against the King.   He for his
part was on his way to invest Lombardy when he heard the
whole story about the Emperor—namely, that he had suffered
a heavy defeat, that part of his army had been butchered
and the rest scattered abroad, that the Emperor himself
after surviving many dangers had been seriously wounded
in several parts of his body whilst fighting magnificently,
but had made a marvellous escape owing to his boldness and

courage. On receipt of these tidings the King turned his horse
and rode back to his native land, considering this a victory
in that he had not exposed himself to danger uselessly. So
this man took the homeward road; and Robert, when he
had reached the King's encampment, did not trouble to
pursue him himself but separated a large detachment from
his troops and sent it in pursuit of the King of Alamania.
He himself gathered up all the booty and made his way to
Rome with the Pope. After establishing the latter firmly
on his throne and in return being nominated King by him,
he returned to Salernum there to repose himself from the many
fatigues of war.

IV Shortly afterwards Bohemund came to him, bearing
witness on his face of the defeat he had sustained. We will
now relate how fate had dealt him this blow. The young
man, mindful of his father's counsels and being moreover
naturally fond of war and of confronting dangers, steadily
pursued the war with the Emperor. Taking his own soldiers
with him and accompanied by all the picked men of the
Romans and by the chiefs of the districts and towns which
had been subdued by Robert (for these threw themselves
heart and soul into Bohemund's cause once they had given
up the Emperor's case as hopeless), he marched through
Bagenetia to Joanina. Here he first drew trenches in the
vineyards outside the town and disposed all his troops in
convenient positions, and then set up his own tent inside the
town. He made a survey of the walls and recognising that
the citadel was in a dangerous condition, he not only hastened
to restore it as far as was possible, but he even built a second
very strong one in another part of the walls where he thought
it would be of more use; he also sent out raiding parties to
plunder the surrounding country and towns. Thereupon
the Emperor without the slightest delay, collected all his
troops, and hurriedly left Constantinople in the month of
May. When he arrived at Joanina, it was the right season
for fighting. As he recognized that his own armies were but
a fraction of Bohemund's forces and knew besides from his
previous battles with Robert that the first onset of the
Frankish cavalry upon their opponents was quite irresistible,
he judged it would be best to have an attack by missiles made
first upon the enemy by a small picked body of peltasts.
By this means he would gain some idea of how much military
experience Bohemund possessed, and by several partial
attacks he would be able to form some opinion of the general

state of affairs, and then, with the knowledge he had gained, engage in battle against the Franks with greater confidence. The two armies were burning with impatience to attack each other. But the Emperor dreading the irresistible first shock of the Latin cavalry hit upon a new device. He had wagons built, smaller and lighter than the ordinary ones, and four poles fixed to each, in these he placed heavy infantry so that when the Latins came dashing down at full gallop upon the Roman phalanx, the heavy-armed infantry should push the wagons forward and thus break the Latins' line.

When the hour of battle approached and the sun had already risen in its brilliance above the horizon, the Emperor drew up his regiments in order of battle and himself took the command of the centre. As soon as the engagement began, Bohemund shewed that he was not unprepared for the Emperor's scheme, but, as if he had foreknowledge of it, he adapted himself to this happening, for he divided his own troops into two divisions, avoided the waggons and attacked the Roman ranks on either flank. Then lines were confounded with lines and men fought men, face to face. After many had fallen on either side in the fierce fight, Bohemund certainly carried off the victory. The Emperor for his part stood like an unshaken tower with darts thrown at him from before and behind, for at one minute he would ride against the advancing Franks, engage in close fights with a few, giving and receiving blows and killing, and at another minute he would be shouting to, and rallying, the fugitives. Finally, however, when he saw his ranks split up into numerous portions, he deemed it wise to seek safety for himself too, not, as some might say, to save himself, nor was he shaken by cowardice, but in order that he might make a second, braver resistance to the valiant Franks, if only he could escape the immediate danger and rally his powers. As he was fleeing from the enemy with a few companions, he fell in with some Franks and again shewed himself the imperturbable general. For after exhorting his companions, he rode down upon the enemy impetuously as if determined either to die that day, or carry off the victory by force ; with his own hand he struck and killed one of the Franks, and the followers of Ares with him wounded many and routed the rest. In this way he escaped from immeasurably great dangers, and once again reached safety by passing through the Swamps to Achrida. There he stayed and after recalling a fair number of the fugitives to his standard, he left them all in those parts with the Great Domestic and him-

self went to the Bardares.   But not for the sake of rest, for
unlike other royalties he did not allow himself imperial ease
and repose.   There he assembled his regiments and mercenaries again and started on his march against Bohemund,
with a new device in his head for overcoming the Franks.
For he prepared iron caltrops, and on the eve of the day on
which he expected a battle, he had them spread over the
intermediate part of the plain, where he guessed the
Frankish cavalry would make their fiercest onslaught, thus
aiming to break the first irresistible attack of the Latins
by piercing the feet of their horses.   And he ordered the
Roman spearsmen who held the front line, to ride forward
at a measured pace in order not to be lamed by the caltrops,
and to part to either side and then turn ;   the light-armed
troops were to send a heavy shower of darts on the Franks
from a distance, and the left and right wings were to fall
upon them in a vehement charge.   These indeed were my
father's plans but they did not escape Bohemund.   For this
is what happened :   whatever plans my father made against
him in the evening, the Frank knew by the morning.   So
he skilfully modified his plans in accordance with what he
had been told, and engaged in battle but did not, as was his
custom, begin with a frontal attack, but forestalling the
Emperor's intention, he raised the din of battle on either
flank, bidding the front ranks keep still for a time.   Then
the battle became a hand-to-hand fight, the soldiers of the
Roman army turned their backs to the Latins and had not
even the courage to look them in the face again, as they had
been thoroughly frightened beforehand by their previous
defeat.   Thus the Roman lines were thrown into utter confusion, even though the Emperor remained undaunted in
hand and heart and offered brave resistance, wounding many
and sometimes too being wounded himself.   But when he
saw that his whole army had disappeared and he was left
with just a few, he decided not to incur danger by carrying
on a hopeless fight.   For when anyone after heavy travail
has no longer the strength to make a stand against his enemies,
he would be a fool if he thrust himself into certain danger.
Now after the left and right wings of the Roman phalanx
had turned to flight, the Emperor was still maintaining the
combat against Bohemund's army, bearing the whole brunt
of the battle himself.   But on comprehending his unquestionable
danger, he deemed it his duty to save himself, so as to be able
to fight once again against his conqueror, and prove himself

a very formidable opponent who would not allow Bohemund
to reap a complete victory. For such was his character,
whether conquered or conquering, fleeing or pursuing, he
never was cowed, nor caught in the snares of despair. Moreover, he had very great faith in God and ever had His name
on his lips, though always refraining from oaths. Now being
tired out as just said, he too turned his back and was pursued
by Bohemund and a few Counts. In so doing he asked
Goules (he was my father's servant) and the others with him,
" How far shall we flee ? " With these words he turned
his horse, drew his sword and hit the foremost of his pursuers
in the face. When the Franks saw this and recognized that
he was quite reckless of his own safety, and as they knew from
experience that men reduced to such a state of mind are
invincible, they were stricken with fear and ceased their
pursuit. And so freed from his pursuers he escaped danger.
Even in flight he did not entirely lose heart but managed to reassemble some of the fugitives and others he jeered at, though
the majority naturally affected not to notice it. Having
in this wise escaped from peril he re-entered the capital
for the purpose of mustering new armies and again taking the
field against Bohemund.

V   After Robert's departure for Lombardy Bohemund,
obedient to his father's behests, carried on the war against
the Emperor, and continually rekindled battles and engagements. Further, he sent Peter, the son of Aliphas, with the
Count of Pontoise to besiege various towns, with the result
that Peter at once took the two Polobi, and the afore-
mentioned Count of Pontoise took Scopia, and on being
invited by the Achridians, he quickly reached Achrida.
But after staying there some time and accomplishing nothing,
for Ariebes was guarding the citadel, he went away to
Ostrobus ; from that town too he was sent away empty-
handed so passed through Soscus and Serbia and came to
Berœa. And after attacking several places repeatedly without success, he reached Moglena viâ Bodina and there
rebuilt a small fort which had long lain in ruins. There he
left a Count, nicknamed " the Saracen," with an ample
garrison and betook himself to a spot on the river Bardares
called the Aspræ Ecclesiæ. And whilst he was spending
three months there, three of the foremost Counts, namely
the Count of Pontoise, Reboldus and a certain Gulielmus
were detected in a plot for deserting to the Emperor. The
Count of Pontoise indeed, became aware of this and escaped

and reached the Emperor, but the other two were captured
and by the Frankish law condemned to ordeal by battle.
Gulielmus was defeated and unhorsed and Bohemund
imprisoned and blinded him ; the other, Reboldus, he sent
to Lombardy to his father, Robert, by whom he too was
deprived of his sight.   Then Bohemund left Asprae Ecclesiae
for Castoria.   The Great Domestic on hearing this, occupied
Moglena, seized and immediately put to death the ' Saracen '
and reduced the fort to complete ruin.   Bohemund, meanwhile, left Castoria and came to Larissa where he hoped to
winter.   When the Emperor reached the capital, as already
mentioned, he at once set to work—being, as he was, a
strenuous worker and never allotting himself any rest—and
asked the sultan for troops as well as for some generals with
long experience.   The latter consequently sent him 7,000
men with highly experienced leaders, among whom was
Camyres who surpassed all in long experience.   While the
Emperor was arranging and preparing these matters, Bohemund selected a certain portion of his own army, all Franks
in full armour, sent them out and they took Pelagonia,
Tricala and Castoria off-hand.   Then Bohemund himself
with his whole army entered Tricala and dispatching a
detachment of brave men took Tzibiscus at first assault.
After this he approached Larissa on the festival of St. George
the Martyr with all his troops, encircled the walls and proceeded to besiege it.   Now the defender of this city was the
son of the Emperor's hereditary servant, Leo Cephalas, and
he put up a stout resistance to Bohemund's engines for six
whole months.   He at once informed the Emperor by letter
of the barbarian's attack.   But the Emperor did not immediately start on his march against Bohemund, though
burning with impatience, but had to postpone his departure
because he was recruiting mercenaries from all quarters.
At length after equipping them all fully, he set out from
Constantinople.   When he was close to the territories of
Larissa and had passed over the hill of the Cells, he left the
public high-road and the hill, Cissabus, so-called locally, on
the right and marched down to Ezeba ; this is a Vlach village
situated close to Androneia.   From this he marched on to a
large village, generally called Plabitza, situated somewhere
near a river called . . . ; here he pitched his camp, entrench-
ing it just sufficiently.   Then on again through the gardens
of Delphinas, and beyond them to Tricala.   And here a
messenger bearing a letter from Leo Cephalas (of whom I

have already spoken), found him. He wrote very freely
as follows: " Know, O Emperor, that up to the present by
evincing extreme zeal I have kept this fortress from being
taken. Now we are deprived of all foods allowed to Christians
and have begun those which are not fitted for us, but even
those are now giving out. Therefore please make haste if
you wish to help us and if you could possibly drive away our
assailants, then thanks be to God. But, if not, I, at least,
have done my duty ; and shortly (for how is it possible to
struggle against nature and its imperious demands ?) we must
bow our heads to necessity and we intend to surrender the
fort to the enemy who are pressing us hard and literally
throttling us. But if this calamity should eventually come
to pass, then may I be accursed ! But I now take the liberty
of speaking openly to your Majesty. If you do not hasten
with all speed to extricate us from this danger, as we are
unable to support the overwhelming burden of warfare, as
well as famine, any longer ; if you, our Sovereign, do not
hasten to bring help when you have the power to do so, then,
I say, you will certainly not escape the imputation of be-
trayal." From this the Emperor realized that in one way or
another he must overcome the foe ; and he was oppressed by
anxieties and speculations. And for a whole day during
which he invoked the aid of God, he worked hard at the
problem of how best to set ambuscades. He also sent for
an old man, a native of Larissa, and sought information from
him about the lie of the land. With intent eyes and pointing
with his finger too, he questioned him carefully about the
places where ravines broke through the plain, and whether
any thick coppices grew beside them. He asked these
questions of the Larissæan because he wished to lay an ambush
and defeat the Latins by craft ; for he shirked an open battle
in the field as in several engagements he had been worsted and
had gained experience of the Frankish method of attack. At
sunset, the Emperor, who had toiled all day long, betook
himself to sleep and a vision appeared to him. He seemed to
be standing in the church of the Protomartyr Demetrius and
heard a voice say " Do not grieve nor groan, to-morrow you
shall conquer." He thought the voice fell upon his ears
from an icon suspended in the temple on which the martyr
Demetrius was painted. He awoke full of joy because of the
voice of his vision, made his prayers to the martyr and
promised besides that, if victory should be granted him, he
would travel to Thessalonica and at several stades' distance

from the town he would dismount and proceed on foot at a smart pace and do obeisance to him in his church. Then he summoned the generals, captains and his relatives and commenced the discussion by asking their individual opinion, and next explained the plan he had formed. And this was to entrust all the divisions to his relatives; as chief commanders he appointed Melissenus Nicephorus and Curticius Basileios, also called 'Little John'; this man was an outstanding figure renowned for his bravery and military skill, a native of Adrianople. But not only the divisions did he entrust to them but also all the royal standards. Moreover he enjoined them to draw up the army on the same plan as he had drawn it up in the foregoing battles, and advised them first to try the vanguard of the Latin army by a skirmishing attack, then to raise their battle-cry and make a general attack. But directly the troops were fully engaged they were to turn their backs to the Latins and flee precipitately as if making for Lycostomium. Whilst the Emperor was giving these orders, suddenly all the horses in the army were heard to neigh. Astonishment seized them all; however, the Emperor and the more intelligent of his audience at once interpreted it as a good omen.

After he had given them these injunctions he left them to the right of Larissa, and after waiting for the sunset, he ordered some picked men to follow him, and went through the narrow pass of Libotanium, skirted Rebenicus and through the so-called "Allage" he reached the left side of Larissa; there he explored the nature of the ground and finding a slight depression, he crouched down with his companions. At the same time when the Emperor, as just related, was on the point of entering the defiles of Libotanium in his haste to place an ambush, the leaders of the Roman divisions selected and sent forward a detachment of the Roman troops against the Franks to draw the latter's attention to themselves and not allow them leisure to spy out whither the Emperor was going. So the Romans descended to the plain, attacked the Franks, and after a short battle, stopped, as night completely prevented further fighting. On reaching the desired spot the Emperor bade all dismount and kneel down and hold their reins in their hands; and he himself accidentally alighted on a bed of germander and bending down likewise lay the rest of the night on his face.

VI At sunrise Bohemund saw the Roman troops drawn up in array, and the royal standards and the silver-studded

spears and the horses with their royal red saddle-cloths,
drew up his own army against them as well as he could,
dividing his forces into two, and leading one half himself
and over the other he put Bryennius[1] as commander, who
was one of the most illustrious Latins and called ' Constable ' by
them. After thus disposing his own forces, he again followed
his usual mode of procedure and thinking the Emperor was
where he saw the imperial ensigns in the middle of the line,
he dashed down upon this deception like a whirlwind. After
a short resistance his opponents turned their backs and he
rushed after them in mad pursuit as in our previous descrip-
tions. Meanwhile the Emperor saw his own troops fleeing
far, and Bohemund in mad pursuit of them, and when he
judged that Bohemund was at a safe distance from the
Roman camp, he jumped on his horse, bade his followers do
the same, and fell upon Bohemund's encampment. Once
inside it he slew a number of the Latins he found there and
carried off all the booty ; then he took another glance at the
pursuers and pursued. And observing that his own men were
really pretending flight and Bohemund chasing after them
and behind him Bryennius, he called George Pyrrhus, a
famous archer, and having detached other brave men, and a
goodly number of peltasts he ordered them to ride quickly after
Bryennius, and when they overtook him, not to start a close
fight, but rather aim at the horses from a little distance and
direct showers of arrows upon them. They did thus overtake the Franks and showered arrows upon the horses so that
the horsemen were reduced to great difficulties. For every
Frank is invincible both in attack and appearance when
he is on horseback, but when he comes off his horse, partly
due to the size of his shield, and partly to the long curved
peaks of his shoes and a consequent difficulty in walking,
then he becomes very easy to deal with and a different man
altogether, for all his mental energy evaporates, as it were.
This, I fancy, the Emperor knew, and therefore ordered them
not to trouble about the riders, but to disable the horses.
As the Franks' horses fell, the men with Bryennius were thrown
into frightful confusion, and from this large whirling mass a
tall, thick cloud of dust rose almost to the sky, so that its
density could almost be likened to the darkness ' that could
be felt ' which befell Egypt long ago. For their eyes were
blinded by the thick dust which also prevented their seeing
whence and by whom the arrows were shot. So Bryennius

[1] = Count of Brienne, Constable of Apulia.

sent three Latins to report the matter to Bohemund. These
found him standing on a little island in the river called Salabrias, eating grapes and also making a boastful pun which is
still popularly quoted. For he kept repeating with his
barbaric pronunciation of " Lycostomium " that they had
driven Alexius " into the wolf's mouth." Thus does arrogance
mislead many even with regard to things directly before their
eyes, and before their feet. But when he heard the news
sent by Bryennius and realized the craftiness and the victory
won by guile he was naturally, indeed, furious with the
Emperor, but in no wise cast down, so brave was he. A few
selected Franks in full armour who were with him, then
mounted a small hill opposite Larissa. Directly our heavy
troops caught sight of them they demanded very eagerly
to be allowed to attack them, but Alexius restrained them
from this enterprise. Nevertheless quite a number from the
different divisions and of various types did join together
and mounted the hill and attacked the Franks, who immediately rushed at them and killed about five hundred. Then
the Emperor guessing at the spot where Bohemund was likely
to pass, dispatched brave soldiers with the Turks and Migidenus
as chief commander, but as they drew near, Bohemund set
upon them and beat them and pursued them to the river.

VII As dawn broke on the following day Bohemund
crossed the river we have mentioned with his attendant
Counts, Bryennius himself among them, and when he found a
swampy place in the neighbourhood of Larissa and a tree-
covered plain between two hills which ran out into a very
narrow pass (this is called a " cleisura "), the plain was named
" the palace of Domenicus," he entered by the pass and
fixed his palisades there. The next day at dawn the leader
of the phalanx, Michael Ducas, my maternal uncle, caught
him there with all the army. This man was celebrated for his
prudence, and in beauty and stature surpassed not only all
his contemporaries, but all who have ever been born ! (for all
who saw him were amazed) ; he was, too, very quick and almost
unrivalled in his conjectures of the future, his investigations
of the actual and in taking action accordingly. The Emperor
gave strict injunctions to this man not to let all the troops
enter the mouth of the " cleisura " ; but to leave the mass of
them outside in squadrons, and to pick out a few of the Turks
and Sauromatians who were skilled archers and allow these to
enter, and to command them to use no weapon but their
arrows. These entered and made cavalry attacks on the

Latins, and the men outside, burning for a fight, vied with each
other as to who should enter the mouth. Bohemund, who was
an expert in strategic science, commanded his men to form in
close order and to stand quietly and protect themselves with
their shields. When the Protostrator saw the men under
him gradually melting away and entering the mouth of the
pass he went in himself. And Bohemund seeing them
come rejoiced as ' a lion who has met with mighty prey,'
to use a Homeric expression, even so he, when he saw the men
and the Protostrator Michael with his own eyes, dashed at
them with all his forces in an irresistible rush, whereupon
they immediately turned and fled. Uzas (who was thus
named after his race), a man famous for his bravery and
skilled, as Homer says, ' in wielding, now right now left, the
tough bull's hide that formed his target,' bent to the right
as he was coming out of the entrance and, turning sharply,
hit the Latin following him, who straightway fell headlong
to the ground. But Bohemund pursued the fugitives as
far as the river Salabrias. During the flight this same Uzas
pierced Bohemund's standard-bearer with his spear and
plucking the standard from his hands waved it aloft a minute,
and then lowered it to the ground. When the Latins saw
their standard lowered, they were confounded and fled along
another path by which they reached Tricala which had already
been seized by some of Bohemund's men who were fleeing to
Lycostomium. And there they entered the town and stayed
awhile and afterwards seized Castoria. But the Emperor
soon left Larissa and entered Thessalonica and with his
usual sagacity very soon began sending offers of rich rewards
to the Counts in Bohemund's train on condition that they
would ask Bohemund for the pay he had promised them,
and that if he could not pay them, they should persuade him
to journey down to the sea and ask his father Robert for it,
or better still, cross the sea himself to fetch it. If they accomplished this, they should all enjoy his respect and numberless benefits. And if any of them were willing to serve under
him as mercenaries, he would enrol them in his army and
give them the pay they required, and to those who preferred
to return to their own homes, he would give a safe passage
through Hungary. In response to the Emperor's suggestion,
the Counts unfeelingly demanded their pay for the last four
years, but as Bohemund had not got it, he temporized awhile.
However, on their insisting in their reasonable demands, he did
not know what to do, so appointed Bryennius Governor of

Castoria, as well as Peter, son of Aliphas, who was guarding Polobi ; and himself journeyed down to Valona.   On receipt of this news, the Emperor packed up and entered the Queen of Cities in triumph.

VIII   When he arrived he found the church in a very perturbed condition, and did not even have a short period of relaxation.   But as he was a true apostle of the church, and now found it vexed by the teachings of Italus, although he was anxious to march against Bryennius (the Frank who had taken Castoria, as we have said) yet even under these circumstances he did not neglect his faith.   For at this time the doctrines of Italus had obtained a great vogue and were upsetting the church.   Now this Italus (for it is necessary to give his history from the beginning) was a native of Italy and had spent a considerable time in Sicily ; this is an island situated near Italy.   For the Sicilians had rebelled against the Roman rule and were preparing for war against them and invited the Italians to join them ; amongst those who came was the father of Italus who brought his son with him, although he was not of military age, and the boy accompanied and tripped along with him and received a military education, as is the custom of the Italians.   That is how Italus spent the early years of his life, and that was the first foundation of his education.   When the famous George Maniaces during the reign of Monomachus mastered and subdued Sicily, the father of Italus with his child only escaped with difficulty and betook themselves in their flight to Lombardy which was still under the Romans.   From there (I do not know how) this Italus came to Constantinople, which was not ill supplied with teachers of every subject and of the art of language. For from the time of Basil Porphyrogenitus down to the Emperor Monomachus, the study of letters, although neglected by the many, had nevertheless not entirely died out ; it blazed up again and revived and was seriously pursued by the lovers of letters in the reign of the Emperor Alexius.   Before that time men for the most part lived luxuriously and amused themselves, and due to their effeminacy they busied themselves with quail-hunting and other more disgraceful pastimes, and treated letters, and in fact any training in arts, as a secondary consideration.   Therefore when Italus found the majority of this character, he consorted with the scholars, gloomy men of uncouth habits (for such were to be found in the capital even then) and after he had gained an education in letters from them he later associated with the renowned

Michael Psellus. This man had not studied very much
under learned professors, but through his natural cleverness
and quick intelligence and further by the help of God (which
he had obtained by his mother's ardent supplications, for
she often spent whole nights in the church of God weeping
and making invocations to the holy picture of the Virgin
on her son's behalf) he had reached the summit of all
knowledge, was thoroughly acquainted with Greek and
Chaldæan literature and grew famous in those days for his
wisdom. Italus, then, became this man's disciple, but he
was never able to plumb the depths of philosophy for he was
of such a boorish and barbarous disposition that he could
not endure teachers even when learning from them. He was
full of daring and barbarous rebelliousness and even before
learning a thing, imagined he surpassed everybody else and
from the very start he entered the lists against Psellus himself.
Being well versed in dialectics he caused daily commotions
in public meeting places by stringing together sophistical
quibbles, putting forward something of the kind and then
maintaining an argument to match it. The reigning Emperor,
Michael Ducas, and his brothers, made a friend of him ; they
certainly placed him after Psellus in their estimation, yet
they were fond of him, and used him in literary contests ;
for the Ducases, the Emperor's brothers, and even the
Emperor Michael himself, were very literary. Italus would
always cast heated, furious glances at Psellus when the latter,
like an eagle, soared above his quibbles.

What happened next ? The war of the Latins and Italians
with the Romans broke out, and the occupation of Lombardy,
nay even of the whole of Italy, was under consideration.
The Emperor of that time sent Italus to Epidamnus on the
supposition that he was his friend and an honest man, and
understood Italian affairs. Then, to cut my story short,
he was detected in treachery to us and an official was sent
to expel him, and Italus getting wind of this, escaped to Rome.
Later, as was his nature, he repented and sent imploring letters
to the Emperor who ordered him back to Constantinople
and gave him as dwelling-place the monastery called Pege,
and the church of the Forty Saints. Later when Psellus
left Byzantium after taking the tonsure, Italus became the
foremost teacher of all philosophy and was styled the highest,
' Hypatus,' of philosophers and he gave lectures explaining
the books of Aristotle and Plato. He was generally supposed
to be very learned. and he undoubtedly was far cleverer than

all others in expounding that most wonderful philosophic system, the Peripatetic, and especially the dialectics of it. But for other branches of literature he had not a very good head, for he stumbled over grammar and had never tasted the nectar of rhetoric. Consequently his language was not adaptable nor at all polished. For the same reason, too, his character was austere and entirely unadorned with grace. His studies too had contracted his brows and he literally exhaled harshness. His writings were crammed full of dialectic exordiums and his language in disputations redounded with 'attempted proofs,' more so in his discourses than in his written works. He was so strong in his arguments and so difficult to beat that his opponent would automatically be reduced to silence and to despair. For he would dig a pit either side of his question and hurl his interlocutor into a well of difficulties. Such skill the man had in dialectics, and by a rapid succession of questions he would overwhelm his opponents by confusing and daunting their minds. And it was impossible for anyone, who had once argued with him, to free himself from these labyrinths. In other ways he was most unrefined, and subject to violent temper; and this fierce temper annulled and obliterated the credit he gained from his learning. For in arguments this man used fists as well as words and he did not allow his interlocutor simply to lose himself in embarrassment nor was he satisfied with sewing up his opponent's mouth and condemning him to silence, but forthwith his hand flew out to tear his beard and hair, and insult quickly followed insult, in fact the man could not be restrained in the use of his hands and tongue. The only unphilosophic trait he had was that after the blow his anger left him, tears and evident remorse followed. If it would interest anyone to know his appearance, his head was large, his brow very prominent, his face open, his nostrils wide and of free exhalation, his beard rounded, his chest broad and his limbs well-knit together, in stature shorter than the very tall. His pronunciation was such as you would expect of a Latin who had come to our country as a young man and learnt Greek thoroughly but was not quite clear in his articulation, for he mutilated his syllables here and there. This want of clearness in his utterance and his dropping the last letters did not escape even ordinary people and made rhetoricians call him 'rustic' in his speech. As a result, although his writings were crammed with dialectical commonplaces, drawn from all sources, they were decidedly not free from faults of composition and solecisms scattered broadcast.

IX This man then was the acknowledged master of all philosophy and the youth flocked to him. (For he expounded to them the doctrines of Plato and Proclus and of the two philosophers, Porphyry and Iamblichus, but especially the rules of Aristotle; and he gave instruction in the system to those who wished, as affording a serviceable tool and it was on this that he rather prided himself and to this he devoted his attention.) Yet he was unequal to exerting a very good influence on his pupils as his violent temper and his general instability of character stood in the way. And look, I pray, at his pupils—there were Solomon John, and an Iasitas and Serblias and others devoted to learning maybe ; most of them I saw myself later, as they often came to the palace. They knew no literary subject accurately, but would pose as dialecticians, making ungainly movements and mad contortions of their limbs, they understood nothing sound but put forth ideas, even those about metempsychosis, in a shadowy way and other similar equally monstrous notions. Is there any learned man who on visiting the court has not seen that holy couple, utterly absorbed in their study of the interpretation of the Divine writings both at day- and night-time ? I mean my royal parents. And here I will tell a little tale, for the laws of oratory allow that. I remember the Empress, my mother, when breakfast was already on the table, carrying a book in her hands and poring over the writings of the didactic Fathers, especially those of the philosopher and martyr Maximus. For she was not so much interested in the physical disputations as in those about the dogmas, because she wished to gain true wisdom. And I was often seized with wonder at her and one day in my wonder I said to her, " How can you spontaneously rise to such sublime heights ? for I tremble and dare not listen to such things even with the tips of my ears ? For the purely abstract and intellectual character of the man makes one's head swim, as the saying goes." She smiled and said " I know that kind of quite laudable dread ; and I myself do not touch these books without a tremor and yet I cannot tear myself away from them. But you wait a little and after you have dipped into other books, you will taste the sweetness of these." The remembrance of these words pricks my heart and I have plunged into an ocean, so to speak, of other tales. But the rules of history forbid them, therefore let us run back to the

tale of Italus—when he was at the height of his popularity
with the students, some of whom I have named, he treated
them all with contempt and turned many of the feebler-
minded to rebellion and made not a few of his own pupils
tyrants. And I could mention several of them, had not time
obliterated their names from my memory. All this took
place before my father was elevated to the throne. On his
accession he found all education here in a very poor way and
the regular study of letters apparently banished afar, he
lost no time in raking the ashes together to see whether some
live sparks might perchance be hidden under them. Those
who were inclined to learning (and they were but few and had
not passed beyond the vestibule of Aristotelian philosophy)
he did not cease from encouraging but bade them prefer the
study of the sacred writings to Greek literature. He found
Italus throwing everything into confusion and leading many
astray, so he deputed the Sebastocrator Isaac to examine
him, as he was very literary and accustomed to undertaking
important duties. When Isaac found that Italus was as
report said, he openly censured him in a public meeting and
then passed him on to the ecclesiastical tribunal by order of
the Emperor, his brother. But Italus was unable to hide
his own ignorance, and there he vomited forth doctrines quite
foreign to the church's, and in the midst of the ecclesiastical
dignitaries he did not cease from acting like a buffoon, and
doing other things of a boorish and uncultured nature ; the
president of the church then was Eustratius Garidas who
condemned him to detention within the precincts of the
great church in the hopes of bringing him to a better state of
mind. But, report says that Garidas would more quickly
have shared the other's evil doctrines than brought him back
to the right path, and Italus won him over entirely to his
side. What was the consequence ? The whole population
of Constantinople surged into the church, shouting for Italus.
Probably he would have been thrown down from the top
into the middle of the church, had he not escaped to the roof
of the sacred edifice and hidden himself in some hole he found.
But as the wrong doctrines he had promulgated were much
discussed by some of the courtiers, and not a few nobles
had been corrupted by those pernicious dogmas, the Emperor's
soul was vexed ; and the heretical doctrines taught by
Italus were summarized in eleven chapters and dispatched
to the Emperor. Then the Emperor made Italus recite these
chapters from the pulpit in the great church with his head

uncovered, and pronounce a curse upon them, while all the congregation listened and repeated the curse. When this had been done, Italus still remained uncontrollable, and again taught these same doctrines to many quite openly, and on being reprimanded by the Emperor, he turned away abruptly and rudely, then he himself was excommunicated. Later on, when he professed penitence, his sentence of excommunication was lightened somewhat. And although his doctrines are still recited and cursed, his name is only mentioned indirectly, as it were, and secretly, and the anathema pronounced on him by the church is not pronounced in a voice audible to the congregation. For in his later years he changed his opinions and repented of the error into which he had been led. Furthermore, he denied a belief in metempsychosis and retracted his insulting words about the holy icons of the saints ; he also remodelled his teaching about " ideas " so as to make it conform to orthodoxy, and it was quite evident that he condemned himself for having formerly strayed from the straight path.

BOOK VI

I

NOW Bryennius was holding Castoria, as told above, so the Emperor who was eager to drive him out and regain possession of the town, called up his whole army again and after fully equipping them with weapons necessary for a siege and also those for engagements in the open he took the road leading to the fort. The situation of the town was as follows : there is a lake called Castoria, into which a promontory runs, which widens out towards the end and terminates in rocky hills. On this neck of land towers and connecting walls were built in the shape of a camp, hence the town's name of Castoria. On arrival the Emperor thought it would be wisest in the first place to made an assault upon the towers and walls with his battering-machines. But as it was impossible to get the soldiers near the walls except from a definite base, he first made a palisaded camp, next built wooden towers and bound them together with iron bands and then from these, as if from a fort, he commenced the battles against the Franks. The siege-engines and catapults he drew up outside the town and then by day and night he fought and broke down part of the walls. However, the besieged resisted most determinedly (they did not surrender even when a breach had been made in the wall) so the Emperor, seeing that he could not achieve his object in that way, conceiyed a plan which was both daring and clever. It was to put some stout-hearted men into boats and make war from both sides simultaneously, that is, from the land and from the lake. As there were no boats he had some light skiffs loaded on wagons and introduced to the lake by means of the narrow causeway. He had noticed that the Latins who mounted the hills at one side, ascended quickly, whereas those who descended at another point spent a longer time over the descent ; so he put George Palæologus in the boat with some plucky soldiers and told him to row to the foot of the hills and when he saw the predetermined signals then to mount to the ridge at the back of the enemy and enter the town by the uninhabited and easier road. Afterwards directly he saw that the Emperor had commenced battle with the Latins on the land-side, he himself was to come as quickly as possible, for the Latins would not be able to carry on the fight equally well on two sides, and as soon as it slackened a bit on one side, they would then more easily be defeated on that same side. George Palæologus therefore anchored off the shores below the hill we have mentioned and stood there ready armed ; he posted a look-out above to watch for the signal to be given by the Emperor and told him directly he saw it, to pass on the same to him. As early as day-break the Emperor's soldiers raised their war-cry and hastened to engage the Latins in battle on the land-side. The look-out seeing the pre-arranged signal, signified it to Palæologus by another signal, whereupon he and his men immediately rushed up the ridge and joined in the fight. When Bryennius saw the besiegers outside and Palæologus raging against them inside he did not surrender even then, but called upon the Counts to be bolder in their resistance. But they behaved very shamelessly to him and said, " You see how calamity is piled upon calamity! Each one of us for the future must secure his own safety, some of us by joining the Emperor and others by returning to their own country." Straightway they translated their words into action ; they petitioned the Emperor to have one standard posted near the shrine of Saint George (for a church dedicated to this martyr had been built there) and a second by the road to Valona. " Thus," said they, " those of us who wish to serve your Majesty, can gather at the turn of the road leading to the church of the martyr, whilst those who desire to return to their own country can assemble near the other on the road to Valona." And with these words they immediately deserted to the Emperor. But Bryennius, being a brave man, absolutely refused to go over to the Emperor, but took an oath never to take up arms against him again, on condition that the Emperor gave him safe conduct to the frontiers of the Roman Empire and there set him free to go to his country. The Emperor at once granted him his request and himself took the road for Byzantium crowned with victory.

II Here I must interrupt the thread of the story a while to relate how the Emperor suppressed the Paulicians. He could not bear the thought of entering the capital without

having first subdued these rebels, but as though presiding over
a second victory after a first, he caused the mass of the
Manichæans to complete the cycle of his achievements.
For it was not even right to allow those descendants of the
Paulicians to be a blemish, as it were, on the brilliant trophy
of his western victories. He did not wish to effect this by
warfare, as in the clash of battle many lives on either side
would be sacrificed, further he knew from of old that these
men were very spirited and breathed defiance against their
enemies. For this reason he was eager only to punish the
ringleaders, and to incorporate the rest in the body of his
army. Hence he proceeded against them adroitly. He knew
those men's love of danger and irrepressible courage in battle
and therefore feared that, if they became desperate, they
would commit some terrible outrage ; and for the moment
they were living quietly in their own country and so far had
abstained from raids and other forms of devastation ; therefore on his way back to Byzantium he asked them by letter
to come and meet him and made them many promises. But
the Manichæans had heard of his victory over the Franks
and naturally suspected that those letters were misleading
them by fair promises ; nevertheless, though reluctant,
they set out to meet him. Alexius halted close to Mosynopolis,
pretending that he was waiting for other reasons, but in reality
he was only awaiting their arrival. When they came he
pretended that he wished to review them and write down
each individual's name. So he presided with a grim face and
commanded the chiefs of the Manichæans not to ride past
promiscuously but in parties of ten, promising a general
review shortly, and then when their names had been inscribed,
to enter the gates in that order. The men whose duty it
was to take them captive were all ready and after taking away
their horses and weapons, locked up the chiefs in the prisons
assigned them. Those who came after were in complete
ignorance of these doings and therefore entered the town
little knowing the fate awaiting them. In this manner then
he captured them, and their property he confiscated and
distributed among the brave soldiers who had shared in the
battles and dangers that had befallen him. The official who
undertook this distribution went to Philippopolis and drove
even the women from their homes and incarcerated them in
the citadel. Within a short time the Emperor took pity
on the imprisoned Manichæans, and those who desired
Christian baptism were not refused even this boon. So

having overreached them by every kind of device he discovered the authors of this terrible madness, and these he banished and imprisoned in islands. The rest he released and gave them permission to go whithersoever they wished. And they, preferring their mother-country to any other, hastened back to it to put their affairs into what order they could.

III Alexius then returned to the Queen of Cities. The mutterings against him in the highways and byways (about his appropriation of Church-treasures) did not escape his notice, and the hearing of them wounded his soul because the number of backbiters railing against him had increased greatly although he had not committed any serious offence. For in a time of dire need and world-upheaval and because of the emptiness of the royal treasury he had recourse to that measure and regarded it as a loan, and most assuredly not as robbery, nor was it the plot of a tyrannical master as his slanderers asserted. Further, he intended after the successful termination of the wars he had on hand, to restore to the churches the ornaments he had taken. So on his return to the Queen-City he could not endure being made the subject of discussion by those who wished to disparage his methods. On this account he summoned the church to a very large conference in the palace of Blachernæ before which he would first present himself as defendant, and as such make his defence. The whole senate was present with the military and all the clergy wondering what this immense gathering was for. The fact was that it was nothing but an enquiry into the rumours which were being bruited about against the Emperor. The priors of the monasteries were present and before them were set up their books (these are generally called 'brevia') in which lists were written of the treasures in each church. In appearance the Emperor, seated on his royal throne, was the judge, but in reality he was about to be examined. First the gifts bequeathed to the holy houses in former times by various donors were read out and then the things that had been taken away later or even by the reigning Emperor. And when it appeared that nothing else had been taken away except the gold and silver ornaments which lay on the tomb of the Queen Zoë and a few other vessels of no great use for the sacred services, the Emperor openly proclaimed himself as the culprit, and as judge anybody who liked. And after a little while changing the tone of his speech, he continued, " I found the Empire surrounded on all sides by barbarians and absolutely deficient in resources for opposing these enemies who were pressing hard upon her ; you know in how many dangers I was involved and only narrowly escaped being slain by a barbarian's sword. And verily the foes who attacked us from either side were many times more numerous than we. You are not ignorant of the incursions of the Persians nor of the raids of the Scythians, and you have not forgotten the spears from Lombardy that were whetted against us. But the money had disappeared together with the arms, and the circle of our rule had been contracted to an indivisible centre. How the whole army has grown, been thoroughly trained, collected from all parts and welded into one, you know ; and that all these things require much money, you all know, and also that what I took was spent usefully after the example of the famous Pericles and for the preservation of our honour. But, if to the censorious among you we appear to have offended against the canons, that is not surprising. For we read that the prophet among kings, David, when reduced to the same need, ate the holy bread with his soldiers, and this, though it was not lawful for a layman to touch the food reserved for the priests. And besides this we learn from the sacred canons that on several occasions holy things were allowed to be sold for the ransom of prisoners of war. If then, when our country was enslaved, when the cities, and even Constantinople itself, were in danger of being captured—if then under this frightful compulsion I laid hands on just a few things which did not at all partake of the dignity of sacred things and used them for our liberation, then, I aver, I have given my detractors no just cause of accusation." With these words he changed his manner of speech, proclaimed himself guilty and himself condemned himself. Then he ordered the guardians of the ' brevia ' to unroll them again with the object of making a clear statement of what had been taken. And he immediately awarded a fairly large sum of gold to the Chapter of the Church of the Antiphonetes to be paid yearly by the trustees of the public fund ; and this payment has remained unchanged to this day ; for the tomb of the Empress aforementioned was there. And to the church in Chalcoprateia he allotted an annual sum of gold from the royal treasury sufficient to pay the regular choristers of that church dedicated to the Virgin.

IV   At the same time a plot against the Emperor was discovered, organized by the leaders of the senate and the chief officers in the army, and it was divulged to the Emperor.

The accusers were confronted with the instigators of the plot and denounced them. Thus their conspiracy was revealed and the legal penalty awaiting them for this offence was heavy, but the Emperor did not wish to impose this punishment upon them, but decreed confiscation of their goods and exile against the ringleaders and to this extent only did he take vengeance for this plot. Now I must return to the point in my history where I broke off.

When Alexius was raised to the rank of Domestic by Nicephorus, Botaniates, he took a certain Travlos, a Manichæan into his staff of intimate servants and after he had honoured him with Christian baptism, he married him to one of the Empress' maidservants. Now this man had four sisters and when he heard of their being driven from their homes with all the other women and imprisoned, and deprived of all their belongings, he was indignant and could not bear it, but began to consider how he could free himself from the Emperor's power. His wife got to know this and seeing her husband ready to run away she revealed the matter to the man entrusted with the supervision of the Manichæans. This fact did not escape Travlos and so one evening he sent for all those whom he had made participators of his secret to come to him. All his kinsmen rallied round him and they took possession of Beliatoba ; this is a little town situated on the top of the hill which overlooks the valley below Beliatoba. Finding this deserted, they looked upon it as their own property and fixed their dwellings there, then they made daily sallies from it, sometimes even as far as their own town, Philippopolis, and returned laden with much booty. But Travlos, not satisfied with this, made a treaty with the Scythians who dwelt by the Danube, and won over the chieftains round Glabinitza and Dristra and the neighbouring districts, and at the same time betrothed himself to the daughter of one of the leading Scythians ; this he did because he desired with all his might to vex the Emperor by an inroad of the Scythians. The Emperor received daily news of his doings and with an eye to the future, he did his best to reconcile him by letters and promises as he suspected the evil that would be wrought by him   Nay, he even issued and sent him a Golden Bull guaranteeing him security and perfect freedom. However, ' a crab never learns to run straight ' ; so Travlos remained the same man as before, continuing to seek the friendship of the Scythians, to send for more from their own countries, and to lay waste all the surrounding regions.

V   When the Emperor had settled this matter of the
Manichæans as a secondary business, he secured their allegiance by a treaty

Bohemund, meanwhile (for we must return to him now),
was still lingering in Valona ; when he received the news
concerning Bryennius and the other Counts, and heard that
some had preferred to serve the Emperor, and the others
had dispersed in different directions, he sought his mother-
country, crossed to Lombardy and found his father at
Salernum, as already said, and by inveighing bitterly against
the Emperor, aroused his father's ire against him.   When
Robert saw him with disastrous tidings plainly written on his
face, and realized that the great hopes he had placed in him
had fallen ' wrong side up like a shell,' he stood dazed for
some time, as if struck by lightning.   After enquiring about
everything and finding that all had happened contrary to his
expectations, he was overcome by dejection.   Yet even at
this crisis he did not meditate anything ignoble or unworthy
of his personal bravery and daring ; but was rather stirred
up all the more to fight, and anxieties and cares, heavier than
the former ones, oppressed him.   For the man was a firm
upholder of his own designs and conceptions and would never
willingly give up anything he had once planned—in a word,
he was undaunted and thought he ought to be able to accomplish everything at the first attempt.   So he soon composed himself and on recovering from his deep despondency
he sent messengers in every direction to announce that he was
crossing again to Illyria to fight against the Emperor, and
summoned all his friends.   In a short time a multitude of
soldiers assembled from all parts, both horse- and foot-,
all splendidly equipped and eager for action.   Homer would
have described this multitude ' as being like tribes of swarm-
ing bees.'   And they flocked together from distant towns
just as much as from nearer ones.   Thus Robert made
great preparations in order to avenge his son's defeat, and
finally sent for his other sons, Roger and another called Gidus.[1]
(The Emperor Alexius wanted to make this son secede from
his father, and had sent to him secretly with an offer of
marriage and promises of high preferment and an extravagant
sum of money ; Gidus had lent a willing ear, but so far had
kept the matter to himself.)   To these two sons Robert
entrusted all the cavalry and dispatched them with orders
to take Valona speedily ; they crossed and did this at once.

[1] = Guido.

Then they left a small number of soldiers as garrison in Valona, marched on with the rest, reached Buthrotum and took this too at the first assault. Robert on his side took his entire fleet, and sailed along the coast opposite Buthrotum, and reached Brindisi with the intention of crossing to Illyria. But when he found out that the strait was narrower at Hydruntum he crossed from that port to Valona. Then with his whole fleet he coasted along from Valona to Buthrotum and was re-united with his sons. As Corfu, which he had conquered before, had revolted again, he left his sons in Buthrotum and sailed for Corfu himself with his whole fleet. So much for Robert—the Emperor when he received the tidings, did not lose heart at all but began preparations for renewing the war against Robert and urged the Venetians by letter to furnish a large fleet, promising them they should have their expenses paid many times over. He himself equipped biremes and triremes and all manner of piratical vessels and sent them out against Robert with hoplites on board skilled in naval warfare. When Robert heard of the arrival of the fleets he, as was his nature, wanted to force on an engagement, so loosed cable and entered the port of Cassope with his whole fleet. The Venetians had anchored in the harbour of Pasari and stayed there a little and on hearing of Robert's arrival, they too quickly made for the port of Cassope. A fierce engagement ensued and a fight at close quarters in which Robert was defeated. But fond of war as he was, and ever lusting for a fight, he would not give in after defeat, but got ready for a second battle and that a more serious one. This the admirals of both the fleets learnt and, emboldened by their recent success, attacked him again on the third day and gained a brilliant victory over him, and after it sailed back to the harbour of Pasari. Then, as so often happens in such cases, they were either over-elated by their previously gained victories or they thought they had driven the vanquished to despair, and consequently relaxed as if they had completed their task, and held Robert in contempt. For they detached all the quick-sailing ships and sent them to Venice to carry the news of Robert's complete defeat. When Robert heard of this from a certain Venetian, Peter Contarinus by name, who had lately deserted to him, he fell into deep despondency and found life scarcely tolerable. He soon, however, thought better of it and recovering his spirits again attacked the Venetians. These were panic-stricken by his unexpected arrival; they at once bound together their larger vessels with ropes in the neighbourhood of the harbour of Corfu, and having thus constructed what is called an ' open sea-harbour ' they drove the smaller vessels into it ; then armed and awaited his coming.   When he came, the battle began, and it was a terrible one and fiercer than the two former for the men fought more madly than before.   So the battle waxed fiery ; and neither side would yield, but on the contrary fought face to face.   The Venetians had previously consumed all their provisions and consequently the boats were empty but for the soldiers ; so the boats, owing to their lightness, floated about as if upheld by the surface of the water, which did not come up even to the second stripe ; the soldiers rushed in a mass to the side of the ships facing the foe, and so were drowned ; they numbered about thirteen thousand.   The other ships were taken, crews and all.   After this signal victory Robert in a fit of harshness treated many of the prisoners most cruelly, for he had the eyes of some gouged out, the noses of others cut off, and some he deprived of their hands and feet, or both. About the rest he sent word to their fellow-countrymen that whoever wanted to ransom a friend for a price might come without fear.   At the same time he asked whether they wished for peace ; and this is the answer they sent : " Know, Duke Robert, that even if we were to see our women and children slaughtered by you, we should not renounce our allegiance to the Emperor Alexius, and certainly we shall never cease succouring him and fighting bravely for him." After a short lapse of time the Venetians equipped some ' dromones ' and triremes and various other small, quicksailing craft and advanced against Robert with a stronger force.   And when they found him stationed at Buthrotum they joined battle with him and gained a great victory over him, killing many and drowning more ; and they very nearly captured his legitimate son, Gidus, and his wife.   Then they sent word to the Emperor of the brilliant victory they had gained over Robert.   He paid their services by liberal gifts and preferments, and honoured the Doge of Venice with the title of ' Protosebastos ' with the salary attached, and on the Patriarch he bestowed the title ' Hypertimius ' with its corresponding salary.   Moreover he decreed that a large sum of gold should be apportioned yearly to all the churches in Venice from the royal treasury, and to the church named after the evangelist and apostle Mark he made all the shopkeepers in Constantinople, who were natives of Amalfi, pay

tribute. He also gave the Venetians all the wharfs running
from the old Hebraic anchorage to that called Bigla and all
the anchorages between these two, as well as much real
property, not only in the capital and in the town of Dyrrachium, but wherever they asked for it. But greatest
gift of all, he ordered that their merchandise should not be
taxed in any of the countries under Roman sway, so that
they could trade freely where they liked, and not pay even
an obol, neither for customs nor for any other tax required
by the Treasury, but should be exempt from all Roman
authority.

VI   As for Robert (for my tale must return to the point
where it digressed and be kept within the bounds of historical
narration) he did not rest even after this defeat. But as he
had already sent one ship with his son to Cephalenia as he
wished to take possession of the town on it, he brought his
remaining ships, with the whole army, to anchor near Boditza
and himself sailed for Cephalenia in a galley with one bank of
oars.   And before he could join his son and the rest of his
forces, whilst he was lingering near Ather (which is a promontory of Cephalenia) he was seized with a violent fever.
As he could not bear the burning of the fever, he asked for
cold water.   His men dispersed in various directions to seek
water when a native said to them, " You see the island there,
Ithaca.   On that a large town was built long ago called Jerusalem, and now it has fallen into ruins from age ; in that town
there was a spring whose water was always fit for drinking
and very cold."   Robert was overcome with fear on hearing
this for by connecting Ather and the town of Jerusalem he
understood that his death was imminent.   For many years
before some soothsayers had prophesied to him the kind of
thing flatterers are wont to tell princes, " As far as Ather you
shall bring all countries under your sway, but from there you
shall depart for Jerusalem and pay your debt to nature."
Whether the fever killed him or whether he died of pleurisy,
I have no means of saying for certain.   At all events he died
in six days.   His wife Gaïta reached him just in time to see
him die and his son weeping over him.   News of this calamity
was then sent to the son whom Robert in his lifetime had
already designated heir to his dukedom.   On hearing the sad
tidings he was overcome at first by uncontrollable grief,
but soon summoning reason to his aid and collecting himself,
he sent for all his followers and, whilst weeping inconsolably
for his father, he told them what had happened, and then

made them take the oath of allegiance to himself. Next he crossed with them all to Apulia. During the crossing he was caught in such a severe storm, although it was summer, that some of the ships were wrecked, and others dashed on the shore and beaten to pieces. The ship carrying the corpse was also half wrecked and the crew only just managed to save the coffin, and convey it safely to Venusia. Robert was buried in the old monastery dedicated to the Holy Trinity, where his brothers had been buried before him. Robert died in the twenty-fifth year of his reign as duke and at the age of seventy. The Emperor, on hearing of Robert's sudden death, was greatly relieved by having such a burden lifted from his shoulders; and very quickly turned his attention to the Normans who were still in possession of Dyrrachium. He aimed at sowing dissension amongst them by letters and other devices, as he thought that would be the easiest means of regaining the city. He also persuaded the Venetians who happened to be in the capital to advise the Venetians, Amalfians and other foreigners who were in Epidamnus to submit to his will and surrender Dyrrachium to him. And he himself did not cease making promises and offering bribes with a view to their surrendering Dyrrachium to him. The Latins allowed themselves to be persuaded (for their whole race is very fond of money and quite accustomed to selling even their dearest possessions for an obol) and with high hopes in their hearts they formed a conspiracy and first of all slew the man who had originally suggested betraying the fort to Robert, and next his fellow-conspirators; and then they went to the Emperor, and handed over the fort to him and in return received immunity of every kind from him.

VII   A certain mathematician named Seth who boasted much of his knowledge of astrology had forecast Robert's fate by an oracle, after his crossing to Illyria, written this forecast on a paper, sealed it and entrusted it to some of the Duke's intimates, bidding them keep it till a certain time. After Robert's death they opened it by the astrologer's order and the prophecy was as follows : " A great enemy from the west shall fall suddenly after having stirred up great confusion." This caused everybody to marvel at the man's knowledge ; and in truth he had delved very deeply into this branch of science, and if I may be allowed to make a short break in the course of my history, the following are the facts about astrological prophecies. The discovery is fairly recent, and the science of it was not known to the ancients. For this method of divination did not exist in the time of Eudoxus, the greatest of all astronomers, neither did Plato have any knowledge of it, and even the astrologer, Manetho, had not brought it to perfection. Now these (astrologers) observe the hour of the birth of the persons about whom they intend to prophesy, and fix the cardinal points and carefully note the disposition of all the stars, in short they do everything that the inventor of this science bequeathed to posterity and which those who trouble about such trifles understand. We, also, at one time dabbled a little in this science, not in order to cast horoscopes (God forbid !), but by gaining a more accurate idea of this vain study to be able to pass judgment upon its devotees. I do not mention this for the sake of boasting, but to prove that during my father's reign many of the sciences made great progress, as he honoured both philosophers and philosophy itself, but towards this teaching of astrology he showed some hostility, I believe because it tended to make people of a guileless nature reject their faith in God and gape at the stars. This was the cause of the Emperor's waging war against the teaching of astrology. Yet in spite of this there was no dearth of astrologers at that time, for the Seth I have mentioned flourished then, and there was also a famous Egyptian, Alexandreus, who was a strong exponent of the mysteries of astrology. He was consulted by many and used to give most accurate forecasts in many cases, not even using the astrolabe, but made his prophecies by a certain casting of dice. There was nothing magical about that either, it was an art practised by the Alexandrians (or by Alexandreus). When the Emperor saw how the young people flocked to him and regarded the man as a species of prophet, he himself consulted him twice and each time Alexandreus gave very correct answers. But the Emperor was afraid that harm might come to many from it and that all would be led away to the vain pursuit of astrology, so he banished him from the capital, assigned Rædestus as his dwelling-place and showed great consideration for him, and his means of living were amply supplied from the imperial treasury. Nay more, the great dialectician, Eleutherius, also an Egyptian by birth, cultivated this art too and carried it to such perfection that he yielded the palm to no one. Later again, a man called Catanances from Athens came to the capital, anxious to carry off the first prize among astrologers and when questioned by some about the date of the Emperor's death, he foretold it as he thought, but was proved wrong in his

prognostication. It happened, however, that the lion which
was kept in the palace died that day, after four days' fever,
so the vulgar considered that the prophecy of Catanances
had been accomplished. After some considerable time he
again foretold the date of the Emperor's death and was
mistaken ; yet the Emperor's mother, the Empress Anna,
died on the very day Catanances had foretold. Because
Catanances had made repeated mistakes in his predictions
about him, the Emperor did not like to banish him as he was
self-convicted, and also it might seem that he banished him
in anger. But now let us return to the point in our history
where we abandoned it, otherwise we shall be thought to be
star-gazers, obscuring the main theme of our history with
the names of astrologers.

Now Robert, as rumour insisted and many said, was a
most exceptional leader, quick-witted, good-looking, courteous
in conversation, ready too in repartee, loud-voiced, easily
accessible, very tall in stature, his hair always close-cut,
long bearded, always anxious to maintain the ancient customs
of his race. He preserved his perfect comeliness of countenance and figure until the end, and of these he was very proud
as his appearance was considered worthy of kingship, he
showed respect to all his subordinates, more especially to
those who were well-disposed towards him. On the other
hand he was very thrifty and fond of money, very business-
like and greedy of gain, and, in addition to all this, most
ambitious ; and since he was a slave to these desires, he has
incurred the serious censure of mankind. Some people
slander the Emperor and say he was faint-hearted and
began the war with Robert too soon. For if, as they allege,
he had not attacked Robert before the right time, he could
have defeated him easily, as Robert was being worried on
all sides by the so-called Albanians and by the natives of
Dalmatia sent by Bodinus. These remarks came from the
back-biters who stood out of shot and hurled envenomed
darts from their lips against the fighters. For all acknowledge Robert's bravery, remarkable skill in warfare and
steadfast spirit ; and he was a man who could not be conquered
easily but only with extreme difficulty, and after a defeat
he seemed to rise again with renewed vigour.

VIII The Emperor, as related above, returned to the
capital in triumph with the Latins from Count Bryennius'
army who had deserted to him on the first of December in
the seventh Indiction. He found his wife in the pangs of

childbirth in the room which had of old been set apart for the
Empresses' confinements, our forefathers called it the ' purple '
room, and from it the name ' Porphyrogeniti '[1] has become
current in the world. And at dawn on a Saturday a female
child was born to them who was exactly like her father, they
said ; that child was I. And once upon a time, I heard the
Empress, my mother, relate that three days before the
Emperor's entry into the palace (for he was returning then
from the war with Robert and his other numerous battles
and labours) she began to feel pains, so she made the sign
of the cross on her womb and said, " Wait a little, child, for
your father's coming ! " When she said that, the ' Protovestiaire,' her mother, scolded her severely and said angrily,
" How do you know whether he will come within a month ?
and how will you be able to bear the pains so long ? " Thus
spake her mother, but the Empress' command took effect,
which signified that even in the womb I felt that affection
for my parents which was manifested so conspicuously in
the future. For afterwards as I grew up and reached years
of discretion I became sincerely devoted to my mother and
also equally to my father. And many can bear witness
to this fact, above all those who know my history. And
further testimony to it are the many struggles, anxieties and
even dangers which I suffered because of my deep love for
them, as I spared neither my honour, money, nor even my
life ; for devotion to them so fired me that I even risked my
life for them several times. But no more of this. Let me
return to the events which took place after my birth. All
the ceremonies usual at the birth of an Emperor's child were
performed most lavishly, that is to say, acclamations and
presents and honours given at such a time to the heads of
the Senate and the army, so that all were more joyful and
exultant than ever before and loud in their praises, especially
the Empress' relations who could not contain themselves for
joy. And when a certain number of days had passed, my
parents honoured me with a crown and royal diadem. Now
Constantine, the son of the ex-Emperor, Michael Ducas, of
whom I have often spoken, was regent together with the
Emperor, my father, and with him signed all deeds of gifts
in red ink ; and wearing a tiara, accompanied him in all
processions, and was acclaimed second in all acclamations ;
as I too was now to be acclaimed, the leaders of the acclamations shouted out " Constantine and Anna " together at the

[1] = Born in the purple.

time for acclamations. And this continued for a good long
time, as I have often heard my relations and parents subse-
quently say. This was perhaps symbolic of what should
befall me later, whether it can be called good, or on the
contrary, ill fortune. When a second daughter was born to
their majesties, bearing a likeness to her parents, and also
showing signs of the virtue and wisdom which were to dis-
tinguish her later, they much desired to have a son as well,
and their prayer was granted. For during the eleventh
Indiction a son was born to them. Thereupon my parents
were indeed overjoyed and no trace of sadness remained, as
their desire had been fulfilled. The whole populace too
rejoiced, seeing their masters so happy, and congratulated
each other and were delighted. Then you would have seen
the palace full of rejoicing and no shadow of sorrow or even
care, for all the well-disposed rejoiced from the bottom of
their heart, whilst the others feigned delight. A people,
as a rule, is ill-affected to its rulers, but by much pretence
and flattery win the favour of their superiors. However
on this one occasion universal joy could be witnessed, as one
and all were really pleased. The child had a swarthy complexion, broad forehead, lean cheeks, a nose neither snub nor
aquiline but something between the two, very black eyes
which betokened, as far as one can judge from an infant's
face, a quick intelligence. As my parents naturally wished
to raise this child to the rank of Emperor and leave him the
empire of the Romans as his inheritance, they deemed him
worthy of being baptised and crowned in the great church of
God. This is what happened to us children, ' born in the
purple ' from the very starting-point of our birth. What
befell us later, shall be narrated in due order.

IX The Emperor Alexius had driven away the Turks
from the shores of Bithynia and the Bosporus and the
Northern provinces and made a truce with Soliman, as I
have recounted earlier ; then he rode off to Illyria where
after many hardships he utterly defeated Robert and his
son, Bohemund, and thus delivered the West from an overwhelming catastrophe. On his return from those parts he
found that the Turks under Apelchasem[1] were not only over-
running the East, but had penetrated as far as the Propontis
and the maritime towns there. And this is the right point
at which to tell how the Ameer Soliman on leaving Nicæa had
left this Apelchasem behind as governor ; how Puzanus was

---

[1] = Abul-kassim.

sent into Asia by the sultan of Persia, and defeated and killed
by Tutuses[1], the brother of the sultan ; and how Tutuses
himself after the defeat of Puzanus, was strangled by his
second cousins. A certain Armenian, Philaretus by name,
conspicuous for bravery and sagacity, had been raised to
the rank of Domestic by the former Emperor, Romanus
Diogenes, and when he saw the latter's downfall and heard
further that he had been deprived of his sight, it was more
than he could bear, for he loved him with an exceeding love,
so plotted rebellion and made himself master of the province
of Antioch. But as the Turks daily laid waste the surrounding
country so that he had no peace, he meditated desertion to
the Turks and circumcision, which they practise. But
his son vehemently opposed him and tried to divert him
from this mad enterprise, but his better counsels were not
accepted. In his grief at his father's refusal he travelled for
eight days to reach Nicæa, and there gained access to the
Ameer Soliman (who had just attained the rank of Sultan)
and roused him to undertake the siege of Antioch and incited
him to war against his father. Soliman lent him a ready
ear, and when starting for Antioch he left Apelchasem as
Governor of Nicæa and also appointed him General-in-Chief
over all the other Generals. Then with Philaretus' son in
his train he rode for twelve nights (for he reposed in the day)
and by the unexpectedness of his arrival took Antioch at
first assault. At the same time Charatices secretly pillaged
Sinope as he had found out that a large sum of gold and
money belonging to the imperial treasury had been stored
there. The Grand Sultan[2] had a brother, Tutuses, who ruled
over Jerusalem, the whole of Mesopotamia, and Aleppo and
as far as Bagdad, and was hoping to secure Antioch ; when he
noticed that the Ameer Soliman was on the point of rebelling,
and had already won the province of Antioch for himself,
he encamped with his whole army midway between Aleppo
and Antioch. On the Ameer Soliman's coming out to meet
him, a tremendous battle broke out at once, and when it
came to hand to hand fighting, Soliman's troops turned their
backs and fled in disorder. In spite of all his protestations
Soliman could not restrain them from flight, so seeing his imminent danger he turned aside from the battle and when he
thought he had reached a safe spot, he placed his shield on
the ground, and throwing himself to the ground, sat down on
it. However he had not escaped the notice of his fellow-

---

[1] Or Tutush or Toutoush.   [2] i.e. Malekshah.

tribesmen ; and some of the satraps followed him and said his uncle Tutuses had sent for him. He refused to go as he scented danger. But the satraps insisted and being unable to restrain them by force, as he was alone, he drew his sword from its sheath and plunged it deep into his bowels ; and thus the wretched man died wretchedly. And the survivors of Ameer Soliman's forces at once joined Tutuses. On hearing of these doings the Sultan feared that Tutuses was growing too powerful, so he sent a Chiauss to the Emperor to ask a Roman princess in marriage for himself and promising, if this were granted, to fetch away the Turks from the maritime towns, to restore him his forts, and to help him whole-heartedly. The Emperor received him, read the Sultan's letter but eluded the question of marriage ; and seeing that the Chiauss was a man of understanding he asked him of his origin and parentage. On the latter replying that his mother was an Iberian but his father a Turk, the Emperor took a great deal of pains to persuade him to accept Christian baptism. The Chiauss consented to this and pledged himself to the Emperor not to return home, after he had received holy baptism. Since he had received instructions from the Sultan by letter that, if the Emperor were willing to arrange a mar-riage for him, he should drive out all the satraps who held the maritime towns by shewing them the Sultan's letter treating of this question, the Emperor suggested to the Chiauss to make use of this letter and after he had expelled them all by shewing them the Sultan's writing, to return to the capital again. The Chiauss with great alacrity went first to Sinope and by shewing Charatices the Sultan's epistle he drove him out of the town without an obol of the Emperor's money in his pocket. This is what happened. As Charatices was going out of Sinope, he desecrated the church dedicated to our Immaculate Lady, the Mother of God, and forthwith he was delivered by the hand of God, as it seemed, to an avenging demon, and fell to the ground foaming at the mouth, and so he went out of the town mad ! The jurisdiction over Sinope the Chiauss handed to Constantine Dalassenus whom the Emperor had sent down there for that purpose, then he successively visited the other towns, shewed the satraps the Sultan's letter, and thus drove them all out and handed the town over to the Emperor's satraps. This business finished, the Chiauss returned to the Emperor, and after receiving holy baptism and revelling in rich presents he was appointed Duke of Anchialus.

X When the suicide of Ameer Soliman became known throughout the whole of Asia, each satrap who was governor over a town or fortress, took that respective place and made it his own. For at the same time that the Ameer Soliman entrusted the Government of Nicæa to Apelchasem on his departure for Antioch, he also apportioned the sea-coast, and Cappadocia, in fact the whole of Asia, to various satraps, for each man to guard his own portion until such time as he, Soliman, should return. Now Apelchasem who was then archsatrap in Nicæa, where the Sultan's palace was, took possession of the town and transferred Cappadocia to his brother, Pulchases, and then lived a care-free life, expecting soon to assume the dignity of 'Sultan,' in fact looked upon it as a certainty. The man was capable and intrepid, and would not be satisfied with what he had, so sent forth foraging parties to lay waste the whole of Bithynia as far as the Propontis. The Emperor then tried his former plan, that is, he dissipated the foragers and forced Apelchasem to sue for terms of peace. But as he found that the latter continued making secret designs against him and postponing the truce, he decided it was necessary to put a strong army in the field against him. So the Emperor sent Taticius (whom I have frequently mentioned) with a respectable force to Nicæa, warning him to use discretion in attacking the enemy if by chance he fell in with any outside the town. Taticius went off and marshalled his army in line of battle close to the walls as no Turks were to be seen then, but they suddenly threw open the gates and a body of about two hundred of them rode down upon him. When the Franks (of whom there were a goodly number) saw them, they dashed straight at them in a tremendous onrush with their long spears in their hands, and after wounding a large number, drove the rest back to the fort. The next day Taticius stood there with his army in the same formation until sunset, and since no Turk shewed himself outside the gates, he marched back to Basileia and pitched his camp at a distance of twelve stades from Nicæa. During the night a countryman came to him and assured him that Prosuch was approaching with fifty thousand men, and had been sent by the newly elected Sultan, Pargiaruch. As others confirmed this report, Taticius, seeing that his forces were insufficient against large numbers, cancelled his former plans and thought it better to preserve his whole army safe and sound rather than lose it altogether by fighting against forces infinitely more numerous and far stronger than his own. Consequently his thoughts turned to the capital, and he settled to return to it viâ Nicomedia. Now Apelchasem from his watch-tower saw him turn off to Constantinople and already on the march, so came out and followed him, intending to attack him if he espied him encamping in some suitable spot. And he overtook him at Prenetus, surprised him and started a violent fight. Taticius quickly drew up his men and allowed the Franks to begin the battle and make the first charge against the enemy. And they, long spears in hand, rode at full gallop and hurled themselves like fire upon the barbarians, cut the phalanxes to pieces and routed them completely. Afterwards Taticius regained the capital by way of Bithynia. Apelchasem, however, could not keep quiet, for he was obsessed with the desire of annexing the Roman Empire, or, if this was impossible, of extending his rule over all the coast-lands and islands as well. In pursuit, then, of these plans he determined first to build some buccaneering vessels, as he had taken Cius (a town on the coast of Bithynia) and when the ships were nearing completion, he thought his plans were maturing well. But he was not unobserved by the Emperor, who quickly fitted out whatever biremes, triremes and other vessels he had at hand, set Manuel Butumites in command and sent him with injunctions to make haste and burn Apelchasem's half-built ships, no matter in what condition he found them. Moreover, he sent Taticius with a considerable army against him by land. These two left the City, and Apelchasem soon saw Butumites approaching by sea at great speed, and heard that others were bearing down upon him by land ; he judged the ground, where he happened to be, unsuitable, as it was rough and narrow, and altogether ill-adapted for his archers, as it would not allow them to act against the Roman cavalry ; so he moved his camp in order to place his troops on suitable ground. This place he found, and by some it is called Halycae and by others Cyparission. Butumites, meanwhile, arrived by sea and set fire to Apelchasem's ships more quickly than can be told. On the following day Taticius too came by land and drawing up his troops in a convenient position, did not cease from morn till eve for fifteen whole days, either skirmishing or engaging the troops of Apelchasem in close combat. But as Apelchasem would not yield but maintained a determined resistance, the Latins grew weary and, although the ground was not to their advantage, yet they worried Taticius to allow them, even unaided, to undertake a pitched battle with the Turks. Finally, although against his own judgment, yet as he saw daily reinforcements coming to Apelchasem, he gave way to the Latins. And about sunrise he set his forces in array and joined battle with Apelchasem. In it many of the Turks were killed, but most were taken prisoners, and still more fled without giving a thought to their personal baggage. And Apelchasem himself rode straight to Nicæa and only just escaped. Taticius' soldiers collected a large amount of booty and returned to their own camp. On receiving this news, the Emperor, clever as he was in winning the souls of men and in softening a heart of stone, at once dictated a letter to Apelchasem advising him to abstain from such vain enterprises and not to beat the air but to come over to him and thus exchange a life of labour for the enjoyment of bounteous gifts and honour. Therefore Apelchasem, when he further heard that Prosuch was besieging towns held by various satraps and would soon be at Nicæa with the object of besieging it, made a virtue of necessity, as the saying is, and boldly accepted the Emperor's offer of peace, although he guessed the latter's purpose. When the truce between them had been concluded, the Emperor who was already scheming to obtain another advantage, and could see no other way of gaining his end, invited Apelchasem to the capital to receive gifts of money, enjoy a life of luxury to the full and then return home. Apelchasem accepted and on his arrival in the capital was treated with much kindness. The Turkish rulers of Nicæa still held Nicomedia (which is the metropolis of Bithynia) and as the Emperor wished to expel them from that town, he thought it well to build a second small citadel near the sea, while the terms of peace were being arranged. Consequently he had all the materials necessary for the construction of the fort, as well as the builders, loaded on transports and dispatched them under Eustathius, the 'Drungaire' of the fleet, to whom he had revealed his secret and entrusted the building. He conjured him to treat any Turks who might pass, very kindly, and give them their fill of needful things, at the same time signifying to them that Apelchasem knew of the building of the forts, but he was to ward off all vessels from the shores of Bithynia to prevent Apelchasem's hearing anything. To Apelchasem the Emperor gave money every day and was profuse in his invitations to him to come to the baths, or horse-races or the chase, and further to view the monuments set up along the highroads. Moreover he gave orders to the charioteers to prepare an equestrian display in his honour in the theatre which Constantine the Great built long ago : and he urged him to go every day and watch the horses being tested, all this was to get time for his builders while Apelchasem wasted his days in the capital. But when the fort was finished and his purpose accomplished, he loaded him with further gifts, honoured him with the rank of " Sebastos " and after again confirming the treaty, sent him home in great state by sea. When the building of the fort was revealed to Apelchasem, although he was wounded deeply by the raising of it, yet he pretended to know nothing and said not a word about it. A similar tale is told of Alcibiades—for he in a similar manner had outwitted the Lacedæmonians when they refused to allow Athens to be rebuilt after it had been destroyed by the Persians. For he told the Athenians to rebuild their city while he went on an embassy to Sparta. There the embassy wasted its time, thus giving the builders an opportunity and after the trick had been successful, the Lacedæmonians learnt of the complete rebuilding of Athens. And the Pæanian[1] somewhere in his writings also mentions this clever deception. So my father's plan was similar, though more sagacious than that of Alcibiades. For he fawned upon this barbarian with horse-races and other delights and by delaying him from day to day he managed to complete the fort and when the work was quite finished he dismissed him from the capital.

XI   Meanwhile Prosuch had come up with an enormous army, as was expected, and was besieging Nicæa, as the countryman who came by night to Taticius said, and for three months he persevered in the siege. Then when the townsmen and even Apelchasem himself saw that things had come to a distressful pass, and that they would be unable to hold out much longer, they sent a message to the Emperor begging him to come to their aid and saying that they preferred to be called his servants than to yield to Prosuch. He immediately picked out the best of the troops that happened to be on the spot, gave them standards and silver-studded sceptres and sent them away to carry succour. Now he did not send this army to help Apelchasem exactly, but in his own heart he hoped that his help might afterwards turn out to be the ruin of Apelchasem. As two enemies of the Roman power were fighting against each other, it was necessary to help the weaker,

[1] = Demosthenes.

not in order that he might grow more powerful, but that he might beat off the other, and then he, the Emperor, would take away the town from the former and make it his own, which at present was outside the orbit of Empire ; after that he would gradually take another and yet another and thus enlarge the boundaries of the Roman Empire which had become very restricted ; more especially since the sword of the Turks had grown so powerful. For there was a time when the limits of the Roman rule were the two pillars which bound east and west respectively, those on the west being called the ' pillars of Heracles,' those on the east the ' pillars of Dionysus ' somewhere near the frontier of India. It is hardly possible to define the Empire's former width. Egypt, Meroë, all the Troglodyte country, and the region adjacent to the torrid zone ; and in the other direction far-famed Thule, and the races who dwell in the northern lands and over whose heads the North Pole stands. But in these later times the boundary of the Roman rule was the neighbouring Bosporus on the east and the city of Adrianople on the west. Now, however, the Emperor Alexius by striking with both hands, as it were, at the barbarians who beset him on either side and starting from Byzantium as his centre, enlarged the circle of his rule, for on the west he made the Adriatic sea his frontier, and on the east the Euphrates and Tigris. And he would have restored the Empire to its former prosperity, had not the successive wars and the recurrent dangers and difficulties hindered him in his purpose (for he was involved in great, as well as frequent, dangers). His idea then, as I said at the beginning, in sending an army to Apelchasem, the tyrant of Nicæa, was not to rescue him from danger, but to gain a victory for himself ; fortune, however, did not favour him. For the matter fell out thus. The troops that were sent reached a small town called after the lord George ; and the Turks immediately opened their gates to them. Then the soldiers went up to the battlements of the wall above the East gate, piled up the standards and sceptres, shouting at the same time and then continuously chanted their war-cries. This noise absolutely terrified the besiegers outside who crept away during the night, thinking that the Emperor himself had come and thereupon the Roman forces returned straightaway to the capital. For they were not a strong enough force to withstand an assault by the Persians who were expected to come up shortly from the depths of the Turkish Empire.

XII The Sultan on his side was awaiting the return of

his Chiauss ; when he noticed that he delayed his return, and then heard all he had done, how he had expelled Charatices by stratagem from Sinope, had accepted Christian baptism and been sent to the west by the Emperor with the title of Duke of Anchialus, he was vexed and distressed. So he resolved to send Puzanus for a second time with troops against Apelchasem, and also to give him a letter for the Emperor treating of the question of alliance by marriage. The tenor of the letter was as follows : " O Emperor, I have heard of thy doings. I know that no sooner hadst thou taken up the reins of government, than thou wast involved in many wars, and that now when thou hast just quelled the turbulent Latins, the Scythians are preparing war against thee, and that Ameer Apelchasem has broken the treaty, made by thee with Soliman, and is ravaging Asia right up to Damalis. If therefore thou art anxious for Apelchasem to be driven out of those countries and to have Asia and even Antioch itself under thy rule, then send me thy daughter as bride for my eldest son. If thou dost this, there will be no more stumbling-blocks in thy path, but thou wilt easily accomplish everything with me as thy coadjutor, not only in the East, but even in Illyria and all the West by means of the forces I shall send thee, and nobody will be able henceforth to stand before thee." This was the tenor of the Persian Sultan's letter. After Puzanus reached Nicæa and made not only one, but several attempts to take it, which were foiled by Apelchasem's valiant resistance, as he had obtained the help he had begged from the Emperor, he turned his attention to the capture of other towns and forts, so left Nicæa and pitched his tents near the Lampe (which is a river near Lopadium). After his departure Apelchasem loaded as much gold as they could carry on fifteen mules and set off to the Sultan of Persia, taking this gift with him in order not to be dismissed from his governor-ship. He came upon the Sultan encamped near Spacha, and as the latter did not deign even to see him, he employed mediators. And as these worried the Sultan, he said " As I have once for all bestowed the province on the Ameer Puzanus I have no intention of taking it away from him again. Let the man go and carry his money to Puzanus and say what he likes to him, and whatever Puzanus settles, will satisfy me." Thus after remaining a considerable time there and taking a great deal of trouble all to no purpose, he started, presumably to go to Puzanus and met the two hundred satraps whom the

latter had sent after him, for his exit from Nicæa had not
passed unnoticed. These took him prisoner, threw a noose
woven of bowstrings round his neck and strangled him.
Now in my opinion this deed was not due to Puzanus, but to
that Sultan who had ordered his men to dispose of Apelchasem
by some such means. That is the story of Apelchasem.
The Emperor read the Sultan's letter but did not think the
offer contained therein worthy of consideration at all. And
how could he have done so ? For if the Emperor's little
daughter, as the letter demanded, had been betrothed to the
barbarian's eldest son, she would assuredly have been unhappy,
if she had gone to Persia and become mistress of a kingdom
which would have brought her greater wretchedness than the
worst poverty. But God forbade it nor did the Emperor ever
intend that such a thing should happen, not even if his
fortunes had sunk to the lowest ebb. Directly after he first
heard the letter he burst into laughter at the barbarian's
presumption with the remark that " Some demon put this
into his mind." This is what the Emperor thought of the
marriage. But as he considered it expedient to keep the
Sultan's mind in suspense by feeding him on vain hopes, he
sent Curticius and three others as ambassadors to him with
letters, in which he pretended to entertain the idea of peace
and to agree to his requests, whilst, on his side, he made other
demands which would occasion further lapse of time. But
before the ambassadors sent from Byzantium had reached
Chorosan they heard of the Sultan's murder, and so returned.
For Tutuses, the Sultan's brother, had killed the Ameer
Soliman and also his own brother-in-law, who had marched
against him from Arabia with an army, and as a result became
puffed up with conceit ; consequently when he learnt that the
Sultan had already begun negotiations for peace with the
Emperor, he contemplated murdering his brother.

So he sent for twelve Chasii, as they are called in Persian,
who breathe murder, and sent them off quickly in the guise
of ambassadors to the Sultan, having first suggested to them
a way of killing his brother. " Go," he said, " and first have
it proclaimed that you have certain secrets to reveal to the
Sultan, and, when you have been granted an audience, go up
close to him as if you wanted to whisper in his ear, and then
slay him quickly." Then these ambassadors, or rather
assassins, went off in very high spirits to kill the Sultan, just
as if they had been invited to a dinner or a festivity. On
arrival they found him drunk, and everything was made

M

easy for them, because the guards entrusted with the watch over the Sultan were standing at some distance, so they approached him, and drawing their swords from under their arm, promptly dispatched the wretched man. For the characteristic of these Chasii is to rejoice in bloodshed, and to consider it a treat to be allowed to thrust their swords through a man's entrails. And if, perchance, others were to attack them at that very minute, and mince them up like sausage-meat, they reckon that kind of death an honour, for they inherit and hand on to their children this trade of assassination, as a species of ancestral heritage. Not one of those fellows returned to Tutuses as they would have lost their own lives in expiation for this crime. Puzanus, however, on hearing of it, returned to Chorosan with all his forces ; and as he was nearing it, Tutuses, the brother of the murdered Sultan, encountered him. At once a close conflict began, as both armies fought bravely and neither would yield the victory to the other, and then Puzanus fell, mortally wounded, after fighting bravely, and causing consternation to his foes ; and his men scattered in flight in different directions, each one thinking only of his own safety. Tutuses entered Chorosan as victor and felt as if he had already risen to the rank of ' Sultan,' and yet danger menaced him. For Pargiaruch, the son of the murdered Sultan, Tapares, met him in battle and rejoicing, as the poet says, ' like a lion who has fallen in with mighty prey,' he attacked him with all his might and main, cut up the whole of Tutuses' forces and vigorously pursued the fugitives. And Tutuses himself, who was puffed up with pride like Novatus,[1] perished too. When Apelchasem had gone to Chorosan with his money to see the Sultan, as was related earlier, his brother Pulchases surprised Nicæa and held it. On receipt of this news the Emperor made him offers of extravagant rewards, provided only he would quit the city and hand it over to him. Pulchases indeed was willing, but hesitated, as he had his eye upon Apelchasem; he sent message upon message to the Emperor, keeping him in suspense, but really waiting for his brother's return. In the interval something like this happened. Before his murder by the Chasii the Sultan of Chorosan had managed to secure the great Soliman's two sons, and after his death they ran away from Chorosan and quickly found their way to Nicæa, where the inhabitants gave them an ovation and received them with the greatest joy. And Pulchases willingly handed over Nicæa to them as being their rightful inheritance, and the

[1] a heretic whose pride had become proverbial.

elder of the two, Clitziasthlan[1] by name, was elected Sultan.
He sent for the wives and children of the men then staying
in Nicæa, and bade them live there, and made this city the
dwelling-place, as one might say, of the Sultans. After
making this arrangement in Nicæa, he deposed Pulchases
from his post, appointed the arch-satrap, Mahomet, chief
over the satraps in Nicæa, and leaving him in charge set out
for Melitene.

XIII So much about the Sultans. Elchanes, the arch-
satrap, with the troops under him, seized Apollonias and
Cyzicus (both these are on the coast) and then laid waste
all the country along the sea. On being informed of this
the Emperor assembled a number of the boats he had (for
the fleet was not ready yet), put siege-engines in them and
brave soldiers, appointed Euphorbenus Alexander, one of
the most illustrious for lineage and famous for valour, over
the expedition and sent him against Elchanes. On reaching
Apollonias he at once besieged it, and after six days and
nights, for he did not at all stop the work at night, he made
himself master of the outer circuit of the fort, which is now
usually called the 'exopolos.' But Elchanes held on stoutly
to the citadel as he expected relieving forces. And indeed
Alexander found out that a large barbarian army was
advancing to the assistance of Elchanes, and seeing that his
own men were but a small fraction of this new army, he
decided that, as he could not conquer, it would be wiser at
least to keep his men unharmed. Since his affairs were in a
precarious state and no road of safety remained, he led his
men off towards the sea. They embarked in their boats,
and intended to sail down the river to the sea. But Elchanes guessing Alexander's intention took possession beforehand of the exit from the lake and the bridge over the river,
on which a shrine to the memory of Constantine the Great was
built of old by St. Helena, and from this the bridge took, and
still takes, its name. At the exit from the lake then and on
this bridge he posted some of his bravest men on either side
with orders to watch for the passing of the fleet. Thus all
our men who were on board these small vessels fell straight
into Elchanes' ambush as they passed through the mouth
of the lake, and losing their heads at sight of the sudden danger
they drove the ships to land and jumped ashore. The Turks
overtook them and a serious battle commenced. Many of
the leaders were captured and many too fell into the river
and were swept away in its eddies. The Emperor could not

[1] = Kilidje Arslan.

brook this defeat, so sent out a considerable army under Opus to march overland against them. Opus reached Cyzicus and took that without trouble ; then he picked out three hundred adventurous men used to storming cities and dispatched them to Pœmanenum. This city, too, they took at first onset and killed some of the inhabitants on the spot and sent the rest as prisoners to Opus, and he, as promptly, sent them to the Emperor. He then left Cyzicus and went on to Apollonias which he beset closely. As Elchanes had no longer adequate forces to contend against him, he surrendered the city of his own free will, and he and all his blood-relations deserted to the Emperor, hence he enjoyed countless privileges, and obtained the greatest of all, namely, holy baptism. Some refused to join Opus, for instance, Scaliarius and he who later was created ' Hyperperilampros ' . . . (for these belonged to the number of illustrious satraps), but when he heard of the Emperor's benevolence and liberal gifts to Elchanes, they came over to him too, and obtained their heart's desire. For the Emperor was essentially a most religious man, and in his life and speech the high priest of all piety. He was very fond, too, of teaching our doctrines and was a real missionary by choice and in his manner of speech; he wanted to bring into the fold of our church not only the Scythian nomads, but also the whole of Persia, as well as the barbarians who inhabit Libya and Egypt and follow the rites of Mohamed.

XIV Enough has been said about the Turks. I now intend to relate a second attack on the Roman Empire, more terrible and greater than the first, and I again resume the story at the beginning, for one subject has come up after another as wave follows wave.

A certain Scythian tribe, who were daily harried by the Sauromatæ, left their homes and travelled down to the Danube. It was, of course, necessary for them to make terms with the dwellers on the shores of the Danube, so by common consent the chieftains met for a conference ; there were Tatus and Chales and Sesthlabus and Satzas (for I must give the names of the highest-born of these, although the elegant appearance of my history is spoiled by them), the last-named was chief over Dristra, the others over Bitzina and neighbouring towns. After having made a truce with the chiefs the Scythians proceeded fearlessly to cross the Danube, and to ravage the surrounding country and also took a few small towns. And in between when they rested a little, they commenced to plough and sowed millet and wheat. But that fellow, Travlos, the Manichæan, with his followers, and his co-religionists who dwelt in the town on the ridge of Beliotaba, with whom this history has dealt at some length already, heard of these Scythians and so brought to birth the plan they had been hatching so long, for they seized the rough roads and passes, sent for the Scythians to help them and then started to devastate the Roman territory. For these Manichæans are by nature ' ever greedy of war ' and, like dogs, ' ever thirsty of human blood.'

On hearing of this, Alexius sent orders to Pacurianus, the Domestic of the West, to take an army and march against them; for he knew he was the ablest man for training and organizing and marshalling it ; with him was to go Branas, another very gallant commander. Pacurianus found that the Scythians had scaled the mountain-pass and planted their palisades this side of Beliotaba, and when he saw their countless host he at once shrank from battle with them, thinking it better to keep his own troops quiet for the present rather than to risk a battle with the Scythians and be defeated and lose many. However, Branas, who was of a very adventurous and daring nature, did not approve of this plan. So the Domestic to avoid the imputation of cowardice for postponing the battle, yielded to Branas' impetuosity, bade his men arm, and after drawing them up in line of battle marched against the Scythians, himself holding the centre of the line. But, since the Roman army was not equivalent even to a small fraction of the opposing host, they were all panic-stricken at first sight. However they did attack the Scythians, and many were killed in the fight and Branas himself fell, mortally wounded. The Domestic fought desperately and made fierce onsets on the foe, but was dashed against an oak and killed on the spot. And the rest of the army scattered in all directions. On receiving these tidings the Emperor mourned for all the fallen, both individually and collectively. But he was most grieved at the Domestic's death and shed floods of tears, for he loved him exceedingly even before his elevation to the throne. Yet in spite of it all he did not lose heart, but called Taticius and sent him with sufficient money to Adrianople to give the soldiers their pay for the year and to collect troops from all quarters so that he might raise a fresh army large enough for the war. He ordered Hubertopoulos to leave an adequate garrison in Cyzicus and taking the Franks only with him to lose no time in joining Taticius. When Taticius saw the Latins and Hubertopoulos, he took courage and as he had already collected a sufficiently large army, he immediately marched straight against the Scythians. When near Philippopolis he pitched his camp on the edge of the river which flows by Blisnus. But when he beheld the Scythians returning from a raid and bringing back much booty and captives, although the baggage had scarcely been brought into the camp, he selected a division of his army and sent it to attack them, then he armed himself, bade all do the same, drew up his lines and then followed the soldiers he had sent ahead. As he observed that the Scythians with their spoils and captives were rejoining the main Scythian body on the bank of the Eurus (?), he divided his army in two and bidding both divisions raise the war-cry he attacked the barbarians amidst loud shouts and clamour. As the conflict grew fierce, the majority of the Scythians were slain but many saved their lives by running away. Then Taticius gathered up all the booty and returned victorious to Philippopolis. There he quartered his whole army and then meditated from what direction and in what manner he could best attack the barbarians again. As he knew that their forces were innumerable he sent out spies in all directions, so that through them he might be kept informed of the Scythians' movements. The spies returned and reported that a great multitude of the barbarians was near Beliotaba and ravaging the country. Taticius who expected the Scythians to come, and had not sufficient forces to pit against such numbers, was at a loss what to do and in great perplexity. Nevertheless he whetted his sword and put courage into the army for a battle. Soon a spy ran in, announcing the approach of the barbarians and adding that they were already close at hand. Taticius quickly snatched up his arms and getting the whole army ready, crossed the Eurus immediately and disposed his regiments in battalions and having formed his plan of battle waited, his own station being the centre of the line. The barbarians who drew themselves up in the Scythian fashion and arrayed themselves for battle, seemed to be eager for a fight and to wish to provoke their opponents to a battle. But really, both the armies were afraid and tried to avoid an engagement ; the Roman army quaked before the overwhelming numbers of the Scythians, while these for their part were alarmed at the sight of all our men in full armour, and the standards, and splendid clothing and the glitter shining over all and gleaming

like starlight. Alone amongst them all the adventuresome
Latins, so daring in battle, wished to be the first to attack,
and they whetted their teeth and their swords at the same
time. But Taticius restrained them ; for he was very level-
headed and very clever in forecasting the trend of events.
So both the armies stood, each waiting for the other to make
a movement, and not a single soldier from either army daring
to ride out into the intervening space ; when the sun began
to set, each of the generals returned to his own encampment.
This was done for two days, the generals got ready for battle
and drew up their men in battle formation, and, as neither
hazarded battle against the other, at dawn of the third day
the Scythians retreated. Directly Taticius learnt this he
hurried after them ; but ' on foot after a Lydian chariot ',
as they say. For the Scythians passed through Sidera (that
is the name of a valley) before him, and as he did not overtake
them there, he led back all his forces to Adrianople. There
he left the Franks and dismissing the soldiers to their homes,
he himself returned to the capital with a portion of the army.

BOOK VII

I

AT the approach of spring Tzelgu (the supreme commander of the Scythian army) crossed the passes above the
Danube with a mixed army of about eighty thousand,
composed of Sauromatians, Scythians, and a number from the
Dacian army (over whom the man called Solomon was leader),
and plundered the towns round about Chariopolis. And
after entering Chariopolis itself and carrying off much booty,
he settled down in a place called Scotinum. On receipt of
this news Nicolas Mavrocatacalon and Bebetziotes (who got
this name from his country) occupied Pamphylum with the
forces under their command. When they saw the villagers
from the districts around hurrying in to the towns and
fortresses in their extreme fear, they moved from the place
called Pamphylum and occupied the small town of Cule with
their whole army. Behind them came the Scythians and
directly they discovered the track of the Roman army (this
is the word used by soldiers) they followed almost in their
footsteps one might say. At dawn of day Tzelgu drew up
his own forces and contemplated battle with Mavrocatacalon.
But the latter climbed up with a few chosen comrades to the
pass overlooking the plain to spy out the barbarian forces ;
and seeing the multitude of the Scythians, he deferred the
battle, although madly impatient for it, as he realized that
the Roman army was numerically far inferior to the Scythian
horde. He returned to the camp and discussed with all the
officers of the army and with Johannaces himself the advis-
ability of attacking the Scythians. As they all urged him
to do so and his own inclination lay in that direction, he
divided the troops into three portions, bade them sound the
attack and engaged the barbarians. In the combat many
Scythians fell wounded, and no fewer were killed ; and
Tzelgu himself who had fought valiantly and thrown the
ranks into confusion, received a mortal wound and gave up

the ghost.   Still more fell as they fled into the stream running between Scotinum and Cule and were trampled under foot by each other and drowned.   Having gained this brilliant victory over the Scythians the Emperor's officers returned to the capital.   Here the Emperor bestowed on them appropriate gifts and honours and afterwards they left with the newly appointed Domestic of the West, Adrian Comnenus, own brother to the Emperor

II   In this manner, then, the Scythians were driven out from the districts round Macedonia and Philippopolis, but they returned and encamped beside the Ister and settled along its banks and plundered our territory as freely as if it were their own.   When the Emperor heard this, he could not endure the idea of their settling within the Roman frontiers, and at the same time he was afraid of their crossing the passes again and perpetrating worse mischief than before.   Consequently he made his preparations, fitted out the army well and marched to Adrianople and thence to Lardea which lies in the plain between Diabolis and Goloë.   Here he appointed George Euphorbenus general and dispatched him by sea to Dristra.   Then the Emperor stayed in those parts for forty days and summoned troops from all sides.   When he had collected a large army, he deliberated whether he should traverse the defiles and commence warfare with the Scythians, " for," said he, " we ought not to allow them immunity at all," and there was justice in this remark in the case of these barbarians.   For the incursions of the Scythians did not begin in one of the four seasons and cease in the following, for instance, starting in summer and finishing in autumn, or even in winter (or late autumn) ; nor was this evil limited to the cycle of one year, but for several years past they had been troubling the Empire, although in the plethora of subjects I have only mentioned them occasionally.   Neither could they be split up by double-dealing, although the Emperor had often tried to seduce them in various ways ; but not one deserted to him even in secret, so unswerving was their loyalty up to that time.   Now Nicephorus Bryennius and Gregorius Mavrocatacalon whom the Emperor had ransomed for forty thousand pieces of money when taken by the Scythians, did not at all approve of waging war along the Ister with the Scythians ; but George Palæologus and Nicolas Mavrocatacalon and all the young, vigorous men pressed the Emperor hard and urged him to cross the passes of the Hæmus and start war with the Scythians on the Danube.   Of this same opinion

were also Nicephorus and Leo, the two sons of the Emperor
Diogenes, who were born to him in the purple room after his
elevation to the throne and were consequently styled " Porphyrogeniti." This purple room was a certain building in
the palace shaped as a complete square from its base to the
spring of the roof, which ended in a pyramid ; it looked out
upon the sea and the harbour where the stone oxen and
lions stand. The floor of this room was paved with marbles
and the walls were panelled with it but not with ordinary
sorts nor even with the more expensive sorts which are fairly
easy to procure, but with the marble which the earlier
Emperors had carried away from Rome. And this marble
is, roughly speaking, purple all over except for spots like
white sand sprinkled over it. It is from this marble, I
imagine, that our ancestors called the room " purple."

Now, as I was saying, when the trumpet with its loud
summons directed all to the road of the Hæmus Mountains,
as if to march against the Scythians, Bryennius, who had tried
his utmost to dissuade the Emperor from this attempt and had
not succeeded, remarked sententiously, " If you cross the
Hæmus, Emperor, you will certainly find out whose
horses are the swiftest." When somebody asked what he
meant by those words, he replied, " When you all flee." For
although this man had had his eyes dug out for rebellion,
yet he was recognized as by far the cleverest strategist, and
most skilful and ingenious in the arrangement of troops.
How this Bryennius was deprived of his sight for desertion,
or rather rebellion, against the Emperor Botaniates, and how,
when captured by Alexius Comnenus, at that time the great
Domestic of the Eastern and Western armies, he was handed
over to Borilus with his eyes uninjured—I must refer those
who wish to know further details to the history of the great
Cæsar. For this Cæsar became the son-in-law of Alexius when
the latter was already Emperor, and he was the descendant of
that Bryennius. But at this point my soul is convulsed and
filled with sorrow, for he was wise in counsel and a very distinguished orator. For everything, strength, swiftness,
physical beauty, in fact all good qualities of mind and body
combined to adorn this man. For in him nature begot and
God fashioned a man most eminent in all ways, and just such a
hero as Homer depicted Achilles among the Achæans, one could
say my Cæsar was, shining forth amongst all those beneath
the sun. And this Cæsar, who was an expert in military matters, had not neglected letters, but had read every book and

applied himself to every branch of learning, and drawn therefrom all the wisdom of our own and of other times. And later he devoted himself to history, and at the suggestion of my mistress mother, I mean the Empress Irene, he composed a work well worthy of attention and worth reading, for he arranged a narrative of my father's deeds before he took up the reins of government. In this history he gives an accurate account of the facts concerning Bryennius ; and there too he narrates his grandfather's many vicissitudes, and his father-in-law's brilliant exploits, and assuredly he never falsified anything for he was related to them both, to the latter by marriage and to the former by blood. I have already mentioned his book in the earlier chapters of this history.

Now the Scythians saw that George Euphorbenus was on his way against them coming up the Ister with a large army and a fleet. (This river flows down from the western mountains, and after a series of cataracts empties itself into the Pontus Euxinus[1] through five mouths ; broad and with a strong current it flows through a vast plain, and is navigable for even the largest and most heavily laden vessels can be carried on its waters. It has not only one name, for in its upper reaches and near its source it is called the ' Danube,' whilst in the lower and at its mouths, the ' Ister.'

To resume, when a portion of the Scythians saw George Euphorbenus coming up this river, and were told that the Emperor too was already marching towards them overland, with a very considerable army, they recognized that it would be impossible for them to fight against both and so looked about for a way of escape from this imminent danger. Accordingly they sent a hundred-and-fifty Scythians as ambassadors to discuss terms of peace, and also to insinuate a few threats and perhaps to promise that if the Emperor acceded to their requests, they would furnish him with thirty thousand horsemen, whenever he required them. But the Emperor, awake to the Scythians' treachery, knew that this embassy was merely to circumvent the immediate danger, and that, at the next opportunity, they would kindle the latent sparks of their malice into a mighty conflagration ; therefore, he refused to receive the ambassadors. In the course of the discussion a certain Nicolas, one of the Emperor's secretaries, came up to him and whispered in his ear, " You may expect an eclipse of the sun to take place to-day," and on the Emperor's

[1] = The Black Sea.

expressing a doubt, he swore with an oath that he was not lying. Then the Emperor, with his habitual quick-wittedness, turned to the Scythians and said, " I appoint God as Judge ; and if a sign appears in the heavens this day, you will know for a surety that I have good reason for suspecting, and therefore not receiving, your embassy because your leaders are not sincere in their overtures for peace. If, however, no sign appears, I shall stand convicted of having been wrong in my surmise." Before two hours had passed, the light of the sun failed, and the whole of its disc was darkened by the moon's passing over it. At that sight the Scythians were terrified, and the Emperor handed them over to Leo Nicerites (he was a eunuch, brought up among the soldiers from babyhood, and much respected) and ordered him to take a sufficient guard and conduct them to the Queen of Cities. And Leo started very willingly on the road to Constantinople. But the barbarians who were throughout intent on regaining their liberty, slew the guards who were keeping a very careless watch over them when they reached little Nicæa, and returned by devious paths to those who had sent them. Nicerites with three others escaped with difficulty and rejoined the Emperor at Goloë.

III   After hearing Leo's tale, the Emperor was afraid that the ambassadors would stir up the whole Scythian army and attack him suddenly ; but he did not require a dream to urge him to battle, as Atreus' son, Agamemnon, did, for he was seething with lust of combat, so he led his legions through the vale of Sidera, and encamped near the Bitzina, a river running down from the adjacent mountains. Here a good many of his soldiers were killed, for in foraging they had strayed too far from the camp and many were captured besides. At dawn the Emperor quickly made for Pliscoba and from there he ascended a mountain peak called Simeon, and also locally ' the Scythians' Parliament House.' Here a similar accident occurred to soldiers who whilst foraging were at a distance from their camp. On the following day he marched along a river flowing at about a distance of twenty-four stades from Dristra and there he piled the baggage and erected his palisades. Here the Scythians made a massed attack upon the Imperial tent and killed not only a number of the light-armed troops but also captured some of the Manichæans who had fought most courageously. Hence a great din and confusion arose in the army and even the imperial tent was overturned by some horse-soldiers careering about wildly, and this fact was looked upon as a bad omen by the Emperor's ill-wishers.

However, the Emperor drove off the barbarians with a detachment of the army to some distance from his tent, so that they should not cause confusion again, then he mounted his horse and quelled the tumult, immediately broke up the camp and marched with all his troops in good order to Distra (this is the best-known of the towns near the Danube) in order to besiege it with engines. Accordingly he set to work, invested the town on all sides, and after breaking down one side of the walls, he entered with his entire army. But the two citadels of this town were still held by the kinsmen of a man called Tatus who had left the town shortly before to try and win over the Comans to come to the help of the Scythians. On the point of leaving and when bidding farewell to his friends this Tatus said, " I know for certain that the Emperor will come and besiege this town. Therefore directly you see him advancing into this plain, make haste to be the first to seize the hill which overlooks it, for it is the most advantageous position, and erect your palisades there, so that the Emperor may not be able to carry on the siege at his leisure, but be obliged to turn his attention to what is happening in his rear through fear of the injury you may do. And throughout the day and night keep on sending relays of troops against him." But the Emperor, hitting upon the right plan, abandoned the siege of the citadels (for it was an arduous and lengthy task), left the town and entrenched himself near a stream, not far from the Ister, and deliberated whether it would be wise to attack the Scythians. Palæologus and Gregorius Mavrocatacalon were for deferring war with the Patzinaks and advised taking an army and capturing the large town Pristhlava. "For," said they, "if the Scythians see us marching in good order fully accoutred, they will certainly not dare to attack us. And should perchance a few horsemen without chariots risk an engagement, you may be sure they will be worsted, and then in future we shall have the large town of Pristhlava as our well-fortified stronghold." This important town, which is situated on the Ister, did not always bear this barbaric name, but a Greek one, for it both was, and was called, a great city, namely, Megalopolis. But from the time that Mocrus, King of the Bulgarians, and his descendants, and finally Samuel, the last of the Bulgarian dynasty (as Zedekiah of the Jewish) overran the West, the town acquired a double name, retaining

' great ' from the Greek language and adding a Slavic word, and was universally spoken of as " Great Pristhlava." " If we have this town as a place of refuge," said Mavrocatacalon's adherents, " and harass the Scythians by daily skirmishes, we shall be punishing them the whole time and not allowing them to come out of their own camp at all either to forage or to fetch any other necessaries." During the bandying of arguments the two young sons of Diogenes, Nicephorus and Leo, who were inexperienced in the difficulties of warfare, slipped off their horses and took off their bridles, gave them a slap and drove them into a field of millet with the remark, " Do not be afraid, Emperor, we will cut them to pieces with our swords." The Emperor who was very adventurous and liked to be the first to start a battle, did not take into consideration the arguments of those who protested against fighting, but put George Cutzomites in charge of the Imperial tent and all the baggage and dispatched him to Betrinum ; then he enjoined the army not to light a lamp or fire that evening, but to keep the horses ready and watch till sun-rise. He himself left his tent at day-break, divided his forces and set them in order of battle, and then reviewed the army. He chose the centre of the line as his post, where he was surrounded by his relations and connections, such as his brother Adrian who was at that time commanding the Latins, and other valiant gentlemen. The left wing was held by Nicephorus Cæsar Melissenus, his sister's husband, and the leaders on the right wing were Castamonites and Taticius, whilst the Sauromatians, Uzas and Caratzas, commanded the allies. Then he chose six men as his own bodyguard and ordered them to attend to him and pay not the slightest attention to anyone else, these six were the two sons of Romanus Diogenes, Nicolas Mavrocatacalon who had had a long and varied military career, Johannaces, Nabites, the prefect of the Varangians, and lastly a certain Gules, a family retainer. But the Scythians too had arranged a plan of battle, for the science of warfare and of ordering troops is inbred in them ; they set ambuscades and connected their ranks in close-ordered array, and built towers, as it were, of their covered wagons, and advanced against the Emperor in squadrons, and hurled missiles from afar. The Emperor adapted his army to meet these squadrons, and forbade the hoplites to move forward or to break the covering formed by their shields, until the Scythians had come quite close. Then when they judged the intervening space between the

two armies to be no more than a bridle's length, they were
to advance against the foe in a body. Whilst the Emperor was
making these preparations the Scythians appeared in the
distance travelling with their covered wagons, wives and children. When the battle commenced, it raged from morning
till evening and the slaughter on either side was tremendous.
And Leo, Diogenes' son, riding too recklessly against the
Scythians, and allowing himself to be drawn closer than was
wise to the wagons, received a mortal wound and fell. And
Adrian, the Emperor's brother, who had been entrusted
with the command over the Latins, seeing that the Scythians'
onset was proving irresistible, gave his horse his head and
charged right up to the wagons and after fighting magnificently
returned with only seven comrades, all the rest had been either
slain or captured by the Scythians.   The result of the battle
was still hanging in the balance, and both armies were fighting
with great spirit, when some Scythian chieftains were seen
in the distance coming with thirty-six thousand men ; the
Romans who could not possibly stand against so many, then
turned their backs to the enemy. The Emperor had advanced
in front of his own army and stood sword in hand ; with
the other he held up as a standard the Pallium of the
Mother of the Divine Word and was supported by only twenty
brave-hearted companions, Nicephorus, Diogenes' son, was
there together with Michael Ducas the Protostrator, and
brother of the Empress, and the servants of his family.   Then
three Scythian foot-soldiers leapt at him, two snatched at his
reins on either side, the third at his right leg. Immediately
he cut one man's hand off, against the other he lifted his sword
and with threatening voice made him fall back, whilst he
struck at the helmet of the man holding his leg.   But he
only gave a rather light blow with his sword nor did he
use his whole strength in making it for he was afraid
that one of two things might happen if, as is often the case,
a severe blow from his sword missed altogether, namely,
that he would hit his own leg, or the horse on which he was
riding, and in that case he would easily be taken by the enemy.
So he quickly gave him a second blow but made the motions
of his hand very cautiously, for in all his actions, words and
motions reason was ever his guide, and he was never carried
away by anger nor led astray by passion. The Scythian's
helmet had fallen off at the first blow so the sword descended
on his bare head, and without a sound he fell straight to the
ground. Seeing the uncontrolled flight of the troops (for

the lines had long since been broken up, as all fled promiscuously), the Protostrator said, " To what purpose, Emperor,
are you trying to hold out here any longer ?   To what
purpose are you risking your life and entirely neglecting your
own safety ? " to which the Emperor replied that he would
rather they should die fighting bravely than seek safety
in ignoble flight.   The Protostrator retorted, " If you
were one of the common herd, your remark would be praise-
worthy, but as your death involves world-wide disaster,
why not choose the better part ?   for if you save yourself,
you can live to fight another day and conquer."

The Emperor seeing himself in instant danger, as the Scythians
were attacking him persistently, abandoned all hope, and said,
" Yes, it is time now for us to take thought for our safety with
the help of God, but we must not pursue the same road as our
fugitives for in that case the Scythians who are pursuing
our men might fall in with us on their return, but," and he
pointed to the Scythians standing in the van of their army,
" we must ride down upon those men there as if we had been
born to-day, and were doomed to die to-day, and then if by
God's aid we get to the rear of the Scythians' lines, we shall
find a different road."   After saying this and encouraging
the others, he was the first to dash like a firebrand upon the
Scythians and struck at the first who encountered him, and
the latter straightway rolled from his saddle.   As the closed
ranks of the Scythians were thus split up, he and his companions reached the country behind the Scythians.   At any
rate the Emperor managed to do this, but the Protostrator
had the misfortune to fall on the ground for his horse slipped ;
but one of his attendants immediately gave him his own horse.
When he caught up the Emperor he never moved more than a
foot's breadth away from him again, for he was so intensely
devoted to him.   In the confusion resulting from one party
fleeing and the other pursuing, a second lot of Scythians
overtook the Emperor ;   he immediately turned round and
hit down his assailant and killed not only him but several
others as well, as those who were present assert.   Another
Scythian who had crept up from the back was on the point
of hitting Nicephorus Diogenes, when the Emperor caught
sight of him and called out :   " Look behind you, Nicephorus ! "   So the latter turned round sharply and struck
the Scythian in the face ; and I have often heard the Emperor
say that he had never seen anything so swift and skilful.   He
used also to say, " If I had not been carrying a standard that

day, I should have killed more Scythians than there are hairs on my head," and this was not bragging, for who ever pushed modesty to such an extreme as he did? But sometimes conversation and the nature of events forced him to speak out about his doings within the circle of his family and intimates, though it was only as the result of much urging on our part; but no one in the world ever heard the Emperor boast of his prowess in public.—As a strong wind was blowing, and the Patzinaks were attacking him he could no longer hold the standard upright. Then a Scythian wielding a long spear in both hands struck him in the buttocks, and though he did not break the skin, he inflicted exquisite pain which lasted for many years. Overcome by these difficulties he furled the standard and hid it in a germander bush so that nobody should see it; and then he rode through the night and came safely to Goloë (and from this the townsmen used to say, "From Dristra to Goloë is a fine feat even for an unwounded man, Comnenus"). During the day he went on to Beroë and stayed there as he wished to ransom the captives.

IV During the flight of the defeated troops that day Palæologus was knocked off his horse and lost it; while standing helpless and well aware of his dangerous situation he gazed about in case he could see his horse anywhere, when suddenly he saw Leo, the Bishop of Chalcedon, of whom we have written above. This man was dressed in priestly garb and was offering him his horse; Palæologus mounted it and continued his flight; but he never saw the holy man again. This priest had really a very frank and open nature, and the right character for a priest of superior rank, but he was somewhat simple-minded and occasionally displayed more zeal than knowledge, and he had no accurate acquaintance with the sacred canons. For these reasons disaster befell him, as has been already related, and he lost his bishopric; Palæologus, however, always adhered to him because of his pre-eminent goodness. So whether it was by reason of his fervent belief in this man that Palæologus was granted this heavenly vision, or whether some other mysterious design of Providence was manifested in this priest, I am unable to say. With the Patzinaks pursuing him, Palæologus ran into a marshy, thickly-shaded place and there fell in with about a hundred and fifty Roman soldiers. As the Scythians encircled them and they saw their case was desperate for they could not fight against so many, they waited upon Palæologus'

N

decision for they knew his bravery and indomitable disposition of old. He advised them to rush headlong at the
Scythians, taking absolutely no thought for their own safety,
and thus, I fancy, purchasing it.   " But first," he said, " we
must confirm this plan by oath, and then if we are all of one
opinion no one must fail to take part in the onset against
the Scythians, but each must regard the general safety and
danger as his own." Thereupon Palæologus made a wild
dash at the foe, and struck the first man he met, who straightway fell to the ground dazed.   But the rest were half-hearted
in their attack, and some of them were killed and others
returned to the covered glade as if to their nest, and saved
their lives by hiding in it. Whilst Palæologus was making
for a certain height he was again pursued by the Patzinaks
and his horse was wounded and fell ; he himself, however,
escaped to the neighbouring mountain. Then he sought
for the road to safety, which under the circumstances it was
not easy for him to find, and so he wandered about for eleven
days, when he fell in with a soldier's widow, who gave him
shelter for several days, and then her sons, who had escaped
with their lives from the battle, pointed out to him the road
to safety. This is the story of Palæologus' adventures.

Now the chieftains of the Scythians were minded to put the
prisoners they held to death, but the majority of the people
absolutely refused to allow this, as they wished to sell them for
a price. And as this proposal gained the day, the Emperor was
acquainted of it by letters from Melissenus who, although he
was a prisoner, had done a great deal to persuade the Scythians
to adopt this course. The Emperor, who was still in Beroë,
at once sent to the capital for the requisite amount of money,
and then redeemed the captives.

V At that time Tatus returned to the Ister with the
Comans he had won over ; directly they saw the amount of
booty, and of captives, they said to the Scythian chieftains,
" We have left our homes and travelled a long way to come
to your assistance on the understanding that we should
share your dangers and your victories. Therefore as we have
done our best it would not be right to send us back empty-
handed.   For it was not by our choice that we arrived too
late for the battle, nor can we in any way be blamed for that,
for it was the fault of the Emperor who hurried on the battle.
Therefore you must either divide all this booty equally with us,
or instead of allies you will find us your enemies."   The
Scythians refused to do this. As the Comans would not

accept their refusal, a violent struggle took place between them and the Scythians were thoroughly beaten, and only escaped with difficulty to the town called Ozolimne. And there they stayed for some time, hemmed in by the Comans and not daring to cross the lake. This lake which we now call " Ozolimne "is the largest in diameter and circumference of all the lakes ever mentioned by geographers and yields to none for size. It lies beyond. the Hundred Hills, and is fed by very large and beautiful rivers ; on its southern half it can carry a number of large merchant-vessels which proves how deep the lake must be in that part. It is called " Ozolimne " not because it emits any bad or offensive effluvia, but because a Hunnish army once lodged near it (this name " Huns " (Ounni) was converted into " Ouzi " in the local patois) and made their camp on its banks, and thus the lake was called Ouzolimne, with the vowel " u " added).

Now in the ancient historians, no mention is made of a Hunnish army ever having come there, but during the Emperor Alexius' reign the whole nation congregated there from all quarters and gave the place its name. These probable facts about the lake are now mentioned by me for the first time in order to prove that owing to the Emperor's many expeditions in many directions many places obtained their names either directly from him or from his enemies who collected there ; and we note that much the same thing happened in the time of Alexander, King of Macedon. For both the Alexandria in Egypt, and the other in India were named after him, and we further know that Lysimachia was named after Lysimachus, one of his soldiers. Therefore it does not surprise me if the Emperor Alexius, emulating Alexander's zeal, occasionally fitted new names to places either from the tribes who assembled there or whom he had summoned, or gave names of his own choosing to places as the result of his own exploits. Let these remarks about Ozolimne be thrown out once for all in the true spirit of history. Now when their provisions ran short, the Comans returned to their homes to get a new supply, and then move against the Scythians once more.

VI In the meantime the Emperor recuperated at Beroë and fitted out the captives he had redeemed and all his hoplites with arms. At that time, too, the Count of Flanders on his way back from Jerusalem visited the Emperor there, and took the customary Latin oath and also promised to send to his succour five hundred horsemen directly he reached

home. Consequently the Emperor showed him great
honour and then dismissed him to his own country. After
wards the Emperor left Beroë with the troops he had amassed
and entered Adrianople. The Scythians next came down
the narrow valleys between Goloë and Diabolis and pitched
their camp near the place called Marcella. Now the Emperor
heard of the doings of the Comans and, as they were expected
to return, he was alarmed because he foresaw danger from
their coming. So he sent Synesius armed with Golden Bulls
to the Scythians to treat with them and say that if they
could be induced to make a treaty and give hostages, though
he would not allow them to enter further into his territory,
yet he would arrange for them to stay in the place they had
taken and provide them liberally with all necessaries. For
Alexius meditated using the Scythians against the Comans
if the latter crossed the Ister again and tried to advance
farther. But if the Scythians could not be persuaded,
Synesius was to leave them and return. This Synesius
accordingly went to the Scythians and after making an
appropriate speech persuaded them to enter into a treaty with
the Emperor ; and he stayed there some time and courted
their favour, thus removing every possible cause of offence.
The Comans returned, fully prepared for war with the
Scythians, but not finding them and learning that they had
come over the passes, occupied Marcella and after arranging
terms of peace with the Emperor, demanded permission to
cross the passes and attack the Scythians. However, the
Emperor refused, as he had already concluded peace with
the Scythians, saying, " We have no need of auxiliaries at
present ; take a satisfactory present and go home ! " He
treated the ambassadors courteously, gave them satisfactory
presents and sent them home in peace. This emboldened
the Scythians who promptly broke the treaty, reverted to
their former cruelty and laid waste the neighbouring lands
and cities. For as a rule all barbarians are unstable, and the
observance of treaties is not natural to them. Becoming
aware of this Synesius returned to the Emperor and himself
informed him of the Scythians' ingratitude and violation of
the treaty. They seized Philippopolis and this placed the
Emperor in a difficulty as against their large numbers his
forces were far too small to allow of his opening battle with
them. But accustomed as he was to find a way out of
difficulties and never in any crisis to feel at all despondent, he
decided that he must endeavour to reduce their numbers by

skirmishes and ambuscades. And so guessing at the places or towns which they were likely to enter in the morning, he anticipated their arrival the evening before ; or if in the evening he heard that they would take possession of a certain place, he occupied that same place in the early morning. And as much as possible, he wore them down from a distance by skirmishes and ambuscades to prevent their gaining possession of the forts. Well, both parties, the Scythians and the Emperor, reached Cypsella. And now, as a mercenary force which he expected had not yet arrived, the Emperor felt very helpless for he knew how quickly the Scythians moved and saw that they were already hastening towards the Queen of Cities. As he had insufficient forces for meeting their immense host, and considering that ' what was not worse, was better,' as the saying is, he again resorted to negotiations for peace. Consequently he sent ambassadors to confer with them about peace, and the Scythians at once fell in with the Emperor's wishes. Before the truce was made, a man named Neantzes deserted to the Romans. Then Migidemus was sent to fetch in recruits from the adjacent regions ; in a battle which occurred later at a place . . . this man's son whilst making a fierce dash against the Pat- zinaks was snared and captured by a Scythian woman and dragged into the circle of their wagons with an iron sickle. His head which they cut off the Emperor bought at his father's request. Overcome by this unforeseen disaster, the father beat his breast for three days and nights with a sling-stone and then died. The interval of peace with the Scythians did not last long, but like ' dogs they returned to their vomit ' ; they then removed from Cypsella and occupied Taurocomus, where they wintered and ravaged the neighbouring village-towns.

VII   On the return of spring they came down from there to Chariopolis. The Emperor who was stationed at Bul- garophygum, wished to no longer delay but set apart a considerable section of the army, all picked men and amongst them too the young soldiers, called " Archontopouli," all with their beards scarcely grown, but irresistible in attack, and ordered them to fall upon the Scythians, who were standing on the tops of their wagons, from the rear.

This band of " Archontopouli " was first formed by Alexius. As the Roman Empire possessed no army owing to the careless- ness of the preceding Emperors, he collected from all sides the sons of soldiers who had fallen in the field, and trained

them in the use of arms and for war and called them " Archontopouli," as though they were the sons of " Archontes " ;
in order that by their name they should be reminded of their
parents' nobility and bravery, and therefore aim at impetuous
valour and prove themselves very brave when circumstances
demanded daring and strength. Such then was the band
of " Archontopouli," and roughly speaking they numbered
about two thousand ; it was much the same as the ' Sacred
Band ' of the Spartans in former days. In obedience to
orders, then, these newly-recruited " Archontopouli " marched
to the attack. But some of the Scythians lying in ambush
in a hollow below the hill, watched their advance ; and when
they saw them falling upon the wagons, they rushed out upon
them with irresistible impetuosity. And during the close
engagement which followed about three hundred of the
" Archontopouli " fell fighting desperately. For some time
the Emperor grieved deeply for them, shedding bitter tears
and calling each by name as if they were absent. After this
victory over their opponents the Patzinaks passed through
Chariopolis and turned to Apros, devastating as they went.
The Emperor then had recourse again to his former plan of
action, and forestalled their entry into Apros ; for, as I have
remarked more than once, he had not sufficient troops to
risk a battle with his enemies. Thereupon, as he knew they
set out on foraging expeditions at daybreak, he sent for
Taticius (he has often been mentioned in this history) and
bade him take the most courageous of the youths and picked
men from his own bodyguard and all the Latins and keep
watch during the night for the Scythians' expedition at
dawn, so that when he supposed that the foraging party was
at a good distance from their camp, he could ride down upon
them at full speed. Taticius carried out these orders, killed
about four hundred and took a large number captive. And
what followed ? The horsemen sent by the Count of Flanders,
about five hundred picked men, arrived and brought as a
present to the Emperor one hundred and fifty selected horses :
moreover they sold him all the horses they did not require
for their own use. The Emperor welcomed them very
graciously and returned hearty thanks. Next he received a
message from the East saying that Apelchasem, the governor
of Nicæa (whom the Persians usually call a ' satrap,' and the
Turks, who now imitate the Persians, an ' ameer '), was all
but starting on an expedition against Nicomedia, so he sent
those horsemen to protect that district.

VIII   At this same time Tzachas who was assured of the
Emperor's manifold troubles in the West and of his continuous
warfare with the Patzinaks, thought that, as the opportunity
offered, he ought to acquire a fleet.   And chancing upon a
certain Smyrniote, he entrusted the building of pirate-vessels
to him for he was experienced in this work.   After he had
built many of these at Smyrna, as well as forty covered
trawlers he embarked experienced men on them, sailed for
Clazomenæ and took the town immediately.   Thence he
sailed to Phocæa and took that too at first assault.   From
that town he sent letters to the Curator Alopus, the administrator of Mitylene, threatening him with dire punishment
unless he left the town very quickly ; he told him also that
he wished him well and had for that reason warned him of the
terrible future that awaited him if he did not depart.   Alopus
was thoroughly scared by Tzachas' threats, so embarked
on a vessel by night and made for the capital.   On hearing
of his flight, Tzachas did not delay but sailed straightway
to Mitylene and took it without any difficulty.   The Emperor
was informed about Tzachas, and immediately dispatched
a large force by boat to fortify Methymna which is situated
on the northern promontory of this island and had not gone
over to Tzachas.   However Tzachas thought Methymna
was beneath consideration, but sailed direct to Chios and
took that also at first assault.   On receipt of this news the
Emperor sent an adequate fleet with plenty of soldiers against
him under the leadership of Nicetas Castamonites.   So he
departed, engaged in battle with Tzachas and was quickly
worsted, and Tzachas also carried off a number of his ships.
When the Emperor was informed of what had happened to
Castamonites, he equipped a second fleet and appointed as
' Duke ' of it, Constantine Dalassenus, a great fighter and
related to him on his mother's side.

Directly he reached the shores of Chios he started the
siege of the citadel, fighting with great energy as he was eager
to take the town before Tzachas could arrive from Smyrna.
So he hammered at the walls with a number of siege-engines
and catapults and destroyed the connecting walls between
two towers.   When the Turks inside perceived this and also
recognized that the Roman forces were hard to resist, they
used the Roman tongue and implored the lord of all to have
mercy.   But the soldiers of Dalassenus and Opus could hardly
be controlled in their eagerness to enter the city, although
their leaders restrained them because they were afraid that

if their men entered the town they would seize all the booty and money that Tzachas had stored there. So they said, "You have heard the Turks clearly proclaiming their allegiance to the Emperor, and you know they have surrendered to us, it would not be right therefore for you to go in and slaughter them mercilessly." When day was almost over and night was at hand the Turks built up another wall in place of the one destroyed, and on its outer side they suspended from it mattresses, hides and any handy garment, so that the impact of the missiles directed against it would be deadened by them and thus slightly diminished.

And Tzachas prepared the fleet he had with him, enlisted about 8,000 Turks and then set off on the road to Chios, while his fleet accompanied him along the coast. When he heard this, Dalassenus ordered the admirals to embark sufficient soldiers and Opus the general, and to put to sea and, if they fell in anywhere with their adversary's fleet, they were to engage them in battle. Tzachas soon left the land and embarked and directed his course straight to Chios, and about midnight Opus met him. (Now Tzachas had got a very long chain and linked all his vessels together so that neither those which wanted to turn back could get away nor those who wished to sail ahead break from their attachment.) When Opus saw this new arrangement of Tzachas' fleet, he was horror-struck and did not even dare to approach it, but turned his helm about and made for Chios. But Tzachas pursued him systematically and did not slacken in rowing. When they approached Chios, Opus managed to anchor his ships first in the harbour of Chios (Dalassenus had before this gained control of it), while Tzachas sailed past this port I have mentioned and stationed his ships close under the wall of the citadel. It was the fourth day of the week. The next day he turned all his men ashore, numbered them and made a list of them. Meanwhile Dalassenus had discovered a small town near the harbour, so levelled there the first palisaded camp he had made and went down there and made a new trench of adequate width and settled his whole army in it. On the following day both armies arrayed themselves and went forth to battle. But the Roman army stood motionless, as Dalassenus had commanded them not to break the ranks. Then Tzachas egged on the larger part of his barbarian army to attack the Romans and bade a very few horsemen follow them up. At this the Latins took their long spears and rode out against them. But the barbarians did not aim their

javelins at the Franks but at the horses and some they
struck with their spears ; thus they killed a great many,
routed the others and drove them into their camp lines, but
they in a mad rush ran out from them towards the ships.
When the Romans saw the Franks in headlong flight, they were
terrified and retreated a little and drew themselves up close
to the wall of the little town. Thus the way was left open
for the barbarians to go down to the coast and capture some
of our ships. Seeing this the sailors loosed the cables, pushed
off quickly from the shore, cast anchor, and waited to see
what would happen. Dalassenus then ordered them to sail
along the coasts to the western part of the island and when
they reached Bolissus, to await his coming there ; now Bolissus
is a small town standing on the headland of the island. But
some Scythians found their way to Tzachas and acquainted
him with Dalassenus' plan. Then he in the first place sent
out fifty spies to let him know at once when Dalassenus' fleet
was getting ready to put to sea, and in the second he sent to
Dalassenus under pretence of wishing to discuss terms. of
peace with him—but really, I believe, because having regard
to Dalassenus' brave and adventurous spirit, he despaired of
victory. The latter promised Tzachas to come to the edge
of his camp on the morrow, when they could exchange views
and hear whatever either had to say. The barbarians agreed
to this, and so in the morning the two leaders met. Tzachas
opened the conversation, addressing the other by name,
and said, " I must tell you that I am the young man who
many years ago overran Asia and though fighting bravely
was trapped through my want of experience and captured
by the famous Cabalicas Alexander. By him I was carried
captive and handed over to the Emperor Nicephorus Botaniates, who at once bestowed on me the rank of ' Protono-
bilissimus ' and rich gifts, and I in return became his vassal.
But ever since Alexius Comnenus assumed the reins of government, all my privileges have been annulled. And I have
come here now in order to explain to you the reasons of my
hostility. Let the Emperor be told of them and, if he wishes
the enmity which has arisen to be brought to an end, then
let him restore to me in full all the privileges due to me of
which I have deen deprived. And if you think favourably
of a marriage between our children, let a form of betrothal
be drawn up in writing as is customary among you and also
among us barbarians. Then if all these conditions I have
mentioned have been fulfilled, I will restore to the Emperor

through you all the islands which I have overrun and taken from the Roman power and, after completing a truce with him, I will return to my own country." Dalassenus looked upon all this as empty talk as he knew well the crafty nature of the Turks, and therefore put off indefinitely the fulfilment of his demands, at the same time he told him plainly the opinion he entertained of him saying, " You will never hand over the islands to me, as you say, nor can I without consulting the Emperor agree to your demands upon him and upon myself. But since the Grand Duke, John, the Emperor's brother-in-law, accompanied by the whole fleet and numerous land-forces, is on the point of arrival, let him hear your terms, and then, if he acts as mediator, I can assure you that your truce with the Emperor will be arranged."

This Duke John had been dispatched to Epidamnus with a strong army by the Emperor, partly to guard Dyrrachium, and partly to carry on war with the Dalmatians. For the chief called Bodinus was a great warrior and full of rascality and would not remain within his own frontiers but made daily incursions on the nearest large Dalmatian villages and annexed them to his own property. Duke John had spent eleven years at Dyrrachium and rescued many forts from the hands of Bolcanus and had also sent many Dalmatians captive to the Emperor, and at last he had engaged in a violent contest with Bodinus and captured him. Now the Emperor had found out from many things that this Duke John was exceedingly brave, skilled in warfare and never disposed to disregard even the slightest of his orders, and as he required a man of this kind to act against Tzachas, he sent for him from Dyrrachium, and dispatched him with a quantity of naval and land forces against Tzachas, after appointing him ' Great Duke ' of the fleet. How many battles he waged with him and how many dangers he incurred before he proved himself victor, this history will tell later on. As Dalassenus was expecting him, he shewed Tzachas in his conference with him that he wished to postpone everything till the Duke's arrival. But Tzachas seemed to reply in the Homeric words, " It is already night ; it is well to obey the voice of night," and he promised to send a large supply of provisions at daybreak. However it was all trickery and deceit, and Dalassenus was right in his supposition. For towards morning Tzachas went secretly to the shore of Chios, and, as there was a favourable wind, he sailed for Smyrna in order to collect more troops and then return to Chios. But Dalassenus proved himself a match for Tzachas' devices. For he embarked with his troops in the ships that were at hand, and went to Bolissus ; there he refitted the ships, prepared more siege-engines, gave his soldiers a rest and collected some more and then returned to the place whence he had started. Then he dashed into a fierce conflict with the barbarians, pulled down the walls and subjugated the town, whilst Tzachas was still dwelling in Smyrna. Afterwards as the sea was calm, he sailed with the whole fleet straight to Mitylene.

IX After thus disposing of the war with Tzachas, the Emperor heard that the Scythians were again aiming at Rusium and had pitched their camp near Polybotum, so he left Constantinople, just as he was, and took possession of Rusium. There accompanied him too the deserter Neantzes who was secretly hatching a horrible design against him, and in his escort were also Cantzus and Catranes, lovers of war and ardently devoted to the Emperor. Seeing a large detachment of the Scythians in the distance, he joined battle with them. Many of the Romans fell in the battle, and others were taken alive and put to death by the Scythians, while a goodly number reached Rusium in safety. But this was only a battle with the Scythian foragers. The Emperor was heartened by the arrival of the so-called Maniacatæ Latins and determined to fight in close combat on the day following with the Scythians. Since there happened to be only a short distance between the two armies, he did not venture to sound the wartrumpet as he wished to spring the battle upon the enemy. Therefore he sent for Constantine, who was in charge of the royal falcons, and ordered him to take a kettledrum in the evening and walk about in the army beating it all through the night, and tell the soldiers that they were to get ready, as with the dawn the Emperor intended without giving any signal to engage the Scythians in battle. The Scythians moved from Polybotum to a place called Hades which they occupied, and pitched their camp in it. Thus from the evening before the Emperor was making his preparations, and when day broke he distributed the troops and drawing them up in phalanxes proceeded against the enemy. But before the armies met and whilst each company was being drawn up into position, Neantzes ascended a hill close by in order to spy out the Scythian army, as he said, and bring the Emperor word of their disposition, but he did exactly the opposite. For in their own language he advised the Scythians to place their wagons in rows, and not to be at all afraid of the Emperor as he was another man as the result of his former defeat and disposed to flee because of his scarcity of troops and allies. After saying this he descended the hill to the Emperor. But a semi-barbarian who knew the Scythian language understood what Neantzes had said to the Scythians and came and reported it all to the Emperor. Neantzes was notified of this and demanded the proof; whereupon the semi-barbarian boldly stepped forward and gave the proof. On the spot Neantzes drew his sword and cut off the man's head in the presence of the Emperor and the troops on either side. I imagine that Neantzes while wishing to exculpate himself from the suspicion of treachery, only brought more suspicion upon himself by slaying the informer. For why did he not wait for the investigation? However it seems as if in his desire to still in anticipation the tongue which would disclose his treachery, he ventured upon a most reckless deed, which was worthy of his barbaric soul, but just as suspicious as it was daring. The Emperor did not immediately proceed against the barbarian nor punish him as he deserved but he restrained himself for the moment, though boiling with rage and indignation, so as not to scare away his prey in advance and spread dismay among his men. But he cherished and dissembled his anger against Neantzes, as from this happening as well as from other signs he had already divined the man's treachery. The issue of the battle stood on a razor's edge, and for this reason the Emperor restrained his boiling wrath for a while, for he was perplexed how to act for the best in the immediate present. Shortly Neantzes approached the Emperor and dismounting from his horse, asked him for another, and the Emperor at once gave him one of the picked horses with a royal saddle-cloth. Neantzes mounted it and when the armies began to move to the encounter made a pretence of riding against the Scythians but turned the point of his spear backwards against our men, and went over to his countrymen and gave them much information about the Emperor's army. They followed his suggestion and engaged in a fierce battle with the Emperor whose army was utterly routed. On seeing the lines all broken and the men scattered in flight the Emperor was perturbed but decided not to endanger himself senselessly, and therefore turned his horse's head and rode to a stream flowing close to Rusium. Here he drew rein and with a few chiefs continued the fight as far as possible against his pursuers, making sorties against them and killing many and occasionally getting wounded himself.

When George, called Pyrrhus, reached the river from another direction in his flight, the Emperor upbraided him and called him to his side. Noticing the headlong recklessness of the Scythians, and how their numbers increased hourly, for other parties kept coming to their assistance, he left George there with the rest and bade them keep up a faint resistance to them until he himself returned. Then he quickly wheeled round his horse, crossed the river and rode into Rusium ; there he collected the fugitive soldiers he found, and all the natives of military age and even the peasants themselves, with their carts, and ordered them to come out with all haste and take their stand along the river-bank. This was done more quickly than one can tell and after arranging them in files he crossed the river again and rode back to George, and this in spite of suffering so from quartan fever that his teeth were chattering with cold. The whole Scythian army had now been gathered together, but when they saw the twofold army and the Emperor's great exertions, and remembered his love of danger and his unwavering spirit in victory or defeat, they felt they could not sustain his attack and consequently remained quiet and did not hazard an engagement with him. The Emperor, partly because he was distressed by his chill and partly because the scattered soldiery had not yet all returned, also stood still, only passing along the lines sometimes, riding at a slow pace and shewing them a bold front. Thus it came about that both armies remained stationary till the evening, and then when night fell, both returned to their own camps without having struck a blow. For they were afraid and not bold enough to fight. Gradually the men who had fled here, there and everywhere in the first battle re-assembled at Rusium, and the majority of them had not taken the slightest part in the battle. Further, Monastras, Uzas and Synesius who were brave followers of Ares, also arrived at Rusium, disabled too, after having traversed the district then called Asprum.

X But the Emperor, who was ill with a chill, as I have said, was obliged to retire to bed for a few days to recover. But even so he could not rest for thinking about what he ought to do on the morrow. As he was meditating on these things, Tatranes came to him. He was a Scythian who had frequently deserted to the Emperor and then gone back to his own people, each time he had been forgiven by the Emperor and in consequence of this forbearance he now bore a deep affection towards him and for the rest of his life he planned and worked for the Emperor with all his heart and soul. He came and said, " O Emperor, I have a presentiment that to-morrow the Scythians will surround the town and then commence a battle with us. You should therefore anticipate them and draw up your lines outside the walls at daybreak." The Emperor thanked him, took his advice and arranged to carry out this plan at sunrise. After giving this advice Tatranes went away and spoke as follows to the Scythian leaders, " Do not be puffed up with pride, because you have recently defeated the Emperor, and when you begin a battle with us do not raise your hopes too high because our numbers are small. For the Emperor's might is invincible and a large mercenary army is expected at any minute. If you will not accept peace with him, the vultures will eat your corpses." This is what Tatranes said to the Scythians. Now the Emperor was planning the capture of the numerous horses of the Scythians which were grazing in the plain, for the Scythians continued ravaging our territory both by day and by night, so he summoned Monastras and Uzas and enjoined them to take some picked horsemen, skirt round the rear of the Scythians and at dawn enter the plain and carry off all the horses and other cattle together with their herdsmen, and he exhorted them to be without fear. " For," said he, " as we shall be fighting the enemy in front, you will easily execute your task." And he was not disappointed, for his words soon became facts. As he was expecting the Scythians to attack he did not sleep at all nor even doze a little, but the whole night long he kept calling for soldiers, especially those who were proficient archers, and told them a great deal about the Scythians, thus stirring them up to battle, as it were, and giving them useful hints for the battle which he expected on the morrow, for instance, how to stretch the bow and direct their darts, also when to hold their horses back and when to let them go, and when to dismount even if necessary. This was his work in the night ; after which he slept for a short time. As day dawned, all the Scythians crossed the river and seemed eager to begin a battle, and thus the Emperor's conjecture was proved correct (he was wonderful in foreseeing what would happen, for from his almost daily battles he had gained wide experience) ; he at once mounted his horse, ordered the attack to be sounded, drew up his lines and himself took his stand before them. When he noticed that the Scythians were coming to the attack more recklessly than of late, he ordered the skilled archers to dis-

mount and proceed on foot and to keep their bows bent
continuously , the rest of the troops followed them and
the Emperor held the centre of the army.   The archers made
a bold attack on the Scythians who, when the battle was
well under way, became frightened either by the thick
clouds of darts or by the sight of the close ranks of our army
and the Emperor's spirited fighting ; and they turned back,
anxious to cross the river in their flight to their wagons.
But the Romans pursued them at full speed, some hit them
in the back with their spears, while others hurled javelins.
Many indeed were slain before they reached the edge of the
river, still more, fleeing with all speed, fell into the torrent and
were carried away and drowned.   The ones who fought
most bravely of all that day were the Emperor's household
retainers, for they were all in the prime of life.   As for the
Emperor he was clearly the champion of the day, and being
proclaimed victor he returned to his camp.

XI   After taking three days' rest there he moved on to
Tzouroulus.   He contemplated remaining there for some
time, and therefore had an entrenched camp made on the
eastern side of the town large enough for the troops he had
with him and stored the imperial tent and all the baggage
inside it.   Then the Scythians in their turn advanced on
Tzouroulus, but on hearing that the Emperor had already taken
possession of the town, they crossed the river running through
the plain somewhere near this town (the local name of which
is Xerogypsos) and fixed their palisades between the river
and the town.   So they were outside and encircled this
town, and the Emperor was cut off inside as if besieged.
When night descended, ' all the gods and warriors with horse-
hair plumes slept,' as Homer's muse says, ' but balmy sleep
did not visit ' Alexius ; the whole night long he lay awake,
revolving schemes for overcoming the Scythians' daring by
craft.   Seeing that Tzouroulus was a fortified town situated on
a fairly steep hill and that the entire barbarian army was
bivouacking down below in the plain, and that his forces
were insufficient to allow of his attempting a pitched battle
against their overwhelming numbers, he devised a most
ingenious plan.   He requisitioned the inhabitants' wagons
and lifted off the bodies from the wheels and axle-trees, and
then suspended the latter, for he had them hung out in order
from the battlements on the outside of the walls and tied
by ropes to the parapets.   He no sooner thought of this
than it was done.   And within an hour there was a circle of

wheels with their axle-trees hanging up, a regular row of circles touching each other and fastened to one another by their axles. In the morning he armed himself and got the army ready and led out his soldiers from the gates and placed them in full view of the enemy. Now it happened that our troops were placed just on that side of the wall where the wheels were hanging, and the opposing army was straight opposite them. Then Alexius stood in the middle of the army and explained to the soldiers that, when the trumpet sounded the attack, they were to dismount and march forward slowly against the foe and by using mostly their arrows and javelins to provoke the Scythians to the attack; and as soon as they saw them drawn on and urging on their horses to the attack, they were to turn hastily and in fleeing wheel off a little to the right and left and thus open to the enemy a clear path for coming close up to the walls. And he had given orders to the men on the walls that when they saw the ranks dividing, they were to cut the ropes with their swords and let the wheels with the axles fall headlong down from above. All this was carried out according to the Emperor's orders. The Scythian horsemen raised their barbaric shout and hurled themselves in a body upon our lines who were marching slowly towards them, the Emperor alone being on horseback. Then our men according to Alexius' plan drew back step by step and, pretending to retreat, unexpectedly split into two parts as if opening a very wide entrance for the enemy into the town. Directly the Scythians had entered this mouth, as it were, of the two parts of our army, the wheels came whirring down. Each wheel rebounded at least a cubit's length from the wall, and through their rims springing back from the wall they seemed to be ejected from catapults and came hurtling down into the midst of the Scythian cavalry with tremendous impetus. Partly owing to their descent in unison caused by their natural weight, and partly because they gained further momentum from the sloping nature of the ground, they fell upon the barbarians with terrific force and crushed them on every side, mowing down, as it were, the legs of the horses. And no matter whether the wheels hit the fore- or the hind-legs of the horses, in either case they forced the horses to sink down on the side they had received the blow and consequently to throw their riders. So the Scythians fell one after another in great numbers, and our men charged them from both sides; the battle pressed terribly on the Scythians from all sides, some were killed by the flying arrows, others wounded by spears, and most of the rest were forced into the river by the violent impact of the wheels and there drowned. The next day when Alexius saw the Scythian survivors preparing for battle again, and noticed that his own men were full of courage, he bade them get ready. He himself donned his armour and, after arranging the order of battle, descended to the slope. There he drew up his lines face to face with the Scythians and halted in order to join battle if possible. He himself held the centre of the line. A fierce engagement ensued and much to their surprise the Romans carried off the victory and then pursued the fleeing Scythians hotly. When the Emperor saw that they were pursuing them for a long distance, he was afraid that they might suddenly fall into an ambush and then, not only would the flight of the Scythians be arrested, but those who were fleeing would unite with the ambush and inflict a severe blow on the Roman army. The Emperor therefore kept riding up to his men and urging them to draw rein and breathe their horses. In this way the two armies parted that day, the Scythians fled and the brilliant victor returned joyfully to his camp. After this decisive defeat the Scythians pitched their tents between Bulgarophygum and little Nicæa. As winter had already overtaken them the Emperor decided that he ought to return to the capital in order to give himself and the larger part of his army some rest after their heavy labours. So he divided his forces and selected the bravest of the troops to remain on guard against the enemy. Over these he placed as commanders Joannaces and Nicolas Mavro-catacalon, of whom I have often spoken in this story; he ordered them to post an adequate number of soldiers as garrison in each town, and to requisition foot-soldiers from all the country together with wagons and the oxen which drew them. For with the return of spring he hoped to renew the war with the Scythians on a larger scale and therefore he made suitable provision and preparations beforehand. When he had carefully arranged everything, he travelled home to Byzantium.

BOOK VIII

I

THE Emperor was now informed that the Scythians had detached a division and sent it against Chœrobacchi, and that their approach was imminent. As he was a man swift to act and ever proved himself ready in sudden crises—in spite of not having had a week's rest yet in his palace nor even taken a bath, nor shaken off the dust of battle—he at once assembled the troops appointed as garrison of the city and all the recruits there were, about 500 in number, and after seeing to their equipment all through the night, he marched out at dawn. On this occasion he made his expedition against the Scythians known, and to all his connections by blood or marriage and to the men of superior fortune who had enrolled themselves in the army (it was then Friday in Septuagesima week) he sent the following orders by his messengers : " I for my part am leaving because I have heard of the Scythians' rapid movement on Chœrobacchi ; you others, however, must march and join us during Quinquagesima week. As I do not wish to appear severe and inconsiderate, I grant you the days from this Septuagesima Friday to the Monday in Quinquagesima week as a short breathing-space." Thereupon the Emperor marched straight to Chœrobacchi, and on entrance closed the gates, and took charge of the keys himself. Then he stationed all those of his servants who were loyal on the battlements of the wall with strict injunctions not to lie down, but to keep a tireless watch all round the walls to prevent anybody's coming up there, stooping down and leaning over to communicate with the Scythians. At sunrise the Scythians, as expected, occupied and took up their stand on the ridge adjacent to the wall of Chœrobacchi. About six thousand of them were afterwards set apart and dispersed for foraging and went as far as Decatum itself which is only some ten stades distant from the Queen of Cities ; it is from this fact, I imagine, that it got its name. The

rest of the Scythians had remained where they were. The
Emperor mounted by the wall to the parapets and carefully
inspected the plains and hills to see whether perchance a
second force was coming to join the Scythians, or whether
they were meditating the planting of ambuscades to impede
anyone who might possibly have the intention of attacking
them. However, he noticed nothing of the kind but saw
at the second hour of the day that they were not prepared
for battle but had turned their attention to food and rest.
He did not dare to engage them in a pitched battle, considering the large number they were, but was indignant at the
thought that they might ravage the whole district and actually
approach the very walls of the Queen of Cities, and that too
when he had quitted the city for the purpose of driving them
out of the country. Consequently he assembled the soldiers
and wishing to test their feelings, said, "We must not let our
courage flag by contemplating the number of Scythians,
but put our trust in God and go to battle with them, and if
only we are all of one mind, I am convinced we shall beat
them utterly." But they all refused absolutely and dissented
from his proposal. Then he aroused greater fear in them
and awoke them to a sense of danger by saying : " If the
foraging party returns and rejoins those who are here, our
peril is clear and manifest. For they will either rush this
fort and we shall be massacred, or maybe they will hold us
of no account and march up to the walls of the capital and
prevent us from re-entering the Queen-City by bivouacking
before its gates. Consequently it behoves us to take the risk
and not die like cowards. So I shall go out at once and
whoever likes can follow me for I will lead the way and dash
into the midst of the Scythians. As for you who cannot,
or will not, do this, do not venture even outside the gates."
With these words he immediately put on his armour and sallied
out by the gate opposite the marsh. After skirting the
walls and turning aside a little, he mounted the ridge from
the back. For he had realized that his men would not follow
him into a regular engagement with the Scythians. He was
the first to seize a spear and push his way into the middle
of the Scythians, and then he struck down the first man he
encountered. And the soldiers, too, who were with him
shewed themselves no less keen fighters, and the result was
that the greater number of Scythians were killed and the
rest taken prisoners. Then with his usual cunning he
clothed his soldiers in the Scythians' garments and bade them

mount the Scythian horses, whilst he entrusted their own horses and standards, and the heads of the Scythians that had been cut off to a few of the most reliable men and ordered them to get back inside the fort and await him. When he had completed these arrangements he marched down with the Scythian standards and his soldiers clad in the Scythians' dress to the river flowing past Chœrobacchi, where he judged that the Scythians would pass on their return from foraging. And the foragers seeing the men standing there, and thinking they too were Scythians, lighted upon them unguardedly and were cut to pieces or taken prisoners.

II When evening had fallen (it was a Saturday) he returned with his captives (to Chœrobacchi) and spent the next day quietly there. At daybreak on Monday he left the fort and divided his men into two parties, in front he placed the men carrying the standards of the Scythians, and behind them the Scythian captives each led by a countryman ; the heads which had been cut off he had stuck on spears and carried aloft by yet other countrymen, and in this order he bade them journey. At a moderate distance behind these he followed with his soldiers and the usual Roman standards. Now Palæologus, who was ardent in military enterprises, had started from Byzantium at dawn on Sexagesima Sunday before the others. As he was aware of the Scythians' rapidity in movement, he was not free from anxiety on his journey, so picked out a few of his accompanying retainers and ordered them to run some distance ahead and inspect the plains, valley and roads, all round, and in case any Scythians were to be seen, to return quickly and report to him. In this order then they travelled ; when the scouts saw in the plain called Dimylia the men dressed in Scythian clothing, and the Scythian standards, they ran back and reported that the Scythians were close at hand. Whereupon he immediately stood to arms. On the heels of the first messenger came a second who affirmed that, at a good distance behind those who looked like Scythians, the Roman standards and soldiers advancing at a double could be seen. These newsbringers guessed a part of the truth indeed, but were also partly wrong. For the army marching in the rear was certainly Roman both in appearance and in reality and the Emperor was in command of it ; but the one in front equipped in Scythian fashion were all members of the Roman army, but dressed in Scythian garments. In the first place, the men dressed up in the way they were by the Emperor's command,

managed as apparent Scythians utterly to deceive the real
Scythians, as I have already described ; and in the second
place, the Emperor made use of this Scythian get-up to cheat
and trick our own men, in order that whoever met these our
own soldiers first should be horror-struck, and think they
had fallen into the hands of Scythians. This would be a
soldier's joke quite free from danger, yet with a spice of fear
in it ; for before they were seriously alarmed, they would be
reassured by seeing the Emperor behind. In this way the
Emperor harmlessly scared those they met. All the men
with Palæologus were overcome with fear at what they saw,
but he himself of far greater experience than they all, and
knowing too how fertile in devices Alexius was, immediately
understood that this was such a device, and therefore regained
confidence himself, and urged the others to do so.

By this time, the whole crowd of his kinsmen and connections was rushing out from the capital, for they were
hurrying, as they thought, to overtake the Emperor according
to their agreement with him. For, as mentioned above,
they agreed to meet him after Sexagesima Sunday in Quinquagesima week. However they did not succeed in leaving the city before the Emperor re-entered it in triumph.
When they met him on arrival they would not have believed
that the Emperor alone had gained trophies and achieved a
victory so quickly, had they not seen the heads of the Scythians
fixed on the spear-heads and many others, who had escaped
the sword, with their hands bound behind their backs, being
dragged and pushed along, one after the other, as prisoners.
People were amazed at the swiftness of the campaign ; but I
heard a little tale about George Palæologus (told me by some
who were present), which was, that he complained bitterly
and blamed himself for having been too late for the battle
and not having been with the Emperor who had reaped so
much glory by his unexpected victory over the barbarians.
For he would have dearly liked to have had a share in that
meed of fame. But with regard to the Emperor one could
say that the words of the song in Deuteronomy were then
visibly accomplished, namely, ' How should one chase a
thousand and two put ten thousand to flight ? ' For at that
juncture the Emperor faced the overwhelming mass of barbarians practically single-handed, and carried through that
whole weighty war successfully right up to victory. And
were one to enquire ' Who or what were his companions ? '
and then compare the Emperor's stratagems and his versa-

tility, combined with his valour and daring with the barbarians' numbers and strength, he would only discover that the Emperor had achieved the victory alone.

III   In such manner did God on that occasion grant the ruler an astounding victory. When the Byzantines saw him enter the city, they shouted with joy for they were astonished at the swiftness, the boldness and the cleverness of the undertaking and the immediate victory, they sang pæans, they leapt, and praised God for having given them such a saviour and benefactor. But Melissenus Nicephorus was annoyed at this and took it ill—such is human nature—and said, "This victory is a fruitless joy to us and a harmless grief to them." And indeed the Scythians, who were innumerable and dispersed all over the West, continued to ravage all the provinces and none of the disasters that had befallen them checked their unbridled audacity in the slightest. Now and again they would even seize small towns in the West, nor did they spare the villages in the neighbourhood of the Queen of Cities, for they even advanced to the one called Bathys Rhyax where stands the sanctuary sacred to the memory of Theodore, greatest of all martyrs. Every day a good many people used to go there to make intercession to the saint, and on Sundays the pious journeyed to the shrine in crowds and spent all day and night there lodging round it, or in the porch, or in the back chamber of the church. But the onward rush of the Scythians prevailed to such an extent that the people who wanted to go to the martyr's church did not even dare to open the gates of Byzantium because of the Scythians' frequent incursions. These indeed were the troubles which beset the Emperor on land in the West, and even at sea matters were far from calm for him, but on the contrary very disturbed as Tzachas had acquired another fleet and was sacking the coast towns. For these reasons, the Emperor was harassed and distressed, for he was beset by troubles on every side. And then news was brought to him that Tzachas had now collected a larger fleet from the maritime districts, and devastated the islands he had previously captured, and that he had further begun to consider an attack on the western provinces, and was sending envoys to the Scythians advising them to seize the Chersonese. The mercenary troops which had come to the Emperor's aid from the East, I mean the Turks, not even these did Tzachas allow to keep their treaty with the Emperor unbroken, but coaxed them with specious promises to desert the Emperor, and come over to him, as soon as he had seized the barley-crop. The Emperor heard this and felt that his affairs on land and sea were in a very parlous condition. And an exceptionally severe winter was blocking up all the roads to such a degree that even the doors of houses could not be opened, because of the weight of snow lying against them (it happened that there had been a very heavy fall, heavier than anyone had ever seen before). Under these circumstances the Emperor did what he could by letters to collect a mercenary army from all sides. But when the sun had reached the spring solstice and the threatening war from the clouds had ceased, and the wrath of the sea was abated, he decided, as his enemies were pressing him hard on either side, that the best course would be to go down to the coast ; there he could easily resist his seafaring enemies, and at the same time conveniently fight against those who approached over land.

He immediately sent off the Cæsar Melissenus Nicephorus with orders to occupy Ænus with all possible despatch. He had previously signified to him by letters to enlist as many soldiers as possible, but not from the veterans (for those had already been distributed throughout the towns in the West to act as garrisons in the more important strongholds). He was partly to levy recruits from the Bulgarians and from the nomadic tribes (called Vlachs in popular parlance) and for the rest whatever horse- or foot-soldiers offered themselves from any country. He himself summoned from Nicomedia the five hundred Franks whom the Count of Flanders had sent, and leaving Byzantium with his kinsmen quickly reached Ænus. There he entered into a coracle, and was rowed past the town whilst he investigated the general lie of the river and its bed on either side and, when he had decided where it would be best to encamp his army, he returned. During the night he assembled the officers and explained to them the nature of the river and of the land on either side and said, " It would be well for you to cross to-morrow and carefully inspect the whole plain. And perhaps you will think the place which I will point out to you not unsuitable for pitching our camp." As they all agreed to this he was the first to cross the river at dawn, and then the whole army followed him. Then he inspected the banks of the river again with the officers, and also the surrounding plain, and shewed them the spot which pleased him. It was quite close to a small town, locally called Chœreni, whose one side was flanked by the river, and the other by a swamp.

Since the unanimous verdict of the soldiers was that this place was sufficiently protected, a trench was quickly dug and the whole army installed there. The Emperor returned to Ænus with a goodly body of light-armed troops, in order to repel the attacks of the Scythians who were advancing from that quarter.

IV When the troops entrenched at Chœreni learnt of the advances of incredibly large Scythian armies, they sent word of this to the Emperor who was still at Ænus. He at once embarked in a coracle and sailing along the coast, entered the river at its mouth and effected a junction with his entire army. As he saw that his own forces were infinitely smaller than the Scythians he fell into great perplexity and fear, for as far as man could see, he had no one to help him. Yet he did not give way or shew weakness but was lost in a welter of reflections. Four days later he saw far off in quite a different direction an army of the Comans approaching, about forty thousand strong. Accordingly he reflected that if these made common cause with the Scythians, they would begin a terrible war against him (from which no other result could be expected than utter destruction), so he judged it wise to conciliate them ; for it was he himself who had previously sent for them. Amongst a crowd of other captains in the Coman army, Togortac, Maniac and a few very valiant men stood out pre-eminent. The Emperor was afraid when he saw the multitude of approaching Comans, for knowing of old their easily-led nature, he feared that his one-time allies might become his foes and enemies, and inflict grievous harm on him. He thought it would be safer to take away the whole army and recross the river, but before doing so he determined to invite the chiefs of the Comans to a conference. They straightway came to him, Maniac himself too, though later than the others as at first he demurred. So Alexius ordered the cooks to spread a gorgeous banquet for them. When they had dined well he received them very graciously and presented them with various gifts, and then, as he was suspicious of their treacherous character, he asked them to give him an oath and hostages. They fulfilled his demands readily, and requested to be allowed to fight with the Patzinaks for three days ; and if God should give them the victory they promised to divide all the booty that accrued to them into two parts and assign one half to the Emperor. He granted them permission to pursue the Scythians, not only for three days, but for ten whole days in whatever way they liked, and gave them permission to keep the whole of the booty they took from them, if within that time God granted them the victory. However the Scythians and the Coman armies remained where they were for some time, while the Comans harassed the Scythian army by skirmishing. Before the expiration of three days Alexius summoned Antiochus (he was one of the nobles who surpassed most in energy), and ordered him to build a bridge. The bridge was quickly constructed by binding boats together with very long planks, then he called for the Protostrator Michael Ducas, his brother-in-law, and the Great Domestic Adrian, his brother, and commanded them to stand at the river's edge, and not allow the infantry and cavalry to cross all together in a confused mass, but first to separate the infantry from the cavalry, and also the baggage-waggon and the sumpter mules. When the infantry had crossed, through fear of the Scythian and Coman troops and their sly attacks, he had trenches drawn with all speed and lodged all the infantry within them; afterwards he ordered the horsemen to cross too, and he stood on the river's brink and watched them cross. Meanwhile Melissenus, acting on the written instructions he had previously received from the Emperor, collected forces from all sides; he had also requisitioned foot-soldiers from the neighbourhood and when these had loaded their own baggage and the necessary commisariat on ox-drawn wagons, he sent them off with all speed to the Emperor. When they had come within range of the human eye, the majority of those who saw them thought they were a detachment of Scythians advancing against the Emperor. One man even had the audacity to point them out with his finger to the Emperor, and insisted that they were Scythians. The latter believed what he said was true and was greatly dismayed as he could not prevail against so many. So in this difficulty he sent for Rodomerus (he was a noble of Bulgarian descent and related to the Empress, our mother, on his mother's side), and bade him go and spy out these new-comers. He quickly accomplished the Emperor's bidding, and returning told him they were men sent by Melissenus. Hereat the Emperor was overjoyed, and when they arrived shortly afterwards, he crossed the river with them, had the newly-made camp slightly enlarged and then united these men to the rest of the army. The Comans at once took possession of the camp from which the Emperor had moved to cross the river with his whole army, and took up their position near there. On

the following day the Emperor moved again intending to
seize the ford lower down the river locally called Philocalus;
but as he met a large body of Scythians he promptly attacked
them, and a vigorous engagement ensued. Many were killed
on either side during the fight, yet the Emperor gained the
victory, and thoroughly worsted the Scythians. After the
battle was concluded in this way, and the armies had retired
to their respective encampments, the Roman army remained
near the spot for the whole of the night. At sunrise on the
morrow they moved on and occupied a place called Lebunium,
which is a hill dominating a plain ; up this hill the Emperor
marched. But as there was not sufficient room on the hill
itself for the whole of the army, he had a trench made at its
foot and a camp, capable of containing the entire army, and
lodged them there. At this moment the deserter Neantzes
with a few Scythians approached the Emperor again ; when
the Emperor saw him he reproached him with his former
ingratitude and several other misdeeds, and had him and his
companions arrested and cast into irons.

V So much then for the Emperor's doings. The Scythians, on their side, kept still in their position on the banks
of the stream called ' Mavropotamos ' and made secret overtures to the Comans, inviting their alliance ; they likewise
did not cease sending envoys to the Emperor to treat about
peace. The latter had a fair idea of their double-dealings,
so gave them appropriate answers, as he wished to keep them
in suspense until the arrival of the mercenary army which he
expected from Rome. And as the Comans only received
dubious promises from the Patzinaks, they did not at all go
over to them, but sent the following communication to the
Emperor in the evening : " For how long are we to postpone
the battle ? know therefore that we shall not wait any longer,
but at sunrise we shall eat the flesh either of wolf or of lamb."
On hearing this the Emperor realized the keen spirit of the
Comans, and was no longer for delaying the fight. He felt
that the next day would be the solemn crisis of the war, and
therefore promised the Comans to do battle with the Scythians on the morrow, and then he straightway summoned
the generals and ' pentecontarchs ' and other officers and bade
them proclaim throughout the whole camp that the battle
was reserved for the morrow. But in spite of all these preparations, he still dreaded the countless hosts of Patzinaks
and Comans, fearing the two armies might coalesce.

Whilst the Emperor was busy with these reflections,

a band of hardy and war-loving mountaineers, numbering about 5,000 in all, deserted to the Emperor and offered him their services. Since the moment of battle could now no longer be postponed, the Emperor invoked the aid of God. At sunset he led the intercessory prayers for help to God, and conducted a brilliant torch-light procession, and sang appropriate hymns. Nor did he allow the army to sleep in peace, for he suggested to the more intelligent individuals that they should follow his example whereas he imposed it as an order upon the more clownish. And thus at that hour you could have seen the sun setting on the horizon, but the whole sky lit up, not as it were with the light of one sun, but as if ever so many more heavenly bodies were contributing their light. For one and all fixed lighted lamps or wax candles, whichever they had, to the tips of their spears. And verily the cries which were sent up by this army must have reached the orb of heaven, I think, or to speak quite truly, they were carried to the ears of our Lord God Himself. From this circumstance, I fancy, one can deduce the Emperor's piety seeing that he thought it wrong to attack an enemy without asking God's help. For he did not place his confidence in men or horses, or military engines, but entrusted all to the Divine decision. These intercessions were continued till midnight ; after which he allowed himself a little bodily rest and then leapt up from sleep. The light-troops he armed more strongly than usual, and some of them he supplied with cuirasses and helmets of silken material of an iron-colour, as he had not a sufficient supply of iron for all. At the first smile of dawn he same out of the gully in heavy armour, and bade them sound the attack. And beneath the hill called Lebunium (this place is . . .) he split up the army and drew up the infantry in troops. The Emperor himself stood in the fore-front breathing fierce wrath, whilst the right and left wings were commanded by George Palæologus and Constantine Dalassenus respectively. On the extreme right of the Comans stood Monastras with his men under arms. For directly they saw the Emperor drawing up his lines they too armed themselves and arranged their line of battle in their own fashion ; to the left of them stood Uzas, and looking towards the west was Hubertopulos with the Franks. When the Emperor had thus fortified the army, so to speak, with the heavy-armed troops and encircled it with squadrons of horse, he ordered the trumpets to sound the attack again. The Romans in their dread of the countless

Scythians and their horrible covered wagons which they used as walls, sent up one cry for mercy to the Lord of All and then, letting their steeds go, dashed at full speed into battle with the Scythians, the Emperor galloping in front of them all. The Roman line was crescent-shaped and at the same instant as if at a signal the whole army of the Comans rushed forward too, so a distinguished chieftain of the Scythians, foreseeing the issue of events, secured his safety in advance, and taking a few men with him went over to the Comans as they spoke the same language. For although these too were fighting fiercely against the Scythians, yet he felt more confidence in them than in the Romans, and approached them in the hope that they would act as mediators for him with the Emperor. The Emperor noticed his secession and grew alarmed lest more should go over and persuade the Comans to make common cause with the Scythians, and to turn their horses as well as their feelings against the Roman army. Consequently, as he was quick in perceiving what was expedient at a critical moment, he ordered the royal standard-bearer to carry the standard and post himself close to the Coman camp. By this time the Scythian array had been completely broken, and the two armies met in hand to hand fight, and then such slaughter of men was seen as nobody had ever witnessed before. For the Scythians were being terribly massacred as if abandoned by the Divine Power, and their opponents who cut them down grew weary of the incessant, heavy mowing with their swords, and were growing faint and relaxing the pursuit. Then the Emperor rode right in among the foe, and confounded all the ranks striking down those who stood in his way, and even overaweing those further off by his shouting. When he saw that the sun was casting its rays vertically as it was about noon, he provided for his troops as follows. He sent for some men, and dispatched them to tell the countrymen to fill their waterskins with water, lade them on their own mules and drive them along to him. When neighbours and friends saw the countrymen doing this they, too, without receiving orders, did the same, and one with a pitcher, another with a skin, and another with whatever vessel he could lay hands on, brought water to refresh the soldiers who were delivering them from the dread hand of the Scythians ; and the soldiers after drinking a little water resumed the battle. That day a new spectacle was seen, for a whole nation, not of ten thousand men only, but surpassing all number together with their wives and children was

completely wiped out. It was the third day of the week,
the twenty-ninth of April; hence the Byzantines made a
little burlesque song, " Just by one day the Scythians missed
seeing the month of May." By the time that the sun was
creeping to the West, and practically all the Scythians had
fallen to the sword, and I repeat the children and the women
too, and many also had been taken alive, the Emperor bade
them sound the recall, and returned to his camp.

These doings might well seem a miracle, especially to
a mind that reflected how not so long ago the men who
left Byzantium to fight the Scythians brought ropes and
straps with which to bind the captive Scythians they meant
to lead home, and then the tables were turned and they
themselves became the prisoners and captives of the Scythians
—this took place when we fought the Scythians near Dristra;
on that occasion God broke the insolent spirit of the Romans.
But later on, at the time I am now relating, when He saw
them full of fear and devoid of all saving hope, as not being
strong enough to prevail against such multitudes, He unexpectedly granted them victory, so that they bound and slew
and captured the Scythians, and not only this (for such things
often happen even in minor battles) but in one single day
they wiped off the face of the earth a whole nation of myriads
of men.

VI   After the Coman and Roman troops had returned to
their respective quarters, and in the early evening the Emperor
was thinking of supper, the man called Synesius came in
very angry and said to the Emperor : " What is this nonsense ?
and what is this new arrangement ? Each soldier has thirty
or more Scythian prisoners. The Comans in their masses
are quite close to us. Now if our soldiers fall asleep as most
certainly they should do, dog-tired as they are, and the
Scythians set each other free, take their daggers and kill
them, what then ? So give orders for most of them to be
put to death at once !" But the Emperor gave him a severe
look and replied, " Even though Scythians, yet they are
men ; and even though our foes, yet worthy of pity. And
I really do not know what you are thinking about to talk
such nonsense." On the other's insisting he dismissed him
angrily. Then he had a proclamation made to the army
that all arms should be taken from the Scythians and deposited
in one place, and that the soldiers should carefully guard their
prisoners. After issuing these orders, he spent the rest of the
night free from anxiety. But during the middle watch of

the night, either by Divine guidance, or for some other unknown reason, certain it is that as if by one accord the soldiers
killed nearly all of them. When the Emperor was told this
in the early morning he at once suspected Synesius, and
therefore had him called directly. After blaming him severely,
he threatened him saying, " This is your work." In spite
of the other's protestations that he knew nothing about it,
he ordered him to be arrested and kept in chains, saying,
" Thus you will learn what an evil mere chains are, and not
to make decisions of this kind against men again." Perhaps
he would have had him scourged too, had not the highest
noblemen, the relations and connections of the Emperor,
united in appealing to him on behalf of Synesius.

Most of the Comans were afraid that the Emperor was
meditating some dreadful stroke against them by night,
because they had taken all the booty, so they went away by
night, taking the road leading to the Danube. To escape
from the stench of the corpses, the Emperor marched away
from his camp at daybreak, and reached another called
' Kala Dendra ' about eighteen stades distant from Chœreni.
On the march thither Melissenus met him. He had been
unable to come in time for the battle, as he had been busy
preparing that crowd of recruits to send to the Emperor.
They naturally embraced and congratulated each other,
and for the rest of the journey spoke about the events connected with the defeat of the Scythians. On arrival at
Kala Dendra, the Emperor heard of the Comans' flight :
thereupon he had all the goods which he had assigned to
them according to their agreement loaded on mules, and sent
them off after them, bidding the drivers make all speed to
overtake them even beyond the Danube, if they could,
and hand over to them what he sent. For throughout his
life he considered it a sin not only to tell a falsehood, but
even to appear to have done so, and he frequently would
discourse at length to all about falseness. This is sufficient
about the fugitives ; as for all the other Comans who followed
him, he saw to it that they feasted royally for the rest of the
day. He judged it wiser not to give these soldiers the reward
due to them on that day, but to let them first sleep off the
effects of the wine they had drunk, so that when they had
regained their clarity of mind, they would appreciate the
gift. On the following day he assembled them all and gave
them not only as much as he had promised beforehand, but
a great deal more. Now when he wanted to dismiss them to

their homes he reflected that they might wander about and turn to plundering on their way and inflict no little harm on the country-towns along the road, so he took hostages from them. They in their turn requested him to give them safe conduct, so he gave them Joannaces (a man of exceptional bravery and prudence) and entrusted him with the care and safe conveyance of the Comans as far as the Zygum.

Thus the Emperor's affairs prospered, thanks entirely to Divine providence. After he had fully settled everything he returned to Byzantium as a ' conquering hero ' in the course of the month of May.

I must now conclude my narrative of the Scythian wars although I have only related a few incidents out of a great number, and have only touched the Adriatic sea with the tip of my finger. But as for the Emperor's brilliant victories, the various defeats he inflicted on his enemies, his individual acts of bravery, the intervening events, and how he adapted himself to all circumstances, and by divers expedients resolved the difficulties that befell him—to relate all this explicitly not even a second Demosthenes would have had the power, nor the whole band of orators, nor even the whole Academy if it combined with the Stoa to celebrate the exploits of Alexius as a subject of prime importance.

VII   Only a few days had elapsed since the Emperor's return to the palace when Ariebes the Armenian and the Frank Hubertopoulos (two noblemen and devotees of Mars) were detected in a plot against the Emperor, in which they had involved a fair number of others. Witnesses came forward and the truth was openly stated. When the conspirators stood condemned, they were punished by confiscation of their property and banishment, as the Emperor remitted the penalty of death, which was prescribed by law.

The Emperor now heard a rumour of an invasion by the Comans, and learnt from another quarter that Bodinus and his Dalmatians had broken the truce and were contemplating an incursion into our territory ; he was divided in mind as to which adversary he should turn his attention first. He decided to proceed against the Dalmatians first, and to anticipate them in occupying, and, as far as practicable, in protecting the valleys lying between their confines and our own. Accordingly he convoked his council and imparted his ideas to them, and as they all approved he left the capital for the purpose of taking charge of affairs in the West. He soon reached Philippopolis where letters were handed to him from the

archbishop of Bulgaria, who wrote about the Duke of Dyrrachium, John, the Sebastocrator's son, as he felt convinced
the latter was hatching rebellion. For a whole day and night
the Emperor was sunk in despondency, at one minute wanting
to adjourn the investigation of the matter because of John's
father, at another fearing lest report spoke true and that, as
John was still a stripling, and at an age when he knew
impulses are uncontrolled, he might start a rebellion and
become the source of intolerable grief both to his father and
uncle. Finally, he concluded that he must in some way
contrive to frustrate his design. For he was exceedingly
attached to the young man. He accordingly summoned the
man who was then Æteriarch'[1] Argyrus Caratzas, who,
though a Scythian, combined great prudence with a love of
virtue and truth, and handed him two letters. The one
addressed to John was conceived in the following terms:
" Our Majesty being informed of the descent of the barbarians
against us through the mountain-passes, has travelled hither
from the city of Constantine to secure the frontiers of the
Roman Empire. Hence we naturally desire your presence
that we may give you instructions with regard to the realm
over which you rule. (I am also somewhat suspicious of
Bolcanus, for he may be hatching some treacherous scheme
against us.)   Further, we wish you to give us a report on the
state of Dalmatia and also to certify whether Bolcanus has
observed the terms of the truce (for most unsatisfactory
rumours about him are brought to us daily).   We shall be
better able to resist his machinations after we have received
reliable information from you ; then we intend to send you to
Illyria after giving you the necessary directions in order that
by attacking the enemy on both sides we may, with God's
help, gain the victory."   This was the tenor of his letter to
John. The other addressed to the leading men in Dyrrachium, ran as follows : " As we were informed that Bolcanus
was once again meditating treachery against us, we have
issued from Byzantium partly to ensure the safety of the
valleys, which lie in the debatable land between our country
and the Dalmatians, and partly too to sift this matter of
Bolcanus and the Dalmatians to the bottom. For this
purpose we deemed it wise to summon hither your Duke, Our
Majesty's dearly beloved nephew, and in his place we send
the man who will hand you this letter, and whom we have
created Duke. Therefore do ye receive him and yield him

[1] (or Heteriarch) = the captain of the foreign guard.

obedience in whatsoever he may command." When he
handed these letter to Caratzas he enjoined him to deliver
the one to John first. Then if John willingly obeyed the orders
in it, he should send him forth in peace, and undertake the
government of the district himself until such time as John
returned. But if John proved recalcitrant or refused to obey,
he was to assemble the leading men of Dyrrachium and read
them the second letter with the object of gaining their help
in arresting John.

VIII Directly the Sebastocrator who was in Constantinople got ear of this, he started off in great haste and reached
Philippopolis in two days and nights. The Emperor was
asleep so he crept noiselessly into the imperial tent and
signifying with his hand to the attendants to keep quiet, he lay
down on the second bed in his brother's tent, and fell asleep
himself. When the Emperor woke up and quite unexpectedly
beheld his brother, he kept quiet for some time and bade the
persons present do the same. When in his turn the Sebastocrator awoke and saw his brother, the Emperor, awake, and
the latter saw him, they arose and embraced each other.
Afterwards the Emperor began to enquire what had brought
him and why in the world he had come. To this the other
replied, " For your sake," and the Emperor retorted, " You
have tired yourself in vain by journeying such a distance so
quickly." To this the Sebastocrator did not reply at the time,
for he was lost in conjectures about the news which would
be brought him by the messenger he had sent on ahead to
Dyrrachium. For the instant the rumours about his son had
come to his ears, he scribbled two words to him, and ordered
him to resort to the Emperor with all speed. He told him too
that he himself was leaving Byzantium and hurrying to
Philippopolis for the express purpose of confuting the state-
ments made to the Emperor about him by putting before his
brother, the Emperor, all likely considerations ; and concluded
by saying he would await his arrival there. The Sebastocrator took leave of the Emperor and went to the tent assigned
to him. And almost immediately the letter-carrier he had
sent to John came running in saying he had returned and
John was on the way. By this news the Sebastocrator was
relieved of his suspicions and regained his former confidence,
but was filled with anger against the persons who had been
the first to denounce his son. Thus disturbed in mind he
went to the Emperor and the latter looked at him and at
once guessed the reason of his disturbance, yet asked him

P

how he felt. And his brother answered, " Badly, and that because of you." For he had not learnt entirely to control his anger when it howled around his heart, and was easily upset sometimes by a mere word. And he added a further remark saying, " I am not so much incensed against your Majesty as against this man " (pointing to Adrian) " who spreads calumnies." To these words that gentle, sweet-tempered Emperor made no answer at all, for he knew how to assuage his brother's boiling rage.

So they both sat down together with the Cæsar Melissenus Nicephorus and a few more of their relations and talked privately to one another concerning the rumours current about John. But when the Sebastocrator observed that Melissenus and his own brother Adrian were indirectly calumniating his son, he was unable to restrain his wrath which was bubbling up again, and darting a fierce look at Adrian he threatened to pull off his beard and to teach him not to try to rob the Emperor of his relations by openly telling lies about them.

Upon this John arrived and was immediately conducted into the imperial tent and heard all the accusations made against him. However, he was not exactly subjected to a cross-examination, but the defendant stood at liberty while the Emperor said to him, " Out of consideration for your father who is also my brother, I cannot bear even to hear mentioned the accusations levelled against you. So go and be free from care as you were before." All this was said inside the imperial tent, with no stranger present, only a few relations. Thus the whole affair which had either been falsely reported or perhaps really planned was hushed up. The Emperor then summoned his own brother, I mean the Sebastocrator Isaac, and his son John, and after a long conversation with them, concluded by saying to the Sebasto-crator, " You go back in peace to the capital to give our mother all the news. As for him," he said, pointing to John, " I am sending him back again to Dyrrachium, as you see, to give his careful attention to the administration of his province." In this manner they parted, and the next day the one took the road to Byzantium and the other was sent to Dyrrachium.

IX   Up to this time the imperial throne was by no means safe. When Theodore Gabras was living in Constantinople, the Emperor who had remarked his violent and energetic nature, wished to remove him from the city and therefore

appointed him Duke of Trapezus,[1] a town he had some time
ago recaptured from the Turks. This man had come
originally from Chaldæa and the upper parts, and gained
glory as a soldier, for he surpassed others in wisdom and
courage, and had practically never failed in any work he took
in hand, but invariably got the better of his enemies ; and
finally after he had captured Trapezus and allotted it to himself, as if it were his special portion, he was irresistible. This
man's son, Gregory, the Sebastocrator, Isaac Comnenus,
affianced to one of his daughters, but as both the children
were under marriageable age, matters only proceeded as far
as a betrothal. After handing over his son Gregory to the
Sebastocrator on condition that, when the children reached
the legal age, the marriage should be celebrated, Gabras took
leave of the Emperor and returned to his own country.
Shortly afterwards his wife paid the debt we all must pay,
and he took to himself a second wife, a high-born woman of
the Alani. Now it happened that the Sebastocrator's wife and
the wife Gabras married, were the daughters of two sisters ;
when this became known, the betrothal of the two children was
broken off as their marriage was forbidden both by the civil
and the ecclesiastical laws. The Emperor, however, who
knew the kind of soldier Gabras was, and the amount of
disturbance he would be capable of creating, did not wish
Gabras' son Gregory to return to his father when the betrothal
was broken off, but desired to retain him in the capital for
two reasons. The one was to hold him as a sort of hostage,
and the second was to win Gabras' affection ; with the idea
that if the latter had been meditating any evil deed, he would
now abstain. He intended to marry Gregory to one of my
sisters ; and for this reason kept postponing the boy's departure. But Gabras came up to the capital again, and as
he had no inkling of the Emperor's intentions, he was planning
to take his son back with him secretly. In the meantime he
kept silent about his plans, although the Emperor did hint
at and indirectly signify to him what he had in mind. But
Gabras perhaps did not understand or owing to the late rupture
of the other engagement he did not care ; however it was, he
asked the Emperor that his son should be allowed to return
with him, and this demand the Emperor refused. Then
Gabras pretended to be quite willing to let him stay and to
leave all plans for the boy to the Emperor. After he had
bidden the Emperor farewell, and was on the point of departure

[1] = Trebizond.

from Byzantium, he was hospitably entertained by the
Sebastocrator close to the chapel built to the memory of the
great martyr Phocas, in the very pretty suburb situated on
the Propontis—this was because of their close connexion
through marriage and their resultant intimacy. After a
very lavish banquet there, the Sebastocrator returned to
Byzantium and Gabras begged to be allowed to keep his
son with him for the next day at least, and to this the other
assented willingly. But when the next day came, and
Gabras (whom I have mentioned so often) ought to have
separated from his son, he asked the tutors to accompany him
as far as Sosthenium, where he intended to pitch his camp.
They agreed and went on with him ; but when the time came
for moving on from there he again asked the tutors the same
thing, whether his son could not accompany him as far as
Pharus ; but they refused. Then he pleaded a father's
affection, and his long absence, and by a string of similar
pleas, he overcame their resolutions, and they let themselves
be over-persuaded and accompanied him. When he reached
Pharus, he revealed his hidden intention, for he seized the boy,
embarked him on a merchant-vessel and entrusted himself
and his son to the waves of the Euxine. On receipt of this
news the Emperor sent off swift ships after him with all
possible expedition, and commanded the captains to hand
Gabras the letters he gave them for him and to bring back
the boy without loss of time with his father's consent, or if
he refused, to inform him that the Emperor would thenceforth count him as an enemy. They departed and overtook
Gabras beyond the town of Æginus, near a town locally called
Carambis. They handed him the Emperor's letter in which
the Emperor stated that he hoped to marry the boy to one
of my sisters, and after a long talk with him, they persuaded
him to send his son back. On his return the Emperor only
ratified the marriage-contract by the usual legal formalities
and gave him into the charge of one of the Empress' attendants,
the eunuch Michael, and as the lad lived in the palace he
bestowed a great deal of care on him, tried to amend his
manners and had him thoroughly trained in all military
exercises. But like most young men, he did not relish having
to obey, and was vexed at not being treated, as he thought,
with sufficient respect. In addition to this he disliked his
tutor and began to consider how he could escape to his own
father, when he ought rather to have been grateful for all
the attention bestowed on him. He did not stop at merely

meditating flight, but tried to put it into execution. Consequently he revealed his secret to a few ; these were George, the son of Decanus, Eustathius Camytzes and the cupbearer Michael, generally called 'Pincerna' by the imperial household. These were all warriors and among the Emperor's close intimates, one of them, Michael, went to the Emperor and acquainted him with the whole matter ; but the latter could not believe it and refused to listen.

When (Gregory) Gabras began to insist and wanted to hurry on his flight, those loyal to the Emperor said " Unless you will guarantee your plot to us by an oath, we will not accompany you." As he assented to this, they showed him where the sacred " nail " was kept with which the lawless soldiers pierced my Saviour's side, and advised him to steal it and bring it out so that he could swear by Him who was pierced by it. Gabras listened to this advice, entered (the church) and secretly abstracted the sacred nail. Then one of the men who had already notified the Emperor of the conspiracy, came running in and said, " Look, here is Gabras, and the sacred nail is in his bosom." Thereupon Gabras was immediately brought in at the Emperor's bidding, and the nail was taken out of his bosom. On being questioned he admitted everything without hesitation, also revealed the names of his fellow-conspirators and the whole scheme. The Emperor found him guilty and sent him to the Duke of Philippopolis, George Mesopotamites, to keep him prisoner in the citadel. George, the son of Decanus, he dispatched with letters to Leo Nicerita who was at that time Duke of the districts round the Danube, ostensibly to help him in guarding the district, but really for Nicerita to keep him prisoner there. As for Eustathius, son of Camytzes, and the rest, he banished and imprisoned them.

BOOK IX

I

IN this wise the Emperor settled the affairs of John and Gregory Gabras; then he started from Philippopolis and visited the valleys lying between Dalmatia and our territory. He traversed the whole narrow mountain ridge of what is locally called the " Zygum," but not on horseback (for the nature of the ground did not allow of this as it was rugged and full of gullies and here and there thickly wooded and almost impassable). So he made his way on foot all along and examined everything with his own eyes; in order that no unguarded corner, through which the enemy could easily force an entrance, should escape notice. In some places he had trenches dug; and in others towers erected made of wood; also wherever the site permitted he ordered small forts to be constructed of bricks or stone while he himself measured out the distance between them, and their size; in some spots too he had exceedingly tall trees felled at the root and laid across the path. After having thus fully blocked the enemy's means of ingress, he returned to the capital. Now all this planning probably sounds but a slight thing when told like this, but many of the Emperor's companions on that occasion are still alive and testify to the hard work and fatigue that journey caused him.

A short time afterwards very accurate information about the doings of Tzachas was brought to him, which was that none of his defeats by land and sea had caused him to abandon his former hope, but that he had adopted the insignia of an Emperor, styled himself Emperor, inhabited Smyrna as if it were his palace, and was now equipping a fleet with which to devastate the islands again and push on to Byzantium, and if anyhow possible, to have himself exalted to the imperial eminence. As these tidings received confirmation daily, the Emperor recognized that he must not lose heart nor show cowardice in face of them, but push on his preparations during what remained of the summer and the ensuing winter,

and then in the following spring start a vigorous campaign
against him and endeavour by all possible means to dash to
pieces all that man's dreams, plans, hopes and enterprises,
and to drive him out of Smyrna as well, and rescue from his
power all the places he had already seized. Accordingly
when the winter was already far spent and spring with its
smiles was near, he sent to Epidamnus for his brother-in-law,
John Ducas, and appointed him 'Great Duke' of the Fleet.
He gave him a picked army of landsmen and ordered him to
make the journey against Tzachas by land, and to entrust
Constantine Dalassenus with the command of the fleet with
orders to sail along the coast so that they might arrive at
Mitylene at the same time, and start the war with Tzachas
conjointly by land and sea. When Ducas reached Mitylene
he at once had wooden towers built, and then, using that
town as a base of operations, he began a vigorous campaign
against the barbarians. Now Tzachas had left his brother
Galabatzes in command of the garrison at Mitylene and,
knowing that the latter had insufficient troops for fighting
against such a famous warrior, he hastened back thither,
formed a plan of operations and opened battle with Ducas.
While the battle was at its height night put an end to it.

From that day on throughout three of the moon's revolutions Ducas never failed to attack the walls of Mitylene
daily nor to engage Tzachas in brilliant conflicts from the
rising of the sun to its setting. And yet Ducas gained no
advantage from his continual toil. The Emperor grew
impatient and annoyed at the news. One day he questioned
a soldier who was on leave from the front and found out that
Ducas did nothing but fight and fight. Then he asked at
what hour of the day they commenced battle with Tzachas ;
the soldier replied, "Directly after sunrise." The Emperor
next enquired, "Which of the two armies faces the East ? "
and the soldier answered, "Ours." From that he understood
the reason, for he often found the clue in some unconsidered
trifle. So he drew up a letter for Ducas advising him to
refrain from battle with Tzachas at dawn, and not to fight
one against two, i.e. against the sun's rays as well as against
Tzachas himself ; but to attack his adversaries when the sun
had passed the meridian and was inclining towards the West.
He handed the letter to the soldier with many recommend-
ations about it, and finally said emphatically, "If you attack
your adversaries when the sun has turned, you will at once
be the victors." The soldier reported everything to Ducas

and as the latter never disregarded the Emperor's advice even in the smallest matter, the next day when the barbarians as usual drew up their lines, none of their opponents appeared. For the Roman troops were remaining quietly in camp according to the Emperor's suggestion, so the barbarians gave up hope of any battle that day, and laid down their arms and stayed where they were. But Ducas was not idle ; when the sun reached the meridian, he and the whole army got under arms. As soon as the sun began to turn, he formed up his lines and with war-cries and tremendous shouting rushed upon the barbarians. However Tzachas was not found unprepared for he quickly had his men fully armed and joined battle with the Roman lines. A very strong wind was blowing at the time and when the battle became very close the dust was whirled in clouds right up to heaven. And thus, firstly because they had the sun shining in their faces, and secondly because the wind somewhat obscured their sight owing to the dust, and also because the Romans drove on the attack more vigorously than ever, the barbarians were utterly discomfited and fled. After this battle Tzachas felt he could not endure the siege any longer and was too weak for continuous fighting, and therefore sued for peace, making only one stipulation that he should be allowed to sail to Smyrna unmolested. Ducas agreed to this, and retained two of the chief satraps as hostages ; whereupon the other asked Ducas for hostages, and on condition that Tzachas on his side would not do injury to any of the Mityleneans before leaving, nor carry any of them away with him on his voyage to Smyrna, and that Ducas on his side would guarantee him a safe voyage to Smyrna, Ducas gave him Alexander Euphorbenus and Manuel Butumites ; both fond of war, and brave men. After giving mutual assurances, the one felt relieved because Tzachas would not injure the Mityleneans before leaving and the other because he would not suffer ill-usage from the Roman fleet on his journey. But ' the crab never learns to walk straight,' no more did Tzachas depart from his former villainy, for he attempted to carry off all the Mityleneans together with their wives and children. While he was arranging this, Constantine Dalassenus, now ' Thalassocrator,' who had up till then not arrived as Ducas had ordered, brought his ships to anchor near a promontory and when he heard what was going on, he went and asked Ducas for permission to engage in battle with Tzachas. But Ducas, respecting his recently pledged word, demurred for a while. However, Dalassenus insisted saying, " You gave an oath but I was not present, so do you keep your promises unbroken, but as I neither swore nor was present and know nothing of what you two arranged between you, I shall now strip myself for combat against Tzachas." So when Tzachas weighed anchor, and without delay sailed straight for Smyrna, Dalassenus overtook him very quickly, and at once attacked and chased him, Ducas too managed to capture the rest of Tzachas' fleet as it was raising anchor, and thus secured the ships and rescued from the barbarians all the prisoners of war and other captives in them. Dalassenus took a number of Tzachas' pirate-vessels, and had everybody in them, rowers and all, put to death. And probably Tzachas himself would have been captured too, had he not with native shrewdness foreseen what was coming and boarded one of the lighter boats, and thus, unsuspected and unseen, got safely away. He had imagined something of this kind might happen to him, and had therefore arranged beforehand for some Turks to stand on a certain headland and watch until he either reached Smyrna safely or, if he fell in with the enemy, steered his ship towards them as toward a safe refuge. Nor did he fail in his object for he anchored his ship there, joined the Turks who were waiting for him, and made for Smyrna. And in very truth he reached it. Dalassenus returned victorious and joined the Great Duke. After securing Mitylene and seeing that Dalassenus was also returning (home), Ducas dispatched the greater part of the Roman fleet to free the islands still held by Tzachas (for he had previously brought a large number into subjection). Then he took Samos and a few other islands off-hand, and afterwards returned to the capital.

II Within a few days, the Emperor heard that Caryces had rebelled and seized Crete, and Rhapsomates Cyprus, so he dispatched John Ducas against them with a large fleet. When the Cretans learnt that Ducas had reached Carpathus, which they knew was not far off, they attacked Caryces, murdered him cruelly and then surrendered Crete to the Great Duke. Ducas organized the administration of the island and left an adequate garrison for its protection, and then sailed down to Cyprus. As soon as he had run his ships ashore, he took Cyrene at first assault, and Rhapsomates informed of this, made great preparations to oppose him. Consequently he left Levcosia, occupied the heights behind Cyrene and fixed his palisades there, but refused battle, for he was ignorant of war and unversed in generalship. For the right thing would have been to fall upon the Romans whilst they were unprepared. But Rhapsomates put off the battle for some time, not really for the purpose of preparing for the clash of arms as if he were not ready (on the contrary he was well prepared and could have engaged in battle at once, had he wished) ; but he acted like one who did not wish to risk an engagement at any time, but had taken up war as children do at play and went about it softly, he kept sending envoys to the Romans as if expecting to entice them over by honeyed words. And I fancy he did this through his ignorance of warfare. (For I have been told that he had only recently handled spear and sword and did not even know how to mount a horse and if by chance he mounted and wanted to ride, he was seized with fright and dizziness, so utterly inexperienced was Rhapsomates in military experience.) It was either for this reason or because the sudden advent of the imperial troops had overwhelmed him, that his mind was in this state of uncertainty. Consequently when he did hazard an engagement, with a kind of despondency, the result did not turn out well for him. For Butumites had won over some of the deserters from Rhapsomates' army and enlisted them in his own. A few days later Rhapsomates drew up his troops and offered battle marching slowly down the steep hillside. When the armies were only a short distance apart, a portion of Rhapsomates' army, numbering about one hundred, detached itself and galloped at full speed to attack Ducas apparently, but they turned the tips of their spears backwards and went over to him. On seeing this Rhapsomates at once turned tail and slacking his reins fled toward Nemesus, hoping to reach that town and find a vessel which would convey him to Syria and to safety. But Manuel Butumites was following fast behind him. So hard pressed by him and foiled in his hope, he reached the mountain on the other side and sought refuge in the church, built of old, to the name of the Holy Cross. Then Butumites (to whom Ducas had assigned this pursuit) captured him there, promised him his life and took him back with him to the Great Duke. Afterwards they all moved on to Levcosia and after receiving the submission of the whole island, they secured it as far as their means permitted and sent a full account of all these doings to the Emperor by letter. The Emperor appreciated their efforts and decided he must take steps to secure Cyprus. For this reason he nominated

Calliparius as judge and assessor; he was (not) one of the nobles, but had a high reputation for just dealing and incorruptibility, combined with modesty. The island also needed a military governor, so he appointed Philocales Eumathius as Stratopedarch, assigning the protection of it to him, and gave him ships of war and cavalry with which to guard Cyprus, both by land and sea. Butumites conducted Rhapsomates and the other ' Immortals ' who had joined him in rebellion and returned with them to Ducas, and thus made his way to the capital.

III Such were the events which took place in the islands, I mean Cyprus and Crete.

Tzachas, however, was too fond of war, and too energetic to be able to keep quiet, and therefore attacked Smyrna after a short interval and took possession of it. And once again he began carefully to equip pirate-ships, 'dromons,' biremes and triremes, and other kinds of lighter vessels, still in pursuit of his former aim. On being informed of this the Emperor did not delay or hesitate, but determined to defeat him utterly by land and sea. So he elected Constantine Dalassenus ' Thalassocrator ' and sent him on this occasion with the whole fleet to oppose Tzachas. He also thought it would be useful to rouse the Sultan to anger against him ; and his letter to the latter ran as follows : " Most glorious Sultan Clitziasthlan, you know that the rank of Sultan is yours by heredity. Now your kinsman by marriage, Tzachas, is preparing war to all seeming against the Roman Empire, and calls himself Emperor, but this is only a transparent pretence. For he is too worldly wise and well informed not to see that the Roman Empire is not for him, and that it would be impossible for him ever to grasp its sceptre. His whole mischievous device is really planned against you. It is your duty therefore not to bear with him, and not be dilatory, but rather to wake up if you do not wish to be deprived of your kingdom. I for my part will, with God's help, drive him out of the countries under the Roman jurisdiction, and in my affection for you, I adjure you, on your side, to take thought for your kingdom and power, and bring that man into subjection, either by peaceful methods, or, if he rejects those, then by the sword." Whilst these preparations were made by the Emperor, Tzachas travelled to Abydos with his troops overland and besieged it with engines and various stone-throwing machines. He had not got his pirate-ships with him for they were not yet fully equipped. Dalassenus, a man ever keen for adventure and full of courage, kept along the road leading to Abydos with his troops.

Directly the Sultan, Clitziasthlan, received the news sent him by the Emperor, he at once set to work, and started on the road to Tzachas with his whole army. For such are all the barbarians ever ready for massacre and war. As the Sultan drew nigh, Tzachas felt very helpless, for he saw foes advancing against him by land and sea, whereas he had not a boat anywhere, for the ships he was building were not yet fitted out, and his forces were insufficient for fighting both against a Roman army and that of his kinsman, the Sultan Clitziasthlan. He was also afraid of the inhabitants and garrison of Abydos, and therefore judged it wise to interview the Sultan, not knowing of the intrigue started against him by the Emperor. The Sultan on beholding him shewed him a cheerful countenance and received him graciously and had a table set before him according to custom, supped with him and obliged Tzachas to drink somewhat too hard. When he saw that the latter was full of wine, he drew his sword and drove it into his side. Thus Tzachas fell dead where he sat ; and the Sultan sent an embassy to the Emperor to arrange peace for the future. And he did not fail to secure his aim. The Emperor consented to his request and, after the terms of peace had been completed in the customary manner, calm was restored in all the maritime provinces.

IV The Emperor had scarcely been relieved of these anxieties, and had not cleared off all the ill-effects caused by Tzachas (for though he was not always present in person, yet he participated and co-operated in all the arrangements and difficulties), before he was hurried into another war.

For now Bolcanus (who ruled over the whole of Dalmatia, and was active in speech and in deed) marched out of his own borders and proceeded to devastate the towns and lands around and actually seized Lipenium itself, set fire to it and burned it down—this was when the sun had twice completed its circuit since the destruction of the Scythians. On receipt of these tidings the Emperor thought them unbearable, so gathered together a considerable army and marched to meet the Serbians along the direct road to Lipenium (this is a small fort lying at the foot of the Zygum, which separates Dalmatia from our territory). He wished if possible to encounter Bolcanus and engage him in a pitched battle and afterwards, if God granted him victory, to rebuild Lipenium and the other forts and restore things to their former state.

But Bolcanus, hearing of the Emperor's advent, moved away from there and occupied Sphentzanium, which is a fort situated above the Zygum, just mentioned, in the borderland between the Roman boundaries and Dalmatia. However, when the Emperor had occupied Scopia, Bolcanus sent envoys with overtures of peace, and absolved himself from all blame for the evil happenings, but laid it all on the Roman satraps by saying, " They are never willing to remain within their own frontiers, but have made frequent inroads which have entailed a great deal of loss on Serbia. I myself will never do anything of the kind again, but will return to my country, send hostages from among my own kinsmen to your Majesty, and not overstep my boundaries again." To this the Emperor agreed, and leaving behind him men appointed to rebuild the ruined towns and receive the hostages, packed up for his return to the capital.

However, Bolcanus when asked for the hostages did not produce them but put the matter off from day to day, and before a full year had passed, he had again marched out to ravage the Roman territory. And, although he received several letters from the Emperor reminding him of the treaty and the promises he had previously made him, he refused even then to fulfil them. Consequently the Emperor summoned John, the son of his brother, the Sebastocrator, and sent him forth against Bolcanus with a large force. Now John, being ignorant of war and lusting for battle, like all young men, started, and after crossing the river of Lipenium pitched his palisades by the foothills of the Zygum, directly opposite Sphentzanium. His movements were not unnoticed by Bolcanus, who again sent to sue for peace, and promised that he would both give the hostages and also keep absolute peace with the Romans from that time forth. These, however, were only empty promises, in secret he was getting ready to attack John. When Bolcanus actually took the road against John, a monk ran ahead and revealed his design to John and assured him that Bolcanus was already close by. But John dismissed him in anger, calling him a liar and deceiver ; however facts quickly proved the truth of his words. For Bolcanus fell upon him in the night, killing many of his soldiers in their tents, and others, fleeing as best they could, were caught in the eddies of the downward rushing river and drowned. Those of more stable character meanwhile posted themselves round John's tent, and with great difficulty saved it by courageous fighting on the spot.

In this way the greater part of the Roman army perished. Bolcanus collected his own men and retired and took up his position on the Zygum at Sphentzanium. John's men were so few when compared with their foes that they could not possibly fight them, and therefore counselled him to recross the river. They did this and reached Lipenium, about twelve stades further on. As he had lost most of his men, and could no longer offer any resistance, John made his way to the capital. Thereupon Bolcanus grew bold, as no opponent was left, and devastated the surrounding lands and towns ; laid the country outside Scopia in ruins and even burnt some of it. As if this was not enough, he even seized Polobus, and proceeding to Branea laid that all waste, carried off a tremendous amount of plunder from it and then returned to his own country.

V These tidings were too bad to be borne by the Emperor, who at once armed himself again, and certainly required no urging, not even from the flute-player Timotheus, for whose Orthian march Alexander waited. The Emperor, I say, armed himself and called to arms all the soldiers who were in the capital, and took in haste the road leading straight to Dalmatia. He wished to rebuild the forts which had just been ruined, to put matters on their former footing and to exact abundant retribution from Bolcanus for the evil he had done. So he started from the capital, reached Daphnutium (an old town about forty stades distant from Constantinople), and there halted waiting for those of his kinsmen who had not yet arrived. The next day Diogenes Nicephorus came, full of anger and haughtiness ; but, as usual, he wore a mask, and had put on, as one might say, a fox-skin, for he assumed a cheerful countenance and pretended to be behaving frankly with the Emperor. And his tent he did not have pitched at the usual distance from the Emperor's sleeping-tent, but close to the slope leading to the Emperor's. Now Manuel Philocales noticed this, for none of Diogenes' schemings ever escaped him, and as if struck by lightning he stood there all shrivelled up. He collected his wits with difficulty, at once went in to the Emperor and said, " This act does not seem free from suspicion to me, and I am oppressed by the fear that an attempt will be made on your Majesty's life at night. I will make some excuse or other, and arrange to make him move from that spot." But the Emperor with his habitual imperturbability refused to allow Philocales to do this, and when the latter continued to urge him, he said, " Let it be,

we must not let the man have any grievance against us. If
he is plotting against us, he must be proved guilty in the
sight of God and men." Philocales went away distressed,
beating his hands together and calling the Emperor rash.
A few hours passed and the Emperor was sleeping peacefully
at the Empress' side, when about the middle watch of the
night Diogenes got up, placed his sword under his arm,
stepped to the threshold (of the Emperor's tent) and stood
there. For while the Emperor slept, the doors were not
bolted nor did a guard keep watch outside—so much for the
Emperor's habits. On his side Nicephorus was at that
moment checked in his undertaking by some divine power.
For he saw a maid fanning their Majesties to drive away the
mosquitoes from their faces, and ' was seized with a sudden
tremor in all his limbs, while pallor overspread his cheeks,'
as the poet says, and he suspended the murder till another
day. This man continued plotting the Emperor's death
without disguise, while the latter was fully aware of what
Diogenes had plotted against him for in the morning the maid
came to him and related the whole occurrence. Consequently
he moved on from that place the next day, and began the
journey before him, all the time pretending to know nothing,
but so arranging matters about Nicephorus, that, whilst he
was on his guard himself, he yet did not give the other any
reasonable occasion [for complaint].

When they came into the region of Serres, Constantine
Ducas Porphyrogenitus, who was accompanying the Emperor,
begged him to come and be his guest at his estate, which was
very delightful and well-watered by cool, drinkable springs,
and had sufficient rooms for the Emperor's reception (its
name was Pentegostis). The Emperor yielded to his wish
and went and stayed with him. But when he wanted to
leave next morning the Porphyrogenitus would not allow it,
but besought him to wait a little longer until he had recovered
from the fatigue of the journey and cleansed his body of dust
by bathing. For he had already made preparations for a
great banquet ; so the Emperor again gave way to the
Porphyrogenitus. Diogenes Nicephorus with his old aspira-
tions after sovereignty heard that the Emperor had bathed
and left the bathroom, and as he was ever watching for an
opportunity to assassinate him, he girt on his short sword
and went into the house as if returning from the chase as
usual. However, Taticius, who had long known of his
intentions, saw him and pushed him out with the reprimand,

" Why do you come in here in this disorderly fashion and wearing your sword ? this is the hour for bathing, not for a journey, or the chase or a battle." So the other retired foiled in his purpose. But apprehending that he was already detected (for our conscience tries us severely), he considered how to ensure his own safety by flight, and escape to the Empress Maria's properties in Christopolis, either to Pernicus or Petritzus, and then to re-arrange his life carefully according to circumstances. For before this the Princess Maria had interested herself in him because on the mother's side he was the brother of her husband, Michael Ducas, the former Emperor, although they had had different fathers. The Emperor departed from Constantine's house on the third day, and left him behind there to rest as he was afraid for the delicate and inexperienced youth who had on this occasion left his own country for the first time to take part in an expedition ; besides this he was the only son of his mother. And in his great concern for the youth the Emperor allowed him to enjoy an easy life with his Queen-Mother, at the same time he loved him exceedingly just as if he were his own child.

VI To prevent my history growing confused, I will relate the story of Diogenes Nicephorus from the beginning. The manner in which his father, Romanus, was raised to the imperial dignity and how he came to his end, has already been treated of by several historians, and those who wish can glean all about him from those books. In any case he died when his sons Leo and Nicephorus were still children ; and from the beginning of his own reign, Alexius took them over as private persons instead of princes (for at his accession to the throne Michael, although he was their own brother, had taken away their red sandals and their diadem and condemned them to banishment in the monastery Cyperoudes with their mother, the Empress Eudocia). Alexius deemed the young men worthy of much consideration, partly because he pitied them for their misfortunes, and partly because he saw they surpassed others in their physical beauty and strength. The first down was showing on their cheeks and chins, they were tall and their breadth was in right proportion to their height ; they exhaled the very bloom of youth ; and to all who were not blinded by prejudice their very appearance proclaimed their high spirits and bravery, for they were like lion-cubs.

Moreover, as Alexius did not judge superficially, nor was blind to the truth, nor a prey to reprehensible passions, but weighed facts in the well-balanced scale of his conscience

and remembered the height from which the two had fallen—
he took them to his bosom as if they were his own children.
Was there any kind word or deed he did not give them?
or did he ever neglect their future? and yet envy cast its
arrows at them and would not let them rest. And if people
tried to incite him against them, the Emperor granted them
his protection all the more, always gave them pleasant looks
as if priding himself upon them, and consistently advised
them to their advantage. Another, perhaps, would have
regarded them as objects of suspicion and done his best to
chase them out of his kingdom by some means or other;
but this Emperor thought nothing of the many tales brought
him about the young men for he loved them dearly; and he
also bestowed gifts on their mother Eudocia and did not
deprive her of the prerogatives due to queens. And to
Nicephorus he actually gave the island of Crete to rule and to
have as his private property. That was how the Emperor
behaved; now of the two young men, the one, Leo, was of a
good disposition and liberal mind, and seeing the Emperor's
kindness to them both, he was content with his lot and rested
happily in his condition according to the advice of the writer:
'You have obtained Sparta by lot, make the best of her.'
Nicephorus, on the contrary, ill-tempered and of a wrathful
disposition, never ceased scheming against the Emperor and
plotting to gain the throne; however, he kept his plans
'under water.' But when he really set to work, he spoke
more frankly to a few companions, and thus a great many
persons came to hear of it; and through them it also got to
the Emperor's ears. The Emperor, however, acting in an
original manner, would send for them at suitable times and
never tell what he had heard, but would talk to them cleverly
and give them timely counsel. And the more he grew to
know of the conspiracy, the more generously he behaved
towards them, hoping thus to win them over. But an
Ethiopian never turned white.' So Nicephorus remained the
same and imparted the contagion to all he approached,
binding some to him by oaths and others by promises. He
did not trouble much about the rank and file of the army,
for all of them were already well-inclined to him; but turned
his attention entirely to the grandees and paid great heed to
the chief officers of the army and the leading men in the
Senate and courted them. For he was keener witted than a
two-edged sword, but unstable throughout, except that in
his desire to be Emperor he displayed immutability. His

Q

words were as sweet as honey and he was pleasant in society,
occasionally clothing himself in humility as if it were a fox-
skin, and then again shewing his courage like a lion ; he was
powerful and boasted that he could wrestle with the Giants ;
his skin was tawny, his chest broad and he stood taller by
the head and shoulders than the men of that time.   If anyone
saw him playing ball, or riding, or shooting an arrow or
brandishing his spear or indulging in horse-exercise, he would
imagine he was looking at a new marvel, stand gaping and be
all but transfixed with wonder.   For this reason above all
he attracted the goodwill of the populace.   In the meanwhile
matters were advancing so fast in accordance with his desires
that he even tried to win over the man married to the
Emperor's sister, namely, Michael Taronites who had been
honoured with the title of ' Panhypersebastos.'

VII   But I must bring back my story to the point where
it broke off, and keep it within the due lines of narration.
After he had discovered Diogenes' conspiracy against him,
the Emperor went over events in his mind and recalled how
from the very beginning of his reign he had treated the two
brothers ; how much kindness and solicitude he had expended
on them for so many years, and, as nothing of all this had
changed Nicephorus' disposition for the better, he felt very
despondent.   For the Emperor reviewed all the facts, namely,
how after his first failure Nicephorus had tried again, and how
he had been repulsed by Taticius ; how he was whetting
his murderous weapon and was eager. to defile his hands in
innocent blood, and that after lying in wait for a while and
watching by night to accomplish the murder he was now
pursuing this object quite undisguisedly.

The Emperor was deeply troubled by these various reflections. He was not at all anxious to prosecute Diogenes, because
he liked him exceedingly and had a sincere affection for him ,
yet looking at things in general and understanding how far
the evil would go, recognizing too that he stood in imminent
danger of his life, he was stricken in heart.   Finally, summing
up everything, he judged it wise to arrest Nicephorus.   The
latter was preparing his meditated escape and, wishing to
start on his way to Christopolis during the night, sent to
Constantine Porphyrogenitus in the evening and begged him
to lend him the swift steed the Emperor had given him.
However, Constantine refused, saying it was impossible to
give away a gift from the Emperor of such value to another
the very same day.   In the morning when the Emperor started

on his projected journey, Diogenes followed in his train, for
God who scattereth plans and setteth at naught the decisions
of nations, confounded this man too, who, though intent on
escape, deferred it trom hour to hour—such are the judgments
of God. So he encamped near Serres, where the Emperor
was also, and buried himself in his usual reflections that he
was already detected and must fear the future. The Emperor
then summoned his brother, the Great Domestic, Adrian,
on the evening when the commemoration of the Great Martyr,
Theodore, was being held. And he communicated to him
again all the facts about Diogenes which the other already
knew, namely how he had come in with his sword, how he had
been turned away from the door, and how he was waiting
anxious to accomplish the deed he had planned so long.
Then the Emperor enjoined the Domestic to summon Diogenes
to his own tent and by gentle words and all manner of promises
to try to persuade him to divulge the whole conspiracy, and
to assure him of immunity and forgiveness in the future
for his wrong doing, on the sole condition that he concealed
nothing, and also confessed the names of all his fellow-
conspirators. And Adrian, though full of despondency,
did as he was bid. So he tried threats and promises and
advice in turn, yet could not induce Diogenes to reveal even
a little of his plot. And what was the result ? the Great
Domestic grew sorrowful and troubled, as he knew into what
dangers Diogenes was running. And before this time Diogenes
had secured him as husband for the youngest of his step-
sisters. For this reason he would not let him go, but besought
him even with tears ; yet even so he could not move him
at all, although he urged him and reminded him of incidents
of past days. For one day when the Emperor was playing
polo in the riding-school of the Great Palace, a barbarian
of Armenian or Turkish descent, came in with a sword hidden
in his clothes. When the man saw the Emperor draw apart
from the other players and drop the reins to breathe his
panting horse, he approached the Emperor, fell on his knees
and pretended to make a petition. The Emperor immediately
drew back his horse and enquired what his request was.
Then the murderer, rather than suppliant, put his hand
under his cloak, took hold of his sword and tried to draw it
from its scabbard. But the sword did not obey his hand.
Once or twice he pulled at his sword whilst stammering forth
imaginary petitions, then in despair threw himself on the
ground and lay there begging for mercy. The Emperor

turned his horse to him and asked for what he was craving forgiveness, and the man pointed to his sword fixed in its sheath ; at the same time he beat his breast in amazement and shouted out these words, " Now I recognize thee as a true servant of God, now I behold with mine own eyes that the great God protects thee. For this sword here I prepared for thy murder, I fetched it from home and came here to plunge it into thy heart. Once, twice, nay thrice, I pulled at it but could not make it obey the strength of my arm." And the Emperor, just as if he had not heard anything strange, had stayed in the same position unalarmed ; suddenly all the others ran up to him either to hear what was being said or in alarm. The Emperor's more loyal companions were about to tear the man to pieces, had not the Emperor checked them by gesture and hand and many expostulations. And what was the end of the matter ? that soldier-assassin obtained full pardon on the spot, and not only pardon but large gifts as well ; and in addition he was allowed to enjoy his freedom. However, many of the King's friends were importunate in their demands that this assassin should be driven out of the capital ; but the Emperor would not listen and quoted, " Except the Lord keep the city, the watchmen wake but in vain. Therefore we must pray to God and ask Him to be our protection and guard." At that time it was whispered abroad that the man had attempted the Emperor's life with the connivance of Diogenes. The Emperor did not give any credence to these stories, but became more angered by them, and continued being patient with Diogenes and pretended to know nothing until the point of the sword was literally almost touching his throat. So much of this. After the Great Domestic had reminded Diogenes of this and yet could not persuade him, he returned to the Emperor and told him that Diogenes was obstinate, and absolutely refused to speak in spite of his many entreaties.

VIII   Then the Emperor sent for Mouzaces and told him to take other armed men with him and fetch Diogenes from the Great Domestic's tent and conduct him to his own and keep him safely there though without applying fetters or any other ill-treatment. And Mouzaces instantly executed this command ; fetched Diogenes and took him to his own tent. And the whole night through he entreated and exhorted him, but so far from persuading him he even found him behaving rudely, and consequently grew very angry and was provoked to act contrary to his orders. For he thought fit to torture him and when he began the torture, Diogenes gave way at the very first touch of pain and assever- ated that he would admit everything, so he at once freed him from his chains and sent for a scribe with his style, and the scribe was Gregory Camaterus, who had lately been engaged as under-secretary to the Emperor. And Diogenes related everything in detail and did not even gloss over the attempted murder. In the morning Mouzaces took this written confession, and other papers addressed to Diogenes which he had found on him as a result of search. From these papers it was evident that the Empress Maria herself had known of Diogenes' attempted rebellion, though she would not entertain the idea of the Emperor's assassination even for a moment, but had diligently sought to divert Diogenes not only from the deed itself, but from the mere thought of it—these papers Mouzaces carried to the Emperor. He read them through and on finding the names of a number he had suspected written down there—and these were all men of high position—he was at a loss how to act. For of a truth Diogenes never troubled much about the common people, for he had them gaping after him with all their soul and well-disposed to him for a long time ; but he had studied to win over all the leading men of the military and political parties. Now the Emperor determined that the Empress Maria's connection with this matter should not be brought to light, so he really played the part of ' the man who knows nothing ' throughout, because of the trust and confidence he had had in her even before he was elected Emperor. It was rumoured everywhere that the Prince Constantine Porphyrogenitus, her son, had informed the Emperor of Diogenes' plot, though the fact of the matter was not so ; for the details of the plot had gradually leaked out from the men who were assisting Diogenes.

After Diogenes had been detected, put into chains and banished, the leading men in his conspiracy who had not already been arrested, knew that they had become objects of suspicion and grew very nervous and anxious about their course of action. The Emperor's friends, perceiving their agitated condition, felt that they themselves were in a difficult situation, for they realized that the Emperor was hardly pressed and that danger was constantly hovering over his head, as for protection he could now only rely on a circumscribed few. The Emperor kept revolving everything from the beginning in his mind, the many occasions Diogenes had plotted against

him and been thwarted by the Divine power, and the fact
that he had actually tried to murder him with his own hand,
and he became very troubled by these numerous recollections.
He changed his mind ever so often, for he recognized that the
entire military and political bodies had been corrupted by
Diogenes' blandishments and he had not sufficient soldiers
to set a guard over so many, nor of a surety did he wish to
mutilate a multitude of people, so finally he banished the
ringleaders Diogenes and Catacalon Cecaumenos to Cæsaropolis.   Here they were simply to be kept in detention in
chains for he did not meditate practising any cruelty on them
although everybody advised him to have them mutilated
(for he had a special liking for Diogenes and still clung to
his former care for him).   He also banished his sister's
husband, Michael Taronites, as well as . . . and confiscated their property.   As for all the others he thought
the safest course would be not to subject them to examination
at all, but rather to soften their hearts by forgiving them.
In the evening each one of those condemned to banishment
heard the place allotted to him, and Diogenes got Cæsaropolis.
Of the others not a single one was moved from his own home
but they all remained where they were.

IX   While matters were in this unhappy condition, the
Emperor decided to hold a public assembly the next day
and carry out his intention.   All of the Emperor's relations
by blood or marriage, who were sincerely devoted to him,
and all his ancestral retainers were present then, men of
fierce passions, quick to see at a glance what was likely to
happen and shrewd in accomplishing what was expedient in
inconsiderable time.   These were afraid that amidst the
popular concourse on the morrow a few men might make
a dash at the Emperor and cut him to pieces on the throne,
as men often carried their swords under their garments, as
that rascal did who in guise of suppliant came to him when he
was playing polo.   (The only way to meet this difficulty
seemed to be to strip the people of all the hopes they had
centred on Diogenes by spreading abroad a rumour that he
had been secretly blinded.)   So they collected and sent out
a few men to impart this news as a secret to everybody,
although such an idea had never yet entered the Emperor's
mind.   And this report, though slight at first, yet proceeded
to do its work, as my story will soon make clear.   When the
sun had stepped over the horizon and leapt up in his glory,
those of the Emperor's suite who had not been parties to

Diogenes' treachery, and the soldiers who from of old were his
appointed bodyguard, came to the Emperor's tent first,
some wearing swords, others carrying spears or their heavy
iron axes on their shoulders and ranged themselves in the
form of a crescent at a certain distance from his throne,
embracing him as it were ; they were all under the sway of
anger, and if they did not whet their swords, they certainly
did their souls. The body of his kinsmen and connections
stood close to the throne, and to the right and left of those
were the armour-bearers. The Emperor sat, an imposing
figure, on his seat, clad in military, rather than imperial,
garb, but did not seem to be seated very high, as his stature
was not tall. But his throne was overlaid with gold, and
gold too was above his head. His brows were drawn together,
and emotion had dyed his cheeks a deeper red, his eyes, tense
with anxiety, were an index to the thoughts that filled his
mind. All crowded towards the tent, in a state of fear, and
by reason of their terror were almost constrained to belch
forth their souls into thin air, some were pricked by their
conscience more sharply than by an arrow, while others
dreaded vain suspicion. Not a sound was uttered by anybody, but they all stood scared, looking fixedly at the man
standing guard at the door of the tent. This man was wise
in speech and powerful in action and his name was Taticius.
The Emperor glanced at this man and by his look signified
to him to let the people outside enter. Whereupon he at
once granted them entrance. And in spite of being frightened
they came in with their eyes averted and walking slowly.
When they had taken up their positions in rows, they waited
eagerly for what would happen, each afraid and feeling as
if he were about to run the last lap of his life's course.

The Emperor himself was not altogether at his ease (I speak
humanly, without regard to the fact that he trusted everything to God), for considering the mixed character of the
meeting he feared that they might be meditating some unforeseen and horrible thing against him. However he composed
himself by vigorous reasoning and once he had braced himself to the struggle he began his speech to them (whilst they
stood more dumb even than fish, as if their tongues had been
cut out). He said, " You know that Diogenes never suffered
any ill-treatment at my hands. For it was not I that snatched
the sceptre of this Empire from his father's hand, but another ;
nor have I ever done anything to cause him hurt or pain.
And when this Empire was transferred to my hands by the

entire will of God, not only did I guard him and his brother alike, but I loved and treated them like my own children. And as often as I have detected Nicephorus plotting against me, so often have I granted him pardon. And although he would not better his ways, I bore with him and concealed most of his outbursts against me, being aware of the general dislike in which they were held. Yet not one of my kind deeds towards him has changed his naturally treacherous disposition, but in return for all of them he decreed my death." At these words all broke into shouts crying that they did not wish to see another man in his place on the imperial throne. This was not the true feeling of the majority, but they made fawning speeches as they were devising by these means to escape from the immediate danger. The emperor grasped the opportunity by the forelock and granted a general pardon to the majority, because the ringleaders of the plot had previously been condemned to banishment. At this a mighty noise arose, such as no ears have heard before or since, so say those that were present, for some were praising the King and marvelling at his forbearance and gentleness, while others traduced the men who had been banished and declared that they deserved to die, for such is the way of men. For the man they load with blessings and escort and hold in high respect to-day, they treat in exactly the opposite way without feeling any shame, when they see the throw of his life's die changed. But the Emperor silenced them by a gesture and again spoke, saying, "There is no need for you to make a noise or try to subvert the decision I have taken. For, as I said, I for my part have granted pardon to all, and shall shew myself the same towards you hereafter as I did before."

While the Emperor was granting pardon to these men, the originators of the plan sent, without the Emperor's knowledge, and had Diogenes blinded. They further decreed that the same thing should be done to Cecaumenos Catacalon as he had been Diogenes' fellow-conspirator. This was the day of the commemoration of the Chief Apostles. This deed has been the subject of discussion from that day until now ; but whether the Emperor was let into the secret by its authors, and gave in, or whether he really initiated it himself, God alone knows ; up to the present I have been unable to find out for certain.

X　Such then were the troubles which beset the Emperor through Diogenes, and the invincible hand of the Highest miraculously preserved him from imminent danger. However his nerve was not weakened by any of these occurrences, but, as he had proposed, he marched straight to Dalmatia. When Bolcanus heard that the Emperor had arrived at Lipenium and saw him in occupation, and realized the impossibility of defying the Roman lines in their close formation and full strategic equipment, he at once asked for terms of peace, promising at the same time to send those long-promised hostages and never again to commit any hostile act. So the Emperor received the barbarian with pleasure, for he hated the idea of, and wished to avert, civil war ; for though they were Dalmatians, they were still Christians. Then Bolcanus took heart, and soon came bringing some relations and the chief of the Zupani with him, and readily handed over his nephews as hostages to the Emperor, Uresis and Stephanus Bolcanus by name, and others as well, bringing up the number in all to twenty. For he could not possibly have made arrangements for the future on any other conditions. The Emperor, having thus peacefully solved what is usually accomplished by blood and iron, returned to the capital.

However he never ceased caring for Diogenes, and was heard to sigh deeply for him ; he displayed great kindness towards him and tried to console him and re-instated him in most of the possessions of which he had been deprived. But Diogenes was frantic with grief, detested town-life and was fond of living on his own estate and devoting himself entirely to the works of the ancient writers which others read aloud to him. For as he was bereft of sight he used the eyes of others for reading. He was a man of such wonderful capabilities that even without eyes he easily understood things that people with eyes find difficult to follow. Then he went through all the later learning, and what is strangest, he even studied that famous science, geometry, under the guidance of a philosopher, whom he ordered to get him the figures made in solid material (*or* in relief). For by feeling these all over with his hands he gained comprehension of all the theorems and figures of geometry, just as the famous Didymus, who by his intellectual keenness reached the very height of music and geometry, although he was blind. Notwithstanding Didymus was led astray into a ridiculous heresy after his studies in these subjects, for his mind was blinded by vain glory, as his eyes were by suffering. Everyone who hears this about Diogenes is astonished, but I have seen the man and marvelled at him and heard him speaking of these subjects ; and being personally not quite untrained in them,

[1] = Zoupans, the feudatory lords.

I recognized that he had an accurate knowledge of the theorems. In spite of his pre-occupation with literature, he never forgot his old grudge against the Emperor, but nourished throughout a smouldering expectation of royal power. Nay, he even told a few friends again of this secret expectation, and one of them went and told the Emperor of his planning. He therefore summoned Diogenes and enquired the details of his plot and the names of those who had joined him in it. Diogenes confessed everything without hesitation and immediately received pardon.

BOOK X

I

AND now the notorious Nilus appeared, shortly after the condemnation of Italus' dogmas, and sweeping over the church like a flood of wickedness, brought restlessness into many a soul, and plunged a number in the eddies of his heterodoxy. (This man sprung I know not whence, had learnt to impersonate virtue very cleverly, and frequented the capital for a while, and alone in a corner, I presume, with God and himself, he had devoted himself to the study of the Holy Scriptures. He was quite uninitiated into Hellenic culture, and never even had a teacher who might from the start have explained to him the deep meanings of the Divine writings; and although he had studied the writings of the saints very closely, yet through never having learnt the art of reasoning he went astray about the meaning of the writings. He had seduced a far from ignoble body of followers, and insinuated himself into some of the big houses as self-elected teacher, partly because of his evident virtue and his austere morals, and partly because of the knowledge which seemed perhaps latent in him.

(Thus, for example, he knew nothing of our Church's teaching of the 'hypostatical union' of the Mystery, he was unable to grasp clearly what 'union' meant, nor did he know clearly what 'hypostasis' is, and as he could not clearly conceive 'union' or 'hypostasis' separately, nor the combination 'hypostatical union,' and had not learnt from holy men how the assumption of human nature was made divine, he was carried far away from the truth and in his delusion he opined that it had been made divine by nature.) The Emperor was not unaware of all this and when he heard of the man, he purposed giving him speedy help and sent for him. He blamed him severely for his audacity and ignorance and, after censuring him on several points, he instructed him clearly in the doctrine of the hypostatical union of the divine and human word, and set before him the manner of the

change and taught him how the assumption of human nature
was made divine by grace from above. But Nilus clung
tenaciously to his own false doctrine, and was quite ready to
suffer ill-treatment, torture and imprisonment, or even the
maiming of his body, rather than refrain from teaching that
the assumption of human nature had been made divine by
nature. At that time there were also a number of Armenians
in the capital and for them Nilus acted as an incentive to
profaneness; consequently there were frequent meetings
with the notorious Ticranes and Arsaces whom Nilus' doctrines
incited to further impiety. What happened next? The
Emperor perceived that this impious teaching was gaining
ground in many minds and that the teaching of Nilus and the
Armenians were involved in each other, and that they were
preaching everywhere and with a loud voice that the assumption of human nature had been made divine by nature—
further that the writings of the Holy Fathers on this subject
were set at naught and that the hypostatical union was
practically ignored. He decided to check the onward course
of this evil, so he assembled the heads of the church and
suggested holding a public synod to deal with these men.
At this synod the whole body of the higher clergy was present,
and the patriarch Nicolas too. Nilus was placed in the centre
with the Armenians and they delivered his doctrines. Next
he expounded tham with a clear voice, and upheld them by
further arguments. What was the result? In order to
release people's minds from this corrupt doctrine, the synod
imposed on Nilus a perpetual anathema, and proclaimed the
hypostatical union according to the tradition of the Fathers
more emphatically. Soon after this, or rather about the
same time, Blachernites was also punished for holding
improper opinions, alien to the church's teachings, although
he was an ordained priest. For he had consorted with the
Enthusiasts[1] and became infected with their mischievous
doctrines, led many astray, undermined great houses in the
capital, and promulgated his impious doctrines. After he
had been frequently brought before, and instructed by, the
Emperor, and yet would not abandon his own pernicious
doctrine, the Emperor handed him also over to the church.
As after a lengthy examination they too recognized him to be
incorrigible, they condemned him and his doctrines to a
perpetual anathema.

[1] They were also called ' Euchites ' and were a sort of Mystics and the
forerunners of the Bogomiles.

II In this manner then like a good pilot the Emperor
had breasted the successive assaults of the waves and washed
from himself much worldly brine, and arranged church matters
satisfactorily, and after that he was carried on to fresh seas
of wars and disturbances. For one thing ever followed close
upon another, or, in other words, sea upon sea and river
upon river of troubles, that scarcely allowed the Emperor
to breathe or even close his eyes, as the saying is. It might
be truly observed that we have only drawn up a small drop
from the Adriatic Sea by our outline sketches, rather than
finished pictures, of a few of the deeds accomplished by the
Emperor at this time, whereas he bore up against all the waves
and billows until he brought the barque of Empire under a
favouring breeze to anchor in a sheltered harbour. And
who could ever sing of all his exploits worthily ? Could the
resonant voice of Demosthenes or the rushing periods of
Polemo or all the Homeric muses ? For myself I should
say that not even Plato himself nor the whole Stoa and
Academy combined could give an adequate philosophic
account of his mind. Before those stormy and complex
wars had ended or the surge had ceased its insolence, another
storm, no whit milder than those already described, burst
upon him. For now a man, not one of the notables but of
the lower class, sprung from the gutter, proclaimed that he
was the son of Diogenes, although this son had been killed
years before in the battle which Isaac Comnenus, the Emperor's
own brother, fought with the Turks near Antioch , whoever
wishes to learn more details about his death, can find them in
the chronicles of our illustrious Cæsar. Many tried to muzzle
the man, but he could not be stopped in any way. He came
from the East, poor and wearing a goat's skin, full of rascality
and versatility, made a house-to-house tour of the city in
all its quarters, telling grand tales about himself and pretending he was Leo, the son of the former Emperor Diogenes,
who had been killed, as already said, at Antioch by a shot
from an arrow. Now this vagabond resuscitated the dead
man, adopted his name, openly aimed at the kingdom and led
away the lighter-headed.

And verily this trouble was an addition to the Emperor's
misfortunes, just as if Fate were adding a tragic play about
this wretched fellow for the Emperor. As the luxurious
have honey-cakes brought in and served to them as dessert
after being sated with a heavy meal, in a similar way, I fancy,
the Fate of the Romans after having danced over so many

ills, became satiated with them and made an extra little play for the Emperor with these pretenders.

The Emperor paid not the slightest heed to this talk. But as this gutter-snipe did not cease talking this nonsense at all seasons in the streets and by-ways, it came to the ears of Theodora, the Emperor Alexius' sister, and wife of that dead son of Diogenes. She could not bear this nonsense and was very annoyed. For after her husband's death in battle, she embraced a solitary life and followed an ascetic life most strictly and devoted herself entirely to God. As that nonsensemonger would not hold his tongue after two or three warnings, the Emperor sent him to Cherson and ordered him to be kept in prison.

While imprisoned there he walked on the wall at night and by stooping over conversed once or twice with the Comans who frequented the place for trading purposes, and for carrying home necessaries from that town; finally after giving and receiving securities he let himself down by ropes one night and thus escaped from the prison. The Comans took him with them and departed to their own country. He bivouacked with them for a considerable time, and gained such an influence over them that they soon styled him ' Emperor.' Then the Comans, who were longing eagerly to gulp down draughts of human blood and take their fill of human flesh, as well as to carry off much booty from our country, used this man as a ' Patroclus excuse ' and decided to invade the Roman territory with their whole army on the pretext of re-establishing him on his paternal throne. This project of theirs was in the air for some time and was not unknown to the Emperor. For this reason he fitted out his troops as well as possible and made preparations for fighting with these barbarians. As we have already told he had previously secured the mountain-passes, which are popularly called ' cleisuræ.' After some time he heard that the Comans with the pretender had occupied the district along the Danube, so he assembled the heads of the army, his relations and connections and deliberated with them about taking the field against the Comans. They all dissuaded him from doing this. Now he did not wish to rely upon himself alone or follow his own judgment, but he referred the whole matter to God and asked Him for a decision. Consequently he summoned all the members of the priestly and military roll, and went up to the great church of God in the evening and the patriarch Nicolas was present. He had lately ascended the patriarchal throne after the resignation of Eustratius Garidas in the course

of the seventh Indiction of the year 6592.[1] The question written
on two writing-tablets whether he should go and attack the
Comans or not, the Emperor, after having sealed them, shewed
them to the chief of all and bade him place them on the Holy
Table. When the all-night singing was ended at early dawn the
Patriarch, who had laid the papers on the Table, went in, fetched
one paper, brought it out, broke it open in the sight of all, and
proceeded to read it aloud. The Emperor, taking the key-note as
if given by the voice of God, threw himself heart and soul into the
expedition, and called up the army by letter from all directions,
and when his preparations were quite complete, took the road
against the Comans. When he had collected the whole army and
occupied Anchialus, he summoned his sister's husband, the Cæsar
Nicephorus Melissenus, and George Palæologus and his nephew,
John Taronites, and sent them to Beroë to keep watch there and
ensure safety for that town and its neighbours. Next he broke up
the army and appointed as commanders to divers sections, the
nobles Dabatenus, George Euphorbenus and Constantine Hubertopoulos, and dispatched them to guard the mountain-passes
round the Zygum. Afterwards he moved on and took up his position
at Chortarea (this is the name of a mountain-pass of the Zygum) and
traversed the whole Zygum to investigate whether the men entrusted with the task had fully carried out the orders he had given
them the last time, or whether anything was only half-done or not
done, and if so, to put it right so that the Comans might not find it
easy to traverse the passes. After putting everything in order he
returned from Chortarea and fixed his palisades by the so-called
Holy Lake close to Anchialus.

At night a certain Pudilus, a Vlach nobleman, came in and
reported that the Comans were crossing the Danube, so the
Emperor judged it wise to assemble the leading men among
his relations and officers at dawn of day and consult on the
steps to be taken. As they were all of opinion that he ought
to be at Anchialus, he at once dispatched Cantacuzenus and
Taticius to the village called Therma with a few barbarian auxiliaries, and Scaliarius, the son of Elchan, and some other picked
men to keep guard over that part of the country, and he himself left for Anchialus. He was then informed that the Comans
were moving towards Adrianople so he sent for all the leading
men of Adrianople, pre-eminent among whom were Catacalon,

---

[1] Of the Byzantine Era — 1048 A.D.

nicknamed Tarchaniotes, and Nicephorus, the son of that Bryennius who once aimed at the throne, and had himself done the same and been deprived of his eyes. The Emperor enjoined these men to guard the fortified city very strictly, and said that if the Comans did approach, they were not to engage in battle with them faint-heartedly, but take a definite aim, and shoot at them from a fixed distance. He also advised that the gates should be kept closed most of the time, and promised them many privileges if they carried out his orders. After recommending these measures to Bryennius and the others he sent them back to Adrianople in good spirits. Next he sent orders by letter to Catacalon Euphorbenus Constantine to take the man called Monastras (he was a semi-barbarian who had picked up much military experience) and Michael Anemas with their respective detachments, and directly he heard that the Comans had come through the passes to follow them up closely and attack them unexpectedly.

III The Comans, however, were shown the paths over the passes by the Vlachs, and by using them crossed the Zygum easily. As soon as they approached Goloë, the inhabitants of that town put the captain of the garrison in chains and handed him over to the Comans, and received the latter with delight and shouts of joy. But Catacalon Constantine, with the Emperor's directions fresh in his mind, fell in with the Comans who had gone out to forage, attacked them vigorously and led off about a hundred of them as captives. The Emperor received him and rewarded him on the spot with the title of 'nobilissimus.' When the inhabitants of the neighbouring towns, Diabolis and the others, saw the Comans in possession of Goloë they capitulated, welcomed them with pleasure, handed over their cities and acclaimed the pseudo-Diogenes. He gradually made himself master of all and then with the whole Coman army marched to Anchialus, intending probably to make an attack upon its walls. The Emperor, who was inside and from youth upwards had acquired long experience in warfare, knew that the position of the town would prevent the Comans from making an attack, for it was an additional defence to the walls, so he divided his forces, threw open the gates of the fortress and drew up his men in troops of close formation outside. Near the tip of the Coman lines . . . a portion of the Roman army with shouts . . . they routed them and pursued them down to the sea. The Emperor observed this, and as his

forces were quite inadequate to oppose such masses he commanded all the soldiers to stand together in close formation
for the time being and said that no one was to move out from
the lines. The Comans drew up their lines too, and stood
right in front of the Romans; however, they did not attack
either. This was carried out for three days from morning
to night; for the lie of the land impeded the Comans in their
longing to fight as did also the fact that not a single Roman
moved out from their lines against them. Now the site of
the fortress Anchialus was like this, on the right lay the
Pontic sea, and on the left the ground was very rough and
impassable and overgrown with vines and did not afford any
foothold for riders. What was the result? The Barbarians
after seeing the Emperor's endurance, gave up their plans in
despair and turned away along another path to Adrianople.
The pretender deceived them by saying, " Directly Bryennius
Nicephorus hears that I have come to Adrianople, he will open
the gate and receive me with delight, he will provide money
and bestow many a kindness on me. For although it was not
a tie of nature, but of choice, he always had a brotherly feeling
for my father. And directly that fortress has been surrendered to us, then we can start on our onward road to the
capital." He used also to call Bryennius ' uncle,' perverting
what had a foundation of truth. For it was a fact that the
former Emperor Romanus Diogenes, knowing that the
man Bryennius excelled all his contemporaries in judgment,
and observing his open disposition and general truthfulness
in word and deed had desired to adopt him as brother. And
as both parties were willing this adoption was effected. These
facts are true and known as such by all, but the Pretender
was so shameless that he actually called Bryennius ' uncle.'

So much then for the Pretender's tricks. The Comans
being barbarians have lightheartedness and changeableness as
natural characteristics, so they listened to his words, reached
Adrianople and encamped outside the city. (Then for
forty-eight days engagements took place daily, for the younger
men who were eager for a fight went out daily and joined in
battle with the barbarians.)

One day Nicephorus Bryennius was called for by the Pretender who stood below, so Nicephorus bent forward over the
wall and said that as far as he could judge from the man's
voice, he did not recognize him as the son of Romanus Diogenes
who had been his brother by choice, as just mentioned and as
often happens, and that Romanus' real son had been killed

R

at Antioch. With these words he dismissed the Pretender in disgrace. As the time dragged on, the inhabitants began to be in want and solicited succour from the Emperor by letter. He forthwith ordered Constantine Euphorbenus to select a sufficient number of the Counts under his command, and with them to effect an entrance into Adrianople at night from the side of Calathades. And Catacalon at once took the road to Orestias with high hopes, thinking he would escape the notice of the Comans. But he was wrong in his conjecture. For they caught sight of him, rode out in vastly superior numbers to the attack, drove him backwards and pursued him fiercely. On this occasion this man's son Nicephorus (who later became the husband of my younger sister Maria Porphyrogenita) wielding a long spear turned round sharply to face the Scythian who was pursuing him, and struck him in the chest, whereupon the latter straightway fell down dead. For of a sooth he knew how to brandish a spear and cover himself with a shield; and anyone seeing him ride, would have conjectured that he was not a Roman but had come from Normandy. For the young man was a marvel on horseback, and a magnificent work of nature; he was strong in his piety to God, and sweet and gracious to men. Forty-eight days had not yet passed before, at the bidding of Nicephorus Bryennius (who had plenary jurisdiction over Adrianople), the gates were thrown open all at once and the brave soldiers marched out against the Comans. A fierce conflict ensued in which certainly a large number of Romans fell fighting bravely in utter disregard of their lives, but they killed still more. Here too Marianus Mavrocatacalon picked out Togortac (the chief commander of the Coman army) for he laid hold of a long spear, gave his horse his head and rode straight at him and was within an ace of killing him, had not the Comans near him rescued him, and very nearly killed Marianus too. Although this Marianus was young and only lately admitted to young man's estate, yet he often rode out from the gates of Orestias and fought with the Comans, and every time he returned in triumph having wounded, or killed, his man. For he was truly a very brave warrior, and had apparently inherited courage as an ancestral heritage, and been born a still braver scion of very brave ancestors. After he had been saved from his imminent peril, he boiled with anger and looked for Pseudo-Diogenes. He found him standing on the further bank of the river, on the very spot where he, Marianus, had been fighting with the barbarians, clad in red and decked in imperial guise and his friends all dispersed, so he lifted up his whip and cut him across the face mercilessly while he stigmatised him as a Pretender-King.

IV   When the Emperor learnt of the persistency of the Comans at Adrianople and the frequent battles there, he judged it necessary to leave Anchialus and go thither in person. So he summoned the chief commanders and the head men of the town and discussed what should be done.   A man called Alacaseus stepped forward and said : " My father was formerly an intimate friend of this Pretender's father.   So let me go and I will take him to some fort and arrest him." Naturally he was asked how he meant to set about this work ; then he imitated Zopyrus, the contemporary of Cyrus, and suggested his device to the Emperor, for he said he would disfigure himself and shave off his beard and hair and go to Diogenes and pretend that the Emperor had had all this done to him.   Now he did not say these things and not do them ;   neither did he promise them and then not fulfil his promise, but directly the Emperor sanctioned the enterprise, Alacaseus shaved himself very closely, disfigured his body and started off to that fictitious Diogenes.   Among other things he reminded him of their old-time friendship, and said, " Now that I have been so badly treated by the Emperor Alexius, I come to you relying on my father's former friendship with your majesty to assist you in your present enterprise."   For he used these terms of flattery in order to attract him the more readily.   And to enlarge a little about his doings—he took a pass from the Emperor Alexius and likewise a letter for the prefect of the garrison of the fort called Putza, which said " Whatsoever the bearer of this letter suggests to you, that do promptly, in accordance with his orders."   (The Emperor had guessed aright that when the Comans moved from Adrianople they would go to that town.)   When these arrangements had been made, Alacaseus, as we have said, approached the Pretender, all closely shaven, and said, " It is because of you that I have been ill-treated, for your sake I have been insulted and thrown into chains, for your sake I have been imprisoned for many days, ever since you crossed the Roman frontier, and I have become an object of suspicion to the Emperor because of my father's friendship with you.   However, I have secretly escaped to you, my real master, after freeing myself from my chains, and will now give you salutary advice."   Diogenes received him well and enquired what he must do to accomplish his object ; to this the other replied, " Do you see this fort and this broad plain which is sufficient for feeding your horses for as many days as you like to rest yourself and your army ? We had better not go on any farther for some time, but stay here a little for you to take possession of this fort, and for the Comans to sally forth and bring in necessaries and then we will commence our march to the capital. And if the idea pleases you, I will see the guardian of this fort who was formerly devoted to me and will arrange for him to surrender it to you without battle." This proposition pleased Diogenes. In the night accordingly Alacaseus tied the Emperor's letter to an arrow and shot it into the fort, and when the Governor had read it, he made ready to hand over the said fort. In the morning Alacaseus approached the gates first and pretended to be talking with the Governor ; beforehand he had arranged a signal with Diogenes and told him that directly he saw it he was to walk straight into the fort. After feigning conversation with the Governor for a little time, and giving the signal he had agreed upon beforehand with the pseudo-Diogenes, the latter on seeing it, took with him some soldiers, not many, and boldly entered. The inhabitants received him with joy, and the Governor of Putza invited him to a bath, which Diogenes accepted at the instigation of Alacaseus. Afterwards they spread a rich banquet for him and the Comans accompanying him. When they had, one and all, feasted exceedingly well, and filled themselves with wine which they gulped down from full skins, they lay on the ground snoring. Then Alacaseus himself and the Governor and a few more went round, took away the horses and their arms, left Diogenes snoring where he lay, but killed his attendants and cast them straightway into some trenches as if into natural graves. Now when Catacalon who followed up the Coman army according to the Emperor's orders, had seen Diogenes enter the fort and the Comans disperse for foraging, he went away and fixed his camp near the town we have just mentioned. As the Comans were dispersed all over the country, Alacaseus did not dare to send the Emperor news about Diogenes, but took him and made straight for Tzouroulus in order to return to the capital. But the Emperor's mistress-mother who was staying in the palace, heard of this and at once dispatched the ' Drungaire ' of the fleet, the eunuch Eustathius Cyminianus with orders to arrest Diogenes and bring him to the capital. Eustathius had with him a certain Turk, Camyres

by name, and made use of this man for the blinding of
Diogenes.

Meanwhile the Emperor, still at Anchialus, heard that the
Comans were dispersed for foraging purposes over the adjacent
territories, so moved away and occupied little Nicæa. Next
he heard that Citzes, one of the commanders of the Coman
army, had collected about twelve thousand Comans whom he
had sent out to plunder, and having in this way gained a
large amount of spoil, had now seized the ridge of Taurocomus. Consequently he marched down with his forces and
halted on the bank of the river which flows across the plain
situated at the foot of this ridge. This place was covered
with germander-bushes and young trees. There he stationed
his forces ; then he selected a large body of Turks, especially
skilled in archery, and launched them against the Comans,
hoping that if they started the fight with them by making
a few sallies they would lure them down the hill. But the
Comans attacked them and pursued them incontinently up
to the Roman lines ; then they drew up their horses for a
few minutes, reformed their lines and got ready to dash at the
Roman army.

The Emperor saw a haughty Coman horseman bound
out from the body of the army, ride along the lines and almost
seem to challenge somebody to come and fight him, so he
could not endure to wait for the right or left wing, but in view
of all he put his horse at the gallop and first transfixed the
barbarian champion with his spear and then driving his
sword right through his chest, hurled him off his horse ;
thus on this day he showed himself more as a soldier than a
general. This deed inspired the Roman ranks with great
confidence, and the Scythians with no less alarm, so that when
he moved towards them like a tower of strength, he soon split
up their army. And now that their serried ranks were broken
they scattered in all directions and fled without restraint.
On that day about seven thousand Comans fell in battle, and
three thousand were taken alive. But the Emperor did not
allow the soldiers of the Roman army to divide all the booty
they had taken among themselves, according to the usual
custom, because it had been recently plundered from the
districts around, but ordered it to be restored to the natives.
The Imperial decree flew like a bird through all the country
round about, and all those who had been robbed, came and
each claimed his own property and carried it off. And with
beatings of breasts and with suppliant hands raised to heaven,

they prayed for blessings upon the Emperor ; and the mingled cries of men and women could be heard rising almost to the disc of the moon. So much for this. Afterwards the Emperor joyfully collected his troops and returned to the aforementioned little Nicæa. There he halted for two days, and on the third he left it and reached Adrianople where he stayed for several days in the house of Sylvester. On the other hand all the leaders of the Comans separated from the rest of their army and with intent to deceive the Emperor, came to him as if of their own will and pretended they would make a truce with him, in order that while time was being wasted over the treaty, the Coman army could advance further.

For three days then they waited and after the third day they left at night and took the road homewards. The Emperor, alive to the Comans' stratagem, sent swift runners to make clear to the men commissioned with guarding the paths through the Zygum that they must not relax but keep a sharp look-out and capture the Comans if possible. But when he was informed that the whole army of the Comans was journeying forwards, he at once took the soldiers that were at hand, and reached a place called Scutarium, eighteen stades distant from Adrianople, and the next day he reached Agathonice. There he heard that the Coman army was still near Abrilebo (this place is not very far from the two towns just mentioned), so he went in that direction and looked from a distance at the countless camp-fires they had lighted, and afterwards sent for Nicolas Mavrocatacalon and the other chief officers of the army and with them considered the steps to take.

It was decided that it would be best to summon the captains of the auxiliary troops, namely, Uzas (he was of the Sauromati), and Caratzas the Scythian, and the semi-barbarian Monastras and arrange that they should go and prepare and light fifteen or more bonfires near every tent, so that when the Comans saw all these fires they would think the Roman army was immense and get frightened and not attack them so boldly in future. This was done and produced great fear in the minds of the Comans. The Emperor got ready in the morning and taking the troops he had, advanced against them, and after a conflict the Comans turned their backs. Then the Emperor divided his army and sent the light-armed troops on ahead and himself rode in rapid pursuit of the Comans who were in mad flight. He caught them up near the Sidera Cleisura and killed many, but took most

prisoners ; the troops that had been sent ahead recovered
all the booty from the Comans and returned. The Emperor
spent the whole night on the mountain-ridge of the Sidera
Cleisura owing to a severe storm, and when day dawned
arrived at Goloë. There he stayed for a day and night, in
order to do honour to the men who had fought bravely, and
reward them with very rich gifts ; and as he had accomplished
his purpose he dismissed them all gratefully to their homes, and
himself regained the palace in two days and nights.

V   After a short rest from his many toils, he found that
the Turks were overrunning the interior of Bithynia and
plundering everything, and that on the other side affairs in the
West were calling for the Emperor's attention. He was more
troubled about the former than the latter (for his business was
naturally to attend to what was urgent) and he devised a
device which was really magnificent and worthy of his brain,
and by this contrivance he safely fenced off Bithynia with a
canal against the Turks' incursions. And it is worth while
describing this contrivance. The river Sangaris[1] and the
coast-line which runs straight as far as the village Chele
and the other which turns to the north enclose within them
a large tract of country. Now this country was easily devastated by the men who from of old have been troublesome
neighbours to us ; that is, the Ishmaelites, for due to the
entire absence of any who could prevent them they came
through the Maryandeni and from beyond the Sangaris,
and they used to cross the river and especially oppress the
town of Nicomedia. The Emperor wished to check these
barbarian inroads and raids upon the country, and above
all to protect the town of Nicomedia. Below the Lake of
Baana he noticed a very long trench, and following it up to
its end he gathered from its position and shape that it had not
been dug out by mere chance, nor been hollowed by nature,
but was the cunning work of some hand. After making close
enquiries about the place, he found out from somebody that
it was indeed Anastasius Dicurus[2] who was the originator of
this trench. With what intent they could not say ; but to the
Emperor Alexius it seemed that the former Emperor had wished
to divert the water from the lake into this artificial canal, and
consequently he was led to the same idea and ordered the
trench to be dug out very deep. He was afraid, however, that
the river might be fordable at the junction of the streams, so
he erected a very strong fort, safe and impregnable on all
sides, by reason of the river and the height and thickness of

---

[1] *or* Sangarius.   [2] i.e. Emperor Anastasius I

its walls ; and from this it got the name of ' Iron.' And now this ' Iron Tower ' is a city in front of a city, and an advanced fortification of a fortification ! The Emperor himself superintended the building of the fort from morning till evening, in spite of the great heat, for the sun had already passed the summer solstice, and he put up with the burning heat and the dust. He incurred great expenses in order to ensure by these means that the fort should be very strong and impregnable, and he lavished money upon the men who dragged the stones, one by one, no matter whether there were fifty, or a hundred, men. Thus it came about that they were not just anybody, but that every soldier and soldier-servant, both native and foreign, was stirred to help with the hauling of these stones by seeing the lavish pay and the Emperor himself presiding like a judge at the games. His craft was also shown in this for by the flocking together of so many men the hauling of these immense stones was made much easier. For the Emperor was ever like that, very deep in his ideas, and magnificent in executing them. The Emperor's reign had proceeded as I have described up to the . . . Indiction of the . . . year.

Before he had enjoyed even a short rest, he heard a report of the approach of innumerable Frankish armies. Now he dreaded their arrival for he knew their irresistible manner of attack, their unstable and mobile character and all the peculiar natural and concomitant characteristics which the Frank retains throughout ; and he also knew that they were always agape for money, and seemed to disregard their truces readily for any reason that cropped up. For he had always heard this reported of them, and found it very true. However, he did not lose heart, but prepared himself in every way so that, when the occasion called, he would be ready for battle. And indeed the actual facts were far greater and more terrible than rumour made them. For the whole of the West and all the barbarian tribes which dwell between the further side of the Adriatic and the pillars of Heracles, had all migrated in a body and were marching into Asia through the intervening Europe, and were making the journey with all their household. The reason of this upheaval was more or less the following. A certain Frank, Peter by name, nicknamed Cucupeter[1], had gone to worship at the Holy Sepulchre and after suffering many things at the hands of the Turks and Saracens who were ravaging Asia,

---

[1] = Peter of the Cowl.

he got back to his own country with difficulty. But he was
angry at having failed in his object, and wanted to undertake
the same journey again. However, he saw that he ought
not to make the journey to the Holy Sepulchre alone again,
lest worse things befall him, so he worked out a cunning
plan. This was to preach in all the Latin countries that
' the voice of God bids me announce to all the Counts in
France that they should all leave their homes and set out
to worship at the Holy Sepulchre, and to endeavour whole-
heartedly with hand and mind to deliver Jerusalem from the
hand of the Hagarenes.' And he really succeeded. For
after inspiring the souls of all with this quasi-divine command
he contrived to assemble the Franks from all sides, one after
the other, with arms, horses and all the other paraphernalia
of war. And they were all so zealous and eager that every
highroad was full of them. And those Frankish soldiers
were accompanied by an unarmed host more numerous
than the sand or the stars, carrying palms and crosses on
their shoulders ; women and children, too, came away from
their countries. And the sight of them was like many rivers
streaming from all sides, and they were advancing towards
us through Dacia generally with all their hosts. Now the
coming of these many peoples was preceded by a locust which
did not touch the wheat, but made a terrible attack on the
vines. This was really a presage as the diviners of the time
interpreted it, and meant that this enormous Frankish army
would, when it came, refrain from interference in Christian
affairs, but fall very heavily upon the barbarian Ishmaelites
who were slaves to drunkenness, wine, and Dionysus. For
this race is under the sway of Dionysus and Eros, rushes
headlong into all kind of sexual intercourse, and is not cir-
cumcised either in the flesh or in their passions. It is nothing
but a slave, nay triply enslaved, to the ills wrought by
Aphrodite. For this reason they worship and adore Astarte
and Ashtaroth too and value above all the image of the moon,
and the golden figure of Hobar in their country. Now in
these symbols Christianity was taken to be the corn because
of its wineless and very nutritive qualities ; in this manner the
diviners interpreted the vines and the wheat. However let
the matter of the prophecy rest.

The incidents of the barbarians' approach followed in
the order I have described, and persons of intelligence could
feel that they were witnessing a strange occurrence. The
arrival of these multitudes did not take place at the same

time nor by the same road (for how indeed could such masses starting from different places have crossed the straits of Lombardy all together ?) Some first, some next, others after them and thus successively all accomplished the transit, and then marched through the Continent. Each army was preceded, as we said, by an unspeakable number of locusts ; and all who saw this more than once recognized them as forerunners of the Frankish armies. When the first of them began crossing the straits of Lombardy sporadically the Emperor summoned certain leaders of the Roman forces, and sent them to the parts of Dyrrachium and Valona with instructions to offer a courteous welcome to the Franks who had crossed, and to collect abundant supplies from all the countries along their route ; then to follow and watch them covertly all the time, and if they saw them making any foraging-excursions, they were to come out from under cover and check them by light skirmishing. These captains were accompanied by some men who knew the Latin tongue, so that they might settle any disputes that arose between them.

Let me, however, give an account of this subject more clearly and in due order. According to universal rumour Godfrey, who had sold his country, was the first to start on the appointed road ; this man was very rich and very proud of his bravery, courage and conspicuous lineage ; for every Frank is anxious to outdo the others. And such an upheaval of both men and women took place then as had never occurred within human memory, the simpler-minded were urged on by the real desire of worshipping at our Lord's Sepulchre, and visiting the sacred places ; but the more astute, especially men like Bohemund and those of like mind, had another secret reason, namely, the hope that while on their travels they might by some means be able to seize the capital itself, looking upon this as a kind of corollary. And Bohemund disturbed the minds of many nobler men by thus cherishing his old grudge against the Emperor. Meanwhile Peter, after he had delivered his message, crossed the straits of Lombardy before anybody else with eighty thousand men on foot, and one hundred thousand on horseback, and reached the capital by way of Hungary. For the Frankish race, as one may conjecture, is always very hot-headed and eager, but when once it has espoused a cause, it is uncontrollable.

VI The Emperor, knowing what Peter had suffered

before from the Turks, advised him to wait for the arrival of
the other Counts, but Peter would not listen for he trusted to
the multitude of his followers, so crossed and pitched his
camp near a small town called Helenopolis.   After him followed the Normans numbering ten thousand, who separated
themselves from the rest of the army and devastated the
country round Nicæa, and behaved most cruelly to all.
For they dismembered some of the children and fixed others
on wooden spits and roasted them at the fire, and on persons
advanced in age they inflicted every kind of torture.   But
when the inhabitants of Nicæa became aware of these doings,
they threw open their gates and marched out upon them,
and after a violent conflict had taken place they had to dash
back inside their citadel as the Normans fought so bravely.
And thus the latter recovered all the booty and returned
to Helenopolis.   Then a dispute arose between them and the
others who had not gone out with them, as is usual in such
cases, for the minds of those who had stayed behind were
aflame with envy, and thus caused a skirmish after which the
headstrong Normans drew apart again, marched to Xerigordus
and took it by assault.   When the Sultan heard what had happened, he dispatched Elchanes against them with a sub-
stantial force.   He came, and recaptured Xerigordus and
sacrificed some of the Normans to the sword, and took others
captive, at the same time laid plans to catch those who had
remained behind with Cucupeter.   He placed ambushes
in suitable spots so that any coming from the camp in the
direction of Nicæa would fall into them unexpectedly and be
killed.   Besides this, as he knew the Franks' love of money, he
sent for two active-minded men and ordered them to go to
Cucupeter's camp and proclaim there that the Normans had
gained possession of Nicæa, and were now dividing everything
in it.   When this report was circulated among Peter's followers, it upset them terribly.   Directly they heard the words
' partition ' and ' money ' they started in a disorderly crowd
along the road to Nicæa, all but unmindful of their military
experience and the discipline which is essential for those
starting out to battle.   For, as I remarked above, the Latin
race is always very fond of money, but more especially when
it is bent on raiding a country ; it then loses its reason and
gets beyond control.   As they journeyed neither in ranks nor
in squadrons, they fell foul of the Turkish ambuscades near
the river Dracon and perished miserably.   And such a large
number of Franks and Normans were the victims of the

Ishmaelite sword, that when they piled up the corpses of the slaughtered men which were lying on either side they formed, I say, not a very large hill or mound or a peak, but a high mountain as it were, of very considerable depth and breadth —so great was the pyramid of bones. And later men of the same tribe as the slaughtered barbarians built a wall and used the bones of the dead to fill the interstices as if they were pebbles, and thus made the city their tomb in a way. This fortified city is still standing to-day with its walls built of a mixture of stones and bones. When they had all in this way fallen a prey to the sword, Peter alone with a few others escaped and re-entered Helenopolis ; and the Turks who wanted to capture him, set fresh ambushes for him. But when the Emperor received reliable information of all this, and the terrible massacre, he was very worried lest Peter should have been captured. He therefore summoned Constantine Catacalon Euphorbenus (who has already been mentioned many times in this history), and gave him a large force which was embarked on ships of war and sent him across the straits to Peter's succour. Directly the Turks saw him land they fled. Constantine, without the slightest delay, picked up Peter and his followers, who were but few, and brought them safe and sound to the Emperor. On the Emperor's reminding him of his original thoughtlessness and saying that it was due to his not having obeyed his, the Emperor's, advice that he had incurred such disasters, Peter, being a haughty Latin, would not admit that he himself was the cause of the trouble, but said it was the others who did not listen to him, but followed their own wills, and he denounced them as robbers and plunderers who, for that reason, were not allowed by the Saviour to worship at His Holy Sepulchre. Others of the Latins, such as Bohemund and men of like mind, who had long cherished a desire for the Roman Empire, and wished to win it for themselves, found a pretext in Peter's preaching, as I have said, deceived the more single-minded, caused this great upheaval and were selling their own estates under the pretence that they were marching against the Turks to redeem the Holy Sepulchre.

VII One Ubus[1], brother of the King of France, and as proud as Novatus of his nobility, riches and power, when on the point of leaving his native land, ostensibly to go to the Holy Sepulchre, sent a ridiculous message to the Emperor, with a view to arranging beforehand that he should

----

[1] = Hugh, Count of Vermandois.

have a magnificent reception. " Know, O Emperor," he wrote, " that I am the king of kings and the greatest of those under heaven ; and it behoves you to meet and treat me on arrival with all pomp and in a manner worthy of my nobility." At the time that this message arrived, John, the son of the Sebastocrator Isaac (of whom mention has been made above) happened to be Duke of Dyrrachium, and Nicolas Mavro-catacalon, a Duke of the Fleet, had anchored the ships at intervals round the harbour of Dyrrachium, and made fre-quent excursions from there and scoured the seas so that no pirate-ships might sail past without his noticing them. On receipt of this message the Emperor at once sent letters to these two, commanding the Duke of Dyrrachium to keep watch over land and sea for the Franks' coming, and to signify the Emperor of his arrival at once by a swift messenger, bidding him also receive Ubus with all ceremony, and exhort the Duke of the Fleet in no way to relax his vigilance or be negligent, but to be on the look-out all the time. When Ubus had arrived safely at the seaboard of Lombardy, he sent ambassadors from there to the Duke of Dyrrachium, twenty-four in number, protected with cuirasses and greaves of gold, together with the Count Tzerpenterius[1] and Elias who had deserted from the Emperor at Thessalonica. They spoke as follows to the Duke, " Be it known to thee, Duke, that our Lord Ubus is on the point of arriving, and is bringing with him from Rome the golden standard of Saint Peter. Under-stand, too, that he is the leader of the whole Frankish army. Therefore prepare a reception for him, and the forces under him, which will be worthy of His Highness, and get ready yourself to meet him." While the envoys were thus speaking to the Duke, Ubus, who, as has been said, travelled through Rome to Lombardy, and was crossing from Bari to Illyria, was caught in a very severe storm and lost the greater number of his vessels, crews, soldiers and all, and only the one skiff on which he was, was spat out, so to say, by the waves on to the coast between Dyrrachium and a place called Palus, and he on it half-broken. After he had been thus miraculously saved, two of the men who were on the look-out for his arrival, found him, and addressing him by name, said, " The Duke is anxiously looking for your coming, and is most desirous to see you." Thereupon Ubus at once asked for a horse, and one of the two men dismounted and very willingly gave him his horse. Thus the Duke met him after his deliverance, and welcomed him and asked him about his journey and his

[1] =Charpentier (?)

country, and heard about the disaster which overtook him on his crossing ; so he comforted him with fair promises, and finally set a rich banquet before him. After the feast he detained him and left him, not without supervision, but certainly free. He speedily acquainted the Emperor with the facts, and then waited to receive further instructions. On receipt of the news the Emperor quickly sent Butumites to Epidamnus (which we have often called Dyrrachium) to fetch Ubus and escort him to the capital, but not to travel along the direct road, but to deviate from it, and pass through Philippopolis. For he was afraid of the Frankish hosts and armies which were coming behind him. The Emperor received him with all honour and shewed him much friendliness, and by also giving him a large sum of money he persuaded him to become his ' man ' at once and to swear thereto by the customary oath of the Latins.

VIII   Now this story of what happened to Ubus may serve as a preface. Bohemund (who has often been mentioned in this history already) crossed scarcely fifteen days later to the coast of Cabalion with various Counts and an army that was beyond all numbering. This Cabalion is a place near Boüsa ; these are the names of places in those parts. Let no one find fault with me for introducing these barbaric names which are a stain on the style of my history ; for not even Homer disdained to mention Bœotians and certain barbarian islands for the sake of accuracy in his history.

Close on his heels the Count of Prebentza[1] came down to the shores of the straits of Lombardy, since he also wished to cross. He hired a three-masted pirate-vessel capable of carrying 10,000 measures, for six thousand gold 'staters,' there were two hundred rowers to it, and three tenders accompanied it. He however did not sail in the direction of Valona, as the other Latin armies did, but fearing the Roman fleet, he loosed his cables, tacked a little and meeting a favouring breeze, sailed straight to Chimara. But whilst trying to avoid the smoke, he fell into the fire. For he did not stumble upon the ships which were watching the straits of Lombardy at different points, but upon Nicolas Mavrocatacalon himself, the Duke of the whole Roman fleet. The Duke had heard about this pirate-vessel from afar, and had consequently taken with him all the biremes, triremes and a few fast cruisers from the whole fleet and stationed himself at Cabalion opposite Ason, the port from which he had sailed out, and

[1] = Provence.

where he had left the large fleet. And he sent the so-called 'second Count' with his own galley (called by the sailors 'excussatum') with injunctions that directly he saw the sailors of the afore-mentioned ship loose the cables and throw them into the sea, he should light a torch. The Count went off and did as he was bid. On seeing the signal the Duke Nicolas at once had the sails of some of the ships spread for sailing, the others, like polypods, he worked with oars and sailed towards the Count who was crossing. And he caught him before he had sailed more than three stades from the mainland and was hurrying towards the opposite coast of Epidamnus, and he had on board one thousand five hundred soldiers besides the eighty horses of the nobles. When the helmsman of the ship saw him he said to the Count of Prebentza, " The Syrian fleet is bearing down upon us, and we risk falling victims to the knife and sword." So the Count at once ordered all to put on their armour and fight valiantly. Though it was the middle of winter, the day of commemoration of Nicolas, the greatest saint in the Hierarchy, yet there was an absolute calm, and the full moon was shining more brightly than in spring. As all the winds had fallen, the pirate-vessel was no longer able to move under sail, so that she lay there motionless upon the waters.

Having reached this point in my history, I should like to descant on the exploits of Marianus. He at once asked his father, the Duke of the fleet, for the lighter vessels, and then steered for the Count's ship, and dashing into its prow, attacked it.

The warriors at once flocked to that spot, as they saw he was strongly armed for battle. But Marianus, speaking in their language, advised the Latins to have no fear, and not to fight against fellow-Christians. But one of the Latins hit his helmet with his cross-bow. This cross-bow is a bow of the barbarians quite unknown to the Greeks; and it is not stretched by the right hand pulling the string whilst the left pulls the bow in a contrary direction, but he who stretches this warlike and very far-shooting weapon must lie, one might say, almost on his back and apply both feet strongly against the semi-circle of the bow and with his two hands pull the string with all his might in the contrary direction. In the middle of the string is a socket, a cylindrical kind of cup fitted to the string itself, and about as long as an arrow of considerable size which reaches from the string to the very middle of the bow ; and through this arrows of many sorts are shot out.

The arrows used with this bow are very short in length, but very thick, fitted in front with a very heavy iron tip. And in discharging them the string shoots them out with enormous violence and force, and whatever these darts chance to hit, they do not fall back, but they pierce through a shield, then cut through a heavy iron corselet and wing their way through and out at the other side. So violent and ineluctable is the discharge of arrows of this kind. Such an arrow has been known to pierce a bronze statue, and if it hits the wall of a very large town, the point of the arrow either protrudes on the inner side or it buries itself in the middle of the wall and is lost. Such then is this monster of a cross-bow, and verily a devilish invention. And the wretched man who is struck by it, dies without feeling anything, not even feeling the blow, however strong it be.

To resume, the arrow from the cross-bow struck the top of Marianus' helmet and pierced it in its flight without touching a hair of his head, for Providence warded it off. Then the man speedily discharged another arrow at the Count, and hit him in the arm; the arrow bored through the shield, passed through his cuirass of scale-armour, and touched his side. A certain Latin priest who happened to be standing in the stern with twelve other fighting men, saw this, and let fly several arrows against Marianus. Not even then did Marianus surrender, but fought fiercely himself and encouraged his men to do the same, so that three times over the men with the priest had to be replaced, as they were wounded and sore-pressed. The priest himself, however, although he had received many blows, and was streaming with his own blood, remained quite fearless. For the rules concerning priests are not the same among the Latins as they are with us; For we are given the command by the canonical laws and the teaching of the Gospel, " Touch not, taste not, handle not ! For thou art consecrated." Whereas the Latin barbarian will simultaneously handle divine things, and wear his shield on his left arm, and hold his spear in his right hand, and at one and the same time he communicates the body and blood of God, and looks murderously and becomes ' a man of blood,' as it says in the psalm of David. For this barbarian race is no less devoted to sacred things than it is to war. And so this man of violence rather than priest, wore his priestly garb at the same time that he handled the oar and had an eye equally to naval or land warfare, fighting simultaneously with the sea and with men. But our rules, as I have just remarked, are derived from the . . . of Aaron and Moses and our first high-priest. After the battle had raged fiercely from the evening till next midday, the Latins surrendered to Marianus, much against their will, after asking and obtaining a promise of immunity.

But that most bellicose priest did not stop fighting, even while the truce was being concluded, but as he had emptied his quiver of darts, he picked up a sling-stone and hurled it at Marianus. The latter protected his head with his shield, but the stone struck the shield and broke it in four pieces and shattered his helmet. And Marianus was overwhelmed by the blow from the stone, and at once fell unconscious, and lay speechless a long time, just as the hero Hector almost gave up the ghost when hit with a stone by Ajax. He recovered with difficulty, and then pulled himself together and by shooting arrows at him, thrice hit the man who had struck him. Yet that polemarch, rather than priest, was not even then sated with fighting, and as he had hurled all the stones he had, he was now utterly unarmed and bereft both of stones and of darts ; so not knowing what to do or how to defend himself against his adversary, he grew impatient, and stormed and raged and twisted himself about like a wild beast ; and directly he saw anything handy he used it. Then he discovered a sack of barley-cakes and began throwing out the barley-cakes from the sack as though they were stones, as if he were officiating and taking a service, and turning war into a sacred celebration. And one barley-cake he picked up, drove it with all his might, aiming at Marianus' face, and hit him on the cheek. So much for that priest and the ship and its crew. The Count of Prebentza, after surrendering himself and his ship and his soldiers to Marianus, immediately followed him. And when they had reached land and were disembarking, that same priest often and repeatedly asked for Marianus and, because he did not know his name, he called him by the colour of his clothes. When he found him, he threw his arms round him and embraced him, whilst saying boastfully, " If you had met me on dry land, many of you would have been killed by my hands." Then he pulled out and gave him a large silver cup worth one hundred and thirty staters. And with these words and this gift he breathed his last.

IX Now Count Godfrey crossed about this time, too, with more Counts, and an army of ten thousand horsemen and seventy thousand foot, and on reaching the capital he quartered his army near the Propontis, and it reached from the bridge nearest to the monastery of Cosmidium right up to the church of St. Phocas. But when the Emperor urged him to cross the straits of the Propontis, he let one day pass after another and postponed doing so on one pretext after another ; the truth was that he was awaiting the arrival of Bohemund and the rest of the Counts. For although Peter for his part undertook this great journey originally only to worship at the Holy Sepulchre, yet the rest of the Counts, and especially Bohemund, who cherished an old grudge against the Emperor, were seeking an opportunity of taking their vengeance on him for that brilliant victory he had gained over Bohemund when he engaged in battle with him at Larissa. The other Counts agreed to Bohemund's plan, and in their dreams of capturing the capital had come to the same decision (which I have often mentioned already) that while in appearance making the journey to Jerusalem, in reality their object was to dethrone the Emperor and to capture the capital. But the Emperor, aware of their rascality from previous experience, sent an order by letter that the auxiliary forces with their officers should move from Athyra to Phileas (a seaside town on the Euxine) and station themselves there by squadrons, and watch whether any messenger came from Godfrey to Bohemund and the other Counts behind, or contrariwise one from them to him, and if so, to prevent their passage. But in the meantime the following incident occurred. The Emperor invited some of the Counts with Godfrey in order to advise them to suggest to Godfrey to take the oath ; and as time was wasted owing to the longwinded talkativeness of the Latins, a false rumour reached the others that the Counts had been thrown into prison by the Emperor. Immediately numerous regiments moved on Byzantium, and to begin with they demolished the palace near the so-called Silver Lake. They also made an attack on the walls of Byzantium, not with siege-engines indeed, as they had none, but trusting to their numbers they actually had the impudence to try to set fire to the gate below the palace which is close to the chapel built long ago by one of the Emperors to the memory of Nicolas, the greatest saint in the hierarchy. Now it was not only the promiscuous mob of Byzantines, who were utterly cowardly and unused to war, that wailed and howled when they saw the Latin troops, and beat their breasts, not knowing what to do for fear, but the loyal adherents of the Emperor, recalling that Friday on which the city was taken, were alarmed lest on this day vengeance might be taken on them for their former actions. All who had military knowledge rushed helter-skelter to the palace. But the Emperor did not trouble to arm himself, did not even put on his corselet of scale-armour, nor take shield or spear in hand, nor gird on his sword, but sat firmly on his throne and with cheerful countenance encouraged and inspired confidence in them all, while deliberating with his kinsmen and generals, about the action to take. To begin with he insisted that not a single person should go out of the city to fight the Latins, firstly, because of the sacredness of that day (for it was the Friday of the greatest and holiest week, the day on which our Saviour suffered an ignominious death for us all) and secondly, because he wanted to avoid civil strife. So he sent frequent messengers to persuade the Latins to desist from their undertaking ; " Reverence," he said, " the God who was slain for us all to-day, who for the sake of our salvation refused neither the Cross nor the nails nor the lance, things fit only for malefactors. But if you really desire war, we shall be ready for you the day after our Lord's resurrection." Not only did the Latins not obey him, but they even placed their troops more closely and sent such heavy showers of darts that one of the men standing by the Emperor's throne was hit in the chest. Seeing this most of those who were standing on either side of the Emperor proceeded to draw back. But he sat on unmoved, consoling and gently chiding them in a way ; this demeanour filled all with amazement. However, when he saw that the Latins approached the walls quite shamelessly and would not listen to sensible advice, he sent first for his son-in-law, Nicephorus, my Cæsar. Him he ordered to take stout soldiers, skilled archers, and station them on the top of the wall, and added the command that they should shoot plenty of arrows at the Latins without taking aim, but should rather miss, so as to terrify them by the frequency of the darts, but by no means to kill. For, as I said above, he respected the sanctity of the day and did not wish for civil war. Then he bade others of the nobles, most of whom carried bows, and others wielding long lances, to throw open the gate of St. Romanus and make a display of a violent assault upon them. They were to draw themselves up in this order, . . . each of the spear-bearers was guarded by two peltasts on either side ; then in this order they were to proceed at a slow pace, but send a few skilled archers ahead to shoot at the Franks from a distance, and to keep

turning about from one side to another. And as soon as
they saw only a narrow space left between the armies, they
were to give the order to the archers accompanying them to
direct a shower of arrows at the horses, not the riders, and to
dash at full speed against the Latins, partly to break the
violence of the Franks' onrush by wounding the horses so that
they could not ride against the Romans, and secondly, which
was more important, to prevent any Christians being killed.
The nobles joyfully fulfilled the Emperor's bidding ; threw open
the gates, and now galloping at full speed against the enemy,
and now checking the horses, they killed many of them while
only a few of their own party were wounded on this day. I
leave them to their perdition.

My lord, the Cæsar, took, as I have said, the experienced
archers and stood on the towers shooting at the barbarians.
And all aimed well and shot far ; for all these young men were
as skilled as the Homeric Teucer in the use of the bow. But
the Cæsar's bow was in very deed the bow of Apollo ; and he
did not after the manner of the Homeric Greeks draw the
string to his breast and place the arrow and fit it to the bow
exhibiting like them the art of the hunter, but like a second
Heracles, he discharged deadly arrows from immortal bows
and provided he willed it, he never missed the mark at which
he aimed. For on other occasions during the time of strife
and battle, he invariably hit whatever object he proposed
himself, and whatever part of a man he aimed at, that part
exactly he always struck. With such strength he stretched
his bow, and with such swiftness he sent his arrows that in
archery he appeared to excel even Teucer himself, and the
two Ajaxes. But although he was so skilful, he respected
the sanctity of the day and took the Emperor's injunction
to heart, and when he saw the Latins recklessly approaching
the walls while protecting themselves with shield and helmet,
he did indeed stretch his bow and fix the arrow to the string,
but purposely shot without aim, launching them sometimes
short of the foe, and sometimes beyond. Even though on
that day he only pretended to aim properly at the Latins,
yet if a reckless and impudent Latin not only aimed several
arrows at them up above, but also seemed to be shouting out
insults in his own tongue, than the Cæsar did indeed stretch
his bow at him. And the arrow did not leap from his hand
in vain, but pierced through the long shield and the corselet
of mail and pinned the man's arm to his side. And he,
as says the poet, at once lay on the ground speechless. And

the cry went up to heaven of our men congratulating the
Cæsar and of the Latins lamenting over the fallen.   As our
cavalry was fighting bravely outside, and our men on the
walls equally so, a serious and severe battle was kindled between the two armies.   Finally the Emperor threw in his own
troops and drove the Latins into headlong flight.

On the following day Ubus went and advised Godfrey to
yield to the Emperor's wish, unless he wanted to have a second
experience of the latter's military skill, and to swear that he
would keep good faith with him.   But Godfrey reprimanded
him severely and said, " You who came from your own country
as a king with great wealth and a great army have brought
yourself down from that high position to the rank of a slave ;
and then just as if you had won some great success you come
and advise me to do the same ? "   The other replied, " We
ought to have remained in our own countries and not have
interfered in foreign affairs ; but as we have come as far as
this where we sorely need the Emperor's protection, matters
will not turn out well for us if we do not fall in with his wishes."
But since Godfrey sent Ubus away without his having effected
anything and the Emperor received news that the Counts
coming after were already near, he sent a selected few of
the generals with their troops, and enjoined them again to
advise, nay even to compel, Godfrey to cross the straits.
Directly the Latins caught sight of them, without waiting
even a minute or asking what they wanted, they betook
themselves to battle and fighting.   A severe battle arose
between them in which many fell on either side, and . . .
the Emperor's . . . were wounded, who had attacked
him too recklessly.   As the imperial troops fought very
bravely, the Latins turned their backs.   In consequence
Godfrey shortly afterwards yielded to the Emperor's wish.   He
went to the Emperor and swore the oath which was required
of him, namely, that whatever towns, countries or forts he
managed to take which had formerly belonged to the Roman
Empire, he would deliver up to the Governor expressly sent
by the Emperor for this purpose.   After he had taken this
oath, and received a large sum of money, he was invited to the
Emperor's hearth and table, and feasted luxuriously, and
afterwards crossed the straits and encamped near Pelecanus.
Thereupon the Emperor gave orders that abundant supplies
of food should be conveyed to them.

X   After this man the Count called Raoul arrived with
fifteen thousand horse and foot and bivouacked by the Propon-

tis near the so-called monastery of the Patriarch with the
Counts under him, and the rest he quartered on the shore
right up to Sosthenium.   He, with the same intention as
Godfrey, put off crossing as he, too, was awaiting the arrival
of the others who were coming after him, but the Emperor
foreseeing what might happen, dreaded their advent, and
tried to hurry on Raoul's crossing by every possible means.
So he sent and had Opus fetched (a man of noble mind and
not inferior to anyone in military experience), and when
he arrived he dispatched him with some other brave men
overland to Raoul with orders to compel the latter to cross
the straits.   But when he found that Raoul would certainly
not obey the Emperor's order, but rather spoke impudently
and most insolently of the Emperor, he drew up his lines
for battle, thinking perhaps to terrify the barbarian, and in
this way persuade him to sail across to the other side.

But Raoul drew up the Franks he had with him more
quickly than can be told, and rejoiced ' like a lion that has
lighted upon a huge carcass,' and straightway commenced
a serious battle with Opus.   Now Pegasius came to the place
by sea in order to transport the Franks, and when he saw the
battle being fought on land, and the Franks attacking the
Roman army very boldly, he disembarked, and himself attacked the Franks from the rear.   In this battle many were
killed, but a far greater number wounded, and consequently the
survivors asked to be put across the sea.   Now the Emperor
in his great prudence reflected that if they joined Godfrey
and related what had happened to them, the latter would
be enraged against him, so he gladly received their request,
put them on boats and transported them by sea to the Saviour's
tomb, at their own urgent request.   To the Counts who
were expected he sent envoys carrying messages of kindly
greeting and holding out great expectations, consequently
on arrival they willingly fulfilled all his orders.   This is
sufficient about Count Raoul.

After him came another innumerable, heterogeneous
crowd, collected from nearly all the Frankish countries,
together with their leaders, kings, dukes, counts and even
bishops.   The Emperor sent men to receive them kindly and to
convey promises of reasonable help, for he was always clever
at providing for the future, and in grasping at a glance what
was expedient for the moment.   He also gave orders to
men specially appointed for this purpose to supply them with
victuals on their journey, so that they might not for any

reason whatsoever have a handle for a quarrel against him.
And they (the Crusaders) hastened on to the capital. One
might have likened them to the stars of heaven or the sand
poured out along the edge of the sea. For these men that
hurried on to approach Constantinople were ' as many as
there are leaves and flowers in the spring time,' as Homer
says. Though I much desire to do so, I cannot detail the
names of the leaders. For my speech is paralysed partly
because I cannot articulate these strange names which are
so unpronounceable, and partly because of the number of
them. And, why indeed should we endeavour to recount
the names of such a multitude, when even the men who were
present were soon filled with indifference at the sight ? When
they finally reached the capital they disposed their armies
at the Emperor's bidding close to the Monastery of Cosmidium
and they extended right up to the Hieron. It was not nine
heralds, as formerly in Greece, who controlled this army
by their shouts, but a large number of brave hoplites who
accompanied them and persuaded them to yield to the
Emperor's orders. Now the Emperor was anxious to force
them all to take the same oath as Godfrey had taken, so he
invited them separately and conversed with them privately
about his wishes, and made use of the more reasonable ones
as intermediaries with the more recalcitrant. As they
would not obey, for they were expecting Bohemund to arrive,
but found various means of evasion by continually making
some fresh demands, the Emperor very easily saw through
their pretences and by harassing them in every possible way,
he forced them to take Godfrey's oath, and sent for Godfrey
from over the sea at Pelecanus that he might be present
during the taking of the oath. Thus they all assembled,
Godfrey amongst them, and after the oath had been taken by
all the Counts, a certain venturesome noble sat down on the
Emperor's seat. The Emperor put up with him and said
not a word, knowing of old the Latins' haughty nature. But
Count Balduinus stepped forward and taking him by the
hand raised him up, rebuked him severely, and said, " It
was wrong of you to do such a thing here, and that too when
you have promised fealty to the Emperor ; for it is not
customary for the Roman Emperors to allow their subjects
to sit beside them on the throne, and those who become his
Majesty's sworn bondmen must observe the customs of the
country." He made no reply to Balduinus, but darted a
fierce glance at the Emperor and muttered some words to

himself in his own language, saying, "Look at this rustic that keeps his seat, while such valiant captains are standing round him." The movement of the Latin's lips did not escape the Emperor, who called one of the interpreters of the Latin tongue and asked the purport of his words. When he heard what the remark was, he said nothing to the Latin for some time, but kept the saying in his heart. As they were all taking leave of the Emperor, he called that haughty-minded, audacious Latin, and enquired who he was and of what country and lineage. "I am a Frank of the purest nobility," he replied, "all that I know is that at the cross-roads in the country whence I come there stands an old sanctuary, to which everyone who desires to fight in single combat goes ready accoutred for single combat, and there prays to God for help while he waits in expectation of the man who will dare to fight him. At those cross-roads I too have often tarried, waiting and longing for an antagonist; but never has one appeared who dared to fight me." In reply to this the Emperor said, "If you did not find a fight when you sought for it then, now the time has come which will give you your fill of fighting. But I strongly advise you not to place yourself in the rear nor in the front of your line, but to stand in the centre of the 'hemilochitæ,' for I have had a long experience of the Turkish method of fighting." It was not to this man only that he gave this advice, but to all the others he foretold the accidents likely to happen on their journey, and counselled them never to pursue the barbarians very far when God granted them a victory over them, for fear of being killed by falling into ambushes.

XI So much then about Godfrey and Raoul and the others who accompanied them. Now when Bohemund reached Apros with the other Counts, he reflected that he was not sprung from the nobility, nor was he bringing a large force owing to his poverty, but he was anxious to win the Emperor's goodwill and at the same time conceal his own designs against him, so leaving the other Counts behind he rode ahead with only ten Franks and hastened to reach the capital. As the Emperor knew his machinations and had been long aware of his treacherous and scheming nature, he desired to talk with him before the other Counts arrived, and to hear what he had to say, and to persuade him to cross into Asia before the others in order that he might not join those who were on the point of arriving, and corrupt their minds also. So when Bohemund entered, he smiled at

him cheerfully and asked him about his journey and where he
had left the Counts. All these things Bohemund explained
clearly as he thought best, and then the Emperor joked and
reminded him of his former daring deeds at Dyrrachium and
his former enmity. To this the other replied, " Though I was
certainly your adversary and enemy at that time, yet now I
come of my own free will as a friend of your Majesty." The
Emperor talked of many things with him, and lightly sounded
his feelings, and as he perceived that he would agree to take
the oath of fidelity, he dismissed him saying, " You must
be tired from your journey and must go and rest now ; to-
morrow we can talk of whatever we like." So Bohemund
went away to Cosmidium where a lodging had been prepared
for him, and a rich table spread for him, laden with all manner
of meats and eatables. The cooks also brought in the un-
cooked flesh of land-animals and birds, and said, " You see,
we have prepared the food in our usual fashion ; but if
those do not please you, see, here is raw meat which shall be
cooked in whatever way you like." For they prepared the
food and spoke in this way by the Emperor's orders. For
he was wonderfully clever in judging a man's character,
clever, too, in penetrating to the heart and ferreting out a
man's thoughts, and as he knew Bohemund's suspicions and
maliciousness, he guessed at the truth. Consequently, to
prevent Bohemund suspecting him, he ordered those raw meats
to be taken to him at the same time in order to allay any suspicion. Nor was he wrong in his surmise. For that dreadful
Bohemund not only refrained from tasting the viands at all,
or even touching them with the tips of his fingers, but pushed
them all away at once, and, though he did not speak of his
secret suspicion, he divided them up amongst the attendants,
pretending to all appearance to be doing them a kindness, but
in reality, if you look at it aright, he was mixing a cup of death
for them. And he did not even conceal his craft, for he
treated his servants with contempt. The raw meats, however, he ordered his own cooks to prepare in the usual Frankish
way. The next day he asked the men who had eaten the
supper how they felt. When they replied that they felt
exceedingly well and had not suffered even the slightest
discomfort from it, he discovered his hidden thought, and
said, " When I recalled my wars with him and that terrible
battle I must own I was afraid that he would perhaps arrange
my death by mixing poison with my food." So spake
Bohemund. I have never seen a wicked man who did not

act wrongly in all his words and deeds ; for whenever a man deserts the middle course of action, to whatever extreme he inclines, he stands far away from goodness.

The Emperor sent for Bohemund and requested him to take the customary oath of the Latins. And he, mindful of his own position, namely, that he was not descended from illustrious ancestors, nor had a great supply of money, and for this reason not even many troops, but only a very limited number of Frankish retainers, and being moreover by nature ready to swear falsely, yielded readily to the Emperor's wish. Then the Emperor selected a room in the palace and had the floor strewn with every kind of riches, . . . and so filled the chamber with garments and stamped gold and silver, and other materials of lesser value, that one could not even walk because of their quantity. And he told the man who was to show Bohemund these things, to throw open the doors suddenly. Bohemund was amazed at the sight and exclaimed " If all these treasures were mine, I should have made myself master of many countries long ere this ! " and the attendant replied, " The Emperor makes you a present of all these riches to-day." Bohemund was overjoyed and after thanking for the present he went away to rest in the house where he lodged. But when these treasures were brought to him, he who had admired them before had changed his mind and said, " Never did I imagine that the Emperor would inflict such dishonour on me. Take them away and give them back to him who sent them." But the Emperor, knowing the Latins' characteristic fickleness, quoted the popular proverb, ' Let bad things return to their own master.' When Bohemund heard of this and saw the porters carefully packing the presents up again, he changed his mind—he, who a minute before was sending them away and was annoyed at them, now gave the porters pleasant looks, just like a polypus that changes its form in an instant. For by nature the man was a rogue and ready for any eventualities ; in roguery and courage he was far superior to all the Latins who came through then, as he was inferior to them in forces and money. But in spite of his surpassing all in superabundant activity in mischief, yet fickleness like some natural Latin appendage attended him too. So he who first rejected the presents, afterwards accepted them with great pleasure. For he was sad in mind as he had left his country a landless man, ostensibly to worship at the Holy Sepulchre, but in reality with the intent of gaining a kingdom for himself, or rather, if it were possible, to follow his father's advice and seize the Roman Empire itself, and as he wanted to let out every reef, as the proverb has it, he required a great deal of money. But the Emperor, who understood his melancholy and ill-natured disposition, did his best cleverly to remove anything that would assist him in his secret plans. Therefore when Bohemund demanded the office of Great Domestic of the East, he did not gain his request, for he was trying to ' out-Cretan a Cretan.' For the Emperor feared that if he gained power he would make the other Counts his captives and bring them round afterwards to doing whatever he wished. Further, he did not want Bohemund to have the slightest suspicion that he was already detected, so he flattered him with fair hopes by saying, " The time for that has not come yet ; but by your energy and reputation and above all by your fidelity it will come ere long." After this conversation and after bestowing gifts and honours of many kinds on them, the next day he took his seat on the imperial throne and summoned Bohemund and all the Counts. To them he discoursed of the things likely to befall them on their journey, and gave them useful advice ; he also instructed them in the Turks' usual methods of warfare, and suggested the manner in which they should dispose the army and arrange their ranks, and advised them not to go far in pursuit of the Turks when they fled. And after he had in this way somewhat softened their savage behaviour by dint of money and advice, and had given them good counsel, he suggested their crossing into Asia. Isangeles[1] he liked especially because of his superior wisdom and genuine sincerity and purity of life, also because he recognized that he valued truth above everything ; for he ' shone ' amidst all the Latins ' as the sun amidst the stars of heaven.' And for this reason he kept him by him for some time. After the Counts had all taken leave of the Emperor and reached Damalium by crossing the Propontis, and the Emperor was relieved from the disturbance they caused, he often sent for Isangeles and explained to him more clearly what he suspected would happen to the Latins on their journey, and he also laid bare to him the suspicions he had of the Franks' intention. He often repeated these things to Isangeles and opened, so to say, the doors of his soul to him and, after stating everything clearly, he enjoined him to be ever on the watch against Bohemund's wickedness and if the latter tried to break his oath to check him and by all possible means frustrate his plans. Isangeles replied to the

[1] = Raymond, Count of St. Giles.

Emperor, "Bohemund has acquired perjury and treachery as a species of ancestral heritage, and it would be a miracle if he kept his oath. However, I will endeavour as far as in me lies always to carry out your orders." And taking his leave of the Emperor, he went away to rejoin the whole Frankish army.

Now the Emperor desired to march against the barbarians with the Franks, but their countless masses terrified him. So he decided it would be wise to go to Pelecanus and stay there, so that being close to Nicæa he could learn how the Franks fared and hear also about the Turks' expeditions outside the city and the state of affairs within. For he considered it would be a pity if in the meantime he did not succeed in some military exploit and he aimed at capturing Nicæa himself, if the occasion seemed propitious, and not receiving it from the Franks in accordance with their pledged word. He kept this plan to himself and the arrangements he made, and the reason for them only he himself understood, and Butumites who was his sole confidant. Him he sent to win over the barbarians inside Nicæa partly by promising them complete immunity beside many other things, and partly by warning them that they would endure terrible sufferings and fall a prey to the sword if the city were taken by the Franks. For the Emperor had found out before this that Butumites was most loyal to him, and very energetic in missions of this nature. These events, then, followed this course from the beginning.

BOOK XI

I

AND now Bohemund and all the Counts joined Godfrey at the place from which they were to cross to Cibotus,[1] and there awaited the arrival of Isangeles. But, as they were a countless multitude, they could not stay in one place because of the scarcity of provisions, although they expected the Emperor to come with Isangeles in order that they might undertake the march to Nicæa in company with him. Consequently they split into two parties, the one travelling to Nicæa through Bithynia and Nicomedia, and the other crossing the sea to Cibotus, and arriving at the same place. After approaching Nicæa by these routes they apportioned its towers and the intervening curtains among themselves, as they intended to carry on the assault on the walls by regular succession so that mutual competition should cause the siege to be conducted very vigorously. The portion that fell to Isangeles they left untouched whilst they waited for his coming. At the same time the Emperor occupied Pelecanus because of his plans about Nicæa which I have already explained. The barbarians inside Nicæa had already frequently implored the Sultan to come to their aid. But, as he still delayed and the siege had by now been carried on for many days from dawn till sunset, and they saw that their affairs were in a very bad way, they decided after discussion that it would be better to surrender to the Emperor than be taken by the Franks. To this intent they approached Butumites who had often promised them in various letters that they would be liberally rewarded by the Emperor if they delivered up Nicæa to him. He now assured them more definitely of the Emperor's kind intentions and shewed them the written promises if they handed over the city, and was gladly welcomed by the Turks who despaired of resisting those immense hordes any longer and considered it better to hand

[1] = Civetot.

over the city of their own free will to the Emperor and receive
money and honour than to fall a sacrifice to the sword.
Butumites had not been in Nicæa three days before Isangeles
arrived and started to make an attempt on the walls with
the siege-engines he had prepared.   In the meantime a rumour
reached them telling of the Sultan's approach.   Directly
the Turks heard it they regained courage and promptly expelled Butumites.   And the Sultan detached and sent on a
part of his army to spy out Isangeles' way of approach and
bade them not refuse battle, if they met any Franks.
Isangeles' soldiers saw them from a distance and joined battle
with them.   Directly the other Counts and Bohemund got
ear of the barbarians' attack, they selected two hundred
soldiers from each Count's army and thus dispatched an army
of imposing size to aid Isangeles' men ; they succeeded in
routing the Turks and pursued them till the evening.   However the Sultan was not at all dispirited by this but armed
himself at break of day and with his whole army occupied
the plain outside Nicæa.   When the Franks became aware
of the Sultan's presence, they armed themselves fully and
rushed upon the Turks like lions.   And then a severe and
terrible battle began.   Throughout the whole day the fate
of the balance swayed equally for both sides, but when the
sun set the Turks were routed and night decided the battle.
Many fell on either side and yet a greater number were
wounded.   After gaining this brilliant victory the Franks
fixed many of the Turks' heads on their spears and marched
back carrying these like standards, in order that the barbarians
should see from a distance what had happened, and lose heart
through being defeated at the start, and therefore refrain
from a strenuous battle.

   These things then the Latins did and devised.   But
the Sultan, after seeing their countless multitude and having
gained experience of their invincible boldness from the battle
itself, sent a message to the Turks inside Nicæa, saying
" Act for the future in whatever way you think best."   For he
had known for some time that they would prefer to surrender
the city to the Emperor than be captured by the Franks.
Isangeles continuing the work he had begun, had a large
circular wooden tower built, which he covered on either side
with hides and with plaited wickerwork round the middle
of it, and made very strong all round and then moved it up to
the side of the tower called Gonates.   This tower obtained
its name long ago when the famous Manuel (father of the

previous Emperor Isaac Comnenus and his brother John, my paternal grandfather) was appointed General-in-Chief of the whole Eastern army by the reigning Emperor Basil in order to compose his differences with Sclerus, either by engaging him in battle, or by using persuasion and inducing him to make peace. But as Sclerus loved war and always delighted in bloodshed he chose war rather than peace ; severe encounters took place daily, partly because Sclerus did not wish for peace, but also because he was striving hard to take Nicæa with the help of siege-engines. He effected a breach in the walls and, as the greater part of the foot of the tower had been cut away, it began to settle down and look as if it had fallen on to its knees, and from this circumstance it obtained its name. Such then is the history of this tower Gonates. When Isangeles had built this tower I have mentioned, very scientifically (it was called a ' tortoise ' by experienced mechanics), he introduced armed men inside it to batter the walls and others who knew how to loosen the tower at its foundations with iron instruments. His idea was that while the one set fought with the defenders on the walls, the other set below would have leisure to undermine the tower. These men substituted logs for the stones they dug out, and, when they had worked their way through to the inner side of the wall and saw the light coming through from it, they set fire to the logs. These were burnt to ashes and caused Gonates to lean forward still more so that it did not lose its name. The remaining part of the walls they encompassed with battering-rams and ' tortoises ' ; the deep trench outside the walls they filled with loose earth in no time, until it was brought up to the level of the plains on either side ; and they prosecuted the siege with all their might.

II The Emperor, who had repeatedly and accurately thought out the matter, realized that it would be impossible for the Latins to take Nicæa, even if they had forces without number, so in the meanwhile he had various sorts of siege-engines built, and most of them not according to the usual designs of the mechanics but on other lines he had thought out himself—a thing which amazed people—and these he sent to the Counts. As already stated, the Emperor had crossed the straits with the soldiers he had at hand, and was staying not far from Pelecanus near Mesampela, where a chapel had been built in former years to the memory of the great martyr George. The Emperor would really have liked to march with the Latins against the impious Turks, but when he pondered over this idea and recognized that no comparison could be made between the countless hosts of the Frankish army and his own Roman army, and as from long experience he knew the Latins' fickleness, he desisted from the enterprise. Not only for this reason, but also because he realized the unstable and faithless nature of these men who were easily swayed in opposite directions like the Euripus, and were often ready because of their covetousness to sell their wives and children for a penny-piece; for these reasons the Emperor held back from the enterprise at that time. He felt that though he could not join the Franks, he ought to give them as much help as if he were with them. As he knew the great strength of the fortifications of Nicæa, he understood that the Latins could not possibly take it; then he heard that the Sultan was conveying sufficient troops and all the necessaries of life into the town quite easily by means of the adjacent lake, and so schemed to get possession of the lake. He had light boats built, such as that water would be able to carry, and then had them piled on wagons and carried to the lake on the side that looks Cius-wards. In them he placed heavy armed soldiers with Manuel Butumites as commander and gave them more standards then necessary to make them appear many times more than they were, as well as trumpets and kettle drums. Such then were the measures the Emperor took about the lake. Then he summoned Taticius and the man called Tzitas from the continent and with two thousand brave peltasts sent them to Nicæa. His orders to them were that directly they disembarked they were to occupy the fort of St. George and pack the load of arrows they carried on mules; dismount from their horses at some distance from the walls of Nicæa, march forward slowly and fix their palisades opposite the tower Gonates, and then by agreement with the Franks attack the walls in close formation. Therefore when Taticius arrived with his army he sent word to the Franks as the Emperor had commanded; and after they had all put on full armour they attacked the walls with much shouting and noise. And while Taticius' men discharged showers of darts, the Franks in one place pierced the walls, and in another hurled stones from catapults incessantly. From the side of the lake too the barbarians were terrified by the imperial standards and trumpets and at the same time they were convoked by Butumites to hear the Emperor's promises, consequently they became so distracted that they did not even dare to look over from the battlements ; and as by this time they had despaired of the Sultan's coming, they considered it wisest to surrender the city to the Emperor and to parley with Butumites about this. After making a suitable speech to them, he shewed them the document sealed with gold which the Emperor had entrusted to him ; they listened to the reading of this document by which the Emperor promised not only immunity, but also rich awards of money and honours, to the Sultan's sister and wife (who was said to be Tzachas' daughter) and without exception to all the barbarians in Nicæa ; consequently they felt encouraged by the Emperor's promises and granted Butumites admission. He immediately sent a letter to Taticius saying, " We already have the prey in our hands ; and you must now get ready to assault the walls. Persuade the Franks to prepare for this too but do not give them any further encouragement than to make an attack on the walls from all sides and tell them to encircle the walls and start the siege at sunrise." This was really advice to make the Franks believe that the city had been taken by Butumites in war and to keep secret the drama of treachery the Emperor had arranged. For the Emperor did not want the Franks to know anything of what Butumites had done. On the following day the war-cry was raised on both sides of the city and on the land-side the Franks started the assault with great vigour, and on the other Butumites mounted to the battlements, fixed the imperial sceptres and standards along the walls and with bugles and trumpets acclaimed the Emperor. And in this way the whole Roman army entered Nicæa. Now Butumites having in mind the number of the Franks, feared on account of their fickleness and impetuosity, that they might enter and take possession of the citadel ; for he observed that the Turkish satraps inside were powerful enough in comparison with the small force he had himself, to imprison and slaughter them all, if they wished to, and accordingly he at once took charge of the keys of the gate. For only one had been used as entrance and exit for some time, the others were all closed through fear of the Franks outside. Now when he had the keys of this gate in his own possession, he decided that he ought to diminish the number of satraps by craft in order that he could easily overpower them and prevent their devising any treachery against him. So he summoned them and advised them to journey to the Emperor if they wished to receive large sums of money from his hands and be rewarded with

T

high titles and granted annual pensions. He persuaded the
Turks, and then opened the gate at night and sent away a
few from time to time over the lake to Rhodomerus and the
semi-barbarian Monastras, who were staying near the fort
named after St. George. He ordered these two to send on
the Turks to the Emperor directly they disembarked and not
to detain them even for a short time so that they might not
join with the Turks who were sent on later in plotting some
mischief against them. Now this was literally a kind of
prophecy and an irrefutable proof of that man's great experience. For as long as the Turks who arrived were sent
on to the Emperor quickly, they (Monastras and Rhodomerus)
were quite safe and no danger threatened them, but when
they had relaxed their diligence, then danger was prepared
for them at the hands of the barbarians whom they had
detained. For as these were now many in number they
schemed to do one or other of two things, either to attack
them by night and kill them, or to take them captive to the
Sultan. As the majority voted for the latter, they attacked
them at night, took them captive according to plan and left
that place. And when they had reached the hill Azalas
(this place is . . . stades distant from the walls of Nicæa)
there, report says, they dismounted from their horses and let
them rest. Now Monastras, being a semi-barbarian, knew
the Turkish language, and Rhodomerus who had once been
captured by the Turks and dwelt some time among them, was
likewise not ignorant of their language. So they repeatedly
started speaking plausibly to them and saying, " Why are
you mixing the cup of death for us, when you yourselves will
not gain the slightest advantage thereby ? All your other
friends have been granted bountiful gifts by the Emperor
and have been assigned yearly pensions, and you are depriving
yourselves of all these advantages. Do not, we pray you,
treat yourselves thus and run headlong into visible peril, when
it lies within your power to live free from peril and return to
your own country pluming yourselves on your riches and perhaps even becoming owners of lands. Very likely too we shall
fall into some Roman ambuscade hereabouts," and they
pointed to the streams and marshy places around, " and then
you will be killed and lose your lives to no purpose. For
undoubtedly a great many are lying in wait for you, not only
Gauls and barbarians but also an immense number of Romans.
Therefore if you will follow our advice, let us turn our horses
and journey all together to the Emperor. And we swear to

you by God that the Emperor will grant you ten thousand gifts and afterwards, whenever you please, you will be at liberty to leave, like free men."

The Turks agreed to their proposition, and after giving and receiving pledges, they hastened along the road to the Emperor. When they reached Pelecanus and the Emperor saw them, he received them all with a cheerful countenance, though inwardly deeply indignant with Rhodomerus and Monastras, but for the moment he sent them away to rest. In the course of the following day all the Turks who expressed readiness to remain in his service, were granted innumerable benefits ; and even those who asked to return to their homes received no inconsiderable presents and were allowed to follow their own will. Later on he censured Rhodomerus and Monastras severely for their thoughtlessness ; but, when he noticed that they did not dare to look him in the face for shame, he changed his tone and tried to conciliate them again. So much then about Rhodomerus and Monastras.

Butumites was appointed Duke of Nicæa by the Emperor, and the Franks asked him for permission to enter the city and visit and worship in its churches. However he, knowing their character, as I have said before, did not allow them all to come in a body, but opened the gates and only allowed ten Franks to enter at a time.

III The Emperor was still staying at Pelecanus and as he wished that those Counts who had not yet sworn fealty to him, should also take this oath, he commanded Butumites by letter to advise all the Counts together not to start on their way to Antioch before they took leave of the Emperor, for if they did so, it might be that they would receive still further gifts. Directly he heard the words 'money' and 'gifts,' Bohemund first of all gave his assent to Butumites' advice and urged all the others to go with him to the Emperor, so insatiably greedy of money was he. When they reached Pelecanus, the Emperor received them with great ceremony, and treated them with much consideration ; later he called them and said, " You remember the oath you all took to me, and if you are not going to be transgressors of it, advise those who you know have not yet sworn fealty to me, to take the same oath." And the Counts at once sent for those who had not yet sworn fealty ; and they all came together and consummated the oath. But Bohemund's nephew, Tancred, a youth of independent spirit, maintained that he owed fidelity to Bohemund alone, and that he would keep it to his death.

His own friends standing by and even the Emperor's kinsmen kept importuning him, and then he said, feigning indifference, as it were, and with a glance at the tent in the front of which the Emperor was sitting (it was larger than any had ever seen before), " If you will give me this tent full of money and as much more as you have given to the Counts, then I too will take the oath." Now because of the respect he bore to the Emperor, Palæologus could not stand Tancred's conceited speech, and turned him away with contempt. Whereat Tancred, who was very hasty, rushed at him and the Emperor observing it rose from his throne and stood between them. Bohemund too held him back with the words, " It is not fitting for you to behave in such an impudent way to the Emperor's kinsman." Then Tancred, ashamed of having acted like a drunken man towards Palæologus and also influenced to a certain degree by Bohemund's and the others' counsel, took the oath. When they had all taken leave of the Emperor, he assigned them Taticius, who was then Great Primicerius, and the troops under his command, partly to assist them on every occasion and to avert danger and partly to take over the towns from them if God allowed them to take any. So the Franks once again crossed the straits the next day, and all took the road leading to Antioch. The Emperor guessed that not all the men would necessarily depart with the Counts and accordingly signified to Butumites to hire all the Franks, who remained behind when their army left, for the garrison of Nicæa.

And Taticius with his army and all the Counts and the innumerable Frankish hosts under their command, reached Leucæ in two days. The vanguard was apportioned to Bohemund at his own request whilst the rest drawn up in line followed him at a slow pace. As he proceeded fairly quickly the Turks in the plains of Dorylæum thought, when they saw him, that the whole army of the Franks had come and despising its size at once commenced a battle with him. Then that swollen-headed Latin, who had dared to sit on the imperial throne, was forgetful of the Emperor's advice, and fought in the front of Bohemund's army and in his stupidity ran ahead of the others. About forty of his men were killed in consequence, and he himself, seriously wounded, turned his back to the foe and made his way back to the middle of the army, thus proclaiming in deed, though he would not in words, the wisdom of the Emperor's advice. As Bohemund saw that the Turks were fighting very bravely, he sent to fetch the

Frankish troops. They came up with all speed, and after
that a serious and terrible battle took place. And the Roman
and Frankish armies carried off the victory. As they travelled
onwards, drawn up in troops, the Sultan Tanisman and
Asan, who alone commanded eighty thousand armed men,
met them near Hebraica. A fierce contest ensued as there
were such numbers of troops, and neither side would yield
to the other ; when Bohemund who commanded the right wing
saw with what courage the Turks were fighting their opponents
he withdrew from the rest of the army and made a headlong
descent upon Clitziasthlan, the Sultan himself, 'like a lion
rejoicing in his strength,' as the poet says. This so terrified
the Turks that it made them turn their backs. Remembering
the Emperor's advice, they did not pursue them far, but
reached the Turks' lines and, after resting there a little,
overtook them again near Augustopolis, and attacked and
routed them utterly. After that the barbarian power collapsed ; the survivors dispersed, one here, one there, leaving
their wives and children behind them, as for the future they
did not dare meet the Latins face to face, but tried to find
safety for themselves in flight.

IV What happened next ? The Latins in company with
the Roman army reached Antioch by the so-called Oxys
Dromos and paid no attention to the country on either side
but drew their lines close to the walls, deposited their baggage
and proceeded to besiege this city during three revolutions
of the moon. The Turks alarmed at the straits which had
overtaken them, sent word to the Sultan of Chorosan begging
him to send sufficient troops to their assistance, in order to
succour the Antiochians themselves, and also to drive off the
Latins who were besieging them from outside.

Now there happened to be an Armenian on the tower
above guarding the portion of the wall assigned to Bohemund. As he often bent over from above Bohemund plied
him with honeyed words, tempted him with many promises
and thus persuaded him to betray the city to him. The
Armenian said to him, " Whenever you like and as soon as
you give me a signal from outside, I will at once hand over
this tower to you. Only be quite ready yourself and have
all the people with you ready too and equipped with ladders.
And not only you yourself must be ready but the whole
army must be under arms so that directly the Turks see you
after you have come up and hear your war-cry, they will be
terrified and turn in flight. And this arrangement Bohe-

mund kept secret. While these matters were in contemplation, a messenger came saying that an immense crowd of Hagarenes sent from Chorosan against them was close at hand, under the conduct of the man called Curpagan.[1] When he heard this, as he did not wish to cede Antioch to Taticius according to the oath he had previously sworn to the Emperor, but rather longed for it for himself, Bohemund planned a wicked plan which would force Taticius to remove himself from the city against his will. Accordingly he went to him and said, " I want to reveal a secret to you, as I am concerned for your safety. A report which has reached the ears of the Counts has much disturbed their minds—it is, that the Emperor has persuaded the Sultan to send these men from Chorosan against us. As the Counts firmly believe this they are plotting against your life. And now, I have done my duty by warning you beforehand of the danger that threatens you. And the rest is your concern, to take measures for your own safety, and that of the troops under you." Then considering the severe famine (for an ox-head was being sold for three gold staters) and also because he despaired of taking Antioch, Taticius departed, embarked on the Roman fleet which was in the harbour of Sudi, and made for Cyprus. After his departure Bohemund, who still kept the Armenian's promise secret, and was buoyed up by the great hope of gaining possession of Antioch for himself, said to the Counts, " You see how long we have already persevered in this siege, and yet have accomplished nothing useful up to the present, and now we are within an ace of perishing by starvation unless we can devise something better for our salvation." On their enquiring what that could be, he replied, " God does not always give victory to the leaders by means of the sword, nor are such things always accomplished by fighting. But what toil has not procured, words have often effected, and the greatest trophies have been erected by friendly and propitiatory intercourse. Let us therefore not spend our time here uselessly, but endeavour to accomplish something sensible and courageous for our own safety before Curpagan arrives. Let each one of us studiously try to win over the barbarian who guards our respective section. And if you like, let there be set as prize for the one who first succeeds in this work, the sovereignty of this city until such time as the man who is to take it over from us arrives from the Emperor. Even in this way perhaps we may not be able to accomplish any-

[1] = Kerboga.

thing worth while." All these things that artful and ambitious
Bohemund did, not so much for the sake of the Latins, and the
common weal, as for his own advancement, and by this
planning and speaking and deceiving he did not fail to gain
his object as my history will shew further on. All the Counts
agreed to his proposition and set to work. And at dawn of
day Bohemund at once made for the tower, and the Armenian
according to agreement opened the gate to him; he immediately rushed up with his followers more quickly than can
be told and was seen by the people within and without standing on the battlements of the tower and ordering the
trumpeters to sound the call to battle.

And then indeed a strange sight was to be seen, the Turks,
panic-stricken fled without delay through the opposite gate,
and the only ones of them who stayed behind were a few
brave men who defended the Cula[1]; and the Franks from
outside ascended the ladders on the heels of Bohemund, and
straightway took possession of the city of Antioch. Tancred
with a small body of men pursued the fugitives, many of whom
were killed and many wounded. When Curpagan arrived
with his countless thousands for the succour of the city of
Antioch and found it already taken, he planted his palisades,
made a trench, deposited the baggage in it and decided to
blockade the city. But before he could start on this work,
the Franks rushed out and attacked him. A fierce battle
then took place between them in which the Turks gained
the victory. Now the Latins were shut up in the city and
were hard pressed on both sides, on the one by the garrison
of the Cula (for the barbarians were still in possession of this)
and on the other, by the Turks encamped outside. That
artful man Bohemund who hoped to win the sovereignty
of Antioch for himself once again spoke to the Counts, pretending to give them advice, saying, "We ought not all to
fight simultaneously both against the enemy outside and the
one inside, but rather split up into two portions in proportion
to the number of the enemy fighting us on one side or the
other, and then carry on the war in that way. And if you
all approve, let my duty be to fight with the defenders of the
Acropolis; and your business will be to fight vigorously
against the foes outside." They all assented to Bohemund's
suggestion. He at once set to work to cut off the Acropolis
from the rest of Antioch by building a transverse wall opposite,
which would be a very strong defence in case of a long war.

[1] = The citadel.

And then he constituted himself the watchful guardian of this wall fighting very bravely on every possible occasion with the garrison within. And the other Counts bestowed the greatest attention to their respective sections, guarding the city continuously and keeping the parapets and battlements of the walls under observation, firstly to prevent the barbarians ascending by ladders at night and capturing the city, and secondly to prevent any of the men inside going up to the wall and from there talking about treachery to the barbarians and betraying the city.

V That is how matters stood at Antioch up till then. But the Emperor, who was very anxious to go to the assistance of the Franks, was in spite of his longing deterred from so doing by the state of devastation and utter ruination of the maritime towns and districts. For Tzachas held Smyrna as if it were his own and a man, called Tangripermes, held the town of Ephesus situated on the coast in which a church was built long ago to the apostle and theologian John. Similarly other satraps held other towns, treated the Christian inhabitants as slaves and spread desolation around. Moreover, they held Chios, Rhodes and some other islands as well and built pirate-vessels in them. Consequently he deemed it wiser first to attend to maritime matters and Tzachas, and to leave strong garrisons on the mainland and a large enough fleet to restrain the Turks' sallies and repel them, and then afterwards with the rest of the army take the road to Antioch and fight with the barbarians on his way to the best of his ability. Accordingly he sent for John Ducas his brother-in-law and handed over to him troops recruited from various countries and a fleet large enough for besieging the maritime towns. He also entrusted to him Tzachas' daughter, who had lately been taken captive at Nicæa with others, and ordered him to proclaim the capture of Nicæa everywhere, and, if it were not believed, to shew Tzachas' daughter to the Turkish satraps and barbarians in the sea-coast towns, so that the men, who held the towns we have just mentioned, on seeing her and being assured of the capture of Nicæa would in despair give up the cities without striking a blow. After supplying John fully with all necessaries he sent him forth.

And now I will proceed to set forth how many trophies he erected over Tzachas and how he drove him out of Smyrna. This Duke, my maternal uncle, took leave of the Emperor, then quitted the capital and crossed to Abydus; there he

summoned a man called Caspax and entrusted him with the
command of the fleet and the whole conduct of the naval
expedition. He promised him that if he fought well then,
when they succeeded in taking Smyrna, he would appoint
him Governor of Smyrna itself and of all the towns on its
borders. So he sent him away by sea, as ruler of the fleet,
and he remained on land in command of the troops. Soon the
inhabitants of Smyrna saw both Caspax approaching with
the fleet and Ducas over land, and then Ducas pitching his
camp at a short distance from the walls, and Caspax anchor-
ing in the harbour. Since they had already heard of the
fall of Nicæa, they had not the slightest wish to resist Ducas,
but preferred to confer about making peace. On condition
that John Ducas was willing to swear that he would allow
them all to depart to their own homes without suffering
any harm, they promised to surrender Smyrna to him without
shedding blood and without striking a blow. Ducas thereupon agreed to Tzachas' proposal, and promised to carry
out everything to the letter. After having driven them out
thus peaceably he invested Caspax with absolute authority
over Smyrna. The following incident occurred by chance.
As Caspax was coming away from John Ducas, a Smyrniote
came up to him, accusing a Saracen of having stolen five
hundred gold staters from him. Caspax ordered them to be
brought up for trial, but the Syrian who was being hauled
along thought he was being led to execution and in despair
of his own safety drew his knife and plunged it into Caspax'
bowels ; and turned round and also wounded Caspax' brother
in the thigh. Hereupon a terrible commotion arose, the
Saracen escaped, and all the men of the fleet, and the crews
as well, rushed into the city pell-mell and killed everybody
mercilessly. It was a pitiful sight, ten thousand killed in a
moment of time. John Ducas was extremely grieved at
Caspax' death and for some time took the whole administration of the fortress upon himself. In this capacity he went
round and inspected the walls and ascertained the opinions
of the inhabitants from men who knew ; and as he felt that
a brave man was needed, he appointed Hyaleas, whom he
thought best of all, Duke of Smyrna. This man was a
devotee of the War-God. Ducas left the whole navy to
protect Smyrna, and then marched with his troops to the
town of Ephesus which was held by the satraps, Tangripermes
and Maraces. When these barbarians saw him advancing
towards them, they got under arms, and arranged their

troops in order of battle on the plains outside the city. And the Duke without any delay and with his army skilfully disposed attacked them. The battle that then began lasted the greater part of the day ; both sides fought well and the issue of the battle hung in the balance till at last the Turks turned their backs and were utterly routed. On this occasion many were killed and still larger numbers were captured, not only of the common soldiers, but of the satraps themselves, so that the total of the captives amounted to two thousand. When informed of this the Emperor ordered them to be dispersed among the islands. The Turks who escaped, crossed the river Mæander and went to Polybotum and were contemptuous of Ducas, thinking him of no account whatever. But this was not so. For leaving Petzeas as Duke of Ephesus, he himself took the whole army and at once started after them according to the Emperor's behest, not in disorderly confusion, but in good order and in the manner that it befits an experienced general to march on the foe. Now the Turks, as already said, travelled to Polybotum by way of the Mæander and the towns along its banks. But the Duke did not follow in their steps, but journeying by the shorter road, took Sardis and Philadelphia off-hand and entrusted these to the guardianship of Michael Cecaumenos. When he reached Laodicea, all the inhabitants immediately came out to him, consequently he treated them kindly as they had joined him of their own accord, and allowed them to stay safely in their homes without even appointing a governor. From there he passed through Coma and reached Lampe and in this town he left Camytzes Eustathius governor. On arriving at Polybotum he fell in with a large crowd of Turks and falling upon them at once whilst they were depositing their baggage, he conquered them completely after a short encounter, and killed many, the amount of booty he took was in proportion to their numbers.

VI Before Ducas had returned, whilst he was still fighting with the Turks, the Emperor prepared to go to the assistance of the Franks in Antioch, and reached Philomelium with all his forces after killing many barbarians on the way and destroying several towns hitherto held by them. Here he was found by men from Antioch, Gelielmus Grantemanes, Stephen, Count of France, and Peter, son of Aliphas ; these had been let down by ropes from the walls of Antioch, made their way through Tarsus and reported to him the terrible straits into which the Franks were driven and upon oath they told him of their utter fall. This news made the Emperor still more anxious to hasten to their assistance although everybody sought to restrain him from this enterprise. And then a report was spread abroad everywhere that an incredible host of barbarians was on its way to overtake him. (For the Sultan of Chorosan, hearing of the Emperor's departure to go to the assistance of the Franks, had collected innumerable men from Chorosan and the further provinces, equipped tham all thoroughly and putting them under the command of his own son, Ishmael by name, had sent them forth with instructions to overtake the Emperor quickly before he reached Antioch.) And thus the Emperor's expedition, which he undertook for the sake of the Franks, and with the desire of wiping out the Turks who were fighting furiously with them, and above all their leader Curpagan— this expedition was stopped both by the report which the Franks had brought and by the news of Ishmael's advance against him. For he calculated what would probably happen in the future, namely, that it was an impossibility to save a city which had only just been taken by the Franks and while still in a state of disorder was immediately besieged from outside by the Hagarenes ; and the Franks in despair of all help, were planning to leave only empty walls to the enemy and to save their own lives by flight. For the nation of the Franks in general is self-willed and independent and never employs military discipline or science, but when it is a question of war and fighting, anger barks in their hearts and they are not to be restrained ; and this applies not only to the soldiers but to the leaders themselves for they dash into the middle of the enemies' ranks with irresistible force, especially if their opponents yield a little. But if the enemy with strategic skill often sets ambuscades for them and pursues them methodically, then all this courage evaporates. In short, the ranks cannot be resisted in their first attack, but afterwards they are exceedingly easy to master both because of the weight of their arms and from their passionate and irrational character. For these reasons, as his forces were insufficient against such numbers, and he could not change the Franks' decision, nor by better advice convert them to their advantage, he considered he had better not proceed any further, lest by hastening to the assistance of Antioch he might cause the destruction of Constantinople. He was afraid, too, in case the countless Turkish tribes overtook him, that the inhabitants of the regions of Philo-

melium would fall victims to the barbarians' swords, so he
arranged to have the approach of the Hagarenes announced
throughout the country. The announcement was immediately made and the order given that each man and woman
should leave their homes before the Turks arrived, and thus
save their persons and as much property as each could carry.
They all elected at once to accompany the Emperor, not only
the men but the women too. . . . This was the arrangement
the Emperor made about the prisoners. Next he detached
a part of the army, broke it up further into several sections
and dispatched them against the Hagarenes, with orders
that, if they met any Turks making advance movements,
they were to engage them and fight fiercely, and thus retard
their attack on the Emperor. He himself, with the whole
crowd of barbarian prisoners and of the Christians who had
joined him, returned to the capital. When the arch-satrap
Ishmael heard of the Emperor's doings, namely, that he had
left Constantinople and effected great slaughter, laid many
small towns he passed through in ruins, collected a large
quantity of spoil and captives, and was now returning to the
capital and had left him nothing to do, Ishmael was at a
loss for he despaired of capturing his prey. Consequently
he turned in another direction and resolved to besiege Païpert
which had been taken shortly before by the illustrious Theodore Gabras, and on reaching the river flowing past the town,
he encamped his whole army there. When informed of this,
Gabras thought of attacking him at night. But the result
of Gabras' enterprise and his origin and character shall be
reserved for a fitting moment in my history ; for the present
we must keep to our subject.

Now the Latins being terribly pressed by famine and the
blockade, went to Peter, the man who had been conquered
at Helenopolis, their Bishop, as has been already explained,
and asked him for counsel. He said to them, " You promised
to keep yourselves pure until you reached Jerusalem, and this
promise, I think, you have broken, and for this reason God
has not been helping you now, as He did formerly. Therefore
you must now turn to the Lord and bewail your sins in sackcloth and ashes, and shew your repentance by many tears
and vigils spent in prayer. I myself too will spend my time
in propitiating the Deity towards you." They obeyed the
bishop's instructions. And after a few days the bishop
inspired by a divine voice assembled the chief Counts and
urged them to dig on the right side of the altar, and there

they would find the Holy Nail.[1] They did as he bade and as they did not find it, they returned all discouraged and announced that they had failed in their quest. He accordingly prayed still more earnestly and bade them conduct their search for the object more carefully. They again did his bidding and when they had found what they sought, carried it headlong to Peter, overcome with joy and awe. And then they entrusted that holy and venerable Nail to Isangeles to carry in battle as he was the holiest of them all. The following day, they sallied out upon the Turks from a secret door. On this occasion the man called Flanders begged the others to grant him just one request, namely, to allow him with three friends only to ride out first against the Turks. This request was granted him, and, when the armies stood drawn up in squadrons on either side and were preparing for the shock of battle, he dismounted and after prostrating himself on the ground three times he prayed to God and invoked His help. Then they all shouted. " God with us ! " and at full gallop he rode straight at Curpagan himself who was standing on a hillock. Speedily they struck with their spears the Turks they encountered, and threw them to the ground. The Turks were so terrified by this, that, even before the battle had commenced, they turned to flight as God was evidently aiding the Christians. Most of the Turks in their flight were in their distraction caught in the eddies of the river and drowned, so that those who came after used the bodies of the drowned in place of a bridge. After pursuing the fugitives for a considerable distance they returned to the Turkish lines where they found the barbarian baggage and all the booty they carried with them, this latter they wanted to remove at once, but it was so much that they scarcely managed to convey it all to Antioch in thirty days. They stayed on the spot for a little time to rest after the hardships of the war, and at the same time they took thought for Antioch and looked for a man to guard it. This man was Bohemund who had asked for this position even before the city was captured. So they conceded him full powers over Antioch and themselves set out on the road to Jerusalem. And on their way they took several of the maritime fortresses, but those, which were very strong and would have necessitated a lengthy siege, they passed by for the present as they were anxious to reach Jerusalem. They encircled its walls and made frequent attacks on them and besieged the

[1] This should be ' Lance.'

town and within one lunar month they took it and killed
many of the Saracenic and Jewish inhabitants. When they
had brought all into subjection and no one resisted them,
they invested Godfrey with supreme authority by unanimous
consent, and called him 'king.'

VII   The tidings of the Franks' expedition was brought
to Amerimnes, Prince of Babylon, and he heard how they had
taken Jerusalem and also occupied Antioch, and several
other towns in its vicinity, so he collected a great multitude
of Armenians, Arabs, Saracens and Hagarenes and dispatched
them to oppose the Franks.   Godfrey announced this to the
Franks who accordingly prepared to meet them, and marched
down to Jaffa and there awaited their coming ; from there
they went to Ramel[1] where the great martyr George suffered,
met the army of Amerimnes advancing towards them and at
once joined battle with them.   And the Franks soon overcame
them.   But on the following day when the vanguard of the
enemy caught them up from behind, the Latins were beaten
and ran for their lives to Ramel.   Count Balduinus alone was
absent from the battle as he had fled, not from cowardice,
but to take measures for his own safety and to prepare an
army to fight the Babylonians.   The Babylonians followed
them and encompassed the town of Ramel and took it after a
short siege.   Many of the Latins fell there, but the greater
number were sent as prisoners to Babylon.   After that the
whole Babylonian army turned round and hurried to besiege
Jaffa.   For such is the barbarian custom.

Meanwhile Balduinus, whom I mentioned above, visited
all the small towns which the Franks had taken, and by
collecting from them a considerable number of foot- and horse-
soldiers, he organized a decent army and marched with it
against the Babylonians and defeated them completely.
When the Emperor heard of the Latins' discomfiture at
Ramel he was very grieved at the Counts being taken prisoners
as he had known them in the bloom of physical strength and
of such nobility of descent as the heroes of old, and could
not bear to think of their being prisoners in a foreign country.
So he sent for a man called Bardales, gave him a
large sum of money for their redemption and sent him to
Babylon with letters about the Counts for Amerimnes.
After reading the Emperor's letter, Amerimnes willingly
set all the Counts except Godfrey free without any ransom.
For Godfrey had already been released for a ransom by his

[1] ▪ Rama.

own brother Balduinus. When the Counts reached the Capital the Emperor received them honourably, gave them much money and after they were sufficiently rested, sent them home full of gratitude. But Godfrey after being again elected king of Jerusalem sent his brother Balduinus to Edessa. Then the Emperor ordered Isangeles to hand over Laodicea to Andronicus Tzintziluces and the forts of Maraceus and Balaneus to the soldiers of Eumathius, at that time Duke of Cyprus; and go on further and do his best to get possession of the other forts by fighting. And this he did in obedience to the Emperor's letter. After having handed over the forts to the men mentioned above he went to Antaradus, and made himself master of it without fighting. Directly this came to the ears of Atapacas of Damascus he gathered a large supply of troops and marched to meet him. As Isangeles had not sufficient forces to face such a number, he conceived a plan which was more clever than courageous. For he said boldly to the inhabitants, " As this fortress is very large, I will hide myself in some corner; and when Atapacas arrives, you must not tell him the truth, but assure him that I fled because I was frightened."

So when Atapacas arrived and asked about Isangeles, he believed the story that he had run away, and being weary from his journey pitched his camp close to the walls. As the inhabitants showed him every kindness, the Turks felt safe and, not suspecting any hostile action, they turned their horses loose into the plain. One day at noon when the sun cast its rays vertically, Isangeles, strongly armed, and his men with him (these were about four hundred) suddenly threw open the gates and dashed right into the middle of their camp. Those of the Turks who were accustomed to fighting bravely did not spare their lives but stood up to him, and submitted to a battle; the rest tried to secure their own safety by flight. Owing to the width of the plain and its not being broken by any marsh or hill or ravine, the Latins were able to overpower them all. Thus all fell victims to the sword, only a few were captured. After overcoming the Turks by this stratagem, he marched to Tripolis. Immediately on arrival he went up and seized the summit of the hill (which is a branch of Lebanon) opposite Tripolis, in order to have his fortified camp there and also to divert the water which flowed down the slopes of this hill to Tripolis. He then wrote a report to the Emperor of what he had accomplished, and begged him to have a well-fortified stronghold built there before more troops arrived from Chorosan and overwhelmed him. The Emperor entrusted the Duke of Cyprus with the erection of such a fort and ordered him to dispatch the fleet quickly with all the requisites and also the masons to build this fort on the spot Isangeles signified to them. This was done while Isangeles was encamped outside Tripolis and never ceased straining every nerve to take it. On the other hand, when Bohemund was informed of Tzintziluces' entry into Laodicea, the enmity which he had so long fostered against the Emperor, burst out openly, and he sent his nephew Tancred with a considerable army to besiege Laodicea. A rumour of this had hardly come to Isangeles' hearing before, without the slightest delay, he rushed to Laodicea and opened negotiations with Tancred, and by various arguments tried to persuade him to desist from besieging the town. But when after a long colloquy he found he could not move him, and only seemed to be ' singing to a deaf man,' he departed and went back again to Tripolis. And the other did not relax the siege in the slightest; consequently when Tzintziluces saw Tancred's determination, and he and his were being reduced to straits, he asked for help from there (or from Cyprus). But the authorities in Cyprus were dilatory, and, as he was now very hard beset both by the siege and the pressure of famine, he elected to surrender the town.

VIII During the course of these events Godfrey died and, as it was necessary to elect another King to take his place, the Latins in Jerusalem at once sent to Tripolis for Isangeles, intending to make him King of Jerusalem. But he kept on postponing his departure for Jerusalem. Consequently when the Latins in Jerusalem heard he had gone to the metropolis and was lingering there, they sent for Balduinus, who was then at Edessa, and appointed him King of Jerusalem. The Emperor received Isangeles with great pleasure and when he heard that Balduinus had accepted the sovereignty of Jerusalem, he kept him with him.

At this time a Norman army arrived whose leaders were two brothers called Flanders. The Emperor repeatedly advised them to travel by the same road as the armies that had gone on before, and to reach Jerusalem by the coast and thus join the rest of the Latin army. But he found that they would not listen as they did not wish to join the Franks, but wanted to travel by another route more to the east and march stright to Chorosan in the hope of taking it. The

Emperor knew that this plan was quite inexpedient and as he did not wish such a large crowd to perish (for they were fifty thousand horse and a hundred thousand foot) he tried ' the next best thing,' as the saying is, when he found they would not listen to him. He sent for Isangeles and Tzitas and asked them to accompany the Normans, to advise them to their advantage and to restrain them as far as possible in their mad enterprises. After crossing the straits of Cibotus they hastened on to Armenia and on reaching Ancyra took it by assault ; next they went over the Halys and reached a small town. This was inhabited by Romans and consequently the citizens feared nothing ; the priests clad in their sacred vestments, and carrying the gospel and crosses went out to meet their fellow-Christians. But the Normans in an inhuman and merciless fashion slaughtered not only the priests but the rest of the Christians also, and then quite heedlessly continued their journey, moving in the direction of Amaseia. But the Turks, long practised in war, seized all the villages and food supplies, and burnt them, and when they caught up with the Normans they attacked them at once. It was on Monday the Turks got the better of them. The Latins fixed their camp on the spot where they were, and deposited their baggage, and the next day both armies met in battle again. The Turks next encamped in a circle round the Latins, and did not allow them to move out either for foraging or even to lead the beasts of burden or horses to water. The Franks now saw destruction staring them in the face, and with utter disregard of their lives, armed themselves strongly the following day (this was Wednesday) and engaged the enemy in battle. The Turks had them in their power, and therefore no longer fought with spears or arrows, but drew their swords and made the battle a hand-to-hand fight and soon routed the Normans, who retreated to their camp, and sought a counsellor. But the excellent Emperor to whom they would not listen when he gave them sensible advice, was not at hand, so they appealed to Isangeles and Tzitas for advice, and at the same time enquired whether there was any place under the Emperor's jurisdiction near by to which they could repair. They actually left their baggage, tents and all the infantry where they were, and rode off as speedily as they could on their horses to the sea-coast of the Armenian theme and Paurae. Then the Turks made a sudden descent upon the camp and carried off everything and afterwards pursued and overtook the infantry and

U

annihilated them completely, except for a few whom they captured and carried back to Chorosan as specimens. Such were the exploits of the Turks against the Normans ; and Isangeles and Tzitas with the few surviving knights reached the capital. The Emperor received them, and gave them plenty of money, and after they were rested asked them whither they wanted to go ; and they chose Jerusalem. Accordingly he lavished more presents upon them and sent them by sea, leaving everything to their discretion. But Isangeles on leaving the capital desired to return to his own army and therefore went back to Tripolis, which he longed to subdue. Afterwards he fell a victim to a mortal disease and, when breathing his last, sent for his nephew Gelielmus[1] and bequeathed to him as a species of inheritance all the towns he had conquered and appointed him leader and master of all his troops. When the news of his death was brought to the Emperor, he immediately wrote to the Duke of Cyprus, and ordered him to send Nicetas Chalintzes with plenty of money to Gelielmus in order to propitiate him and influence him to swear on oath that he would maintain unbroken fidelity to the Emperor just as his deceased uncle Isangeles had preserved his to the end.

IX　Soon the Emperor learnt of the seizure of Laodicea by Tancred, and therefore sent a letter to Bohemund which ran as follows : " You know the oaths and promises which not only you but all the Counts took to the Roman Empire. Now you were the first to break them, by retaining possession of Antioch, and then taking more fortresses and even Laodicea itself. Therefore withdraw from Antioch and all the other cities and do what is just and right, and do not provoke more wars and troubles for yourself." Now Bohemund after reading the Emperor's letter could not reply by a falsehood, as he usually did, for the facts openly declared the truth, so outwardly he assented to it, but put the blame for all the wrong he had done upon the Emperor and wrote to him thus, " It is not I, but you, who are the cause of all this. For you promised you would follow us with a large army, but you never thought of making good your promise by deeds. When we reached Antioch we fought for three months under great difficulty both against the enemy and against famine, which was more severe than had ever been experienced before, with the result that most of us ate of the very foods which are forbidden by law. We endured for a long time and while

[1] William.

we were in this danger even Taticius, your Majesty's most
loyal servant, whom you had appointed to help us, went away
and left us to our danger. Yet we captured Antioch unexpectedly and utterly routed the troops which had come
from Chorosan to succour Antioch. In what way would it
be just for us to deprive ourselves willingly of what we
gained by our own sweat and toil?" When the envoys
returned from him the Emperor recognized from the reading
of his letter that he was still the same Bohemund and in no
wise changed for the better, and therefore decided that he
must protect the boundaries of the Roman Empire, and as
far as possible, check his impetuous advance. Accordingly
he sent Butumites into Cilicia with numerous forces and the
pick of the military roll, all very warlike men and devotees
of Ares, amongst them too Bardas and the chief cup-bearer
Michael, both in the flower of youth with beards newly-
grown. These two the Emperor had taken to himself from
childhood and trained thoroughly in military science; he
now gave them to Butumites as being more loyal than the
rest besides another thousand men of noble birth, Franks
and Romans, mixed, who were to accompany him and obey
him in everything and also acquaint him himself by secret
letters of the hourly happenings. His desire was to subdue
the whole province of Cilicia and thus more easily carry out
his designs upon Antioch. Butumites started with all his
forces and reached the city of Attalus; there he noticed that
Bardas and the chief cup-bearer, Michael, would not comply
with his wishes and to prevent the whole army perhaps
mutinying, and all his labour being in vain, and his being obliged
to return from Cilicia without accomplishing anything, he at
once wrote to the Emperor full details about these men, and
asked to be relieved of their company. The Emperor vividly
aware of the harm that is wont to result from such beginnings,
turned them and the others he suspected into another direction
by writing to them to go to Cyprus with all speed and join
Constantine Euphorbenus, who held the position of Duke of
Cyprus at the time, and obey him in everything. On receiving
the letters they gladly embarked for Cyprus. But after
they had been a short time with the Duke of Cyprus, they
began their usual impudence with him, in consequence of
which he looked upon them askance. But the young men
mindful of the Emperor's affection for them wrote to the
Emperor and ran down Euphorbenus, and asked to be recalled
to Constantinople. After perusing their letters the Emperor,

who had sent several of the richer men (of whom he was suspicious) with these two to Cyprus, was afraid lest these might from annoyance join the two in rebellion, and straightway enjoined Cantacuzenus to go and bring them back with him.   Directly Cantacuzenus arrived in Cyrenea he sent for them and took them back.   This is what happened to those two, I mean Bardas and the chief cup-bearer Michael.

Butumites meanwhile with Monastras and the picked officers who remained with him, reached Cilicia and found that the Armenians had already concluded a truce with Tancred.   So he passed them by and seized Marasin and all the neighbouring villages and forts ;   then he left the semi-barbarian Monastras (who has often been mentioned in this history) as governor with sufficient troops to protect the whole country, and himself returned to the capital.

X   When the Franks moved out of Jerusalem to take the cities of Syria, they promised the Bishop of Pisa[1] large rewards, if he would assist them in their proposed object.   He agreed to their request and stirred up two others who dwelt on the coast to do the same ;   and then without any delay equipped biremes and triremes and ' dromones ' and other fast-sailing ships amounting to nine hundred and sailed forth to meet them.   He detached a number of the ships and sent them to pillage Corfu, Leucas, Cephalenia and Zacynthus.   On hearing this the Emperor ordered ships to be furnished by all the countries under the Roman sway.   He had a number built in the capital itself and would at intervals go round in a monoreme and instruct the shipwrights how to make them   As he knew that the Pisans were skilled in sea-warfare and dreaded a battle with them, on the prow of each ship he had a head fixed of a lion or other land-animal, made in brass or iron with the mouth open and then gilded over, so that their mere aspect was terrifying.   And the fire which was to be directed against the enemy through tubes he made to pass through the mouths of the beasts, so that it seemed as if the lions and the other similar monsters were vomiting the fire.   In this manner then these ships were prepared ; he next sent for Taticius, newly returned from Antioch, and gave him these ships and named him their supreme head.   But the whole fleet he put under the command of Landulph and raised him to the dignity of Great Duke, as he was the most experienced in naval warfare.   They left the capital in the course of the month of April and sailed to

[1] = The Archbishop of Pisa, Daimbert.

Samos with the Roman fleet. There they disembarked and
hauled the ships up on land in order to make them stronger
and more durable by tarring them over. But when they
heard that the Pisan fleet had sailed past, they heaved up
their anchors and hurried after them towards Cos; and
reached that island in the evening while the Pisans had reached
it in the morning. As they did not meet the Pisans they
sailed to Cnidus which lies on the Eastern Continent. On
arriving there, although they missed their prey, yet they
found a few Pisans who had been left behind and enquired
of them whither the Pisan fleet had gone, and they answered
'to Rhodes.' So they immediately loosed their cables and
soon overtook them between Patara and Rhodes. When the
Pisans caught sight of them they speedily arranged their
fleet in battle-order and whetted their minds, as well as their
swords, for the fray. As the Roman fleet was drawing near,
a certain Peloponnesian count, Perichytes by name, and a
very expert navigator, had his ship of a single bank of oars
rowed very quickly against the Pisans directly he saw them;
and he passed right through the midst of them like fire, and
then returned to the Roman fleet. The Roman fleet however
did not venture upon a regular sea-battle with the Pisans,
but made a series of swift, irregular attacks upon them.
Landulph himself, first of all, drew close to the Pisan ships
and threw fire at them, but aimed badly and thus accomplished
nothing but wasting his fire. Then the man called Count
Eleemon very boldly attacked the largest vessel at the stern,
but got entangled in its rudders, and as he could not free
himself easily he would have been taken, had he not with great
presence of mind had recourse to his machine and poured
fire upon the enemy very successfully. Then he quickly
turned his ship round and set fire on the spot to three more
of the largest barbarian ships. At the same moment a squall
of wind suddenly struck the sea and churned it up and
dashed the ships together and almost threatened to sink them
(for the waves roared, the yard arms creaked and the sails
were split). The barbarians now became thoroughly alarmed,
firstly because of the fire directed upon them (for they were
not accustomed to that kind of machine, nor to a fire, which
naturally flames upwards, but in this case was directed in
whatever direction the sender desired, often downwards or
laterally) and secondly they were much upset by the storm,
and consequently they fled. That is what the barbarians
did. The Roman fleet for its part ran to a little island,

locally called Seutlus, and when day dawned sailed away
from there and entered the harbour of Rhodes. There they
disembarked and led out all the prisoners they had succeeded
in taking, amongst them Bohemund's nephew, and tried to
frighten them by saying they would either sell them as slaves
or kill them. As they noticed the prisoners were quite
unmoved by these threats and thought nothing of slavery,
they slaughtered them all on the spot. The survivors of the
Pisan fleet turned their attention to pillaging whatever
islands they touched and especially Cyprus; Philocales
Eumathius happened to be there and advanced against them.
At this the sailors were so distraught by fear that they did
not even give a thought to the men who had gone away from
the ships for foraging, but left the greater number on the
island, hurriedly loosed their cables and sailed away to
Laodicea to Bohemund. When the sailors who had been
left on the island to collect plunder returned and did not see
their own fleet, they threw themselves into the sea in desperation, and were drowned.

The commanders of the Roman fleet including Landulph
himself met in Cyprus and decided to make overtures for peace.
As all agreed to this, Butumites was sent to Bohemund. The
latter saw him and detained him quite fifteen days, then
famine oppressed Laodicea, and as Bohemund was still Bohemund and not changed at all, and had not learnt to speak
words of peace, he sent for Butumites and said, " You did
not come here for the sake of peace or of friendship, but in
order to set fire to my ships. Be gone now ; and you have
reason to be thankful that you get away from here unharmed."
So he sailed away and found the men who had sent him in
the harbour of Cyprus. From his report they recognized
more fully Bohemund's wicked disposition, and the impossibility of peace being made between him and the Emperor,
so they left Cyprus and with all sails set they sailed over the
watery ways to the capital. But opposite Syce a great
tempest and violent sea arose and the ships were dashed on
shore and half-broken, all except those Taticius commanded.
Such were the events connected with the Pisan fleet. Bohemund with his extreme natural astuteness was afraid that the
Emperor might proceed to seize Curicum, keep the Roman
fleet in its harbour and thus protect Cyprus and at the same
time prevent his allies from Lombardy coming to him along
the eastern coast. Because of these considerations he decided
to rebuild the town himself and occupy the harbour. For

Curicum had formerly been a very strongly fortified town, but allowed in later times to fall into ruin.

The Emperor had already thought of this and anticipated Bohemund's plan by sending the eunuch Eustathius (whom he promoted from the rank of Canicleius[1] to Great Drungaire of the fleet) with orders to occupy Curicum with all speed. Further he was to rebuild it quickly, and the fort Seleucia as well, which was six stades distant, then leave an adequate garrison in each and appoint Strategius Strabus Duke over them, a man of small body, but of long and varied military experience. He was moreover to have a large fleet at anchor in the harbour and order them to keep a careful look-out for the men coming from Lombardy to Bohemund's aid, and also to help to guard Cyprus. So this Drungaire of the fleet I have mentioned went forth, and anticipating Bohemund's intentions, repaired the town and restored it to its former condition. He also rebuilt Seleucia and made it surer by digging trenches all round, and left a good number of troops in each town under the Duke Strategius. Finally he went down to the harbour and left a considerable fleet in it according to the Emperor's instructions and then travelled back to the capital, where he received great commendation from the Emperor and lavish rewards.

XI   Such then were the doings at Curicum. After the lapse of a year Alexius was informed that the Genoese Fleet was also preparing to enter into alliance with the Franks and foresaw that they would be likely to cause great injury to the Roman Empire. Hence he dispatched Cantacuzenus by land with a considerable force, and Landulph by sea with the fleet which had been hurriedly prepared and ordered him to get to the most southern parts of the coasts as quickly as possible in order to open battle with the Genoese who had to pass there. After these two had departed on the routes indicated, a severe and intolerable storm caught them, by which many of the ships were badly battered. They hauled them up on the dry land again and carefully applied a coating of wet pitch. Then when Cantacuzenus was informed that the Genoese fleet was close at hand sailing southward, he proposed to Landulph to take the eighteen ships (the only ones he then had at sea as the others were drawn up on land) and sail to the promontory of Malea; there to wait, according to the Emperor's advice, and when the Genoese fleet passed, to engage them in battle at once if he had the courage

---

[1] = The keeper of the red ink used for imperial signature.

to fight with them ; but if not, then to secure safety for himself and ships and their crews by landing at Corone.   He sailed away and when he saw the large Genoese fleet he abandoned the idea of fighting with them and hastened to Corone.   But Cantacuzenus gathered the whole Roman fleet, as was right, and called up all the men who were there with him and then sailed in pursuit of the Genoese as fast as he could.   He did not catch them and therefore went to Laodicea as he wished to prosecute the war with Bohemund with all his might and main.   And indeed he began his task at once by taking possession of the harbour, and then by day and night he carried on the siege of the town.

However he accomplished nothing, for his countless attacks were as regularly repulsed, and he could neither win over the Franks by persuasive arguments nor gain anything by fighting.   Then in three days and nights he built a circular wall of stones without mortar between the sea-shore and the walls of Laodicea, and after that by using this wall as a fortification, he quickly erected a second citadel inside it of such material as came to hand, in order that from this as a base he might carry on the siege more rigorously.   He also built two towers on either side of the harbour's mouth and threw an iron chain across from them and by this means erected a bar against the ships which were perhaps expected to come by sea to the succour of the Franks.   During this period he took a number of the forts on the coast, the one called Argyrocastron, Marchapin, Gabala and others right up to the confines of Tripolis ; these places formerly paid tribute to the Saracens, but in this last year had been regained by the Emperor for the Roman Empire at the cost of much toil and labour.   Now the Emperor considered that Laodicea ought to be besieged from the land-side as well ; as he had lengthy experience of Bohemund's wiliness and machinations, and was clever at grasping a man's character in a short time, and had accurate knowledge of the man's treacherous and rebellious nature, he sent for Monastras.   Him he dispatched overland with the requisite forces, so that while Cantacuzenus besieged Laodicea by sea, he should do the same on land. Before Monastras arrived, Cantacuzenus had taken possession of the harbour and the town ; but the citadel, which it is now the usual custom to call Cula, was still held by five hundred foot-soldiers and one hundred horse of the Franks. When he learnt of the seizure of these towns, and was also informed by the Count in command of the citadel of Laodicea, that he was in need of food, Bohemund united all his forces to those of his nephew Tancred and Isangeles, loaded mules with all kinds of provisions, reached Laodicea and introduced them into the Cula very expeditiously. Then in an interview with Cantacuzenus, he asked him, "What object had you in view in the erection of these walls and buildings ? " He replied, " You know that you all promised service to the Emperor and agreed in accordance with your oath to hand over to him the cities you took. Then you transgressed your oath, disregarded also the terms of peace and after taking this town and handing it over to us, you changed your mind again and kept possession of it, so that my journey hither to take over the towns you had captured, is bootless." Then Bohemund asked, " Did you come in the expectation of taking these towns from us by money or by the sword ? " and the other replied, " The money has been given to our brave followers to make them fight bravely." Then Bohemund said in a rage, " Let me tell you that you will never be able to take even a tiny fort from us without money." After that he incited the troops under him to ride right up to the gates of the town. Cantacuzenus' men kept the wall and discharged arrows thick as a snowstorm against the Franks when they approached the walls, and forced them to retreat a little, so Bohemund immediately recalled them all and entered into the Acropolis. And because he suspected the Count in charge of the town and also the Franks under him he appointed another in his place and sent the former away. At this time he also had the vineyards near the walls up-rooted, so that they might not be an obstacle in future to the Latins when on horseback. After making these arrangements he left and returned to Antioch. Cantacuzenus on his side did not neglect carrying on the siege in various ways and by numberless machines and devices and siege-engines he greatly disturbed the Latins in the Acropolis. And now Monastras who was coming overland with the cavalry seized Longinias, Tarsus, Adana, Mamista, in fact, the whole of Cilicia.

XII Bohemund was now getting alarmed by the Emperor's threats and had no means of protecting himself (for he had neither an army on land nor a fleet at sea ; and danger menaced him from both sides), so he devised a plan which was exceedingly sordid, and yet exceedingly ingenious. First of all he left the town of Antioch to his nephew Tancred, the son of Marceses, and had a report spread about himself, which said that Bohemund had died, and while still alive he arranged that the world should think of him as dead. And the report spread more quickly than a bird can fly and proclaimed that Bohemund was a corpse ! And when he found that the report had taken good hold, a wooden coffin was soon prepared and a bireme, in which the coffin was placed, and also he, the living corpse, sailed away from Sudei, which is the harbour of Antioch, to Rome. Thus Bohemund was carried across the sea as a corpse, for to all appearance he was a corpse to judge by the coffin and the demeanour of his companions (for wherever they stopped the barbarians plucked out their hair and mourned him ostentatiously), and inside he was lying stretched out dead for the time being, but for the rest inhaling and exhaling air through unseen holes. This took place at the sea-ports ; but when the boat was out at sea, they gave him food and attention ; and then afterwards the same lamentations and trickeries were repeated. And to make the corpse appear stale and odoriferous, they strangled or killed a cock and placed it with the corpse. And when a cock has been dead for four or five days its smell is most disagreeable for those who have a sense of smell. And this smell seemed to those who are deceived by outward appearance to be that of Bohemund's body ; and that villain Bohemund enjoyed this fictitious evil all the more ; I for myself am astonished that he being alive could bear such a siege of his nostrils, and be carried about with a dead body. And from this I have learnt that the whole barbarian nation is hard to turn back from any undertaking upon which they have started, and there is nothing too burdensome for them to bear when they have once embarked upon difficult tasks of their own choice. For this man, who was not dead except in pretence, did not shrink from living with dead bodies. The device of the barbarian was unique in the world of our time, and was directed towards the downfall of the Roman hegemony. Never before this time did any barbarian or Greek devise such a plan against his enemies nor, do I fancy, will another such ever be seen in our lifetime. When he reached Corfu, it was as if he had reached some mountain-ridge and peak of refuge in this Corfu, and was now safe, so he arose from the dead and left the corpse-bearing coffin there and basked in more sunlight and breathed purer air and wandered about the town of Corfu. And the inhabitants seeing him in his foreign and barbaric garb asked his lineage and his fortune, and who he was, whence he came and to whom he was going. However, he treated them all with contempt and asked for the Duke of the town. The Duke happened to be a certain Alexius of the Armenian theme. When Bohemund saw him he looked at him haughtily and with haughty bearing and speaking haughtily in his barbarian language ordered him to give Alexius the Emperor the following message. " This message I send to thee, I, that Bohemund the son of Robert, who has in these past years taught thee and thy Empire how strong I am in courage and perseverance. God knows that, wheresoever I may go and whatever crisis of fortune I experience, I shall never bear patiently the wrongs that have been done me. For ever since I passed through the Roman Empire, and took Antioch and enslaved the whole of Syria by my sword, I have had my fill of bitter treatment from thee and thy army, disappointed in one hope after another and involved in countless misfortunes and barbaric wars. But now let me tell thee that, though I died, I have come to life again, and have slipped through thy hands. For in the guise of a dead man I eluded every eye and hand and mind, and now, alive and moving about and breathing the air, I send thee from this town of Corfu news which will be very distasteful to thy Majesty, and which thou wilt certainly not receive with overmuch joy. To my nephew Tancred I have entrusted the city of Antioch and have left him as a worthy opponent to thy generals. But I myself, who was reported to thee and thine as dead, am going to my own country as a living man to myself and mine and full of dire intentions against thee. For to shatter the Roman Empire under thy sway, I died when alive, and came to life when dead. For as soon as I reach the continent opposite and see the men of Lombardy, and all the Latins and Germans and the Franks, our subjects and most warlike men, I shall fill thy towns and countries with many murders and much bloodshed until I plant my spear on Byzantium itself." To such a pitch of arrogance was the barbarian carried.

BOOK XII

I

NOW the deeds that were done consequent on Bohemund's first crossing, and all the schemes he devised against the Emperor in his desire to win the sceptre of the Roman Empire for himself, and the manner in which he effected his retreat by cunning, but certainly with great success, in that he made the voyage by being conducted as a corpse and so reached Corfu—may be regarded as described fairly in the foregoing. And now my history must relate Bohemund's further doings. After the odoriferous corpse reached Corfu, as has been said, and sent a threatening message to the Emperor by the Duke of that island, as already told in this history, he crossed over into Lombardy and set to work. For he intended to occupy Illyria again and was anxious to collect more allies than before for this purpose. And after conferring about a matrimonial alliance with the King of France, the latter gave him one of his daughters in marriage, and sent another by sea to Antioch to be united in marriage to Bohemund's nephew, Tancred. Next Bohemund collected innumerable forces from all quarters and every town and country, and sent for the Counts with their respective armies and hurried on his crossing to Illyria.

Directly the Emperor received the message forwarded to him through Alexius, he sent letters to the various states, Pisa, Genoa and Venice to warn them beforehand and prevent their being seduced by Bohemund's false words, and joining him. For Bohemund did in truth visit all the towns and countries, inveighing bitterly against the Emperor and calling him a pagan and an enemy of the Christians. During the time that countless hosts of Franks crossed from the West into Asia and were proving a scourge to Antioch, Tyre and all the surrounding towns and countries, the Babylonian[1] had managed to capture three hundred Counts and was keeping them bound

[1] = The Sultan of Cairo.

in prison where their treatment was as cruel as it used to be
in olden times. When the Emperor heard the details of
their capture and the consequent sufferings that had befallen
them, he was cut to the heart and occupied himself entirely
with their deliverance. Accordingly he sent for Nicetas
Panucomites and dispatched him to the Babylonian with
money and also handed him a letter in which he begged
for those captive Counts and promised the Sultan many
benefits if he would release them from their chains. After
seeing Panucomites and hearing from him the message sent
by the Emperor, the Babylonian read the letter and immediately freed the captives from their bonds and had them
brought out of prison. However he did not grant them
absolute liberty but handed them over to Panucomites to
conduct to the Emperor and this without accepting even a
farthing of the money that had been sent. Whether this
was because he did not consider the sum sufficient for the
ransom of so many men or whether he was anxious to avoid
the imputation of corruptibility and did not wish to appear
to have sold them for a price, but to have conferred a pure
and genuine favour on the Emperor, or whether he aimed at
further rewards, God alone can say. When the Emperor
saw these men arrive, he was overjoyed and marvelled at the
barbarian's decision ; he questioned them minutely about all
that had befallen them and learned how they had been kept
in prison for a very long time and many months without
ever once seeing the sun or being freed from their chains ,
and besides this they had remained all that time without
tasting any kind of food except bread and water. In pity
for their sufferings the Emperor shed a bitter tear and at once
shewed them much kindness, giving them money, providing
clothes of all sorts, conducting them to the baths and en-
deavouring in every way to help them recover from their
ill-treatment. The Counts were delighted at the kind
way they were treated by the Emperor, they his former foes
and opponents, who had broken their promises and oaths to
him, and they appreciated his forbearance towards them.
After some days he sent for them and said, " For the future I
give you permission to stay as long as you like in this city
with us. But if anyone of you has a longing for home and
wishes to return thither, he can start on his homeward journey
without let or hindrance, after taking leave of us, and in
addition being well provided with money and every other
necessary for the journey. I simply wish to give you per-

mission to go or to stay and to do what you like according to your own judgment as free men." For some time already, as I have said, they had received great attention from the Emperor and were reluctant to leave him. But when, as before mentioned, Bohemund reached Lombardy and was busy gathering together larger armies than his former ones, and was going round to all the towns and villages decrying the Emperor and loudly proclaiming him a pagan who was assisting the pagans with all his might—the Emperor on hearing this gave the aforementioned Counts lavish presents and sent them off home. He did this, firstly because they themselves had already begun to wish to return home, and secondly, in order that they might refute the tales which Bohemund had been publishing about him. But he himself departed hurriedly for the city of Thettalus, partly in order to train the recruits in military exercises, and partly to hinder Bohemund from his reputed desire of crossing from Lombardy into our Empire. The Counts when they left became most trustworthy evidence against Bohemund, they called him a cheat who never spoke the truth even in ordinary cases, they often refuted him to his face and denounced him in every town and village, and were in themselves credible witnesses.

II As Bohemund's crossing was being spoken of on all sides and the Emperor recognized that he still required many more forces to have an army of proportionate size to oppose to the Frankish masses, he did not delay or hesitate, but sent for the men from Cœlo-Syria, I mean Cantacuzenus and Monastras; for the former was holding Laodicea and the latter Tarsus. Now when he summoned these men, he did not leave the towns and provinces under their care unprotected, but sent Petzeas with other troops to Laodicea, whilst to Tarsus and all the towns and provinces under Monastras he sent Aspietes. This man was a noble descended from an Armenian family, renowned for its bravery, as report said at that time, though the crises which then arose did not prove him to be anything of the kind, at least as regards strategic ability. For Tancred, the governor of Antioch, who, as we have already told, was now in Syria, repeatedly spread the rumour abroad, that he would descend on Cilicia very soon to besiege its towns and wrest it from the Emperor's hands, as it was his own, and he had taken it from the Turks by force of arms. He did not only disseminate such rumours, but even threatened far worse things by letters, which were daily handed in to Aspietes. And he did not merely threaten, but did a few things, illustrative of his threats, and undertook to do still more. He collected troops from all sides from the Armenians and Franks, drilled these daily, and trained the army gradually to form up in line and engage in battle; sometimes he sent it out on foraging expeditions, thus symbolizing the smoke which precedes a fire; he was also preparing siege-engines and getting himself ready in every way for a siege. So much then for his doings; but the Armenian Aspietes, just as if nobody were threatening and terrifying him or menacing him with such terrible danger, sat carelessly at his ease and nightly indulged in heavy drinking. And yet he was very brave and a most valiant soldier; but when he was put into Cilicia, far away from a master's hand and had full authority, he abandoned himself to all sorts of wantonness. Consequently when the moment of the siege arrived, that wretched Armenian, who was steadily growing more effeminate and leading a loose life, shewed that he had become quite helpless in face of that most patient soldier, Tancred. For his hearing was not disturbed by the thunder of his threats and when Tancred came wielding the thunderbolt through scenes of devastation to Cilicia, he did not even glance up at the lightning.

Tancred suddenly led out his enormous army from Antioch and, forming it into two divisions, sent half overland to the towns of Mopsus,[1] the other half he embarked on triremes and took them by sea into the mouth of the river Saron. This river runs down from the Taurus mountains, and flows between the two cities of Mopsus, the one in ruins, the other newly built, and empties itself into the Syrian sea. Tancred's ships sailed from this sea and when they had entered the mouth of this river, they went up it as far as the bridges which unite the two cities. In this way the city was encircled and attacked on both sides. For Tancred's men were able easily to fight against the city from the sea on the one side, while on the other the army could fight and harass it from the land. As if nothing out of the common were happening, and no mighty swarm of soldiers were buzzing round the city, Aspietes most strangely, and in a manner quite unworthy of his courage, paid little heed to these things. This caused him to be most heartily hated by the imperial army. What then was likely to be the fate of the Cilician cities when captured by such a man? for besides being the strongest of all his contemporaries

---

[1] = Mopsuestia *or* Malmistra.

and one of the most respected for military experience, Tancred
was most deadly in the art of besieging a town.   Now any one
reading as far as this might wonder that the Emperor was not
aware of Aspietes' lack of military experience.   But I would
say in defence of my father that the nobility of his descent
influenced the Emperor and that the brilliance of his ancestry
and the fame of his name contributed much to Aspietes'
receiving this appointment.   For he held the highest rank
among the Arsacidæ and was born of royal blood.   It was
for this reason that my father appointed him Stratopedarch
of the whole East and promoted him to very high honours,
especially after he had had a proof of his courage.   Once
when the Emperor, my father, joined battle with Robert, as
we have related, in the heat of that battle a certain Frank
exceedingly tall, directed his spear, spurred on his horse and
fell upon Aspietes like a thunderbolt.   The latter grasping
his sword received the Frank's terrific onslaught and was
wounded most severely, for the spear pierced his lung and
passed out through his spine.   However Aspietes was not
perturbed by the blow nor unhorsed, but settling himself
more firmly in his seat, struck the barbarian on his helmet
and cut both the helmet and the head in half.   And then both
fell from their horses, the Frank dead and Aspietes still breathing.   His attendants picked him up, all drained of blood,
tended him well and then carried him to the Emperor,
shewed him the spear and the wound and reported the death
of the Frank.   The Emperor was for some reason or other
mindful of this former act of bravery and daring and taking
it in conjunction with his descent and consequent reputation
sent him as a [presumedly] able general to Cilicia to oppose
Tancred and appointed him Stratopedarch, as I have just
written.

III   This is sufficient about these men.   To the various
generals engaged in the West he sent other letters enjoining
them to march to Sthlanitza without delay.   What happened
next ?   Did he after summoning the protagonists, relapse
nto ease, and enjoy his leisure and the pleasure of the baths,
as the Emperors who prefer a bestial life, are wont to do ?
No, certainly not, why he could not even endure staying in
the palace any longer.   He left Byzantium, as stated above,
travelled through the western countries, and reached Thessalonica in the month of September in the fourteenth Indiction
and in the twentieth year of his taking up the reins of government.   And he constrained the Empress to go with him

against her will. For her disposition was of such a nature
that she did not willingly appear much in public, but generally
kept at home and attended to her duties, such as reading the
books of the Saints and communing with herself and doing
acts of kindness and charity to men, especially to those who
were, as she saw from their conduct and manner of life, true
servants of God, and she persevered in prayers and a succession
of hymns. Whenever it behoved her to appear in public
as Empress on some very necessary occasion, she was overcome with shyness and her cheeks were mantled with blushes.

Similarly the philosopher Theano, when her forearm once
became uncovered and somebody jokingly said, " What
a beautiful forearm ! " replied " Yes, but not a public one."
And so the Empress, my mother, the image of dignity, the
temple of holiness, did not only dislike shewing her arm or
eyes to the public, but did not even like her voice to be
carried to unaccustomed ears. Such a wonderful example of
modesty was she ! But since, as it is said, not even the
gods can fight against necessity, she was obliged to accompany
the Emperor on his frequent expeditions. Her natural
modesty would have kept her at home in the palace, but her
devotion and ardent love for the Emperor drove her out of it
even against her will for various reasons, the first of which
was that the illness, which had attacked his feet, necessitated
very constant care. For in consequence of this gouty
affection, the Emperor had piercing pains and would not
submit to anybody's touch as readily as my mother's, for by
touching him carefully and rubbing skilfully she could assuage
the pains to a certain extent. (And now let nobody accuse
me of bragging, for I admire domestic virtues, nor suspect
me of telling falsehoods about the Emperor, for I am only
telling the truth.) The Emperor in very truth ever considered
his own comfort and affairs as secondary to the welfare of the
cities. For nothing could separate him from his love of the
Christians, neither pains nor pleasure nor the miseries of wars,
nor anything either great or small, neither the blazing heat of
summer, nor the biting cold of winter, nor any barbarian
attack. He was quite undaunted by all these things, and if
he did sink under a combination of diseases he would spring up
again at the call for help. The second and more important
reason why the Empress accompanied the Emperor was
because so many plots cropped up on all sides that he needed
constant guarding, and literally a many-eyed protecting power.
For, as night wove plots for him, so did the middle of the day ;

the evening would bring forth some fresh evil and the morning devise the worst ; God is witness of this. Was it not necessary therefore that the Emperor against whom so many wicked men conspired, should be watched over by a thousand eyes ? for some aimed their arrows at him, others whetted their sword in secret, and others, if opportunity for action was wanting, let loose their slanderous tongue and malicious talk. Who had more right to be by the Emperor's side to help him than she, his natural counsellor ? Who better than she looked after the Emperor and suspected the conspirators ? for she was quick in seeing what would be to his advantage, but still quicker in detecting his enemies' intrigues. For these reasons my mother was all in all to the ruler, my father, she was a sleepless eye at night, a most illustrious guardian by day, a good antidote to dangers at table and a salutary counterpotion to mischiefs arising from food. These were the reasons that thrust aside this woman's innate shyness, and gave her the bold eyes of a man (or encouraged her to meet the eyes of men) ; yet even in these circumstances she did not lose her usual modesty, but by her quiet looks and silence and by her self-respect remained little known to the majority. The only thing that shewed the Empress was following the army was a litter borne by two mules and covered with the imperial curtains, for the rest her divine body was concealed from view. One thing alone all acknowledged, namely, that some most excellent foresight conducted everything to do with the Emperor's malady, and that she was his tireless guardian, an ever-wakeful eye which never slumbered over its duties. And such of us as were well-disposed to the Emperor aided and abetted the mistress, my mother, in her care to the utmost of our respective ability, nor did we ever relax. I have written this especially for those who are fond of scoffing and reviling. For they bring a charge even against the innocent (the Homeric Muse, too, knew this human trait) and they disparage noble deeds and find fault with the faultless. And thus on the expedition which took place at that time (the Emperor was marching to meet Bohemund) she accompanied him, partly against, and partly of, her own will. For it was not necessary for the Empress to take part in the attack on the barbarian army. For how could she ? that would have been all very well for Tomyris and the Massagetan Sparethra, but not for my Irene. Her courage was used in another direction and though she was fully armed it was not with Athena's spear or the helmet of Hades, but her shield and

buckler and sword were for standing up bravely against
the chances and vicissitudes of life to which she knew rulers
were always exposed ; her activity in business, her stern
resistance to passion and her genuine loyalty were such as
Solomon lauds.

Thus my mother was prepared for wars of that kind, but in
other respects she was as peaceful as her name.

But since the moment for the struggle with the barbarian
was impending the Emperor was busy preparing everything
for this struggle, and saw to the forts being made secure and
where necessary, further strengthened ; in a word, he did his
best to get everything in good trim against Bohemund's arrival.
And he took the Empress with him partly for his own sake
and the reasons we have given, and partly because there was
no danger at the moment, and the time for war was not yet at
hand. The Empress took with her all the gold and coined
money of other quality she had as well as some of her other
precious possessions and left the city. And throughout the
journey she gave with lavish hand to the beggars, the men
clad in leather and the naked ; no one who asked of her went
away empty-handed. Even when she reached the tent
appointed for her, she did not immediately enter and lie down
to rest, but threw it open and gave the beggars free access.
For to this class she was very accessible, and allowed herself
to be both seen and heard by them. And she did not only give
money to the poor, but also good advice. If she noticed any
of strong physique who led a lazy life, she urged them to find
work and employment and earn the necessaries of life in that
way, rather than grow lax through sloth and go about begging
from door to door. And no juncture kept the Empress away
from such work. Now David is known to have mixed his
drink with tears ; but this Empress could be seen to mix her
food and drink daily with pity. I could have said a great deal
about this Empress, were it not that a loved daughter's testimony might have been suspected of falsehood and flattery of
her mother. But for those who have such suspicions, I will
adduce facts in corroboration of my words.

IV Directly the men of the western provinces heard
that the Emperor had arrived in Thessalonica, they all
assembled round him there, exactly as heavy bodies are
drawn by gravity to the centre. This time, indeed, a locust
did not precede the advent of the Franks as it did before ;
but a large comet appeared in the sky, the largest of all
that had ever been seen before, and some pronounced it to be
a beam-meteor, and others a javelin-meteor. For it was only

right that some unusual signs, predicting the strange things that were shortly to happen, should be sent from above. And this comet was to be seen shining brightly for a whole forty days and nights; and it seemed to rise in the West and travel across towards the East. All who saw it were dumbfounded and asked of what this meteor was the portent. The Emperor did not as a rule pay much attention to such matters, for he was of opinion that they arose from some natural cause, yet even he questioned the men who understood these things; and summoned Basilius (this man shewed great devotion to the Emperor), who had lately received the honourable post of Prefect of Byzantium, and consulted him about the comet which had appeared. Basilius said he would defer his answer till the next day, and he returned to his lodging (which was a chapel built long ago in honour of the evangelist John) and watched the comet when the sun was about setting. While he was thus worried and wearied with calculations, he happened to fall asleep, and in his sleep beheld the saint dressed in priestly robés. All overjoyed, he fancied he ' saw no illusive dream, but a reality.' Hence on recognising the saint he was fearful and begged him timidly to make known to him the message of the comet. And the saint replied that it foretold the movement of the Franks and ' its setting denotes their destruction in the same quarter of the globe.' Such is the story of the comet that appeared. The Emperor arrived in Thessalonica, as already stated, and there prepared for Bohemund's crossing by training the recruits in stretching the bow and shooting arrows at a mark and protecting themselves with their shields; by means of letters he was also procuring troops from foreign countries so that they might come quickly when required. He also showed great care for Illyria, strengthened the city of Dyrrachium and appointed Alexius, the Sebastocrator Isaac's second son, prefect of it. At the same time he ordered the Cyclades, and all the maritime towns of Asia and even of Europe, to get a fleet ready; and when several objected to building a fleet as Bohemund was in no haste to cross yet, he would not listen to them, but said that a general must be a watchful guardian, and not only be prepared for immediate happenings, but look far ahead, and by no means be caught unprepared when danger threatened through having stinted money, especially if he knew that the enemy was advancing. After having settled these matters very cleverly, he left Thessalonica for Strubitza and went on from there to Slopimus. On

hearing that John, the Sebastocrator's son, who had been
sent ahead previously had been defeated by the Dalmatians,
he sent enough troops to succour him.　Bolcanus meanwhile,
who was very guileful, at once opened negotiations for peace
with the Emperor and sent him the hostages he had demanded.
The Emperor lingered on in those parts for a year and two
months, and then he was informed that Bohemund was
still staying about in Lombardy and as winter was already
setting in, he dismissed all the soldiers to their homes and himself returned to Thessalonica.　Whilst he was journeying to
Thessalonica, the first son of the prince John Porphyrogenitus
was born at Balabista and a little girl was born at the same
time.　The Emperor attended the services of the commemoration of the Proto-martyr Demetrius in Thessalonica and then
returned to the Capital.

Here the following incident occurred.　Nearly in the
middle of the Forum of Constantine there was a bronze statue
looking towards the East standing on a conspicuous purple
pillar and holding a sceptre in its right hand, and in its left
a sphere fashioned of bronze.　This was said to be the
statue of Apollo, but the inhabitants of Constantinople
used to call it Anthelius, I believe.　But that great one
among kings, Constantine, the father and master of the city,
changed its name to his own, and called it a statue of the
Emperor Constantine.　Yet the name given originally
to the statue persisted, and everybody called it Anelius or
Anthelius.

Suddenly a very violent south-west wind arose, blew this
statue off its pedestal and hurled it to the ground, the sun
was then in the sign of the Bull.　Most interpreted this as a
bad omen, especially the Emperor's ill-wishers ; for they
whispered that this accident portended the Emperor's death.
But he said, " I know only one Lord of life and death, and do
not believe for a minute that the fall of an image can cause
a death.　For come, tell me when a Pheidias or any sculptor
by hewing stone produces a statue can he bring the dead to
life or bring forth living creatures ?　and, if he can, what will
be left for the Creator of all things ?　For ' It is I that will
kill and I will make alive,' He says, and not the fall or the
erection of this or that statue."　And indeed he always referred everything to the great providence of God.

V　And now a fresh potion of ills had been mixed again
for the Emperor ; this one was not prepared by ordinary
people, but certain men, very proud of their courage and

brilliant descent, who breathed murder, plotted against the imperial life. And at this point of my history I stop to wonder how it came about that the Emperor was surrounded by such a crowd of dangers. For there was nothing and no quarter from which agitations did not arise against him. At home disaffection was rife, and abroad rebellions never ceased. And at a time, when the Emperor had not yet over-come the difficulties at home, all the world outside burst into a blaze just as if Fortune were making the barbarians abroad and the pretenders at home spring up simultaneously like the self-grown Giants. And this in spite of the Emperor's administrating and managing the government in a very peaceful and humane way, and overwhelming everybody with kindnesses. For some he gladdened with honours and promotions, and never ceased enriching by handsome gifts; while as for the barbarians of whatever country they were, he never gave them any pretext for war nor enforced the necessity of it upon them, but when they made a tumult he checked them; for it is bad generals who in a time of universal peace purposely excite their neighbours to war. For peace is the end of every war, but to choose war in every case instead of peace for the sake of anything . . . and always to dis-regard the good end, this is the characteristic of senseless generals and demagogues and men who are working for the destruction of the state.

Now the Emperor Alexius used to do just the opposite and was exceptionally desirous of peace, and . . . when it existed he always did his utmost to maintain it, and when it was broken, often lay awake thinking how to restore it. By nature he was peaceful, but under the compulsion of cir-cumstances, very warlike. And I can boldly assert of this man that after imperial dignity had long been absent from the Roman Court, it returned in a certain degree under him and him alone, and was then first entertained as a guest by the Roman ruler. But, as I said at the beginning of this chapter, I cannot but be astonished at the influx of wars; for everything both at home and abroad was seen to be in a state of tumult. However, the Emperor Alexius perceived his enemies' secret and hidden plans beforehand, and by various devices he warded off their harmful effects. Both when he was fighting against the pretenders at home or the barbarians abroad, he ever anticipated the plots of the plotters by his keen instinct, and thus frustrated their attempts. From all these things I infer that Fate . . . the kingdom

because dangers accumulated from every direction, and the
body politic was disturbed, and every foreign nation was
raging against the Roman Empire ; it was as if a man were
so unfortunately placed as to be attacked by enemies from
without, whilst he was being exhausted physically by cruel
pains, and yet Providence roused him up to make a stand
against these manifold ills ; as was to be observed in this
case.

For the barbarian Bohemund, whom we have mentioned so
frequently, was preparing for his attack on the Roman throne
by collecting an immense army, and on the other side this
party of pretenders rose against the Emperor, as we said
before in the preface. The originators of the conspiracy
were four in all, by surname Anemades, and their Christian
names were Michael, Leo, . . . and . . . They
were brothers, firstly by birth, and secondly by disposition ; for they all agreed on this point, to kill the Emperor
and seize the sceptre. Others of the nobility associated
themselves with them, namely, the Antiochi of illustrious race,
and the two called Exazeni, that is Ducas and Hyaleas, the
boldest men in battle that ever were, and besides them
Nicetas Castamonites and a certain Curticius and George
Basilacius. These were all leaders in the military party,
and of the Senate there was John Solomon. Because of the
latter's superfluity of riches and brilliant lineage, Michael,
the leader of the Anemades quartette, deceitfully promised
that Solomon should be appointed Emperor. Now this
Solomon, who was the head of the senatorial body, was shortest
in stature and lightest in mind of the senators as well as of
his fellow-dupes. He thought he had completely exhausted
the doctrines of Aristotle and Plato, but he had not really a
good store of philosophic knowledge, for he was puffed up by
his extreme lightheadedness. For the rest he directed his
course towards the throne under full sail as if wafted along
by the Anemades. But they were utter impostors. For
Michael and his brothers had not the slightest intention of
raising him to the throne, far from it, but they used the
man's wealth and his levity for their own purpose. They
continually helped themselves to his stream of gold, and by
puffing him up with promises of the throne, they rendered him
quite subservient to themselves. They intended, if they
were successful and fortune smiled upon them, to elbow him
out of the way, and leave him fluttering on the sea, and when
they themselves had grasped the sceptre, they would assign

him but little glory and prosperity.   And when speaking
about the plot in his presence, no mention was made of the
Emperor's murder or the drawing of a sword, or of a battle or
war, so as not to alarm this man, for they knew of old that he
was a great coward in anything to do with war.   Accordingly
they embraced Solomon as if he were the chief leader of the
party.   Involved in this plot were also Sclerus, and Xerus,
who had then completed his term of office as Prefect of Constantinople.   Now, as said above, Solomon was of a light-
headed disposition and as he understood nothing of what
was meditated by Exazenus and Hyaleas and the Anemades
themselves, imagined he already held the Roman Empire in
his grasp, and would talk to people and try to win them over
by promises of gifts and honours.   Once Michael Anemas,
the chief actor in the drama, went to him and seeing him
talk to somebody asked what he was saying ; Solomon with
his usual simplicity replied, " He asked me for a certain
post, and on my promising it he agreed to become one of us
in the plot."   Michael cursed his foolishness and grew very
frightened as he realized that the other was incapable of holding
his tongue, and consequently did not visit him as frequently
as before.

      VI   Now the soldiers, I mean the Anemades, the Antiochi
and their fellow-conspirators, planned mischief against the
Emperor and arranged that directly they found an opportune
moment, they would at once carry into execution the Emperor's
premeditated murder.   But since Providence denied them
opportunity and time was running on, and they were afraid
they might be detected, they imagined they had found the
occasion they sought.   For, on awaking from sleep in the
early morning, in order to dissipate the humours (*lit.* : ' sweeten
the brine ') engendered by his many anxieties the Emperor
occasionally played at chess with one of his relations (this
game was invented by the luxurious Assyrians, and brought
thence to us) ;   so these men, with arms in their plotting
hands, intended to pass through the royal bedroom and get at
the Emperor in their longing for his murder.   This imperial
bedroom, where the Emperors then slept, was situated on the
left side of the chapel in the palace dedicated to the Mother
of God ; most people said it was dedicated to the great martyr
Demetrius.   To the right was an atrium paved with marble.
And the door leading to this from the chapel was always
open to all.   They intended, therefore, to enter the chapel
by this door, to force open the doors which shut off the

Emperor's bedroom and thus to enter and despatch him by the sword.

This indeed is what those guilty men purposed against him who had done them no wrong. But God wrecked their plans. For somebody revealed the plot to the Emperor, who at once summoned them all. First he had John Solomon and George Basilacius introduced into the palace to a place close to the small room in which he happened to be with his family around him. He wanted to ask them a few questions, and as he had long known that they were very simple-minded, he thought he would easily learn the details of the plot. But in answer to his repeated questions they denied everything ; then the Sebastocrator Isaac approached them and nodding to Solomon said, " Solomon, you know well the goodness of my brother, the Emperor. Now if you will give a full account of the plot you will be granted an immediate pardon, but, if not, then you will be handed over to horrible tortures." Solomon looked fixedly at him, and then at the barbarians standing in a circle round the Sebastocrator, brandishing their one-edged axes on their shoulders, and forthwith fell to trembling, and revealed everything and gave the names of his fellow-plotters, but insisted that he knew nothing about any intention to murder. They were then handed over to the men assigned to guard them and put into separate prisons. Afterwards the Emperor and his brother questioned the rest about the plot ; they confessed everything and even avowed their intention to murder. When it was found that the soldiers had arranged this, or rather Michael Anemas, the ringleader of the plot, who had murderous feelings against the Emperor, they were all banished, and their property confiscated. However, Solomon's house was given to the Empress, as it was very beautiful. But she, with her usual kindness, took pity on Solomon's wife, and gave it back to her without taking the slightest thing out of it. And Solomon was kept imprisoned in Sozopolis. But Anemas and the others who were the prime authors with him, had their heads closely shaven and their beards cut off, and then the Emperor ordered them to be led through the middle of the Agora and afterwards have their eyes gouged out. So the masters of the ceremonies took them and dressed them in sacks and decorated their heads with the entrails of oxen and sheep as if they were fillets, then placed them on oxen, not astride, but sideways, and conducted them through the court of the palace. Lictors gambolled before them, singing

a ridiculous song suitable to the procession in a loud voice ;
it was expressed in rude language, and its meaning was somewhat like this . . . . . .   For the song aimed
at bidding all the public come out and look at these
horn-bearing pretenders who had whetted their swords
against the Emperor.   So people of every age flocked together
to view this spectacle, and even we, the Emperor's daughters,
went out to see it secretly.   When the people saw Michael
looking up to the palace and raising suppliant hands to
heaven, and by gestures asking that his arms should be torn
from his shoulders, and his legs from his buttocks, and his
head be cut off, every creature was moved to tears and
lamentations, and we, the Emperor's daughters, more than
all.   And I in my desire to rescue the man from such misery
repeatedly implored the Empress, my mother, to come and
see the procession.   For to tell the truth we were concerned
about the men for the Emperor's sake, for in them he would
be deprived of such good soldiers, especially Michael on whom
the heaviest sentence had been pronounced.   Accordingly,
when I saw how humbled he was by his misfortune, I tried to
force my mother, as I was saying, in order that the men
might perchance, be saved from the danger which stood so
near them.   For the conductors were leading the procession
very slowly with the purpose of giving an opportunity for
pardon being granted to the guilty.   But as she delayed coming (for she was sitting with the Emperor and they were conjointly making intercessions to God before the Mother of God)
I went down and standing fearfully outside the doors, for I
did not dare to go in, I tried to draw her out by signs.   And
finally she was persuaded and came out to see the sight.
When she saw Michael she pitied him and ran back to the
Emperor, shedding bitter tears, and besought him, not
once or twice, but repeatedly, to spare Michael's eyes.   He
at once dispatched a messenger to stop the executioners ;
and, by hurrying, the man got there just before they had
passed inside the ' Hands ' as they were called ; for he who
has once passed them, can no longer be saved from his fate.
For the Emperors had fixed up these bronze hands in a very
conspicuous place on a lofty stone arch with the fixed intention that if a man, condemned to death by law, should
be short of them, and on the way receive a pardon from the
hand of the Emperor, he was to be freed from his punishment.
For the Hands signified that the Emperor took the men back
into his arms and held them firmly, and did not loose them

from the hands of his mercy.   But if they passed the Hands,
this was a sign that in all truth the imperial majesty rejected
them.   The fate of men under punishment is therefore in the
hands of fortune, which I interpret as the decree of God, and
it is right, therefore, to implore His help.   For either mercy
reaches them short of the Hands and the wretches are delivered from danger, or they have passed beyond the Hands
and are far from salvation.   But I attribute it all to God's
providence, which on this occasion delivered the man from
the gouging out of his eyes.   For it seems probable that it was
God who moved us on that day to take pity on the man.
For the messenger of salvation hastened and reached this side
of the arch on which the bronze Hands are fixed, gave the
letter granting the pardon to the men leading Michael, took
him and came back with him, and on reaching a tower,
built close to the palace, confined him there, for such were his
orders.

VII   Michael had not yet been liberated from prison
before Anemas' prison received Gregory again.   For this tower
was one of those in the city-walls near the palace of Blachernæ,
and was called the ' Tower of Anemas ' just as if it had got
this name by fate as Anemas was first to be confined there in
chains and was to spend a long time in it.   For in the course
of the twelfth Indiction the Gregory already mentioned who
had long been hatching rebellion, on being appointed Duke
of Trapezus, disclosed his secret on his journey to Trapezus.
For he met Dabatenus (who was returning to Constantinople
after handing over the post of Duke to Taronites), took
him prisoner and kept him in jail in Tebenna ;   and not
Dabatenus only, but also several of the leading Trapezuntines,
among them the nephew of Bacchenus.   As they were not
released from imprisonment, they all united, subjected the
jailers put over them by the rebel to ill-treatment, led them
outside the walls and drove them some distance away.   Then
they appropriated Tebenna and held it.   The Emperor
sent many letters to recall him and at other times advised
him to desist from his wicked doings if he wished to obtain
mercy and be restored to his former status ;   or again he
would threaten him if he did not obey.   But Gregory
so far from listening to the Emperor's wise counsel, actually
sent him a letter of many pages in which he attacked, not
only the most important members of the Senate and the
army, but even the Emperor's relations and marriage-connec-
tions.   From this letter the Emperor became certain that

Gregory was daily going on the downward path, and was heading towards complete madness and consequently despaired of him. In the fourteenth Indiction he sent his nephew John, the son of his eldest sister, and the rebel's cousin on his father's side to him; he was at first to give him salutary advice, for he thought Gregory would listen to him because of their bond of kinship and consanguinity. But if he would not listen, John was to oppose him with a large force and resist him manfully by land and sea. When Gregory Taronites heard he was coming he at once left for Colonea (a very strong and impregnable fort) in order to call Tanismanes to his aid. John was informed of this as he was starting, so he detached the Franks and some picked Roman troops from his army, and sent them against Gregory. They overtook him and engaged him in a fierce battle, in which two brave soldiers attacked him with their spears and struck him down from his horse. They then conducted him to John, who led him captive to the Emperor though he had sworn not even to see him, still less to deign him worthy of conversation on the way. And yet he interceded strongly for him to the Emperor, who pretended that he intended to deprive him of his eyes. At last the Emperor reluctantly avowed his hypocrisy, yielded to John's prayers but exhorted him repeatedly not to let their conversation be divulged. Three days later, he had Gregory's hair and beard shaven off close to the skin and led in that condition through the middle of the Agora and then imprisoned in the tower of Anemas of which I have just spoken. Since even in prison he was still foolish and uttered words of madness daily to his jailers the Emperor bestowed great care upon him for a long time, in the hope of making him change and give proof of repentance. However he was the same as before and often asked for my Cæsar as in former days he had been friendly with us. Consequently the Emperor gave my Cæsar permission to visit him in order to lift him out of his deep despondency and give him good advice. But the other seemed very slow in changing for the better, and for that reason he remained prisoner for a long time. When he was granted pardon, he enjoyed such kindness and gifts and honour as never before, for such was the Emperor's clemency in these matters.

VIII Having thus attended to the matter of the conspirators and the rebel Gregory he did not on account of these forget Bohemund, but summoned Isaac Contostephanus, and promoted him to be Great Duke of the fleet, and sent

him to Dyrrachium and further threatened him that his
eyes would be put out if he did not manage to arrive in
Illyria before Bohemund crossed.

He also continually sent letters to his nephew Alexius,
the Duke of Dyrrachium, stirring him up and bidding him
keep a sharp look-out and to order those who were at guard
on the sea to do the same, to prevent Bohemund's crossing
secretly, but to send word of his crossing at once by letter.
That is what the Emperor did.

Now Contostephanus' only orders were to watch the
straits of Lombardy carefully and to prevent the ships
crossing which Bohemund was sending ahead to carry all
his apparatus from the one coast to the other—in fine, not
to allow anything whatever to be conveyed from Lombardy
to Illyria. When he departed he did not even know the like-
liest spot from which the ships would sail across to Illyria, and
not only that, but he disregarded orders and crossed to Hydruntum, which is a town situated on the coast of Lombardy.
This town was commanded by a woman, Tancred's mother,
it was said, whether she was the sister of Bohemund (so often
mentioned in this history already) or not, I cannot say positively, for I do not know for certain whether Tancred was
related to Bohemund on his mother's side, or his father's.
When Contostephanus reached the town and brought his ships
to anchor, he made an attack on the walls [of Brindisi] and
very nearly captured the city. But the woman inside who had
a sound mind and a determined character, directly he had
anchored his ships there, sent for one of her sons and bade
him come with all speed. By now the whole fleet was in
great spirits, thinking the town was theirs, and all began
shouting acclaim to the Emperor ; and the woman in this
difficulty ordered the inhabitants to do likewise. At the
same time she sent envoys to Contostephanus confessing her
allegiance to the Emperor, and promised to make terms of
peace with him, and said she would come out to Contostephanus
to consult him about them so that he could explain everything
to the Emperor. She devised all this to keep Contostephanus
in suspense, hoping that perchance in the meantime her son
might arrive, and then she would throw off the mask, as they
say of the tragedians, and attack him in battle. Thus while
all the men inside and outside the town were hurrahing
and the shouts filled the whole neighbourhood, and that
martial woman, as I said, was holding Contostephanus in
suspense by her messages and promises, the son she expected

actually arrived with his fellow-counts, at once attacked
Contostephanus and routed him completely. All the men
of the fleet being unversed in land-fighting threw themselves
into the sea.   Now there were a goodly number of Scythians
in the Roman army and some of these (as is the barbarians'
custom) had run ahead during the battle to forage, and in
this way it happened that six of them were taken captive.
They were sent to Bohemund and, when he saw them, he
considered them a very great asset, and went straightway
with them to Rome. There he approached the apostolic
seat, and conversed with the Pope and raised his fierce ire
against the Romans and fanned the ancient grudge of those
barbarians against our race.   And in order to excite the Pope's
and his Italians' rage still further, Bohemund brought in the
captured Scythians as a convincing proof that the Emperor
Alexius was hostile to the Christians, as he used unbelieving
barbarians and monstrous mounted archers to wield weapons
and draw their bows against Christians.   And in every conversation of this kind he drew the Pope's attention to those
Scythians who were in Scythian dress and, as usual, looked
extremely barbaric ; and all the time he kept calling them
' pagans ' ;   as the Latins' habit is, and mocking at their
name and appearance.   Very cunningly, as you see, he handled
this affair of the war against the Christians, in order that he
might convince the high-priestly mind that he had good
reason to be aroused to enmity with the Romans ;   at the
same time wooing the support of a voluntary army of the
more rustic and stupid men.   For who among the barbarians close by, or further off, would not come of his own
accord to a war against us when the high-priest gave his
consent, and an apparently just cause aroused every horse,
man and soldierly arm ?   The Pope was constrained by
Bohemund's arguments, and agreed with him, and sanctioned
his crossing into Illyria.   And now I must return to the subject in hand.

The land-soldiers did indeed put up a valiant fight, but
the others were engulfed in the waves of the sea. Consequently the Franks had a brilliant victory in hand, but our
braver soldiers, especially those of the higher rank, pre-eminent
among whom were Nicephorus Exazenus Hyaleas and his
cousin Constantine Exazenus, called Ducas, and that
most courageous man, Alexander Euphorbenus, and others
of similar worth and rank—these, I say, mindful of ' impetuous valour ' turned back, drew their swords and fought

with all their might and main and revived the battle and carried off a brilliant victory over the Franks. In this way Contostephanus obtained relief from the attacks of the Franks and slipped his cables and sailed away with his whole fleet to Valona. When he had first come to Dyrrachium he had posted his ships of war all about from Dyrrachium itself up to Valona and even up to the place called Chimara (now Dyrrachium is one hundred stades distant from Valona and Chimara is sixty stades further away from Valona). But now that he heard that Bohemund's crossing was imminent, and as he surmised that he would probably cross to Valona, for the passage to Valona was shorter than that to Dyrrachium, he decided that a stricter guard must be kept over Valona. So he sailed with the other Dukes and kept a careful watch on the intervening straits from Valona ; he placed scouts on the ridge of the hill called Jason to keep a look-out over the sea and watch for the ships. A Frank who had just crossed from Italy assured them that Bohemund was on the very point of starting. On being informed of this, the Contostephani who shrank with dread from a naval battle with Bohemund (and were indeed terror-stricken by the mere thought of it) pretended they were ill and must therefore go to the baths. Landulph, commander of the whole fleet, who had a long and varied experience of sea-craft and of naval battles, kept exhorting them to be continually on their guard, and to expect Bohemund's arrival. But the Contostephani, when leaving for Chimara to take the baths, left the man called the second Drungaire of the fleet with the monoreme Excussatum on watch near the promontory Glossa which is not very far from Valona. And Landulph remained at Valona with a suitable supply of ships.

IX After making these arrangements the Contostephani on their side went off to take the baths, or so pretended. Bohemund on his side arranged twelve pirate-vessels around his own, all biremes, with a large number of rowers, who by the regular beat of their oars made a loud, echoing noise. In a circle round this fleet he placed merchant ships on either side, like a fence inside of which he enclosed the ships of war. And if you had seen it, viewing it even from afar from some headland, you would have likened this fleet under sail to a floating city. For Fortune also favoured him to a certain degree. For the sea was quite calm except for a gentle southerly breeze which just rippled the surface and swelled the sails of the merchant vessels. This just enabled them to sail with the wind while the ships that were rowed kept level with the sailing vessels and from the middle of the Adriatic sea the noise this fleet made was audible on both continents. So this barbarian fleet of Bohemund's was a sight well fitted to inspire awe, and, if the sailors of the Contostephani shrank from it in horror, I cannot blame them, nor would I accuse the men of cowardice. For even the famous Argonautic fleet would have been afraid of him and his fleet arranged in this fashion, much more so then the Contostephani, the Landulphs and other such folk. Indeed, when Landulph saw Bohemund crossing the sea with this dread array and with transports carrying myriads of men, as we have already more accurately described, he sailed away a little from Valona as he was unable to fight against such numbers and gave Bohemund a free entry. The latter made use of his good fortune and crossed from Bari to Valona and disembarked all the army he had brought over the sea on the opposite coast, and then first of all devastated the whole sea-coast. For he brought an incredibly large army of Franks and Gauls, and men from the island of Thule who usually fought for the Romans, but through force of circumstances had on this occasion joined him ; and besides this there were many of the Germanic race and of the Celtiberians. Next he dispersed all these troops which he had mustered over the whole country along the Adriatic sea and after ravaging that systematically he attacked Epidamnus, which we call Dyrrachium ; for his intention was to take this town and then devastate all the country right up to Constantinople. Now Bohemund was skilled above all men in the art of sieges even surpassing the famous Demetrius Poliorcetes, and as he had set his whole mind on Epidamnus, he moved up all his engineering contrivances against that town. First he encompassed with his army and besieged all the places close to, and those at some distance from, the town of Dyrrachium ; at times the Roman armies would oppose him, and at others there was nobody at all to interfere with him. After several battles and encounters and massacres he contemplated, as we said before, besieging the town of Dyrrachium itself.

But before speaking of the tyrant Bohemund's fight for Dyrrachium it is necessary to explain the position of the city. It is situated on the very shores of the Adriatic sea. In front of it lies the deep, long sea which in breadth stretches across to the opposite coast of Italy; in length by turning to the north-east it goes right up to the barbarian Vetones, opposite whom lies the province of Apulia. These form the boundaries of the Adriatic. The town Dyrrachium, or Epidamnus, an ancient Greek city, lies somewhat lower than Elissus and on its left side, for Elissus stands higher and more to the right. This Elissus is either named after some river Elissus, a tributary of the great river Drymon, or the fortress was simply given that name, I cannot say which it was. Now Elissus is a fort built on a hill and quite impregnable, and looks down upon Dyrrachium in the plains, as the saying is; and it is so secure that both by land and sea it can afford great assistance to Dyrrachium. Of this fort Elissus the Emperor Alexius made use in order to help the city of Epidamnus both from the side of the river Drymon which was navigable, and from the land-side he strengthened Dyrrachium and brought in necessaries by land and water, everything, in fact, that was required for the sustenance of the soldiers and citizens in it or in the way of arms and equipment for fighting. This river Drymon (for I must add a few words about this stream) runs down from the lake Lychnis through some hundred channels, which we call 'bridges.' The present corrupted language calls this lake Achris, after the King of the Bulgarians, who lived in the time of the Emperors Constantine and Basilius Porphyrogeniti, and was at first called Mocrus, and latterly Samuel. For separate rivers amounting to one hundred in number come out of this lake as if from different sources, they never fail and flow separately in this way until they join the river near Deure, from which point it is called Drymon, and when united to this they widen it out and make a very big river of it. It flows past the extreme end of Dalmatia, and goes north, then it bends to the south, washes the feet of Elissus, and empties itself into the Adriatic gulf.

Let this be sufficient about the position of Dyrrachium and Elissus and the security of both places. Whilst still lingering in the capital the Emperor heard by letters from the Duke of Dyrrachium of Bohemund's crossing and therefore hastened his departure. For the Duke of Dyrrachium was most vigilant and did not even allow himself any sleep, and when he knew for certain that Bohemund had sailed across to the plains of Illyria, disembarked from his ships, and pitched his camp there, he sent a Scythian, a 'winged' messenger as they are called, to the Emperor to announce his crossing. He found the Emperor returning from the chase, and running in at full speed and bowing his head to the ground he shouted out in a piercing voice that Bohemund had crossed. All those present stood stark-frozen each in his place, for at the mere name of Bohemund they lost their wits.   But the Emperor, full of courage and resource as ever, loosed the strap of his shoe and said, " For the present let us go to lunch, afterwards we will discuss the matter of Bohemund."

BOOK XIII

I

WE were, one and all, astounded at the Emperor's dignified attitude. But although outwardly he pretended for the sake of those present to receive that message with disdain, yet inwardly he was deeply perturbed by it. Then he decided that he must leave Byzantium again and this although he knew that things at home were not going on well for him ; yet he arranged matters in the palace and the Queen of Cities and appointed as guardians the eunuch Eustathius Cymineanus, the Great Drungaire of the Fleet, and Nicephorus, called the son of Decanus. Afterwards he left Byzantium with a few companions—and those his relations—on the first day of November in the first Indiction and occupied the imperial purple tent at Geranium outside the city. But he was anxious because at his departure the Mother of God had not displayed the usual miracle in Blachernæ. For this reason after spending four days in the same place, he took the return journey with his wife at sunset and secretly entered the church of the Mother of God with a few attendants. After singing the correct hymns and making more than usually lengthy prayers, the customary miracle was shewn and consequently he left the church with high hopes. On the following day he commenced the journey to Thessalonica, and when he reached Chœrobacchi he appointed John Taronites governor of it. This man was of noble birth, had been adopted by the Emperor as a child and served him a long time as under-secretary ; he was of a very energetic disposition and an expert in Roman law, and extolled the Emperor's decrees provided the orders he gave were consonant with His Majesty. For he had a free tongue and though he never expressed himself impudently when he found fault, yet he was such as the Stagirite commands a dialectician to be. After leaving Chœrobacchi the Emperor continually sent letters to Isaac, the Duke of the Fleet, and his fellow-officers, I mean Ducas Exazenus and Hyaleas, to keep a perpetual look-out and prevent boats sailing over to Bohemund from Lombardy. When he reached Mestus, the Empress wished to return to the palace, but the Emperor compelled her to go further ; and after they both had crossed the river called Eurus, they pitched their tents at Psyllus. There the man who had just escaped one assassin would have been like to fall under the hands of another, had not the Divine hand held back the murderers from the deed. For a certain man who traced his descent on one side, although he was illegitimate, from the famous Aronii[1] urged on the disaffected party to murder, and revealed this secret plot to his own brother Theodore. Whether others of the disaffected were also aware of this plan, I do not wish to say. Anyhow, they had suborned a Scythian slave, Demetrius by name, to perpetrate the murderous deed (this slave's master was none but Aaron himself). They fixed the Empress's departure as the moment for its accomplishment and told the Scythian to seize an opportunity then and drive his sword into the Emperor's side either when he met him in a corner or if he could catch him sleeping. And Demetrius with murder in his heart whetted his sword and got his bloody right hand ready. But Justice then staged something new. For, as the Empress did not leave the Emperor soon but kept on accompanying him as he enticed her further day after day, those murderers grew wearied when they saw that the Emperor's sleepless guardian, I mean the Empress, still lingered near, so they wrote some libellous stuff (*famosa*) and threw it into the Emperor's tent. (The men who threw it were not seen ; and the word '*famosa*' denotes scurrilous writing.) The writing advised the Emperor to proceed with his journey and the Empress to return to Byzantium. Now the law punishes such libels very severely ; for it burns them in the fire and subjects their authors to the most excruciating punishments. But as they had missed their aim, they descended to the foolery of libelling. After the Emperor had lunched and the majority of his attendants had retired and only Romanus the Manichæan and the eunuch Basilius Psyllus and Theodore, Aaron's brother, were present, a libel was again found thrown under the Emperor's couch ; it contained a fierce invective against the Empress because she accompanied the Emperor and had not gone back to the capital sooner. For their design was to secure complete

[1] The descendants of Aaron or Araon, a prince of Bulgaria.

freedom of action. But the Emperor knew who had thrown
it, and said very angrily with a nod to the Empress, " Either
you or I or one of these here present threw this." At the
bottom of the paper was written " I, a monk, write this ;
at present, Emperor, you do not know me but you shall
see me in your dreams." Now one Constantine, a eunuch,
who had been the table-servant of the Emperor's father and
now waited on the Empress, was standing outside the tent
one night about the third watch and singing the appointed
hymns when he heard someone shout, " If I do not go in and
tell him all you have planned and also all about the silly
libellous writing you threw in, then let no one any longer
count me a man ! " Constantine at once ordered his own
servant to go and catch the man who was talking. He
went, recognized Aaron's servant, Strategius, bound him and
led him to the Prefect of the table. Directly he was brought
in, he disclosed all he knew ; and Constantine took him and
conducted him to the Emperor. But at that moment their
Majesties were asleep. However, he met the eunuch Basilius
and compelled him to go and report all he had told him about
Aaron's man Strategius. So Basilius went in at once and took
Strategius with him. Directly the latter was questioned,
he disclosed with great clearness the whole drama of the
foolish libels, also named the man who had arranged the
murder and even the very fellow hired to assassinate the
Emperor, " My master Aaron," he said, " conjointly with
others, of whom thy Majesty is not quite ignorant, have
plotted against thy life, O Emperor. And as thy murderer
they suborned Demetrius, my fellow-slave, a Scythian by
origin, with a very murderous disposition and strong arms,
ready to dare anything, and of a very bestial and cruel mind.
To this man they have handed a double-edged sword and
given him this inhuman order that he is to come up close
and with unflinching boldness drive the sword into thy
Majesty's entrails." But the Emperor (who was never
ready to believe such tales) said, " Is it not perhaps because
you hate your masters and your fellow-servant that you have
woven this accusation ? Come now, tell me as much as you
know of the truth. For in case you should be found to be
lying, your accusation will not be to your advantage."
But the fellow asserted that he was telling the truth, so was
handed over to Basilius in order that he might give the latter
the libellous writings. Basilius took him away and led him
into Aaron's tent where everybody was asleep, and there

the man picked up a military wallet full of such writings and handed it to Basilius. By this time the day had broken, the Emperor glanced through the writings and recognized that his assassination had been arranged, and sent orders to the governors of the city that Aaron's mother should be banished to Chœrobacchi, Aaron to . . . and his brother, Theodore, to Anchialus. This matter retarded the Emperor's onward journey for five days.

II Whilst on his way to Thessalonica, where the contingents from all the various districts were assembled, he thought it would not be amiss to hold a review of the troops drawn up in battle array. In a short time the legions were drawn up in companies with their captains in front and the rear-guard and those who held the middle of the line followed in order, all in gleaming armour (and the array was an awesome sight), and fitted close to each other like the wall of a city. You would have fancied you were looking at bronze statues and metal soldiers as they all stood absolutely still on the plain with only their spears quivering as if longing to taste flesh. The Emperor arranged them in this order and moved them about and made them manœuvre how they would advance to the spear-side or to the shield-side. Then he separated the newly-recruited corps from the whole army and appointed as commanders over these soldiers the men whom he himself had especially brought up and trained in military exercises. These were three hundred in all, every one of them young and tall, in full physical vigour, with beards scarcely grown and very adroit in the use of the bow and very steady in throwing the spear. They had been chosen from various races and formed a kind of select army within the general Roman army directly under the command of the Emperor as General, for he was to them not only their Emperor but General and teacher as well. From these he further picked out the cleverest and appointed them leaders of their companies and sent them into the valleys through which the barbarian army was expected to pass. But he himself was wintering in Thessalonica. Now, as we have said, the tyrant Bohemund crossed with an enormous fleet from the other side into our country and then poured his whole Frankish army over our plains. From there he marched on Epidamnus in battle-order thinking he might perhaps be able to take it without a blow; but, if not, he would capture the city by means of siege-engines and stone-throwing machines. This at least was his intention. He bivouacked opposite the gate that opens to the East on which there stands an equestrian statue in bronze, and after reconnoitring he began the siege. For the whole of that winter he made plans and examined every corner to see at which point Dyrrachium could be taken. But when spring began to smile, since he had made his troops cross once for all, he set fire to his ships of burden, his cavalry-transports and, as I might say, his military ships. This was partly a strategic movement to prevent his soldiers from looking towards the sea, partly too it was due to the compulsion of the Roman fleet ; and then he gave his whole attention to the siege. To begin with he surrounded the city completely with his barbarian army and indulged in skirmishing. (In reply to this the archers of the Roman army shot at them, sometimes from the towers of Dyrrachium and sometimes from a distance.) He would also send out divisions of the Frankish army who would engage us in battle or be engaged by us. He took Petroula and the fort called Mylus, which lies on the other side of the river Diabolis, and other such towns in the neighbourhood of Dyrrachium he received as his portion by the law of war. These things he did by military force ; but at the same time he was constructing machines of war, building movable sheds (*or* ' tortoises ') with towers and battering rams, and other sheds to protect the diggers and the sappers, he worked all the winter and summer, and by his threats and deeds terrified the men who were already terrified. But even so he could not shake the Roman power in the slightest. And the question of commissariat was becoming very difficult for him. For all the food-stuffs he had originally brought in as plunder from the country round Dyrrachium had been used up already, and the sources from which he had hoped to get further supplies were blocked by the Roman soldiery who occupied the valleys and passes and even the sea-board itself. Consequently a severe famine overtook them, consuming both horses and men alike, as the horses had no fodder and the men no food. In addition to this the barbarian army was seized with a disorder of the stomach, apparently due to some unsuitable cereal, that is millet ; but in reality the wrath of God swooped down upon this innumerable and irresistible army and caused continuous deaths.

III   However, this misfortune seemed light to the man of tyrannical mind who threatened to destroy the whole world. In spite of it he still went on contriving, and gathered himself together like a wounded beast, and, as we have said, his whole mind was concentrated on the siege. First he completed a tortoise with a battering-ram,[1] an indescribable object, and rolled it up to the eastern side of the city. And merely to look at it was a fearsome sight, for it was built in the following manner. They made a small shed, fashioning it in the shape of a parallelogram, put wheels under it, and covered its sides, both above and laterally, with ox-hides sewn together, and thus, as Homer would say, they made the roof and the walls of the machine ' of seven bull's-hides,' and then hung the battering-rams inside. When the machine was ready, he drove it up to the wall by means of a large number of men pushing it along from inside with poles and bringing it close to the walls of Dyrrachium. When it seemed near enough and at an appropriate distance, they took off the wheels, and fixed the machine firmly on all sides with wooden pegs, so that the roof might not be shaken to pieces by the blows. Afterwards some very strong men on either side of the ram pushed it violently against the wall with regular co-ordinated movement. The men would push forward the ram violently with a single movement and the ram thus brought up against the wall shattered it, then it rebounded, and returning made a second shattering. And this it did several times as it was swung several times in either direction, and did not cease making holes in the wall. The engineers of old who invented this thing near Gadira[2] probably named it a ' ram ' by taking the metaphor from our rams who exercise themselves by butting at each other. But the inhabitants laughed at this futile battering of the wall by the barbarians and at the men working the ram, and at their ineffective siege, and they threw the gates open and bade them come in, for they utterly despised the blows made by the ram. " For," said they, " the ram will never make such a large opening by its battering, as the one this gate presents." Consequently this work was shown to be futile owing to the bravery of the inhabitants and the confidence of the governor Alexius, the Emperor's nephew ; and the enemy themselves relaxed and abandoned the siege as far as this part was concerned. For the bravery of the inhabitants and their opening the gates to the barbarians and shewing them a bold face had made cowards of them and they abandoned that machine. So the work round the battering-ram stood still. None the less, fire was thrown down from above on to this engine which

[1] *Or* a belfry.   [2] = Cadiz.

now stood idle and immovable for the aforesaid reasons,
and converted it into ashes. Desisting from this, the
Frankish crowd turned its thoughts to another more terrible
machine which was placed against the north wall opposite
the ducal residence, called the Prætorium. The configuration
of this locality was as follows. The Prætorium stood on a
hill, not a hill of rock but of earth, and the wall of the city
ran over it. Opposite this hill Bohemund's men now began
to dig in a definite direction. For the besiegers had devised
this new mischief against the city and invented a new
knavish siege-engine to apply to the town. For as they dug,
they went along under the ground like moles boring holes
in the soil and in places protecting themselves by sheds
with high roofs against the stones and arrows which were
thrown from above, and in others propping up the earth above
them with poles, and thus they went on in a straight line.
So they made a very broad and long tunnel and always carried
away the earth from their diggings in wagons. When they
had bored through sufficiently far, they rejoiced as if they
had accomplished a great task. But the men in the city
were not negligent for at some distance from the other they
dug out the earth and made a good-sized tunnel and then
posted themselves along its whole strength to watch for the
spot where the besieging party would break through from
their tunnel to ours. And soon they found it, for they heard
them knocking and digging and undermining the base of
the walls and, above all, their . . . Then they opened
up a little hole opposite and when they saw the quantity of
workers by means of this peep-hole, they burnt their faces to
ashes with fire. Now this fire is prepared from the following
ingredients. The readily combustible rosin is collected from
the pine and other similar evergreen trees and mixed with
sulphur. Then it is introduced into reed-pipes and blown
by the man using it with a strong continuous breath and at
the other end fire is applied to it and it bursts into flame and
falls like a streak of lightning on the faces of the men opposite.
This fire the men of Dyrrachium used directly they were face
to face with the enemy, and burnt their beards and faces.
And the enemy could be seen, like a swarm of bees which
has been smoked out, rushing out in disorder from the place
they had entered in good order. Since this labour had also
been expended in vain and this idea of the barbarians had
not resulted in any good, they devised a third expedient.
This was a wooden tower, and report says that the building

of this siege-apparatus was not commenced after the failure
of the devices already tried, but a whole year before.
Evidently this was the real work, and the other devices
afore-mentioned were only accessories. Before proceeding
I must describe in a few words the appearance of the city of
Dyrrachium. The walls were flanked by towers standing
up above it all around and rising as high as eleven feet, which
were ascended by a spiral stair and strengthened by battlements. Such was the appearance and the defence of the city.
The thickness of the walls was remarkable, in fact so great
was its width that more than four horsemen could ride abreast
on it quite safely. These few cursory words about the wall
had to be said so that what I am going to relate now may be
clear. The construction of this towering edifice, which
Bohemund's barbarians built like the tower of a shed, is
difficult to describe and was fearful to look at, as men who saw
it told me, not to speak of those whom the horrible monster
approached. It was fashioned in this wise. A wooden tower
was built on a square base and carried to such a height
that it overtopped the towers of the city by five or six cubits.
The wooden tower had to be constructed in the way described
in order that by letting down the hanging drawbridge, the
soldiers could run down easily to the tower-level of the city
wall. And then they thought the natives would be continually
pushed backwards, and unable to stand up against their
violent onrush. And it really seems that the barbarians
besieging Dyrrachium had a very good knowledge of the
science of optics, for without that science they could not
have measured the height of the walls ; anyhow if they did not
know optics, they understood the use of optical instruments.
The tower was certainly terrible to look at, and when moving
seemed still more terrible. For its base was raised on a
number of wheels, and, as it was levered along with crowbars
by the soldiers inside, it caused amazement, as the source of
its motion was invisible and it seemed to be moving of its
own accord like some towering giant. It was completely
covered in from top to base and divided into several floors,
and all around were openings in the shape of loop-holes
through which arrows were shot. On the top floor stood
high-spirited men, fully armed, with swords in their hands
ready to stand on defence. When this terrific object drew
near the wall, the men under Alexius, the military governor
of the city of Dyrrachium, lost no time, but whilst Bohemund
was building this machine outside the walls, to be an infallible

captor of the city, they built a counter one inside. For
seeing to what a height that self-moving tower reached and
where they had planted it after taking off the wheels, they
fixed opposite the tower four very long beams which stood
up like a scaffold from a square base. Then they introduced
some flooring between these upright beams and thus made
an erection which exceeded the wooden tower outside by
one cubit. And the structure was left open all round for it did
not require any protection except at the top where it was
roofed over. Next Alexius' soldiers carried up the liquid
fire to the top story of the open structure with intent to shoot
it against the wooden tower opposite. But this idea and its
execution did not seem sufficient for the complete destruction
of the machine. For the fire when directed against it would
only catch the extreme top of the tower. So what did they
devise ? they filled the space between the wooden tower
and the city-tower with all kinds of inflammable material
and poured streams of oil upon it. To this they applied fire,
namely torches and fire-brands, which smouldered for a short
time, then flared up a little and finally burst into tall
flames. As the fiery streaks of the liquid fire also contributed
their share, that whole terrific construction all made of wood
caught fire, and made an immense noise and was a terrible
sight for the eyes. And that enormous fire was seen for
thirteen stades round. The tumult and the confusion of the
barbarians inside was tremendous and hopeless, for some were
caught by the fire and burnt to ashes, and others threw themselves to the ground from the top. And there was also much
shouting and wild confusion among the barbarians outside
who re-echoed their cries.

IV This is enough about the gigantic tower and the
siege of the barbarians ; and the story must now revert to
the Emperor.

When spring set in the Empress returned from Thessalonica to the capital and the Emperor continued his onward
journey and by way of Pelagonia he reached Diabolis which
lies at the foot of those impracticable passes of which we
have spoken before. As he had thought out a new plan of
campaign against the barbarians, he judged it absolutely necessary to avoid a general battle. For the same reason he did not
wish for any close fighting but left the impassable valleys
and roads which had no outlet as border-land between the
two armies, and then posted all the most loyal officers along
the hill-tops with sufficient forces and thus initiated his new

plan of campaign, which was that neither his men should be able
to reach Bohemund easily nor letters pass or messages be
conveyed from Bohemund's camp to our men, for these
are generally the means by which conciliation is effected.
For the Stagirite says that many friendships are dissolved
through neglecting friendly greetings. He knew Bohemund
to be a man of consummate guile and energy and, although
he was quite willing to accept open battle with him, as I have
said, yet he never ceased working against him by every other
possible means and device. For the aforesaid reasons,
although he was longing for a fight (for the Emperor, my
father, was fond of, and long accustomed to, danger, yet
ever let reason be his guide in all matters), he was anxious
to overcome Bohemund by other methods. For I hold that
a general ought not always to try to gain victory for himself
by drawing the sword, but that, when opportunity and circumstances permit, he should occasionally have recourse to
wiliness and thus ensure complete victory for himself. For,
as far as we know, it is the prerogative of generals not only
to deal with swords and fighting but also with treaties. And
besides when opportunity offers, it is as well to rout the
enemy by playing the rogue with him, and this is what the
Emperor seems to have been busy about at that time. For
in his desire to sow discord between the Counts and Bohemund
and to weaken, or entirely break, their alliance with each
other, he staged the following drama. First he sent for
Marinus Sebastus from Naples (he belonged to a family of
Maëstromilii[1]; and although he did not always preserve his
oath to the Emperor intact, through being beguiled by false
words and promises, yet in as far as Bohemund was concerned
the Emperor felt confident he could disclose his secret plan
to him). At the same time he summoned Roger (a noble
Frank) and Peter Aliphas, a man renowned in war who
kept his loyalty to the Emperor unbroken throughout. In
council with them he sought a plan by which he could so
dispose matters with regard to Bohemund as utterly to rout
him, and he also asked them who were Bohemund's most
loyal followers and most in sympathy with him. When they
had told him, he said he must by some means or other win
these men over. "And if this is done, then with their help
discord can be introduced and that will split up the body
of the Frankish army." This plan he communicated to the
men just mentioned, and begged each of the three to lend him

[1] = Magistri militum.

one of their trusted servants who knew how to hold his tongue ; and they willingly agreed to give him their best servants. When the men came, he invented the following scheme. He composed letters which were apparently answers to some of Bohemund's most intimate friends and were conceived on the assumption that the others had already written to him, wooing his friendship and revealing the tyrant's secret intentions. So he sent them these letters in which he pretended to offer them most grateful thanks and to be ready to accept their kind feelings toward him. These men were Guido, Bohemund's own brother, and another called Coprisianus, one of the most renowned men, the third was Richard, the fourth Principatus, a brave man who held the highest rank in Bohemund's army, and several others. To these he addressed the false letters. For the Emperor had not received any letter of the kind from the other side, either from Richard or anybody else, with suggestions of good-will and trust; but he alone out of his own brain conceived this species of letter. The object of this dramatic business was that, if the treachery of these men of such high-standing should come to Bohemund's ears, and he believe that they had become disaffected towards him and gone over to the Emperor's side, he would in his perturbation revert to his natural barbarity, treat those men ill and compel them to break with him and then in consequence of Alexius' trick they would do what had never entered their heads, namely, secede to the latter. For methinks the General knew that every opponent is strong, provided the whole tribe is welded and bound together, but when at odds and split into several parties it becomes feebler and in consequence falls an easy prey to those warring against it. Such was the deep conception and hidden guile of those letters. Alexius carried out the affair as follows. He sent each letter to those men by a different messenger with orders to deliver it personally. Those letters did not merely convey his thanks but spoke of gifts and royal presents and extravagant promises, and coaxed them to bear and show good-will to him in the future and not conceal any secret from him. On their heels he sent one of his most trusty servants to follow the messengers without being seen and told him that when he saw they were close to the camp he was to slip past and outrun them and find Bohemund. To him he was to pretend that he was a deserter and had come over to him because he hated being with the Emperor, and while professing friendship and a certain goodwill to the tyrant, he was to accuse those men openly to whom the letters were addressed. Saying that such and such a one, enumerating them all by name, had broken their pledge of loyalty to him and had become the Emperor's friends and well-wishers and studied his interests, and that Bohemund should be on his guard lest they should suddenly commit some violence, long since planned against him. Moreover the Emperor told him that the plan had been devised in order that Bohemund should do no harm to the letter-carriers. For the Emperor was concerned to keep the men he had suborned safe and, still more, to upset Bohemund's affairs thoroughly. And he did not merely say and counsel this without actual effect, but the man mentioned approached Bohemund and, after ensuring the letter-carriers' security on oath, he disclosed everything to him according to the Emperor's promptings. When questioned where he thought they would be now, he said they must have passed Petroula. So Bohemund sent and detained those letter-carriers and after opening the letters turned quite faint and nearly fell, for he believed they were true. Then he arranged that those men should be closely guarded and he himself remained in his tent, without coming forth for six days, debating with himself what he ought to do. He revolved many plans in his head ; ought he to call for the constables and openly tell his brother Guido the suggestion made against him ? and ought they to be brought to him after examination or without examination ? and—another question—whom was he to appoint constables in their place ? For he reflected that, if these men who were pre-eminent for valour, were removed, his cause would suffer great injury, so he settled the matter in the only permissible way (and I fancy he suspected the hidden meaning of the letters), for he met them cheerfully and with full confidence allowed them to retain their positions.

V   After the Emperor had posted a considerable number of troops under picked leaders on all the mountain-passes, he further blocked all the paths against the Franks with large piles of timber, called ' xyloclasiæ.' He speedily appointed Michael Cecaumenos to be the tireless guardian over Valona, Hierico and Canina. Petroula received as governor Alexander Cabasilas with a mixed body of infantry—he was a man of intrepid spirit who had routed many Turks in Asia. Devra was held by Leo Nicerites with an adequate garrison, and to Eustathius Camytzes had fallen the duty of guarding the

passes near Arbanum. From the very starting-line, as the
saying is, Bohemund had sent his brother Guido and a Count
called Saracenus and Contopaganus against Cabasilas. When
some small towns bordering on Arbanum fell into Bohemund's
hands, their inhabitants, who were intimately acquainted
with all the roads round Arbanum, came to him and explained
the exact position of Devra and showed him the hidden
paths. Guido thereupon divided his army into two parts ;
he himself opened battle with Camytzes in front, and ordered
Contopaganus and the Count Saracenus to take the Devriots
as guides and fall upon him from the rear. They both
approved this scheme and while Guido was fighting in front,
the other Counts attacked Camytzes' army from the rear and
wrought terrible carnage upon it. He could not possibly
fight against them all, so when he saw his men put to flight,
he too followed their example. Many of the Romans fell
in this battle, among them Caras who even from childhood
had been received and enrolled among the Emperor's nobility ;
and also the Turk Scaliarius, formerly one of the most brilliant
chieftains in the East, who had afterwards deserted to the
Emperor and received Holy Baptism. That then is what
befell Camytzes. Alyates, who with other picked men was
guarding Glabinitza, went down to the plain, whether to fight
or to examine the lie of the land, God alone knows. All of
a sudden there accidentally met him some Franks on mail-
clad horses, valiant fellows, fifty in number ; they formed
themselves into two parties, one attacked him from the front
with a tremendous dash at full gallop, while the others followed
him noiselessly at the rear ; for the spot was marshy. Now
Alyates did not notice the soldiers coming behind him but
was struggling with might and main against the enemy in
front and was quite unaware of the danger into which he had
fallen. For now the men in his rear attacked him and fought
fiercely with him. A Count called Contopaganus met him
and thrust at him with his spear in such wise that he straightway fell down dead. A number of his companions were
killed too. On receiving this news the Emperor sent for
Cantacuzenus, knowing that he was very skilful in military
enterprises. He had just reached the Emperor for, as I
said, he had been recalled from Laodicea. As proceedings
against Bohemund admitted of no delay, he gave him a large
army and accompanied him, when he marched out of the
camp, as if spurring him on to fight. When they reached the
pass, locally called Petra, he stayed there awhile, supplied

him with much advice and strategic plans, gave him useful counsel and then sent Cantacuzenus forth with high hopes to Glabinitza, while he himself returned to Diabolis. On his way Cantacuzenus came to a small fortress, called Mylus' fort, and immediately set up siege-engines and besieged it. And the Romans approached the walls unconcernedly, some threw fire on the gates and burnt them down, while others climbed up the wall and reached the battlements. Directly the Franks encamped on the other side of the river Buses noticed this, they ran towards Mylus' fort. Cantacuzenus' scouts (who were barbarians as I have explained) saw them, ran back to him in disorder and did not inform him privately of what they had seen but began shouting it out from afar and telling of the Franks' advance. When the soldiers heard of the Franks' approach—although they had scaled the walls and burnt down the gates, and were on the point of capturing the fort—they were panic-stricken and each ran off to find his horse, but such was their terror and confusion of mind that they jumped on to each other's horses. Cantacuzenus certainly made strenuous efforts and kept riding up to the terrified men and shouting, " Be men ! " or quoting the poet's words " Remember ' impetuous valour.' " But as he could not persuade them, he cleverly stilled their excitement by saying, " We must not leave our siege-engines for the enemy to use against us, but rather set fire to them and then retreat in good order." At once then the soldiers did as he ordered with a very good will, and burnt not only the siege-engines but also their boats on the river Buses to prevent the Franks finding easy means of crossing it. Then he retired a little and coming upon a plain bounded on the right by the river called Charzanes, and on the left by marshy, swampy country, he used both these as defences and fixed his palisades there. The Franks we mentioned came down to the river's bank and saw the burnt boats, and being disappointed in their expectations went back. When Bohemund's brother, Guido, learnt from them what had happened, he changed his route, and picking out the bravest of his soldiers, sent them forward to Hierico and Canina. They reached the valleys which the Emperor had appointed Michael Cecaumenus to guard, and availing themselves of the nature of the ground, attacked the Romans boldly and routed them completely. For if the Frank meets his enemy in a confined space, he becomes invincible, just as on the plains he is easily captured.

VI Then emboldened by this victory, they ran back

again with the idea of attacking Cantacuzenus. But when
they realized that the ground where, as told, Cantacuzenus
had already pitched his stakes would not be advantageous
to them, they grew faint-hearted and postponed the battle.
But he had noticed their approach and throughout the night
he was busy and transferred the whole army to the other side
of the river. And before the sun had risen above the horizon
he himself was fully accoutred and had armed the whole
army too ; he placed himself in front of the centre of the line
of battle with the Turks on his left ; while Rosmices Alanus
commanded the right wing with his fellow-countrymen under
him. He sent the Scythians ahead with orders to draw on
the Franks by shooting at them from a distance, and at one
minute to shoot continuously, at the next to flee backwards
and then run forward again. They set off readily but accomplished nothing, as the Franks were drawn up in close
order and did not break their line at all but marched on slowly
in set order. When the two armies had approached to the
right distance for battle, the Scythians were unable to shoot
their arrows any longer as the Franks rode down upon them
at full speed, so they immediately turned their backs to the
Franks. In their desire to help them the Turks next attacked,
but the Franks did not think them of much account either
and fought the more fiercely. As Cantacuzenus saw the
Turks were completely overcome, he ordered the Exousiocrator
Rosmices who held the right wing with his men to join battle
with the Franks (they were Alani and very warlike men).
But he, too, after he attacked, seemed to be drawing back,
although raging terribly against them like a lion. When
Cantacuzenus saw him also being worsted, he took courage
as if from some stimulant and dashed into the front of the
Frankish line and after breaking up the army into several
bits he routed the Franks and pursued them hard as far as
Mylus' fort. After killing many of the second rank and also
of the higher, and taking a few of the illustrious Counts alive,
such as Ubus and his brother Richard and Contopaganus,
he returned victoriously. In order to present this victory
in a vivid way to the Emperor, he fixed several of the Franks'
heads on spears, and sent them to him at once, as well as the
more important captives, namely Ubus and the man called
Contopaganus.

I had got as far as this and was toiling with my pen
about the time of lamp-lighting, when I noticed that I
was dozing a bit over my writing, as the subject was losing

z

its interest. For when it is absolutely necessary to make
use of the barbarian names and to narrate various successive
events, the body of my history and the continuity of my
writing is like to be cut up into paragraphs ; but my kind
readers will bear me no grudge for this.

The warrior Bohemund now saw that his affairs were in
a sorry way as he was being attacked both from the sea and
the land and also that he was in utter want through the
complete lack of necessaries; accordingly he detached a fair-
sized army and dispatched it to plunder all the towns situated
near Valona, Hierico and Canina. However Cantacuzenus
was on the watch nor did ' sweet sleep overtake the man,'
as the poet says, but with great alacrity he sent Beroïtes with
a large army to oppose the Franks. He met them and defeated
them and on his way back set fire to Bohemund's ships as a
sequel. But the fierce tyrant was not at all depressed when he
heard that the men he had sent had been defeated but was
just as if he had not lost a single soldier. On the contrary
he seemed even more courageous and again detached horse
and foot soldiers who were very keen fighters numbering six
thousand, and dispatched them against Cantacuzenus, thinking
that at the very first shout they would capture Cantacuzenus
himself together with the Roman army. But the latter
always had scouts keeping a watch on the Frankish hosts
and directly they told him of their approach he armed himself
and the army fully during the night as he was lusting to attack
them at dawn. So when the Franks arrived, tired out, at
the banks of the river Buses and lay down for a little rest, he
surprised them there almost before the first smile of the
morning, attacked them immediately, took many alive and
killed more. The rest were caught in the eddies of the river
and drowned, for trying to escape a wolf, they fell in with a
lion. He sent all the Counts to the Emperor and afterwards
returned to Timorus, a marshy and inaccessible spot. Here
he waited for six days and sent out a number of spies in
different directions to observe Bohemund's movements and
forward information to himself, so that by knowing
Bohemund's doings he might form a more accurate judgment.
These spies accidentally came upon a hundred Franks building
some rafts on which they intended to cross the river and
capture the small town situated on the opposite side. They
fell upon them suddenly, took nearly all of them alive, one
of them being Bohemund's cousin, a man standing ten foot
tall and as broad as a second Heracles. Indeed it was a

strange sight to see that great giant, who was really pro-
digious, held captive by a little dwarf of a Scythian. When
sending away the captured, Cantacuzenus ordered that the
Scythian pigmy should lead in that monster bound in chains
to the Emperor, thinking perhaps to amuse the Emperor.
As soon as the Emperor heard of their arrival, he seated
himself on the imperial throne and ordered the prisoners to
be brought in ; amongst them came the Scythian scarcely
reaching to the waist of the gigantic Frank he dragged in
chains. Immediately all present burst into a roar of laughter.
The other Counts were consigned to prison. . . .

VII The Emperor had barely time to light up with a
smile at Cantacuzenus' success before a second, most calami-
tous message arrived, announcing an incredible slaughter
of the Roman divisions under Carnytzes and Cabasilas. The
Emperor's spirit did not fail at all though he was smitten
to the heart and worried, often sighing over the men that had
fallen and occasionally even weeping for some individual.
But he summoned Constantine Gabras, a true follower of
Ares, a fire-breather against his enemies, and ordered him
to go to the place called Petroula to find out by what road
the Franks had entered the valleys and wrought such carnage,
and to bar this passage against them for the future. But
Gabras was discontented and, so to say, worried by the job
(for he was a self-conceited person and longed to take a
hand in great enterprises). Consequently he sent Marianus
Mavrocatacalon, the husband of my Cæsar's sister, a man of
very war-like spirit who had shewn it in many valiant deeds
and was dearly beloved by the Emperor, and with him a
thousand very brave men. He also selected to accompany
them a number of the servants of the Porphyrogeniti and my
Cæsar who were longing to fight. However this man too was
rather afraid of the task, but yet he went to his own tent
to think about it. About the middle watch of the night
letters arrived from Landulph. who was at that time with
Isaac Contostephanus the Thalassocrator ; in these he
inveighed against the Contostephani, namely Isaac, and his
brothers Stephen and Euphorbenus, for neglect in guarding
the straits of Lombardy, and for frequently going off to the
mainland for a rest. Part of the letter ran, " Even if you,
O Emperor, try to prevent the raiding parties and excursions
of the Franks with all your might and main, yet, if these men
fail and go to sleep over their duty of guarding the straits of
Lombardy, it naturally follows that the ships sailing across

to Bohemund and conveying the necessaries of life can do so at their leisure. A little while ago the men who sailed across from Lombardy to Bohemund waited for a favourable wind to blow (for a strong south wind is most useful for crossing from Lombardy to Illyria, whereas the north wind is unfavourable). Then they winged their ships with their sails and boldly sailed over to Illyria. But as the south wind was blowing very strongly it prevented their landing at Dyrrachium, and compelled them to sail past the coast of Dyrrachium and run into Valona. There they brought their huge merchant-ships to land and thence conveyed to Bohemund the large supplies of horse and foot-soldiers they had carried over, and all the wants of life. And from these they set up a number of stalls where the Franks could buy in abundance everything for their maintenance." The Emperor was very enraged and censured Isaac severely and by threatening him in case he did not do better he succeeded in making him keep an untiring watch. But Contostephanus did not accomplish anything as he intended (for though he endeavoured more than once to intercept the ships sailing to Illyria he failed in his object ; for he held the middle of the straits and when he saw the Franks sailing along under a favourable wind with all their sails set and going at a great pace he was quite unable to fight against the Franks and the wind at the same time, as the breeze was contrary and not even Heracles could fight against two, they say ; and thus he was driven backwards by the violence of the wind). At this news the Emperor was cut to the heart, for he recognized that Contostephanus did not station his fleet in the right spot and consequently the south winds which favoured the Franks' crossing hindered him. He therefore made a map of the coast of Lombardy and of Illyria, putting in the harbours on either side, and sent it to Contostephanus, and explained to him by letter where he ought to post his ships and from which place he could start with a favouring wind against the Franks who were crossing. He again encouraged Contostephanus and urged him to tackle the work. So Isaac took heart and went and anchored his ships where the Emperor had advised him to. Then he waited for his opportunity and one day when the men from Lombardy were sailing across to Illyria with a quantity of stores, and the right wind was blowing, he caught them in the middle of the strait and set fire to some of the freight-ships, while sending the greater number to the bottom, crews and all. Before he heard of this but had his mind full of what Landulph and even the Duke of Dyrrachium had written, the Emperor changed his mind and sent for Marianus Mavrocatacalon (who was mentioned above) and appointed him Duke of the Fleet and entrusted the Petroula business to another man. So Marianus went off and by sheer good luck at once ran into pirate- and freight-ships sailing from Lombardy to Bohemund and captured them and they were all full of provisions. And for the future he was a sleepless guardian of the straits between Lombardy and Illyria, and did not allow any Franks at all to sail across to Dyrrachium.

VIII The Emperor meanwhile was encamped near Diabolis at the foot of the passes, and for one thing he kept in check the men who longed to desert to Bohemund and for another he sent messengers as thick as snow-flakes to the officers keeping the passes and directed them as to the number of soldiers they were to send down to the plain of Dyrrachium to fight against Bohemund, and the order of battle in which they were to arrange their men for the fight. Most of them were to make an attack on horseback and then ride back again, and to do this repeatedly and use their bows and arrows; the soldiers carrying spears were to advance at slow march behind them, so that if by chance the archers were forced back too far, these soldiers could receive them and also strike at any Franks that came to blows with them. He furnished them abundantly with arrows and exhorted them not to use them sparingly, but to shoot at the horses rather than at the Franks. For he knew that the Franks were difficult to wound, or rather, practically invulnerable, thanks to their breastplates and coats of mail. Therefore he considered shooting at them useless and quite senseless. For the Frank-ish weapon of defence is this coat of mail, ring plaited into ring, and the iron fabric is such excellent iron that it repels arrows and keeps the wearer's skin unhurt. An additional weapon of defence is a shield which is not round, but a long shield, very broad at the top and running out to a point, hollowed out slightly inside, but externally smooth and gleam-ing with a brilliant boss of molten brass. Consequently any arrow, be it Scythian or Persian, or even discharged by the arms of a giant, would glint off such a shield and hark back to the sender. For this reason, as he was cognizant both of the Frankish armour and our archery, the Emperor advised our men to attack the horses chiefly and ' wing ' them with their arrows so that when the Franks had dismounted, they could easily be captured. For a Frank on horseback is invincible, and would even make a hole in the walls of Babylon, but directly he gets off his horse, anyone who likes can make sport of him. Knowing the perverse nature of his followers the Emperor did not wish to cross the passes, although, as he often told us in former days, he was dearly longing to engage Bohemund in a general battle. For with regard to battles he was sharper than any sword, fearless of spirit and absolutely undaunted ; however late events which grievously oppressed his soul deterred him from such an attempt.

And now Bohemund was sorely pressed both by land and sea. (For the Emperor sat like a spectator watching the events in the Illyrian plain, yet with his whole heart and soul he stood by the side of his soldiers and shared all their exertions and labours—or even underwent more, one might say. He spurred on the chiefs he had posted at the heads of the passes to fresh combats and battles, and suggested to them the manner in which they should attack the Franks. And Marianus was watching the pathways of the straits between Lombardy and Illyria, and entirely prevented men crossing from Italy to Illyria, for he did not allow a three-masted boat or a large merchant-vessel or even a light two-oared pirate-boat to cross to Bohemund.) Now that the provisions which used to be brought by sea failed Bohemund and he was hard pressed on land, for he saw the war was being waged with great skill (for whenever any soldiers left the palisades to forage or fetch in other things or drive out the horses to water the Romans at once attacked them and killed the majority, so that his army was gradually wasting away), he sent envoys to Alexius, Duke of Dyrrachium, and began to treat for peace. Moreover one of Bohemund's high-bred Counts, Gelielmus Clareles, observing that the Frankish army was perishing from starvation and disease (for a terrible disease had swooped down upon it from above) consulted his own safety and deserted to the Emperor with fifty horse. The Emperor welcomed such a guest, enquired about Bohemund's affairs and on being assured that famine was breaking up the army and that the Franks' position was really desperate, he conferred the rank of Nobilissimus on him on the spot and repaid him with many gifts and attentions. He next heard by letter from Alexius that Bohemund had sent an embassy to sue for peace. As he was aware that the men about his person were always plotting some evil against him and reflected how frequently they had rebelled, and that he was really more exposed to foes at home than to enemies abroad, he decided to leave off fighting against both parties with both hands. Accordingly he made a virtue of necessity, as the saying is, and judged it wise to accept peace with the Franks and not reject Bohemund's offers, for he was afraid of advancing further for the reason which this history has already stated. So he remained where he was, resisting both parties, and bade the Duke of Dyrrachium by letter answer Bohemund as follows. "You know very well how often I have been deceived when trusting to your oaths and promises. And did not the divine law of the gospel command Christians to forgive each other all offences, I should not have opened my ears to your proposals yet it is better to be deceived than to offend God and to transgress divine laws. For this reason only I do not reject your request. If you yourself too really desire peace and detest the foolish and impracticable task you have undertaken and no longer wish to find pleasure in shedding the blood of Christians, not for the sake of your own country or on behalf of Christians, but simply and solely for your own gratification, then, as the distance between us is but short, come here yourself with as many soldiers as you please. And whether our respective wishes coincide, as the result of an agreement, or whether they do not, in either case, as I have said, you shall return to your own camp unharmed."

IX On receiving this letter Bohemund asked that hostages from among the noblemen should be given to him, on the condition that they should be free but guarded by his Counts in his camp until he himself returned ; for otherwise he would not dare to come to the Emperor. Thereupon the Emperor summoned the Neapolitan Marianus and Roger Francus, renowned for his bravery, prudent men with long experience of Latin customs, and Constantine Euphorbenus (he had both physical and moral courage and had never failed in any of the tasks assigned him by the Emperor) and a certain Adralestus who knew the Frankish language. These men, as has been said, he sent to Bohemund with the admonition to try in every possible way to persuade him to go to the Emperor of his own free will in order to acquaint him with what he wished and asked of him. And if his demands were pleasing to the Emperor, he would naturally obtain them ; but if not, then he would return to his own camp unharmed. After giving them these instructions the Emperor sent them off, and they took the road leading to

Bohemund.   When he heard of their approach he was afraid
they might notice the collapse of his army and speak about
it to the Emperor, so he rode out and met them at some
distance from the camp.   They rendered the Emperor's
message to him as follows : " The Emperor says that he has
not at all forgotten the oaths and promises which were made
not only by you yourself, but by all the Counts who passed
through his kingdom at that time.   And now you can see
clearly that your transgression of these oaths has not resulted
in any good to yourself."   To this Bohemund replied,
" Enough of this talk.   If you have brought me any other
message from the Emperor, let me hear it."   And the ambassadors said, " The Emperor who desires your safety and that
of the army under you sends you this intimation by us.
You are aware that after much labour you have neither
succeeded in subduing the town of Dyrrachium nor have you
gained any advantage for yourself or the men under you.
Therefore if you do not wish to bring about your own and
your people's destruction, come to our Majesty without fear
and explain what it is you wish and listen on the other hand
to our wishes.   Then if our opinions should happily coincide,
thanks be to God ; but if not, I will restore you to your own
camp unharmed.   Moreover all those of your people who
desire to go and worship at the Holy Sepulchre, shall be
safely conveyed by me ; whereas those who choose to return
to their country, shall be gratified by liberal presents from
me and be free to depart to their home."   Then he replied
to them, " Now I really feel that the Emperor has sent me
men fit to give and render reason.   I beg therefore to be
fully assured by you that I shall be received with due honours
by the Emperor.   The nearest of his blood-relations must
come to meet me six stades from the town, and when I approach
the imperial tent, directly I enter the door, he must rise
from his seat and receive me honourably.   He must also not
make any reference to our former treaties nor put me on my
trial but I must have full liberty to say as much as I like and
what I like.   In addition to this the Emperor must take my
hand and seat me at the head of his couch ; I must make my
entry with two soldiers and not bend my knee or my neck in
the slightest as sign of obeisance to the Emperor."   When
they heard this proposal the above-named ambassadors
would not accept the idea of the Emperor rising from his
throne, but dismissed the request as superfluous ; not only
did they reject that but also Bohemund's saying that he

could not bend his knee or neck in obeisance to the Emperor. The other requests they did not reject ; for instance that some of the Emperor's less close relations should go a decent distance and receive him on his coming to visit the Emperor for the sake of paying him respect and attention ; as also that he should enter with two soldiers ; and further that the Emperor should touch his hand and set him at the upper end of the Emperor's couch. After this conversation the ambassadors departed to go to the place where their rest-quarters had been prepared ; they were guarded by a hundred sergeants so that they might not go out by night and spy out the state of the army and as a result bear themselves more disdainfully towards him. On the following day he arrived with three hundred horsemen and all the Counts at the place where he had conferred with the aforementioned ambassadors the day before, there he picked out six noblemen and took them with him and went off to the ambassadors ; the rest he left there to await his return. The former day's discussions were resumed and as Bohemund was persistent, one of the highest-born Counts, Ubus by name, said to Bohemund, " Not one of us who came with you to wage war against the Emperor, has ever yet struck a blow at any one with his spear. So leave all this talking—you must exchange peace for war." Many words were bandied to and fro, and Bohemund considered it a great slight that all he had asked for from the ambassadors should not be granted. They consented to some things, but refused others, finally Bohemund gave way, making a virtue of necessity, as they say; next he asked them to give their oath that he would be received honourably and that, if the Emperor did not agree to his terms, he should be sent back to his own camp unharmed. So the Holy Gospels were placed on the table and he asked that hostages should be handed over to his brother Guido and retained by him until such time as he himself returned. The ambassadors agreed to this and then they mutually exchanged oaths to ensure the safety of the hostages. Bohemund assented to this, and after oaths had been taken and given he handed over the hostages, the Sebastus Marianus, the man called Adralestus, and Roger Francus, to his brother Guido, on the understanding that, whether he came to terms of peace with the Emperor or not, he should comply with the oaths and send them back to the Emperor safe and sound.

X When they were on the point of starting on their journey to the Emperor in company with Euphorbenus

Constantine Catacalon, Bohemund said that he wanted to move his army because, owing to its having remained for a long time in the same place, there was a frightful stench in it, but he would not like to do even this without their advice. For the Frankish race is unstable like that, and turns to one extreme or the other in the twinkling of an eye ; at one moment you can hear one and the same man boasting that he will upset the whole world, and at the next he is desperate and bowed down to the very dust, especially if he comes into contact with firmer characters. The ambassadors would not allow him to move the army more than twelve stades and " If you like " they said to Bohemund, "we will come with you and examine the site." Bohemund agreed to this, so they at once notified the keepers of the passes by letter that they must not make sorties and inflict hurt on them. And Constantine Euphorbenus Catacalon begged Bohemund for permission to enter Dyrrachium and on its being granted, quickly made his way there ; then sought out the governor of the city, the Sebastocrator Isaac's son, Alexius, and reported to him the messages which the Emperor had entrusted to him and the other military chiefs who had accompanied him.

For they were not able to lean forward over the top of the wall because of the contrivance the Emperor had ordered to be placed on the battlements. This contrivance was planks specially prepared without nails for this purpose and skilfully fitted into the battlements of the fort so that if by chance some of the Latins tried to clamber up by ladders, they would not stand firmly when they got on to the battlements, but would slip down, planks and all, and fall inside, as I said above. So Euphorbenus talked to the men of Dyrrachium, and gave them the Emperor's message, and inspired them with confidence ; then he enquired about the condition of the fort and found that things had been arranged in the best possible manner and that in consequence they still had abundant supplies of necessaries and took no account of Bohemund's machines. After this he returned to Bohemund who had transferred his camp to the place he had chosen, and joining him, started on his way to the Emperor. In accordance with the previous arrangements the rest of the ambassadors remained behind with Guido, and Catacalon sent Manuel Modenus, his most loyal and trusty servant ahead, to announce to the Emperor that Bohemund was on the way to him. When the latter drew near to the imperial tent, all the details of his reception were carried out, as the ambassadors had agreed upon with him. Directly he entered, the Emperor stretched out his hand and grasped his, gave him the customary greeting for kings, and placed him near the imperial throne. Now the man was such as, to put it briefly, had never before been seen in the land of the Romans, be he either of the barbarians or of the Greeks (for he was a marvel for the eyes to behold, and his reputation was terrifying). Let me describe the barbarian's appearance more particularly —he was so tall in stature that he overtopped the tallest by nearly one cubit, narrow in the waist and loins, with broad shoulders and a deep chest and powerful arms. And in the whole build of the body he was neither too slender nor over-weighted with flesh, but perfectly proportioned and, one might say, built in conformity with the canon of Polycleitus. He had powerful hands and stood firmly on his feet, and his neck and back were well compacted. An accurate observer would notice that he stooped slightly, but this was not from any weakness of the vertebræ of his spine but he had probably had this posture slightly from birth. His skin all over his body was very white, and in his face the white was tempered with red. His hair was yellowish, but did not hang down to his waist like that of the other barbarians ; for the man was not inordinately vain of his hair, but had it cut short to the ears. Whether his beard was reddish, or any other colour I cannot say, for the razor had passed over it very closely and left a surface smoother than chalk, most likely it too was reddish. His blue eyes indicated both a high spirit and dignity ; and his nose and nostrils breathed in the air freely ; his chest corresponded to his nostrils and by his nostrils . . . the breadth of his chest. For by his nostrils nature had given free passage for the high spirit which bubbled up from his heart. A certain charm hung about this man but was partly marred by a general air of the horrible. For in the whole of his body the entire man shewed implacable and savage both in his size and glance, methinks, and even his laughter sounded to others like snorting. He was so made in mind and body that both courage and passion reared their crests within him and both inclined to war. His wit was mani-fold and crafty and able to find a way of escape (*lit.* " handle ") in every emergency. In conversation he was well informed, and the answers he gave were quite irrefutable. This man who was of such a size and such a character was inferior to the Emperor alone in fortune and eloquence and in other gifts of nature.

XI The Emperor only reminded him of past events by a cursory and veiled remark and at once turned the conversation into other channels. But Bohemund, whose conscience pricked him, carefully avoided making any objection to his words, and merely remarked, " I have not come to be examined about the past, for in that case I also should have had a good deal to say. But as God has brought me hither, I leave everything for the future to your Majesty." To which the Emperor replied, " We must leave the past now. If you really wish to make peace with me, you must first become one of my subjects, and then order your nephew Tancred to do the same, and to deliver up Antioch to the men I shall send according to the former agreement made between us. Further you must promise to keep both now and for the future all the agreements formerly made between us." After the Emperor had said, and listened to, a great deal more than this, Bohemund, who was still the same as ever and unchanged, said, " It is quite impossible for me to make any such promise." And to other demands made by the Emperor he only replied by requesting to be allowed to return to his own army according to the agreement made with the ambassadors. Then the Emperor said to him, " I have no one better than myself to re-conduct you in safety." And as he spoke he openly gave orders to the leaders of the army to get their horses ready to ride with him to Dyrrachium. On hearing this Bohemund went out to go to the tent assigned to him and asked to see my Cæsar, Nicephorus Bryennius, who had lately been honoured with the rank of Panhyper-sebastos. Nicephorus came and used every persuasive argument (for he was unrivalled in public oratory as well as in private conversations) and finally persuaded Bohemund to give his assent to most of the Emperor's claims. Then he took him by the hand and led him back to the Emperor. The following day Bohemund took the oath from his own choice and in his own way and completed the agreement, which was couched in the following terms.

XII " The former agreement which I made with thy divinely crowned Majesty at the time when, with a very numerous army of Franks, I stayed in the Royal City on my way from Europe to Asia for the liberation of Jerusalem, has become invalid owing to various vicissitudes, therefore it must be annulled and not be held effective since it is condemned as invalid because of the change of circumstances. And thy Majesty must not have any rights against me because of it nor contend with me about the points agreed upon and written down in the same. For since I declared war against thy divinely appointed Empire and broke the agreement, thereby the charges held by thy Majesty against me were cancelled as well. But now as if moved by remorse and like a stricken fisherman I have recovered my sanity and, I might almost say, been rendered more discreet by thy spear, remembering too the defeat and the wars of former years, I come to make this, the second agreement with thy Majesty by which I will become the liegeman of thy sceptre, or to express it more clearly and plainly, thy menial and subject, as thou too hast determined to drag me under thy right hand and art willing to make me thy liegeman. Therefore from now on according to this second agreement, which I intend to observe for ever and so swear by God and all His saints, since with them as witnesses these presents are being written and said, I shall be the faithful liegeman of thy Majesty and of thy dearly loved son and sovereign lord, John Porphyrogenitus. And I will arm my right hand against any who oppose thy power, be he who lifts his hands against thee of the Christian race or a stranger to our court, one of those whom we call 'pagans.' So that a clause which was contained in the afore-mentioned pact and pleased both parties, your Majesties and myself, that clause alone of all the others which have been annulled, I wish to transfer here and I insist and cling fast to it, namely that I shall be the slave and liegeman of both your Majesties, thus renewing as it were what had been abolished. And, no matter what may happen, never will I disregard this clause ; nor shall there be any clause or any means, open or secret, by which I shall be proved to have transgressed this treaty and this present agreement. But since I am to receive a region, expressly to be named herein, in some district of the East by a Golden Bull from thy Majesty, signed by thy Majesty with thy signature in red ink, and a copy of this same Golden Bull will also be given to me, I receive the countries given to me as a gift from your Majesties : and my right to this gift derives force from this Golden Bull, and in return for these certain countries and towns I pledge my faith to your Majesties, that is to say, to thee, the great Emperor and Lord, Alexius Comnenus, and to thy thrice-longed-for son, the Emperor and Lord John Porphyrogenitus, and this faith I promise to maintain, like a firm anchor, unshaken and un-moved. And, to repeat my promise more clearly and to guard the individuality of those who make this agreement in writing, behold, I, Bohemund, the son of Robert Guiscard, make an agreement with your Empire, and I wish to keep this pact inviolate with your Majesties, that is with thee, the Emperor of the Romans, the Lord Alexius and the Emperor, thy son the Porphyrogenitus, to be thy true and genuine liege as long as I breathe and am counted among the living. And I will take arms against the enemies that may arise in the future against you and your Majesties of the ever-venerable august Emperors of the Roman hegemony. And wherever I shall be ordered by you to go, I shall unhesitatingly serve you with the whole army under me according to your instant need. And all such as may be inimical to your Empire, provided only they be not like the immortal angels and invulnerable by our spears or endowed with adamantine bodies, against all such I shall make war on behalf of your Majesties. And as long as I am in good bodily health and not occupied with any barbarian or Turkish war, I myself in person with the army that follows me will undertake any war on your behalf. But if I am hindered by any severe illness, many of which befall us mortals, or an imminent war requires my presence, then of a surety I promise to send as large reinforcements as I possibly can from the brave men around me so that they may make up for my absence. For my genuine pledge which I give to-day to your Majesties is that either by my own arm or by that of others, as just said, I will preserve the terms of this pact unmutilated. And I swear I will keep this genuine pledge both generally and in particular on behalf of your Empire and your life, I mean your life here below on this earth. For on behalf of this temporal life of yours I shall stand under arms like a statue of iron, wrought by the hammer. But I also extend my oath to the protection of your honour and your imperial limbs and if any guilty enemy plots mischief against them, I will do my best to destroy them and check them in their evil design. But I will also fight on behalf of every country of yours, or town, small or great, and of the islands themselves or, in general, of every land and sea that is under your sway, namely, from this Adriatic sea to the farthest East and throughout the length of great Asia, wherever the Roman boundaries are. And I further agree, and to this God will listen and be my witness that I will never at any time take and hold any country which either now or formerly has been brought under thy sway, nor hold and take any

town or island, and, in general, not to take any possession
of all those which formerly comprised or are now held by the
Empire of Constantinople, be they in the East or the West,
except only such as are expressly given to me by your divinely
appointed Majesties and which shall be stated by name in this
present writing.   But whenever I shall be able to subdue a
country which once belonged to this Empire by driving
out the present occupiers of that country, I am bound to
refer the administration of that country to your decision.
And if indeed you wish to make me the administrator of the
re-conquered country as you - liege and faithful slave, so be it,
but if not, then I would surrender it without any delay to
whatever man your Majesties should appoint.   And if anyone
else should offer me a country, town or small town which was
at some time or other within the jurisdiction of the Empire,
to appertain to me, I will not accept it.   But all that were
taken by a siege or without a siege, as they were yours, shall
be yours again, and I shall not advance any plea whatsoever
for them.   And I will not even ask for an oath from any
Christian nor take one with anybody else or make any agreement whatever which would tend to your harm or to the
detriment of yourself or your Empire.   Nor shall I become
the ' man ' of anyone else or of any other government, be
it greater or smaller, without your authority.   But the one
lordship which I promise to serve is thy Majesty and that of
thy dearly-loved son.   And if any man of thy Empire come
to me saying that they have risen in revolt against thy
Empire and wish to serve me, I will hate them and send
them away, or rather take arms against them.   And as for
the other barbarians . . . if they still wish to come under my
sword, I will accept them but not on my own rights, but I
will make them swear an oath to you and your much-beloved
son and I will take over the countries from them by the right
of your Majesties and whatsoever you prescribe for them all,
I promise to do unhesitatingly.   This then is all that concerns
the towns and countries which happen to be under the sceptre
of the Romans.   With regard to those that have never yet
been subject to the Roman Empire, I hereby take my oath
that the countries which fall to me without war or by war and
fighting I will consider as given to me by your Majesties, be
they Turkish or Armenian or as one would say who understood our language, Pagan or Christian, and the men of those
nations who join me and wish to serve me, I will accept on
the condition that they too will agree to become thy Majesty's

men, and my agreement with thy Majesty and the oaths that have been ratified should extend to them too. And if of these your Majesties wish some to be subject to me, let them be so subjected ; and those whom you wish to be sent to your Empire, I will send, if they are willing, but if they are not willing and refuse allegiance to you, I will not receive them either. Moreover on Tancred, my nephew, I will make implacable war unless he is willing to abandon his hostility towards your Majesties and free from his power the cities that belong to your Empire. And when, with his consent or without it, the towns have been freed, I myself by your permission will be lord over the towns given to me by the Golden Bull, which shall be expressly enumerated, but the other towns together with Laodicea in Syria all these, except those given to me, shall be attached to your sceptre. Again I will never receive any fugitives from your Empire, but will compel them to retrace their steps and return to your Empire. Further, in addition to what has been said above, I also promise this to make the agreement more sure. That is I agree to give guarantors for these agreements so that they may remain unbroken and unshaken in perpetuity, namely, those liegemen of mine who are going to hold in my right the country given me by thy Majesty and the cities and towns which shall be set forth by name. For I shall arrange for these men to take the most fearful oaths in order that they too will keep their faith unswerving to your Empire and to all the land over which the Roman law extends and acquiesce very strictly in all the things contained in this present agreement. And I shall make them swear by the heavenly powers and the insufferable wrath of God that, if I should ever conspire against your Majesties, which God forbid ! O Saviour, and O Justice of God, forbid it ! they would first endeavour by every possible means throughout a period of forty days to bring me back from my self-exaltation to the fidelity due to your Majesties. This would happen, if indeed it were allowed to happen, when downright madness and frenzy had seized me, or if I had clearly taken leave of my senses. And if I am insensible and unmoved by their advice and madness rushes violently upon my mind, then at last they shall renounce me and utterly reject me and shall be transferred to your Empire and hand and judgment, and the countries which they hold by my right, they shall snatch away from my power and surrender them to you and your portion. And they will be compelled to do this by their oaths and they will keep the same faith and allegiance and good-will to you as I have agreed to keep ; and on behalf of your life and earthly honour they will take arms, as well as also on behalf of your imperial person so that they may not be hurt by any enemy, and they will not cease from desire of fighting for at least as long as they have knowledge of any conspirators or dangerous persons. These things I swear and I call God and men and the highest angels to witness that I will truly compel these men by binding them with fearful oaths to do and work as far as in them lies. Likewise, on behalf of your forts and towns and countries, in a word, all the portions of the countries under your rule, that the West contains or the East comprises, they shall agree under oath to all the points on which I too have made an agreement with you ; these things they shall do, be I alive or be I dead, and your Empire shall have these men as your subjects and shall ordain to them all that you would to trusty servants. And those of my followers who happen to be staying here with me now, shall give their pledges on security of oath and their pacts now at once, to your august Majesties, the Lord Alexius, Emperor of the Romans, and the Porphyrogenitus Emperor, thy son. With regard to those of my horsemen and heavy-armed soldiers, whom we generally call 'chevaliers', who are absent, let thy Majesty send a man to the city of Antioch and there those others shall take the same oaths and the man sent by thy Majesty shall tender them, whilst I, I swear this, will see to it that the men swear and agree to keep the same agreement without any change. Further, I agree and I swear, that as often as your Majesty desires me to raise my hands and to organize a war against the holders of towns and countries, which were once subject to the Empire of Constantinople, this I will do and arm myself against them. But those against whom it is not in thy mind to send an army, then neither will we ourselves march against them. For in all things we wish to serve thy Empire and to let every deed and every wish depend upon thy will. As for any of the Saracens or Ishmaelites who come over into thy kingdom of their own free will and surrender their cities, I will not hinder them nor make any efforts to win them over to myself unless indeed their territory after being subdued by my sword and reduced to extreme straits, should look to thy Empire in the moment of danger and wish to ensure their own safety by submitting to you. But all such and all others who through fear of the Frankish sword and in dread

of imminent death call for help upon your august Majesties
. . . not for this reason will you lay claim to our
captives, but clearly only to those who without any toils or
pains of ours, shall enter into subjection to you of their own
free will. In addition to the foregoing, I also agree to this;
that all soldiers who wish to cross the Adriatic from Lombardy
with me, shall themselves also swear and agree to subjection
to thy Majesty and shall all give their oaths hereto to the man
of your Empire whom you yourselves will send for this same
purpose to the other side of the Adriatic. But if they do
not take the oath, I will not allow them to cross at all as they
refuse to be like-minded with us. And it is necessary that
the countries and towns bestowed on me in the Golden Bull
by your divinely-appointed Empire should be set out in this
writing. They are these:—the city of Antioch in Cœle-
Syria with its fortifications and its dependency together
with Suetium situated on the sea-coast; Dux with all its
dependencies, together with the place called Cavcas; the
place called Lulu; and the Mons Admirabilis and Phersia
with all the country belonging to it; the military district St.
Elias with all the small towns belonging to it; the military
district of Borze and the small towns belonging to it; all
the country round the military district of Sezer, which the
Greeks call Larissa; likewise the military districts of Artach
and Teluch with their respective fortifications; also Germanicia
with its small towns; the Maurus Mons and all the castles
dependent on it, and all the plain that lies at its foot except
only the territories of the Rupenii, Leo and Theodore the
Armenians, who have become subjects of your Empire.
Besides those already written down, the military districts
of Pagras and that of Palatzas, the province of Zoum and
all its dependent castles and small towns and the country
pertaining to each. For all these places are also contained
in your Majesties' Golden Bull as being given to me by the
divine power until the end of my life and after my removal
hence, they are bound to revert to the Empire of the New
Rome and the Queen of Cities, Constantinople, on condition
that I keep unsullied faith and sincere goodwill through you
the ever-revered august Majesties to its Empire and that I
am the servant and subject liege of its throne and imperial
sceptre. And I agree and I swear by the God that is
worshipped in the church of Antioch, that there shall never
be a patriarch of Antioch of our race but he shall be one whom
your Majesties shall appoint from among the disciples of the

great church of Constantinople. This man shall sit on the
throne in Antioch and perform all arch-hieratical offices
in the elections and the other ecclesiastical functions according to the privileges pertaining to this throne. But there
were also parts cut off from the ducal province of Antioch
by your Majesties who wished to incorporate these in the
Empire ; these are, the province of Podandum . . .
and further, the military district of the city of Tarsus, and the
city of Adana and Mopsuestiæ, and Anabarza and, to put it
concisely, all that part of Cilicia which is bounded by the
Cydnus and the Hermon ; likewise too the military district
Laodicea in Syria and further that military district of Gabala,
which we speaking like barbarians call Zebel, and the military
district of Balaneus and Maraceus and Antaradus together
with Antarto ; both these are military districts. These are
the places which your Majesty cut off from the whole ducal
province of Antioch and took them away and joined them to
the orb of your Empire. And I am content with what has
been given me and likewise with what has been taken away.
And I will hold fast to the rights and privileges I have received
from you, nor will I lay claim to those I have not received.
Nor will I transgress my boundaries, but will remain within
those given to me and enjoy them, as long as my life shall
last, as has been already explained. After my death, this
too has already been written down, they shall return to your
own rule by whom they were given for my possession. For
I shall give injunctions to my stewards and men in the last
expressions of my will to give back all the said countries to
the sceptre of the Roman rule without making any trouble
about giving them back or entering into any controversies
about them. This too I swear and I strongly ratify this
agreement that they shall carry out my orders without delay
and without ambiguity. Let this too be added to the agreements that whereas with regard to the districts that have
been taken away by your Empire from the rule of Antioch
and the duchy of the city I made intercession to your throne
to grant some compensation and the Peregrini also made
intercessions to your Majesty, your Empire had consented
to give me in compensation certain provinces and lands and
towns situated in the East. These too must be mentioned
here by name so that neither your Majesties should be in
doubt on any point, nor I have reason to strive for more.
They were these ; the province of the whole land of Casiotis,
whose capital is Berrœa, called Chalep in the barbarian tongue ;

the province of Lapara and all the small towns belonging to it, namely Plasta, the castle of Chonium, Romaïna, the castle Aramisus, the small town of Ameras, the castle of Sarbanus, the fort of Telchampson ; with these also the three Tilia, Sthlabotilin, and the two others, the fort Sgenin and the castle Caltzierin ; as well as also these towns, Commermœri and the other called Cathismatin, and Sarsapin and the small town, Necran. These are all situated in Hither-Syria. The other provinces are in Mespotamia, situated somewhere near the town of Edessa, namely, the province of Limnii and the province of Ætus with all their respective fortifications. These points about Edessa must not be left unmentioned, nor the yearly talent assigned to me by your divinely guarded Empire. I mean the two hunded pounds of the coinage of the Emperor Michael. In addition to all these there has been given to me by the sacrosanct Golden Bull of your Majesties the duchy of . . .[1] in its entirety with all the forts and lands pertaining thereto, and this ducal dignity is not confined to my person alone ; for permission is given me by the same sacrosanct Golden Bull to bequeath it to whomsoever I myself may desire, that is, if he also is willing to bow to your Majesties' commands and wishes as being the liegeman of the same Empire and the same kingdom and being of the same will and agreement with you, as I was.

And from henceforth, when once I have become your ' man ' and belong to the circle of your Empire, it is my right to receive as yearly gift from the imperial treasury two hundred talents of money of the right quality and bearing the impress of the former Emperor, the Lord Michael, and they shall be sent to me by an envoy of mine from Syria who will also bear letters to you to the Queen of Cities in order that he may receive these monies for our person. And you on your side, you the ever-revered Majesties, the Sebasti and Augusti of the Roman Empire will observe, I presume, all that is written in this Golden Bull of your pious Majesties and keep its promises. I on my side by this my oath do ratify all the agreements made by me with you. For I swear by the passion of Christ, our passionless Saviour, and by His unconquerable Cross, which He endured for the salvation of all men, and on these all-holy Gospels, which lie before me, which have brought the whole world into their net; holding them in my hand, and in my spirit, I include with them the most precious cross of Christ and His crown of thorns and the

---

[1] *Perhaps* ' of Edessa.'

nails and the lance which pierced His divine and life-giving
side, I swear to thee, our most powerful and holy Emperor,
the Lord Alexius Comnenus, and to thy fellow-Emperor,
the much-desired Lord John Porphyrogenitus that I will
observe all the conditions to which I have agreed and spoken
by my mouth and will keep them inviolate for all time and
the things that are for the good of your Empire I care for now
and will for ever care for and I will never harbour even the
slightest thought of hatred or treachery towards you, but will
abide by the agreements here made by me and not in any
way whatsoever will I be false in my oaths to you or try to
annul my promises nor will I think upon anything that tends
to war, neither I myself nor any of those who are with me and
under my jurisdiction and form the body of my soldiers.
But on behalf of . . . and against thine enemies we
will don our corselets and take arms and spears and to thy
friends we will give our right hands ; and everything that is
for the benefit and honour of the Roman rule that I will
both think of and execute. Thus may I enjoy the help of
God, and of the Cross and of the holy Gospels.

These things were written and the oaths were completed
in the presence of the witnesses whose names are signed
below in the month of September in the second Indiction
of the year then drawing to its close, six thousand six hundred
and seventeen.[1]

But the witnesses who were present and have signed below,
before whom these things were done, are as follows ; the
bishops most dear to God, the bishop Mavros of Amalfi and
Renardus of Tarentum and the clerics with him ; the most
reverend abbot of the holy monastery of St. Andrew in
Lombardy which stands on the island of Brindisi ; and two
monks of the same ; the chief men of the Peregrini who made
their marks below with their own hands, and whose names
were written against their marks by the hand of the bishop
of Amalfi, most dear to God, who had come to the Emperor as
ambassador from the Pope.[2] Those of the imperial court
were : the Sebastus Marianus, Roger the son of Tacupertus,[3]
Peter Aliphas, Gelielmus Ganze, Richard Printzitas, Iosphre
Male,[4] Hubert the son of Raoul, Paul the Roman, the envoys
who had come from Dacia from the Cral,[5] the Queen's relation,
Zupanus Peres and Simon and the envoys of Riscardus

---

[1] 6617 of the Byzantine Era = 1109 A.D.
[2] *Then* Pascal II.   [3] = Dagobert.   [4] *Probably* Geoffroi de Mailli.
[5] = the Prince of Bulgaria.

Siniscardus, the Nobilissimus Basilius, a eunuch, and the notary Constantine."

This oath, then, put down in writing the Emperor received from Bohemund, and in return he gave him the above-mentioned Golden Bull signed in red ink, as was the custom, by the imperial right hand.

BOOK XIV

I

THUS these matters were brought to an end conformably
with the Emperor's wishes and Bohemund ratified by
oaths the agreement which has been set out at length
above with the holy Gospels in front of him and the lance,
with which the lawless soldiers pierced our Saviour's side.
Then he asked to be allowed to return to his own country,
and placed all his forces in the power and at the discretion
of the Emperor, requesting at the same time that they should
pass the winter within the Roman dominions and be supplied
abundantly with all necessaries, and that when the winter
was over and they had recovered from their many toils,
they should be allowed to go wherever they wanted. These
requests he made and the Emperor immediately gave his
consent to them. After being then and there honoured with
the rank of Sebastus and receiving a large sum of money he
returned to his own army. And Constantine Euphorbenus,
usually called Catacalon, accompanied him so that no injury
should be done to him on the road by any soldiers of ours,
but more especially to take forethought for a camp for the
Frankish army in some suitable and safe spot, and to listen
to, and grant, any requests the soldiers might make. When
Bohemund reached his own camp and had handed over his
army to the men sent with him by the Emperor for this
purpose, he embarked on a ship with one bank of oars and
landed in Lombardy. He lived only six months longer and
then paid the debt that all must pay.

The Emperor was detained for some time by his care
for the Franks; and when he had arranged everything
satisfactorily for them, he took the road home to Byzantium.
But after his return he did not give himself entirely to rest
and repose, for, when he reflected how the barbarians had laid
the whole sea-coast of Smyrna in ruins right up to Attalia,
he thought it would be a disgrace if he could not restore the
cities to their pristine state, bring back their former prosperity

and re-people them with the inhabitants who were now scattered far and wide. Not but what he was also concerned about the city of Attalus but he gave much thought to it. There was a man, Philocales Eumathius, who was very energetic, and not only belonged to the nobility by birth, but excelled most in prudence ; he was liberal in mind and hand, faithful to God and his friends, singularly devoted to his masters but absolutely uninitiated in military training, for he neither knew how to hold a bow and draw its string to his breast, or how to protect himself with a shield. In other ways he was very clever as, for example, in setting ambuscades and in worsting the enemy by various devices. This man went to the Emperor and earnestly besought him to give him the governorship of Attalia. Knowing the man's subtlety in inventions and undertakings and the good luck which always attended him (whatever that is or is supposed to be), for he never put his hand to any undertaking without attaining his object, the Emperor let himself be persuaded by these reasons, and gave him a good supply of troops, and also many suggestions and bade him above all be very discreet in his enterprises. On reaching Abydus Eumathius at once sailed across the intervening straits and reached Atramytium.[1] This was formerly a very populous town ; but when Tzachas was laying waste the country round Smyrna, he laid it in ruins and rased it to the ground. On observing the complete disappearance of this town which looked as if man had never dwelt in it, Eumathius forthwith rebuilt it and restored it to its former appearance and recalled the inhabitants from all sides, at least such of the original ones as had escaped, and sent for many from other parts and settled them in the town, and thus gave it back its former appearance. Then he enquired about the Turks and learnt that they were at the moment near Lampe, so he separated a detachment from his forces and sent it to meet them. They attacked them and after a fierce battle carried off the victory without delay ; and they treated the Turks so cruelly that they even threw new-born infants into kettles of boiling water ; they killed many and others they took alive, and returned to Eumathius with rejoicing. The surviving Turks put on black clothes as they wished to represent their misfortunes to their countrymen even by their garments, and travelled through all the country occupied by the Turks and with shrill lamentations, related the horrors that had befallen them and by their very dress

[1] = Adramyttium.

they moved all to pity and roused them up to avenge them. Eumathius who had betaken himself to Philadelphia was rejoicing at the success of his enterprise. But a certain leading satrap, Asan by name, who was in possession of Cappadocia and treated the inhabitants like purchased slaves, heard of the calamity that had befallen the Turks of whom we have spoken, so collected his forces, sent for more from other places and brought up his army to twenty-four thousand, and then marched out to meet Eumathius. Now Eumathius, being a clever man, as already said, was not living in unconcern in Philadelphia, nor had he fallen into idle ways directly he got inside its walls, but kept on sending out scouts in all directions and to prevent their becoming careless, he sent a second lot after the first to rouse them into wakefulness, with the result that they watched all night long and kept an eye on all the by-ways and plains. One of these scouts saw the Turkish army in the distance and came running to bring Eumathius the tidings. As he was quick-witted and swift at grasping the needful and in giving effect to his decisions without a moment's loss, he immediately bade all the gates of the city to be made secure because he felt that his forces were insufficient against such numbers, and ordered that nobody at all was to be allowed to go up to the walls, or shout or play on the flute or lyre. In a word he gave such an appearance to the town, that passers-by would have thought it was quite uninhabited.

On reaching Philadelphia Asan encircled it with his army and remained there for three days. But as not a single inhabitant could be seen looking out, and the gates were securely fastened and he had neither siege-engines nor catapults, he concluded that Eumathius' army was small and for this reason did not dare to venture out, so he con-demned those within severely for weakness and turned in another direction in utter contempt of Eumathius. Con-sequently he dispatched ten thousand of his own army against Celbianum, and . . . others toward Smyrna and Nymphæum, and the rest to Chliarâ and Pergamus; he sent them all out to forage and himself followed the troops that were going to Smyrna. Philocales, however, guessing Asan's intention, sent all the forces he had in pursuit of the Turks. They followed up the division that was proceeding to Celbianum and surprised them sleeping unheedingly, so attacked them at dawn of day and cut them down without mercy; and also liberated all the prisoners taken by the

Turks. Afterwards they pursued the Turks marching to Smyrna and Nymphæum ; some of the troops ran on ahead and opened battle with them from the front and the two flanks and routed them completely. They killed many and took many captive ; the few that were left fell into the streams of the Mæander in their flight and were immediately drowned. This is a river in Phrygia, the most winding of all rivers, for it twists hither and thither the whole way. Emboldened by their second victory they pursued the third division, but could do nothing more as the Turks had already travelled on too far ahead. They therefore returned to Philadelphia. When Eumathius saw them and heard how gallantly they had fought and made a point of not letting one of the enemy slip through their fingers, he rewarded them lavishly and promised them further favours in the future.

II After Bohemund's death Tancred kept a tight hold on Antioch for he considered that it belonged to him, so he kept the Emperor entirely out of it. The Emperor meanwhile reflected that the barbarian Franks had broken their oaths in the case of this city, that he himself had spent a great deal of money and suffered many inconveniences in transporting those myriad hosts from the Western countries into Asia, in spite of his finding them a stiff-necked and sharp-tempered people. He had also sent many Roman armies out with them to fight against the Turks, and this for two reasons, firstly, to prevent their falling a prey to the Turkish sword (for being Christians he was concerned for them), and secondly, in order that they with our co-operation should destroy some of the Ishmaelites' cities, and give others under a truce to the Roman Emperors, and in this way the portions of the Romans would be enlarged. But no good had accrued to the Roman rule from these innumerable toils and dangers and gifts, for the Franks kept a tight hold on the city of Antioch, and did not give us back the other cities either so he felt he could not bear it nor restrain himself any longer from returning evil for evil and taking revenge for their horrible inhumanity. For that Tancred should enjoy those countless presents and those heaps of gold and the Emperor's unending care of the Franks and the quantities of armies he had sent as auxiliaries to them, whilst the Roman kingdom reaped no benefit from all this and the Franks considered the prize their own and disregarded and counted as naught the treaties and oaths they had made with him—this thought rent his soul asunder and he did not know how to bear the insult. Consequently he sent ambassadors to Tancred the governor of Antioch, to accuse him of injustice and the violation of oaths and to say that he would no longer submit to being despised by him but would take vengeance upon him for his ingratitude to the Romans. For it would be disgraceful, and more than disgraceful, if after spending countless sums of money, and sending the finest regiments of the Roman army with them to take the whole of Syria and Antioch itself, and striving with all his heart and might to enlarge the boundaries of the Roman Empire, it should be Tancred who luxuriated in his, the Emperor's, money and labours.

When the Emperor's ambassadors brought this message, that mad and demented barbarian would not listen, even with the tips of his ears, to the truth of their words and the free speech of the ambassadors, but acted like the men of his race and being puffed up with vanity boasted that he would place his throne above the stars and threatened to bore a hole through the walls of Babylon with the tip of his spear, and sang the praise of his power for being undaunted and irresistible in onslaught, and reiterated that, no matter what happened, he would never give up Antioch, not even if the soldiers set to fight against him had hands of fire. He further likened himself to Ninus, the great king of Assyria, and said he was a big, irresistible giant, a dead weight standing upon the earth, and he considered all the Romans ants and the weakest of all creatures. The ambassadors left him and returned and after they related the Frank's mad talk, the Emperor became filled with rage and could hardly be restrained but wanted to start for Antioch on the spot. He then convoked the men of the highest repute in military circles and all the members of the senate and asked them for their advice. They immediately and unanimously rejected the idea of the Emperor's marching against Tancred. They said that he ought first to win over the other Counts who were masters of the towns round about Antioch, and also Balduinus, King of Jerusalem, and find out their opinions and whether they would be willing to assist him in an expedition against Antioch. Afterwards if he were sure that they were all hostile to Tancred, he could advance against him with full confidence ; but, if not, the matter of Antioch must be managed in some different way. The Emperor commended this advice and shortly summoned Manuel Butumites and another man

who knew the Latin language and sent them to the Counts
and to the King of Jerusalem, after giving them full instructions on the subject about which they were to converse
with the Counts and also with Balduinus himself, the King of
Jerusalem. As it was imperative that they should have
money to use in their mission to these Counts, because the
Latins are so covetous, he handed Butumites orders for
Eumathius Philocales, at that time Duke of Cyprus, telling
the latter to supply them with as many ships as they needed ;
he also bade him give them plenty of money of all kinds, of
every shape and coinage and of varying qualities to be used
as gifts for the Counts. He also enjoined on the men
mentioned, more especially on Manuel Butumites, that
after receiving the money from Philocales, they should anchor
off Tripoli and visit the Count Pelctranus,[1] the son of the
Isangeles who has often been mentioned in this history, and
remind him of the faith which his father had always kept
with the Emperor, and hand him the Emperor's letters at
the same time. And they were to say to him, " You must
not shew yourself inferior to your own father, but preserve
faith with us just as he did. I would have you know that I
am going to Antioch to take my vengeance on that man who
has violated the solemn oaths he made to God and to me. Be
careful not to give him assistance in any way and do your
best to induce the Counts to pledge their faith to us so that
they may not for some reason or other espouse Tancred's
cause." So they made their way to Cyprus and, after collecting the money there and as many ships as they wanted, they
sailed straight to Tripoli. They moored their ships in its
harbour, disembarked and had an interview with Pelctranus
and recited to him the messages with which the Emperor
had charged them. They found him very well-inclined and
ready to fulfil any wish of the Emperor's, and willing even to
suffer death for his sake if that should be necessary, and he
promised that when the Emperor arrived in the neighbourhood
of Antioch, he would come down and do obeisance to him.
Then with his consent they deposited the money they had
brought with them in the episcopal palace of Tripoli, as the
Emperor had suggested. For he feared that if the Counts
found out they were carrying money with them, they would
take the money but send them away empty-handed, and use
the money for themselves and Tancred. He therefore
judged it wiser that the ambassadors should first go empty-

---

[1] = Bertram, son of Raymond of Toulouse.

handed and test the Counts' feelings but also tell them how
much the Emperor had destined for them, and promise the
gift of the money and require an oath from them and, if in
the meanwhile they shewed themselves willing to yield to
the Emperor's demands, then only to hand the money over
to them. So Butumites and his fellows deposited the money
in the bishop's residence at Tripoli, as we have said. But
on Balduinus' hearing of these ambassadors' arrival in Tripoli,
he at once, through desire for the money, sent his own cousin
Simon to forestall their coming and invite them. They with
Pelctranus' consent left the money behind there and accompanied Simon who had been sent from Jerusalem and found
Balduinus besieging Tyre. He received them with pleasure
and shewed them much friendliness, and as they had reached
him on the Carnival, he kept them there through the whole
of Lent whilst he, as we said, was besieging Tyre.

Now this city was protected by impregnable walls as well
as by three outworks which enclosed it in a circle. For the
outmost circle encompassed the second, and this in its turn
the innermost or third one. They were like three circles,
enclosing each other and set like girdles round the city.
Balduinus knew well that he must first destroy these outworks
and only then take the city; for they were like corselets
placed in front of Tyre and hindered the siege. He had
already destroyed this first and second belt by means of
machines of destruction and was at work on the third, but
after tearing down its battlements he had grown idle, for he
could have taken this one too, if he had set his mind to it.
But, thinking that after this he could ascend into the city
by the help of a few ladders, he lost interest in the siege,
just as if he already had the town in his power. This fact
brought salvation to the Saracens; and the man who had
had victory almost in his hand, was utterly beaten off from
it, and the men who were inside the net, escaped from its
meshes. For the interval spent by Balduinus in idleness was
most diligently used by them as a time of recovery. They
devised the following cunning trick. To all seeming they had
an eye to making terms of peace and sent embassies to Balduinus about it; but in reality while the terms of peace were
under discussion, they were preparing their defence, and while
they kept him buoyed up with hope they were forming
machinations against him. For having noticed his great
slackness in the war, and also that the soldiers outside the
walls had lost heart, one night they filled a number of clay

jars full of liquid pitch, and hurled them down on to the
engines standing round the city.   As the jars were necessarily
broken to pieces in their fall, the liquid was poured all over
the woodwork, and on to that they threw lighted torches.
Then they brought other jars containing a great deal of
naphtha which caught the fire and made the flames shoot
up into the air and converted the Franks' engines into ashes.
And the light of the breaking day mingled with the light
from the towering blaze of the wooden sheds.   Thus Balduinus'
soldiers reaped the fruits of the carelessness in which they
had indulged and of which they repented now that the smoke
and fire shewed them the result.   Some of the soldiers standing near the sheds were taken captive, six in number, and on
seeing them the Tyrian governor had their heads cut off and
shot into Balduinus' camp from catapults.   When the soldiers
saw the fire and the heads they were seized with panic,
jumped on their horses and fled as if utterly terrified by those
heads, although Balduinus rode to and fro among them and
called back the fugitives and tried to embolden them in every
way.   But ' he was singing to deaf men ' ;   for once they
had abandoned themselves to flight, they kept steadily on
their course and seemed swifter than any bird.   And the
goal of their course was the fortress locally called Ace,[1] for that
appeared to those cowardly runagates like a tower of refuge.
Then in despair and at an utter loss Balduinus, though unwillingly, followed the fleeing soldiers and likewise ran away
to the city mentioned.   Meanwhile Butumites embarked
on his Cyprian ships (they were twelve in all) and sailed along
the coast towards Ace, and there met Balduinus and then
reported to him all the Emperor had ordered him to say ;
but he supplemented his speech by saying that the Emperor
had already reached Seleucia.   This was not true at all but
just an artifice to frighten the barbarian and make him dismiss
him quickly.   But Balduinus was not deceived by this dodge,
and rebuked Butumites sternly for having lied.   For he had
already received information from elsewhere of the Emperor's
doings, namely that he had gone down to the long coast,
suppressed the pirate-ships which were ravaging those shores,
and then returned home from there because he was ill (about
this we will speak more in detail later on).   With this information Balduinus contradicted Butumites, and after censuring
him for his false statement, said, " You must come with me
to the Holy Sepulchre and from there I will send ambassadors

[1] = Acre.

to carry our decisions to the Emperor." Directly they reached the Holy City, he demanded the money which the Emperor had sent. Butumites said, " If you promise that you will help the Emperor against Tancred and thus keep the oath which you made with him when you passed through, then you shall receive the money which was sent for you without delay." Balduinus however was anxious to get the money although eager to help Tancred and not the Emperor, and when he did not get it, he was annoyed. The whole barbarian race is like that, it is always agape for presents and money, but is very little inclined to carry out the purpose for which the money is given. So he merely handed Butumites some letters and dismissed him. The ambassadors also met the Count Iatzulinus,[1] on the day of our Lord's resurrection, who had come to worship at the Holy Sepulchre, and discussed what was fitting with him. But when they discovered that he answered in the same strain as Balduinus, they left Jerusalem without having accomplished anything.

When they found that Pelctranus was no longer among the living, they asked for the moneys they had deposited in the episcopal palace. But Pelctranus' son and the bishop of Tripoli delayed giving them back the money for some time, so at last the ambassadors threatened them saying, " If you do not give back the money to us, you are not true servants of the Emperor and you are proved not to observe the same fidelity to him as Pelctranus and his father Isangeles did. Very well then, you shall not have an abundant supply of necessaries from Cyprus in the future, nor shall the Duke of Cyprus come to your aid, and then you will perish by famine." After they had ' let out every reef,' as the proverb says, and tried first honeyed words and then threats and yet could not persuade Pelctranus' son to give up the money, they judged it expedient to make him take a solemn oath of fidelity to the Emperor, and then to give him only the gift destined for his father, consisting of gold and silver stamped money and garments of divers kinds. On receipt of these the son took the solemn oath of fidelity to the Emperor. The rest of the money they took back to Eumathius and with it purchased well-bred horses from Damascus and Edessa and even Arabia. From there they crossed the Syrian sea and gulf of Pamphylia and then gave up sailing as they considered the land safer than the sea, and made their way to the Chersonese where

[1] = Joscelin de Courtenay.

the Emperor was, and after crossing the Hellespont they reached the Emperor.

III   And now troubles fell upon him one after the other, like a snowstorm, for at sea the chiefs of Pisa, Genoa and Lombardy were preparing to lay waste all the sea-board by means of their fleet ; and on land in the East the Ameer Saisan[1] was again trying to get hold of Philadelphia and the maritime districts.   Consequently the Emperor decided he must leave the capital and go to some place from which he could carry on the war against both parties.   So he went to the Chersonese and called up troops from all parts both from land and sea, and set apart a goodly army to go over the Scamander to Atramytium or even Thracesium and stay there.   At that time the governor of Philadelphia was Constantine Gabras who had sufficient men to garrison the town ; the semi-barbarian Monastras (who has often been mentioned in this history) held Pergamus and Chliara and the towns round about it, and all the other towns along the sea were governed by men renowned for daring and military experience. The Emperor sent them frequent messages exhorting them to keep a constant watch and to send out spies in all directions to observe the barbarians' skirmishings and bring their news quickly.   Having thus made things in Asia secure he turned his attention to the war at sea ; he ordered some of the sailors to anchor their ships in the harbours of Madytus and Cœli and keep a steady watch on the straits opposite and also make excursions with light cruisers and keep a continual look-out over the sea-ways in expectation of the Frankish fleet.   Others were to sail among the islands and guard them without at the same time overlooking the Peloponnese, but to give that too the requisite protection.

As he wished to stay in those parts for a considerable time, he had some dwellings constructed in a suitable spot and spent the winter there.   When the fully-equipped fleet from Lombardy and the other places loosed its cables and sailed forth, the admiral of it picked out five biremes and sent them out to catch some ships and from them learn the Emperor's whereabouts.   But when they reached Abydos, it fell out that only one ship returned to the man who sent them forth, as the rest were captured, crews and all.   From this ship the admirals of the said fleets learnt of the Emperor's doings, namely that after making everything very secure on land

[1] *Or* Melek.

and sea, he was wintering in the Chersonese in order to hearten up all his men. Since they were unable to fight successfully against the Emperor's subtle plans, they put their hands to their rudders and went off in another direction. One Frank alone from among these admirals took his own monoreme which was very swift and sailed away to Balduinus. He found him besieging Tyre and related to him all that we have just said about the Emperor (I fancy he had sailed with the other admirals' consent); and also told him that the Roman fleet had succeeded in capturing the scout-ships, as told above. And he even confessed without a blush that when the leaders of the Frankish fleet discovered that the Emperor was all ready to meet them, they retreated, thinking it better to return without accomplishing anything than to fight with the Roman fleet and be beaten. All these things that Frank, who was nervous and still in dread of the Roman fleet, recounted to Balduinus. That then is what happened to the Franks at sea ; but on land things did not settle down without distresses and worries for the Emperor. For a certain Michael from Amastris who was the governor of Acrunus, was meditating defection and took the town and began to ravage the surrounding country terribly. On being informed of this the Emperor sent George, the son of Decanus, against him with an adequate force. After a siege of three months George took the city and sent the rebel to the Emperor without delay. The Emperor entrusted the care of the fortress to another man, but at Michael he shot a severe glance, threatened him with many things and apparently had doomed him to death ; thus he instilled great fear into the man, and yet very soon relieved the soldier of his dread. For the sun had not set below the horizon before the prisoner was a free man, and the man condemned to death was the recipient of many gifts. Such was my father, the Emperor, on all occasions, and yet later on he met with much ingratitude from the whole world. Just in the same way our universal Benefactor was once treated, our Lord who rained down manna in the wilderness, gave food to men in the mountains and made them pass through the sea with dry feet, and yet later He was set at naught and insulted and beaten and finally condemned to be crucified by the impious. But as I write this my tears gush out before my words, and I long to speak of these men and make a list of the ungrateful, but I restrain my tongue and beating heart and continually repeat to myself the words of the poet, " Bear up, O heart, for thou

2B

hast borne more horrible things already ! " This is enough
about that ungrateful soldier.

The Sultan Saisan sent troops from Chorosan, some
of whom marched through the lands of Sinaus, and the others
through what is properly called Asia. On receipt of this
news, Constantine Gabras, then Governor of Philadelphia,
collected his troops and overtook the Turks at Celbianum ;
he was the first to dash upon them at full gallop and ordered
the others to do the same and thus they routed the barbarians.
When the Sultan who had dispatched these troops heard
how many had been killed, he sent ambassadors to the Emperor to treat about peace, confessing at the same time
that he had long desired to see peace between Mussulmans and
Romans. For from afar he had heard of the Emperor's
prowess against all his foes, and on making trial of it himself
he had ' recognized the cloth by its edge,' and the ' lion by
its claws,' and though against his will had turned aside to
thoughts of peace. Now when the Ambassadors from
Persia arrived, the Emperor, a formidable figure, seated
himself on his throne and the men, whose business it was,
arranged the soldiers of every nationality and the axe-bearing
barbarians in their proper order, and then brought in the
ambassadors to the imperial throne. The Emperor first
asked them the conventional questions about the Sultan,
and, after listening to the messages they brought, he confessed that he welcomed and desired peace with the whole
world. He next enquired about the Sultan's proposals and
when he recognized that some of his requests would not
be expedient for the Roman rule, he wrapped up very persuasive arguments in many words and made a very clever
defence of his actions to them, and by his long speech persuaded them to concur with his wishes. Then he dismissed
them to the tent prepared for them with injunctions to
think over his words and said that if they agreed whole-
heartedly with them the treaty between them should be
concluded on the morrow. They shewed themselves very
ready to accept the Emperor's terms, and the treaty was
concluded on the following day. In this the Emperor was
not thinking only of his own interests but of the Roman
Empire. For he was more solicitous of the universal welfare
than of his own, and in all his arrangements he only regarded,
and referred everything to, the dignity of the Roman sceptre,
in order that treaties might last on even after his death to
future years—and yet he failed in his object. For after

him things were different and everything was turned into confusion. In the meantime all disturbing elements had been laid to rest and we looked forward to perfect peace, and we had peace from then to the end of his life. But all that was most desirable vanished together with the Emperor, and his efforts were all rendered vain after his departure by the stupidity of his successors to the throne.

IV After receiving trustworthy information about the Roman fleet from the survivors of the five cruisers, as we have related, and learning that the Emperor had equipped his fleet and was staying in the Chersonese in expectation of their arrival, the admirals of the Frankish fleet abandoned their first plan and had no longer the slightest desire to approach the coasts of Romania. The Emperor wintered in Calliopolis with the Empress (who, as we have mentioned several times, accompanied him because of the severe pains in his feet) and after waiting for the season in which the Frankish fleet usually sailed home he returned to the capital. But only a short time elapsed before news was brought of the advance of a Turkish host, collected from all the countries of the East, even from Chorosan itself and numbering about fifty thousand men. For never throughout his whole reign did the Emperor enjoy even a short time of rest, as enemies after enemies kept continually cropping up. Consequently he called up his whole army from all sides, and choosing the time of year when the barbarians were wont to make their expeditions against the Christians, he crossed the straits between Byzantium and Damalis. And not even the increasing pain in his feet could deter him from this undertaking.

Now this disease had never attacked any of his ancestors, so that one might think it had been passed on to him by heredity ; nor was it due to soft living which often gives it to those who are intemperate in their life and pleasures. But I will relate the real origin of this affection of his feet. One day for the sake of exercise, he was playing at polo with Taticius, of whom I have often spoken. Taticius was caused to swerve by his horse and fell against the king, whose knee-cap was injured by the weight of the impact and the pain extended right down the leg. But, as he was used to endurance, he said nothing about the pain, and only had the leg slightly attended to, and as the pain soon passed he pursued his usual routine. This was the original cause of the Emperor's sufferings in his feet ; for the local injury drew the rheumatics to the injured part. But the second and more active source of all this trouble was the following. Who has not heard of those countless hosts of Franks who arrived in the Queen of Cities when they had quitted their own homes and invaded ours ? By them the Emperor was engulfed in an immense sea of worries, for he had long grasped the fact that the Franks were dreaming of the Roman Empire ; and he saw their multitude exceeding the sand and the stars in number, and then looked at the Roman forces which did not equal a fraction of theirs, even if they could all be concentrated on one spot. But on the contrary most of them were dispersed, for some were keeping guard in the valleys of Serbia and in Dalmatia ; others were protecting the lands along the Ister against the inroads of the Comans and the Dacians, and many again were entrusted with the guarding of Dyrrachium so that it might not be re-taken by the Franks—when he considered all this the Emperor bent his whole attention to the Franks and relegated everything else to the second place. And the barbarians who were moving about secretly and had not yet openly declared their enmity, he appeased by titles and gifts. By all possible means he tried to check the Franks' aim, and when he reflected not less, but rather more, on the internal disaffection, he did his utmost to guard himself by skilfully bringing their plots to naught. But who could describe the welter of ills which overtook him ? Therefore he made himself all things to all men, and by re-arranging matters as far as possible, according to circumstances, he applied himself to the most pressing need, just as a good physician who follows the rules of his art. In the morning, as soon as the sun had leapt above the eastern horizon, he sat on the imperial throne and gave orders that all the Franks should come in freely every day, partly because he wished them to state their requests, and partly too because he was manœuvring by arguments of various kinds to bring them to accede to his own wishes.

Now the Frankish Counts are naturally shameless and violent, naturally greedy of money too, and immoderate in everything they wish, and possess a flow of language greater than any other human race ; and they did not make their visits to the Emperor in any order, but each Count as he came brought in as many men as he liked with him ; and one came after another, and another in turn after him. And when they came in, they did not regulate their conversation by a waterglass, as the rule was for orators formerly, but for as long as each wished to talk to the Emperor, be he even a mere

nobody, for so long he was allowed to talk. Now, as this was
their character, and their speech very long-winded, and as
they had no reverence for the Emperor, nor took heed of the
lapse of time nor suspected the indignation of the onlookers,
not one of them gave place to those who came after them,
but kept on unceasingly with their talk and requests. Their
talkativeness and hunting instinct and their finicking speech
are known to all who are interested in studying the manners
of mankind, but we who were then present learnt them more
thoroughly from experience. For even when evening came,
the Emperor who had remained without food all through
the day, rose from his throne to retire to his private bedroom ;
but not even then was he freed from the Franks' importunity.
For one came after the other and not only those who had
not been heard during the day, but the same came over
again, aways preferring one excuse after another for further
talk, whilst he stood unmoved in the midst of the Franks,
quietly bearing their endless chatter. And you could see
him all alone and with unchanging countenance ever giving
a ready answer to all their questions. And there was no
end to their unseasonable loquacity. If any one of the
ministers tried to cut them short, the Emperor prevented
him For knowing the Franks' natural irritability he was
afraid lest from some trifling pretext a great fire of scandal
should be lighted and great harm ensue to the Roman rule.
And really it was a most wonderful sight. For like a hammer-
wrought statue, made perhaps of bronze or cold iron, he
would sit the whole night through, from the evening until
midnight perhaps, and often even till the third cock-crow,
and very occasionally almost till the sun's rays were bright.
All his attendants were dead-tired and would retire and rest
and then come back again grumbling. Not one of his courtiers
could remain as long as he did without resting, but all kept
fidgeting in one way or another. For one would sit, another
would rest his head on something and lie down, and another
would prop himself against the wall. The Emperor alone
presented an unyielding front to all this labour. And what
words would properly describe his patience ? For in this
babel of tongues each one spoke at length and ' wrangled on
unbridled of tongue,' as Homer says ; then he would stand
aside for another and give him the opportunity of speaking,
and he passed it on to another and so on from one to the
other. And they only stood at intervals, but he had to
retain his position unceasingly up to the first or second

cock-crow. After a short rest he was again seated on his throne when the sun rose and then fresh labours and new contentions succeeded those of the night. Clearly it was from this reason that the pain in his feet attacked the Emperor. And from that time on to his death the rheumatism visited him at periodical intervals, and caused him exquisite agony. But he endured it so patiently without ever uttering a word of complaint, but only said, " I deserve the pain ; it comes upon me justly because of the multitude of my sins." If perchance a word of despondency had escaped his lips, he at once made the sign of the cross against the miscreant demon, and said, " Away from me, thou wicked one ! Perdition to thee and thy machinations against Christians ! " I have said sufficient about the pains in his feet for the present.

But perhaps there was a person who contributed to this disease and increased the sufferings he bore from this cup of his, so full of bitterness; however I will only suggest it in a few words, but not tell the whole story. Although the Empress smeared the rim of the cup with honey and contrived to make much of his suffering slip down easily, through being his ever-watchful guardian, yet this man must be added to our description and may be called a third reason of the Emperor's malady ; and he was not only the immediate but the most effective cause, to use the traditional language of physicians. For he did not only attack him once and then disappear, but he was always present and his companion, just as the most subtle humours are present in the blood-vessels. Nay more, if one reflected on that man's nature, he was not only the cause of disease, but actually a malady itself and its severest symptom. But it behoves me to bite my tongue and restrain my words and not run off the track, however eager I may be to leap upon those villains. But I will reserve my story about him to a fitting moment.

V Now let my history resume its narrative. The Emperor had crossed to Damalis on the opposite coast and was in camp there, and there our narrative had left him. And soon all flocked to him like a snowstorm, and crossed to him who was staying in that place, partly because he was awaiting the arrival of them all, and partly in the hope that his excessive pains would diminish. The Empress was with him taking care of him and lightening the pains in his feet by various kinds of tendance. When he saw the full moon, he said to her, " If the Turks really think of sallying forth to plunder, now is the fittest time for it, and I am annoyed that I have missed this opportunity." He said this in the evening and at dawn the eunuch in attendance on their Majesties' bedchamber announced that the Turks had made an attack upon Nicæa, and shewed them a letter from Eustathius Camytzes, at that time governor of that city, describing what they had done. Immediately, without waiting a little or delaying at all, and as if oblivious of his continuous pains, the Emperor started in a war-chariot for Nicæa, holding the whip himself in his right hand. The soldiers too picked up their spears and marched in orderly bands on either side. Some ran along at his side, some went ahead and others followed, all in high spirits at his marching against the barbarians, but saddened because his pains prevented his riding (on horseback). And he inspired all with confidence by his signs and words, for he smiled sweetly and talked to them. After three days' journey they reached a place called Ægiali, from which he intended to cross to Cibotus. As the Empress saw that he wished to hurry on the crossing, she bade him farewell and returned to the capital. On the Emperor's reaching Cibotus a messenger came to him saying that the chief satraps of the forty thousand had separated, and some of them had gone to ravage Nicæa and the lands around it, whilst Monolycus and .   .   . were devastating the countries along the sea. The troops which had laid waste all the districts adjacent to the lake of Nicæa, as well as Prusa and Apollonias, had pitched their camp by the town and brought all their booty together there. Then they had moved forward in a body and laid waste Lopadium and the surrounding districts, and, as the messenger said, had even taken Cyzicus at the first assault from the seaward side, as the governor of the town had not offered even the slightest resistance, but fled ignominiously from the place.

Further, Contogmen and the Ameer Muhumet, the archsatraps of the picked troops, had proceeded by way of Lentiana to Pœmanenum, dragging along with them much booty and very many captives, both men and wretched women and children whom the sword had spared. After crossing the river Monolycus (locally called Barenus, which flows down from a mountain named Ibis, in which many other rivers take their rise, namely the Scamander, the Angelocomites and the Empelus), they turned off to Parium, and Abydus on the Hellespont and then marched through Atramytium and Chliara with their whole train of prisoners without shedding a drop of blood or fighting a single battle. On receipt of this news the Emperor sent letters to Camytzes, then acting as Duke of Nicæa, ordering him to follow up the barbarians with five hundred soldiers and keep him informed by letter about them, but to avoid an engagement with them. He marched out from Nicæa, overtook Contogmen and the Ameer Muhumet and the rest near the place called Aorata, and as if forgetful of the Emperor's instructions, at once attacked them.

Now they were expecting the Emperor and, thinking it was he who had fallen upon them, they fled in a panic. But they had captured a Scythian prisoner and when they learnt the truth from him, and found it was Camytzes, they crossed the mountains and took heart and by means of kettledrums and shouts recalled their tribesmen who had scattered in all directions. And these recognizing this signal of recall, all flocked back to them. Then they returned to the plain which lies immediately below the place called Aorata and reassembled there. But Camytzes, after taking all the booty from them, did not wish to push on to Pœmanenum where he could have arranged matters well (for it was a very strongly fortified town), but loitered round Aorata without noticing that he was plotting his own destruction. For the barbarians who had secured a safe position did not forget Camytzes but lay in wait for him all the time. And when they found out that he was still staying at Aorata arranging about all the booty and the prisoners they drew up all their forces in companies and fell upon him at early dawn. Directly they saw the vast crowd of barbarians which had attacked them, the greater part of Camytzes' army thought good to ensure their own safety by flight, but Camytzes himself with the Scythians and the Franks and the braver of the Romans fought valiantly. And there the greater number of them fell ; yet Camytzes, with a few survivors, still continued the fight. But when the horse on which he was riding received a fatal blow, he was thrown to the ground, whereupon his nephew, Catarodon by name, jumped off his own horse and gave it to him. But as he was a tall, heavy man Camytzes did not find it easy to mount the horse ; so he stepped back a little and then propping himself against an oak, drew his dagger ; he despaired of any hope of safety, but did not cease hitting at the helmet, shoulders or even the hands of any barbarians who dared approach him. When the barbarians saw him maintaining his resistance so long and killing many and also wounding many, they admired the man's boldness and marvelled at his steadiness and decided to save him for this reason. The arch-satrap, Muhumet by name, who had known him formerly and now recognized him, checked the attack of the men who were fighting with Camytzes, and dismounting from his horse, as did also the men with him, went up to him and said, "Do not choose death in preference to your safety, but give me your hand and be saved!" Then Camytzes, seeing the numbers by which he was surrounded and feeling unable to cope with so many, gave his hand to Muhumet, who had him put on a horse and his feet bound so that he could not easily run away. This, then, was the fate which overtook Eustathius.

The Emperor guessing the route by which the barbarians would come took another, passed through Nicæa and Malagina and the so-called Basilica (these are narrow valleys and very difficult paths lying on the mountain-ridges of Olympus) and then descended to Alethina and next reached Acrocus as he was hurrying to get ahead of the Turks and attack them from the front and thus start a pitched battle with them. But the Turks in absolute forgetfulness of the Roman army found a reed-bed along the valley, and scattered themselves about in it and rested. When the news was brought to the Emperor as he was starting out against them that the barbarians had occupied the plains of the valley, he drew up his army in battle-order at a suitable distance. In the van he placed Constantine Gabras and Monastras, the rest of the troops he arranged in squadrons on either flank, and the rear he entrusted to Tzipoureles and Abelas who had had long and varied military experience. The centre of the line he held himself and falling upon the Turks like a thunderbolt he threw all their troops into confusion and commenced a pitched battle with them. Many of the barbarians were killed on that occasion, after a very close fight and many too were taken by the spear. Those who sought refuge in the reed-bed, were safe for a time; but after securing a brilliant victory over the others the Emperor turned to the reed-bed and tried to drive the men there out of it. However his soldiers did not know how to do it as they could not go in because of the swampy nature and density of the reed-bed. So the Emperor put a ring of his soldiers round the reed-bed and ordered a fire to be lighted on one side of it. This was done and the flames rose to a great height; the Turks inside while fleeing from the fire fell into the soldiers' hands; and some of them fell to the sword while others were led alive to the Emperor.

VI This is what happened to the Turks who had come down from Carme. When the Ameer Muhumet heard of the disaster which had overtaken the Turks from Carme, he at once marched in pursuit of the Emperor after joining up with the Turcomans, who dwelt in Asia, and the rest; and thus it came about that the same man was both pursuer and pursued. For the barbarians with Muhumet pursued the Emperor by following his tracks while he was marching after the Turks from Carme and was thus caught between the two. However he had already conquered the one lot, and the pursuers were quite free from danger. When Muhumet suddenly attacked the Emperor's rear he first fell in with Abelas. As he was within sight of the Emperor this gave him greater confidence and being moreover a rash man, he did not wait a little for his troops to come up so as to receive the Turks' attack with a properly arrayed army, but dashed against Muhumet. And Tzipoureles followed him. When the two had reached an old fort, but their men had not yet arrived, Muhumet, a very determined man, met them, and wounded Abelas' horse, but not its rider, with an arrow and so unhorsed him. And when the Turks saw him on foot they surrounded and killed him. Likewise on seeing Tzipoureles riding fearlessly against them they 'winged', so to say, the horse on which he was riding with their arrows and unseated him and straightway dispatched him with their swords. Now the soldiers of the rear-guard whose duty it was to protect the wearied baggage-carriers and the horses and drive off as much as possible any who worried them, saw the Turks making this attack, so rushed upon them and routed them completely. Camytzes was there with the Turks, as a prisoner, and when he noticed the confusion that had arisen in the battle and saw that the Turks were now fleeing and our men pursuing, he, being a determined man, planned his escape and took to the road, and fell in with a Frank in full armour who gave him his horse. He found the Emperor encamped in the plain of the valley lying between Philadelphia and Acrocus which was large enough, not only for one, but for several armies. When he saw Camytzes he received him with great joy and after offering thanksgiving to God for having delivered him, he sent him off to the capital, saying, " Tell them all you have suffered and seen and report to our relations that, thanks to God, we are alive." On being told of the death of Abelas and Tzipoureles the Emperor was deeply grieved in soul about their death and said, " We have gained one, but lost two." For, whenever he had been victorious in war, it was his wont to enquire whether any of his soldiers had been captured or fallen a victim to the enemy's hands, and even though he had routed whole phalanxes and carried off the victory, yet had it happened that any one even of the lowest rank of soldiers had perished, he considered that victory as naught but regarded it as virtually a Cadmean one, and a loss instead of gain. After that he constituted certain officers, George Lebunes and others, custodians of that country and left them his troops and then returned to the capital as victor.

Camytzes meanwhile reached Damalis and got into a little boat about the mid-watch of the night, and, as he knew that the Empress was in the upper part of the palace, he went there and knocked at the door next to the shore. When the porters asked who he was, he did not want to declare his own name, but only asked them to open the doors to him. And directly he gave his name he was permitted to enter. The Empress was overjoyed and received him outside her bedroom-door (this balcony was formerly called 'Aristerion'), but when she saw him dressed in Turkish clothes and limping on both feet through having been beaten during the battle, she first enquired about the Emperor and then bade him be seated. Next she asked him about everything and when she heard of the Emperor's recent and unexpected victory and saw the prisoner free before her, she did not know what to do for joy. She allowed him to rest till daytime and then go out and proclaim to the whole world what had happened. So he got up in the morning and mounted a horse in the same clothes in which he had arrived after his marvellous deliverance from captivity, and rode down to the Forum of Constantine. And the whole city at once ran out to him, partly to know what he was doing, and partly because they were still more anxious to have news of the Emperor. Then surrounded by a number of horse- and foot-soldiers he related the events of the war in a loud voice and all that had befallen the Roman army, and the plans the Emperor had made against the barbarians and the brilliant victory he had gained whereby he had avenged himself several times over; and concluded with his own miraculous escape from the barbarians. The whole populace applauded his speech and the noise of their applause reached the skies.

VII After this had been done, Constantinople was full of the news of the Emperor's successes. For in very truth, to what an extent had fate involved him in difficult affairs which were adverse to him and the Roman state, and in general by what a number of misfortunes was he encompassed! Yet his valour and vigilant and energetic nature resisted and struggled manfully against every misfortune. For not one of the former Emperors right down to the present day were ever met by such a complication of affairs and such wickedness from all kinds of men, both at home and abroad, as we have found to be the case with regard to this Emperor. For either it was decreed by God's permission that the Roman state should be oppressed by ills (for I should never consider our fate as dependent upon the revolution of the stars) or the Roman dynasty had been reduced to such a state by the foolishness of the previous Emperors that a crowd of business and a heavy swell of confusion was accumulated on the time of my father's reign. For at one and the same moment the Scythian rose against him from the North, the Frank from the West, and the Ishmaelite from the East, to say nothing of the dangers of the sea, and the barbarians who ruled the sea, and the countless pirate-ships, some of which were built by the wrath of the Saracens, and others by the covetousness of the Vetones and their dislike to the Roman Empire. For all cast envious glances at it. For being by nature mistress of the other nations the Roman Empire is regarded as an enemy by her subjects, and, whenever an opportunity offers, either the one or the other rushes upon her either from the land or from the sea.

Now the difficulties during the reigns before our time were very slight and fairly tolerable; but in the case of my father directly he mounted the imperial'chariot dangers of every kind streamed down upon him from all quarters at the same time. For the Frank was moving and shewing the tip of his spear, the Ishmaelite was stretching his bow, and all the nomadic and Scythian tribes with their myriad wagons were rushing upon him. But perhaps someone who has lighted upon this history and read so far will say that my tongue has been corrupted by nature. But verily that is not so; I swear by the dangers the Emperor underwent for the welfare of the Roman Empire, and the struggles and disasters my father suffered on behalf of the Christians, I most certainly do not describe and write of these things in order to favour my father. And, wherever I perceive that my father made a mistake, I unhesitatingly transgress the natural law and cling to the truth, for though I hold him dear, I hold truth dearer still. For, as some philosopher has said, when two things are dear, it is best to prefer the truth. But I follow up the facts themselves, without adding anything of my own or slurring over events, and thus I speak and write. And the proof is close at hand; for I am not writing about things of ten thousand years ago, but there are many still living to-day who knew my father and tell me of his doings; and no small part of my history has been gathered from them, for one will relate one thing which he happens to remember and another another, and all are of the same opinion. And as a rule I was with my father and mother and accompanied them. For it was not my lot to be kept at home and brought up in the shade and in luxury; but even from my cradle (I call my God and His Mother to witness!) toils and afflictions and continual misfortunes beset me, some from without and some from within. What my physical appearance was I cannot say, that the attendants of the women's apartments can describe and tell at length. But as for all the external ills which happened to me before I had even completed my eighth year, and the many enemies the malice of men aroused against me it would require the Siren of Isocrates to tell, or the eloquence of Pindar, the breeziness of Polemo, the Calliope of Homer, the lyre of Sappho or some other power beyond all these. For there is no terror either great or small, from near or afar that did not throng around us. And verily the floods overwhelmed me and from that time until now, up to the very time that I am writing this history, the sea of calamities rushes over me and waves follow upon waves. But unconsciously I have been drawn to speak of my own troubles; now having returned to my senses, I will swim upstream again, as it were, and return to my first subject.

Part of my history, as I said, I derive from my own memory and part from the men who accompanied the Emperor on his expeditions and told me divers things about them, and who by means of ferrymen conveyed the news to us of what had happened in the wars; but most I gathered first-hand as I often heard the Emperor and George Palæologus talking about them. In this way I collected much of my material, but most during the reign of the third successor to the imperial throne after my father, when all flatteries and lies about his grandfather had expired together, for the whole world was flattering the present occupant of the throne and nobody shewed any sign of adulation for the departed, but related the naked facts, and spoke of things just as they had received them.

But now I am bewailing my own misfortunes and lamenting the deaths of three Emperors, my Emperor and father, my Empress and mistress-mother, and alas! my own husband and Cæsar; so I mostly keep in a corner and occupy myself with books and God. And I shall not allow even the most insignificant of men to approach me unless they be men from whom I can learn of things which they happen to have heard of from others, or they be my father's intimate friends. For during these last thirty years, I swear it by the souls of the most blessed Emperors, I have neither seen nor spoken to a friend of my father's, this is due partly to many of them having died and partly to many being prevented by fear. For the powers that be have condemned us to this ridiculous position so that we should not be seen, but be a general object of abhorrence. And what I have added to my history, let God and His Mother my Mistress be my witnesses, I have collected from some absolutely unpretentious, simple commentaries, and from a few old men who were soldiers when my father seized the Roman sceptre but have fallen upon evil times and retired from the turmoil of the world to the calm life of monasteries. For the commentaries which fell into my hands were simple in diction and incurious and strictly truthful and displayed no style and were free from all rhetorical pretensions. And the narrations of the old men were like the commentaries both in phrase and scope, and I judged the truth of my history from them by comparing and examining what I had written with what they told me, and what they told me with what I remembered from having often heard the accounts both from my father himself and from my paternal and maternal uncles. From all these sources I wove the whole fabric of my truthful history. And now let me return to the point in my history of which I was speaking above, namely Camytzes' escape from the barbarians and his speech to the citizens.

He, as I have said, recounted all that had happened, and the devices the Emperor employed against the Ishmaelites; and the inhabitants of Constantinople with one voice and mouth shouted their applause, hymned the Emperor and made a god of him and blessed him for his generalship and could not restrain their pleasure in him. And after escorting Camytzes homeward in high spirits, they welcomed the Emperor a few days later as a triumphant victor, an invincible general, an undefeated King and a revered Emperor. That was how the people acted; but he after entering the palace and offering thanksgiving for his safe return to God and the Mother of God, recommenced his usual mode of life. For as he had settled his enemies abroad and put down the rebellions of pretenders he now turned his attention to the courts of justice and the laws. For he was at the same time the best administrator both of peace and of war. For he judged the case of orphans, had right done to widows, looked very severely on any case of injustice and only occasionally sought physical refreshment in the chase or other relaxations. For as in other matters he acted as a philosopher, in this too, in subduing his body and making it subservient to him. During the greater part of the day he devoted it to labours, and then again would recall it from labours. But even his relaxation was a second labour, the reading and studying of books and the careful observance of the precept, ' search the scriptures.' The chase and the game of polo were but of secondary, or tertiary, importance to my father, even while he was still a young man and before that monster, the affection in his feet, had fastened itself upon him like a sinuous serpent, and kept ' biting his heel,' as it says in the curse. But directly this disease commenced and began to increase then certainly he gave himself up to gymnastics, and horse-exercise and other games for he was ordered to do this by medical science in order that by regular horse-exercise some of the fluid which descended might be dispersed and he might be relieved of the weight which pressed upon him. For as I have said above, this racking affliction of my father's arose from no other cause than his labours and fatigues for the glory of the Romans.

VIII Not a year had passed before the Emperor heard a rumour that the Comans had crossed the Ister ; consequently at the commencement of the eighth Indiction in the month of November in the beginning of autumn he left the Queen of Cities after calling up all his forces and stationed these, some in Philippopolis and in the towns called Petritzus and Triaditza and in the province of Nisus and some as far away as Branizoba (or Buranitzobe) on the banks of the Ister. He enjoined them to bestow great care on their horses so that they should grow stout and strong enough to carry their riders in time of battle. He himself remained in Philippopolis, a town in the centre of Thrace, which is washed by the Eurus on the side of the North wind.

This river flows down from the extreme end of Rhodope, makes many twists and turns, flows past the town of Adrian and after many tributaries have joined it, empties itself into the sea near the town of Ænus. When speaking of Philip I do not mean the Macedonian, the son of Amyntas, for the city is younger than that Philip, but I mean the Roman Philip, an extremely tall man whose physical strength nobody could resist. At first it was a small town called Crenides before Philip's time, and by others Trimus. But that very large man Philip enlarged the town and girt it round with walls and made it the most famous town in Thrace, for he built a very large circus in it and other admirable edifices, the traces of which I saw myself when I once stayed in the town with the Emperor for some purpose or other. The city stands on three hills and each hill is surrounded by a strong and high wall, and on the side where it slopes down to the plains and level ground there is a moat running along-side of the Eurus. From all appearances it must once have been a large and fine city. After the Tauri and Scythians enslaved the city in bygone days, it was reduced to the condition in which we found it during my father's reign and conjectured that it must have been very large. The chief of its misfortunes was the residence of so many heretics there. For the Armenians took possession of the city and the so-called Bogomils (I will speak of them and their heresy later at an opportune moment), and even those most godless Paulicians, an offshoot of the Manichæan sect, founded as their name shows by Paul and John, two men who had imbibed the undiluted heresy of Manes and handed it on to their followers.

I rather wished to treat lightly of the doctrine of the Manichæans and to explain it very concisely, and even attempt a refutation of their most godless doctrines. But I will omit these as I know that everybody considers the Manichæan heresy an absurdity and also because I wish to hasten on with my history. Moreover I know that not only men of our own court have refuted them, but that Porphyrius, our great opponent, reduced the nonsensical doctrine of the Manichæans to utter absurdity when in several chapters he very scientifically examined the question of two principles, although his doctrine of the unity of God compels his readers to support Plato's " Unity " or " the One." We do indeed worship the unity of the Divine nature, but not that Unity which contains only one Person. Nor do we accept the ' One ' of Plato ; that which is with the Greeks, the ' Mysterious ' and with the Chaldeans the ' Ineffable ' ; for from it they make many other principles dependent, both mundane and hyper-mundane.

Now these followers of Manes and of Paul and John, the sons of Callinice, who were very uncivilized and cruel and would not hesitate to shed blood, were conquered in war by that most admirable of Emperors, John Tzimisces; then he led them as slaves out of Asia and transported them from the regions of Chalybes and Armenia to Thrace and compelled them to take up their abode near Philippopolis. This he did firstly to drive them out of their strong cities and forts which they held as despotic rulers, and secondly to post them as trustworthy guards against the inroads of the Scythians by which the country of Thrace was often oppressed; for the barbarians crossed the passes of the Hæmus and overran the plains below.

This Hæmus is a very long mountain range running along a line parallel to Mount Rhodope. The range begins at the Euxine sea, leaves the cataracts a little on one side and continues right into Illyria; there it is cut through by the Adriatic Sea, I fancy, and emerges again in the opposite continent and finishes right away in the Hercynian forests. On either side of its slopes dwell many very wealthy tribes, the Dacians and the Thracians on the northern side, and on the southern, more Thracians and the Macedonians. In olden days the Scythian nomads would cross the Hæmus, before Alexius' spear and his many battles brought them almost to extermination, and spoil the Roman territory with their large armies and especially the nearer towns, of which the chief one was the formerly renowned city of Philippopolis. But John Tzimisces converted our opponents of the Manichæan heresy into our allies, as far as arms are concerned, by opposing them as redoubtable forces to these Scythian nomads, and from that time the cities had a respite from most of their incursions. However the Manichæans, being naturally free and unruly, soon acted as usual and reverted to their original nature. For, as all the inhabitants of Philippopolis were Manichæans except a few, they tyrannized over the Christians there and plundered their goods, caring little or naught for the envoys sent by the Emperor. They increased in numbers until all the inhabitants around Philip-popolis were heretics. Then another brackish stream of Armenians joined them and yet another from the most polluted sources of James. And thus, metaphorically speaking, it was a meeting-place of all evils; for the rest disagreed

2C

indeed with the Manichæans in doctrines, but agreed with them in disaffection. But my father, the Emperor, arrayed his long military experience against them too and subdued some without fighting and others he reduced to slavery by fighting. How much that valiant man did and endured over this truly apostolic work! For what reason could anyone forbear to praise him? perhaps because he was negligent in his military duties?—nay, he filled the East and the West with his exploits as general. Or is it because he was indifferent to argumentation?—nay again, for he had studied the Holy Writings more than anybody else in order to sharpen his tongue for wrestlings with the heretics. He alone commingled arms and arguments, and conquered the barbarians with his arms, and subdued the impious by his arguments; as in this present instance he engaged the Manichæans in a contest that was apostolic rather than military. I for my part should call him 'the thirteenth apostle.' Although some ascribe this glory to Constantine the Great; yet I am of opinion that Alexius should be ranked equal to the Emperor Constantine or, to prevent contentiousness, let him be placed second to Constantine both as apostle and Emperor.

For, as we were saying above, he went to Philippopolis for the reasons given and, as the Comans had not yet appeared, he made the secondary purpose of his journey more important than his actual task and began turning the Manichæans from their brackish religion and instilling into them the sweet doctrines of the Church. So from the morning till afternoon or even evening, and sometimes till the second or third watch of the night he would send for them and teach them the orthodox faith and refute their distorted heresies. Present with him were Eustratius, the bishop of Nicæa, a man of wide knowledge of religious and secular literature and pluming himself on dialectics more than those who frequent the Stoa and Academy, and also the incumbent of the archiepiscopal throne of Phillippopolis. In addition to all the others and in preference to them the Emperor had as his coadjutor my Cæsar, Nicephorus, whom he had trained in the study of the sacred books. Consequently many of the Manichæans on that occasion went to the priests without any hesitation, confessed their sins and received divine baptism. But many too could be seen who with a tenacity exceeding that of the Maccabeans of old clung to their own religion and quoted passages and proofs from the sacred writings, thinking thereby to confirm their own detestable doctrine. But by the Emperor's

continuous arguments and frequent admonitions the majority
of these too were convinced and accepted divine baptism.
For from the first rays of the sun in the East to deepest night
very often the controversy was continued and he would not
desist from the conference but often remained without food
and this too in summer-time in an open-air tent.

IX   While this was going on and that wordy disputation
with the Manichæans was being hammered out, a messenger
came from the Ister and announced that the Comans had
crossed.   Without delay the Emperor started for the Danube,
taking with him what soldiers he had.   On reaching Bidyne
and not finding the barbarians (for they had already crossed
back directly they heard of the Emperor's approach) he at
once detached a band of brave soldiers and bade them go
in pursuit of the barbarians.   So they crossed the Danube
and started off after them.   They pursued them for three
days and nights but when they found that the Comans had
crossed the river beyond the Danube on rafts, they returned
to the Emperor without having effected anything.   The
Emperor was indeed somewhat annoyed that his soldiers
had not overtaken the barbarians, and yet he considered it a
species of victory that by the mere sound of his name he had
driven the barbarians away, and converted many from the
Manichæan heresy to our faith.   So he set up a double
trophy, one for a victory over the barbarians by means of
arms, and the other over the heretics by most pious discourses.
Then he returned to Philippopolis and after a short rest
applied himself to fresh contests.   For Culeon and Cusinus
and with them Pholus, the chief upholders of the Manichæan
heresy, and in other respects like the rest of the Manichæans,
but clever at maintaining their heterodoxy, were adamantine
against all verbal persuasion ;   they were also exceedingly
able in pulling the Scriptures to pieces and in interpreting
them perversely ;   so the Emperor summoned them every
day and engaged in a war of words with them.   Then could
be seen a double contest—on the one side, the Emperor
contending with all his might for their salvation, and on the
other, these three men disputing earnestly to gain, if possible,
a so-called Cadmean victory.   For the three stood there
sharpening each other's wits, as if they were boar's teeth,
intent upon rending the Emperor's arguments.   And if any
objection escaped Cusinus, Culeon would take it up ;   and if
Culeon was at a loss, Pholus in his turn would rise in opposition;
or they would, one after the other, rouse themselves against

the Emperor's premises and refutations, just like very large
waves following up other large waves. But the Emperor
swept away all their objections as if they were a spider's web
and quickly closed their impious mouths. But as he could
not convince them at all, he finally wearied of these men's
silliness and dispatched them to the Queen City, allotting
to them as their abode the verandahs which surrounded the
great palace. And yet his hunting had not been all in vain
in spite of his not having captured those leaders by his words ;
for every day he brought to God, maybe a hundred, maybe
even more than a hundred ; so that the sum total of those
he had captured before and those whom he won now by the
words of his mouth would amount to thousands and ten
thousand souls. But why should I linger to speak of that
which the whole world knows and to which the East and West
bear testimony ? for whole towns and districts infected by
various heresies he brought back by divers means to our
orthodox faith. Upon the more eminent Manichæans he
bestowed great gifts and enrolled them among the picked
soldiery. But the more vulgar, such as were diggers or had
to do with ploughing and cattle, he gathered together and
transplanted them with their wives and children to a town
he built for them near Philippopolis on the other side of the
river Eurus. There he settled them and called the town
Alexiopolis, or a name more generally used, Neocastrum,
and to one and all he distributed plough-lands and vineyards, horses and immovable property. Nor did he leave
these gifts unsecured, so that like the gardens of Adonis they
should bear flowers one day and fall away the next, but by
Golden Bulls he confirmed these gifts to them and he did not
limit his benefactions to them only but made them trans-
missible to their sons and sons' sons ; and, in case the males
failed, the women could succeed to the inheritance. In this
wise did the great man confer his benefits. Let this be
sufficient on this subject, although a great deal has been
omitted ; and let no one revile this history as if it were
corrupt. For many of the people still living can testify to the
truth of what I have related and I could not be convicted
of falsehood.

After arranging all matters as was best the Emperor left
Philippopolis and went back to the Queen City. And there he
renewed his continual discussions and arguments with Culeon
and Cusinus and their followers. And he captured Culeon,
for he, I fancy, was the more intelligent and able to follow

the true arguments closely, and he became a very tame lamb
in our fold. But Cusinus and Pholus became savage and,
like iron, they were hammered upon by the Emperor's frequent
discourses and yet they remained of iron and turned away
from him and would not be led by him. Therefore as they
were the most blasphemous of all the Manichæans and clearly
drifting into melancholy madness, he had them cast into the
prison called Elephantine, and while supplying them liberally
with all necessaries, he allowed them to die in company with
their sins alone.

BOOK XV

I

THE doings of the Emperor in Philippopolis and with regard to the Manichæans were such as I have related; after that a fresh potion of troubles was brewed for him by the barbarians. For the Sultan Soliman was planning to devastate Asia again and assembled his forces from Chorosan and Chalep[1] to see whether he might possibly be able to resist the Emperor successfully. As the whole of the Sultan Soliman's plan had already been reported to the Emperor, he contemplated advancing as far as Iconium with his army and there forcing him into a closely contested battle. For that town formed the boundaries of the Sultanicium of Clitziasthlan. Therefore he solicited troops from foreign countries, and a large mercenary force, and called up his own army from all sides. Then, whilst these two generals were making preparations against each other, the old trouble in his feet attacked the Emperor. And forces kept coming in from all quarters, but only in driblets, not all together, because their countries were so far away, and the pain prevented the Emperor not merely from carrying out his projected plan, but even from walking at all. And he was vexed at being confined to his couch not so much because of the excessive pain in his feet, but by reason of the postponement of his expedition against the barbarians. The barbarian Clitziasthlan was well aware of this and consequently despoiled the whole of Asia at his leisure during this interval and made seven onslaughts upon the Christians. Never before had the Emperor suffered so severely from that pain ; for before this it had only come on him at long intervals but now it did not come periodically but was continuous and the irritation unending. Now Clitziasthlan's followers thought that this suffering was only a pretence at illness, not really an illness, and that hesitation and indolence were disguised under the cloak of gout ; and therefore often joked about it when drunk or drinking, and as natural orators the bar-

₁ = Berrœa (*now* Aleppo).

barians wove moral talks about the Emperor's sufferings
in his feet, and the trouble in his feet became the subject of
comedies. For they would impersonate doctors and other
people busied about the Emperor and place the Emperor
himself in the middle, lying on a couch, and make a play of it.
And these puerile games aroused much laughter among the
barbarians. These doings did not escape the Emperor and
they made him boil with anger and provoked him still more
to war with them. After a short interval he was relieved
from pain and commenced his projected journey. He ferried
over to Damalis, then sailed across the straits between
Cibotus and Ægiali, disembarked at Cibotus and went on to
Lopadium to await the arrival of his armies and the mercenary
army he had engaged. When they were all assembled he
moved away from there with all his forces and occupied the
fort of Lord George close to the lake outside Nicæa, and
thence on to Nicæa. Then after three days he returned and
encamped on this side of the bridge of Lopadium near the
fountain of Caryx as it was called ; for he thought best
to send the army over the bridge first to pitch their tents in
a suitable spot and then to cross himself by the same bridge
and erect the imperial tent in company with all the army.
But the wily Turks were devastating the plain lying at the
foot of the Lentianian hills and the place called Cotœræcia,
and on hearing of the Emperor's advance against them, they
were terrified and immediately lighted a number of beacon-
fires, thus giving beholders the illusion of a large army.
And the sky was lighted up by these fires and frightened
many of the inexperienced soldiers but nothing of all this
troubled the Emperor. Then the Turks collected all the booty
and prisoners and went away ; and at dawn the Emperor
hastened after them to the plain [already mentioned] with the
desire of overtaking them on the spot, but he missed his
quarry. On the contrary he found a number of Romans
still breathing, and many corpses, which naturally enraged
him. But he was very anxious to pursue the Turks so as not
to lose all his prey, and, as it was impossible for the whole
army to follow up the fugitives quickly, he pitched his palisades on the spot near Pœmanenum and selecting at once a
detachment of brave light-armed soldiers, he entrusted them
with the pursuit of the barbarians and told them which road
to take after the wretches. These soldiers overtook the Turks
with all their booty and captives at a place called Cellia by
the natives and rushed upon them like fire and soon killed

most of them but took a few alive and after collecting all the
booty there they returned brilliantly victorious to the
Emperor. After welcoming them and learning of the total
destruction of the enemy he returned to Lopadium. When
he reached it he stayed in that town for three whole months,
partly because of the want of water in the districts he would
have to pass through (for it was the summer-season and the
heat was intolerable) and partly because he was waiting for
part of the mercenary army which had not yet arrived.
But when they had all assembled, he shifted his camp and
quartered his army between the ridges of Olympus and of the
mountains called Malagni and himself occupied Aër. The
Empress meanwhile was lodging at Principus, as from there
she could more easily have news of the Emperor after his
return to Lopadium. Directly the Emperor went to Aër,
he sent the imperial galley to fetch her, firstly because he was
always dreading the pain in his feet, and secondly through
fear of his bosom enemies who were accompanying him, and
thus he wanted her both for the extreme care she took of
him, and for her most vigilant eye.

II   Three days had not yet passed before the attendant
of the imperial bedchamber came in towards morning and
stood close to the royal couch. The Empress woke up and
when she looked at him he said, " I have come to report that
the Turks are upon us." When he further told her that they
had already reached what was called George's fort, she
motioned to him with her hand to be silent so as not to wake
the Emperor. He had however heard all that was said, but
remained for some time in the same position and unmoved,
and when the sun rose he betook himself to his usual occu-
pations, though his mind was completely absorbed by this
man's warning. Before the third hour had passed another
messenger came to say that the barbarians were already quite
near. The Empress was still with the Emperor and though
naturally frightened yet she awaited his decision. When
their Majesties were hurrying to their lunch, yet another came,
all blood-stained, and bowing himself to the ground at the
Emperor's feet he swore on oath that the danger was imminent,
for the barbarians were already at his heels. Then the
Emperor immediately gave the Empress permission to return
to Byzantium, and she was dismayed but hid her fear in her
inmost heart and did not shew it either by word or manner.
For she was courageous and steady-minded, like the woman
sung of by Solomon in the Proverbs, and shewed no feminine

cowardice such as we see so many women generally give way
to directly they hear any terrible news. And even the
colour of their face proves the cowardice of their soul and often
too they utter shrill screams as if the danger threatened them
closely. But although that Empress was afraid, her fear
was for the Emperor lest an accident should befall him ;
and fear for herself came second. So on this occasion she did
not do anything unworthy of her bravery but took leave of
the Emperor though unwillingly, and often turned round to
look at him again, yet she pulled herself together and braced
herself up, so to say, as she reluctantly tore herself away from
him. She went down from there to the sea and embarking
on the galley set apart for their Majesties, she sailed past the
coast of Bithynia, then was caught in a tempest and so
anchored off Helenopolis and stayed there for a time. So
far about the Empress.

The Emperor and all the soldiers and kinsmen who were
with him at once got under arms ; and then mounted and rode
towards Nicæa. But the barbarians had caught an Alanian
and on hearing from him of the Emperor's advance against
them they fled back along the paths by which they had come.
But Strabobasilius and Michael Stypiota (let no one though
when he hears this name think of Stypiota the semi-barbarian,
for the latter was this man's bought slave and was afterwards
given as a present to the Emperor, whereas this Stypiota
belonged to the nobility), these two, who were very warlike
and already counted among famous men, waited about on
the ridges of the Germii and watched the roads around, in
case perchance the barbarians might fall into, and be caught in,
their nets, like a wild beast. When they had learnt of the
Turks' approach they went down to the plains called . . .
offered them battle and met them in a fierce fight in which
they worsted them completely. The Emperor occupied
first the fort of George (which has been frequently mentioned)
and then the village called Sagudai by its inhabitants but did
not come across the Turks. But when he heard what had
happened to them at the hands of the brave men afore-
mentioned, I mean Stypiota and Strabobasilius and had
expressed his appreciation of the Romans' daring from the very
start and their victory, then he himself fixed his palisades
in a spot outside that same fort. And on the following day
he went down to Helenopolis to meet the Empress who was
still held up there as the sea was not navigable. Then he
related to her all that had happened to the Turks and how in

their desire for victory they had met with misfortune, and
fancying themselves to be the masters had on the contrary
been mastered and got the opposite to what they had expected.
Having thus relieved her deep anxiety he left again for Nicæa ;
there he heard of a fresh inroad of the Turks, so went on to
Lopadium. Here he stayed a little and on learning that a
large Turkish army was on its way to Nicæa he collected his
forces, turned off to Cius and, as he was informed that the
Turks were marching on towards Nicæa all through that
night, he moved his camp again and passed through Nicæa to
Miscura. Here he learnt for certain that the whole Turkish
army had not yet arrived but that some few men had been
sent by Monolycus and were lingering around Dolylum and
Nicæa in order to watch for the Emperor's arrival and to
send Monolycus information about him continually. Consequently he sent Leo Nicerites with the troops under his
command to Lopadium and bade him keep a sharp look-out
the whole time, to watch the roads round about, and to let
him know by letter whatever he found out about the Turks.
The rest of the army he settled in suitable places and then
decided that it would be better not to advance against the
Sultan at present, for he guessed that the barbarians who had
escaped would spread the news of the Romans' attack upon
them amongst all the Turks in Asia, and would tell how they
had met and attacked the Romans at various . . . ,
how they resisted valiantly, and how they had been worsted
and some of them captured and others killed and only a few
wounded had escaped. From this tale the barbarians would
realize, he thought, that he was approaching, and consequently
retreat even beyond Iconium, and thus all his trouble would be
in vain. For these reasons, he turned round and marched
to Nicomedia through Bithynia, with the idea that the
barbarians would in consequence no longer expect his attack
and each return to the place where he had formerly dwelt.
Afterwards when they had regained courage and again
dispersed for skirmishing, as was the Turks' way, and the
Sultan himself recommenced his old tricks, and his own
soldiers had had a brief rest and the horses and beasts of burden
had fattened, he would shortly carry on the war against him
more vigorously and attack him fiercely in battle. For these
reasons he made for Nicomedia, as said, and taking with him
all the soldiers he had, he billeted them in the villages close
by so that the horses and beasts of burden might have
sufficient food, as the land of Bithynia was rich in grass,

and the soldiers themselves too could easily fetch everything
necessary for their use from Byzantium and its neighbourhood
by crossing the bay. He enjoined them to give their full
attention and much care to the horses and beasts of burden
and not to use the horses for hunting or riding, so that when
the need arrived they should be in good condition and able
to carry their riders easily and would be useful for making
cavalry-attacks upon the enemy.

III Having made all these arrangements he sat down
at a distance, like a look-out, after posting guards on every
path. And as he intended remaining in that place for a
good many days he sent for the Empress for the reason I
have given several times, so that she might be with him until
he was notified of the barbarians' incursions and should wish
to move away from there. She came to Nicomedia with all
haste ; she noticed that some of his opponents were exulting,
as it were, over the Emperor's having done nothing and were
everywhere slandering him and muttering that in spite of
his grand preparations for advancing on the barbarians
and collecting large forces, he had accomplished nothing
of importance, but retired to Nicomedia. This was not only
whispered in corners but spoken of brazenly in the squares
and on the high roads and cross-roads, and annoyed and
vexed her. But the Emperor who divined that the issue
of his attack upon the enemy would be propitious (and he
was clever in these ways), thought nothing of his adversaries'
denunciations and malice but despised all that kind of thing
as childish play and laughed at their infantile minds. And he
cheered up the Empress by his sensible arguments and assured
her that the very thing they sneered at would be the cause of
a greater victory. Now I consider it courage when anybody
gains a victory through using sound judgment ; for high
spirits and energy without judgment are to be condemned,
and are rashness and not courage. For we have courage in
war against men whom we can conquer ; but we are rash
against those whom we cannot overcome, and thus, when danger
impends over us, we hesitate to attack from the front.

. . . and then we handle the war in a different way and
endeavour to conquer the enemy without fighting. And
the chief virtue of a general is to know how to obtain a
victory without danger ; for ' by skill,' as Homer says,
' one charioteer prevails over another.' For even the proverb
derived from Cadmus disparages a victory fraught with
danger, to me it has always seemed best to carry out some

wily, yet strategic, move even during the battle itself, whenever one's army is not adequate compared with the strength of one's opponents. Anyone who likes can gather from history that a victory is not always achieved in the same way, or by the same means, but that from olden days down to the present it is gained by various efforts, hence we conclude that victory is indeed one and the same, but that the means by which generals obtain it, are diverse and varied in nature. For some of our former celebrated generals seem to have conquered their enemies by sheer strength . . . in this way; whereas others used different means and gained the victory. Now my father, the Emperor, sometimes overcame his adversaries by prowess, and at others by his quick wit, for even during a battle he occasionally thought out some clever device and by daringly using it at once carried off the victory. By making use of stratagems on some occasions, and on others by hard fighting he often and unexpectedly set up trophies. If there ever was a man who was fond of danger, it was he, and dangers could be seen continually rising up in his path, and at times he would walk into them bare-headed and come to close quarters with the barbarians, and at others again he would pretend to decline battle, and act the frightened man, if the occasion demanded it and circumstances advised it. Or to put the whole matter concisely, he prevailed when he fled, and conquered when he pursued, and falling he stood, and dropping down he was erect on the principle of caltrops which always stick upright however you throw them. But here again I must deprecate being censured on the score that I am caught bragging; for in my defence I have several times said that it is not love for my father that suggests these remarks, but the nature of the circumstances. For does anything on the side of truth itself prevent a person being fond of his father and fond of truth also? for I have chosen to write a truthful history and that of a good man; but if that man happens to be the father of the historian, let the father's name be added to it as a mere appendage; but the history must be dedicated to natural truth. In other matters I have declared my love for my father and by so doing have sharpened the spears and whetted the swords of the ill-disposed against myself, as all those know who are acquainted with the facts of my life. But in shaping my history I would certainly not betray the truth. There is a time for shewing love to a father (and at such time I have shewn courage) and another time when

truth is the main consideration and now since that time has
fallen my way, I cannot regard it lightly. But if, as I have
said, this time also combines to shew me fond of my father,
I do not fear men's censure for having suppressed the truth.
However my story must now go back to its subject.

As long as the Emperor pitched his tent there (in Nicomedia) he had nothing else to do besides enrolling recruits in
the army and training them carefully in the art of stretching
the bow, wielding the spear, riding on horseback, and making
various formations. He also taught the soldiers the new
system of marshalling the lines which he had invented himself; now and again he would ride with them and review
the phalanxes and give seasonable suggestions. But the sun
was now returning from its large circuits, and as the autumn
equinox was passed, it was already inclining to the more
southern circuits, this seemed a season well-adapted for
taking the field, so with all his forces he marched straight for
Iconium according to the plan he had originally proposed to
himself. Then on reaching Nicæa he detached a body of
light troops with experienced leaders from the rest of the
army and ordered them to go on ahead and in separate
divisions make sallies upon the Turks and go foraging. But,
if God gave them the victory and they routed the enemy,
he advised them in no case to continue their raid, but be
satisfied with the victory given them and at once make an
orderly retreat. So they all with the Emperor occupied a
place situated . . . and locally called Gaïta, and there
the one lot went off, while he moved on from there with
all his forces and held the bridge over the river Pithecas.
Then in three days' march by way of Armenocastrum and the
so-called Leucæ he reached the plains of Doryleum. He saw
that these were large enough for marshalling his troops and
being anxious to review them all and find out exactly his
military strength, he seized this opportune moment and drew
up his soldiers, in very reality in the battle-order for which
he had so long been yearning and so often described on paper
when planning this arrangement (for he was well-versed in
Ælian's tactics); and then he set up his camp in the plain.
For he knew from very long experience that the Turkish
battle-order did not agree at all with that of other nations,
for with them " shield did not rest upon shield, and helmet
upon helmet and man upon man " as Homer says, but the
Turks' right and left wing, and centre were quite disconnected
and the phalanxes stood as if severed from each other. Con-

sequently if you attacked the right or left wing, the centre
would swoop down upon you and all the rest of the army
posted behind it, and like whirlwinds throw the opposing
body into confusion. Now for their weapons of war :—they
do not use spears much, as the Franks do, but surround the
enemy completely and shoot at him with arrows, and they
make this defence from a distance. When he pursues, he
captures his man with the bow ; when he is pursued he
conquers with his darts ; he throws a dart and the flying
dart hits either the horse or its rider, and as it has been dispatched with very great force it passes right through the
body ; so skilled are they in the use of the bow. Having
noticed this from long experience the Emperor arranged his
lines and phalanxes in such a way that the Turks should
shoot from the right side, the side on which the shields were
advanced, and that our men should shoot from the left, the
side on which the Turks' bodies were unprotected. And
he himself imagined that this order of battle would be invincible, and marvelled at its strength and looked upon it as
an arrangement directly inspired by God and a marshalling
due to the angels. And everybody else admired and rejoiced
in it and took fresh courage from the Emperor's invention.
And when he himself thought about his forces and the plains
through which he was soon to pass and reflected that his
battle-order was solid and not easily broken, his hopes rose
high and he prayed to God to bring them to fulfilment.

IV   In this order of battle he reached Santabaris   . . .
and distributed all the leaders of this array [over the country] ;
Camytzes he sent to attack Polybotum and Cedrus (this was
a very strongly fortified town held by the satrap Pucheas) ;
Stypiota he ordered to march on the barbarians in Amorium.
. . .   Two Scythians got wind of this plan and deserted
to Pucheas and brought word to him of Camytzes' advance
and also of the Emperor's approach. He was so stricken
with fear at this that at midnight he left the city and departed
with all his countrymen. As day was dawning, Camytzes
reached the place and found no Pucheas nor indeed any Turk
at all. He found the fort, I mean Cedrea, full of spoil but
did not waste any time over that for he was annoyed as
huntsmen are when they lose the prey which was almost in
their grasp. So without delay he turned his horse's head and
marched to Polybotum. This he attacked unexpectedly and
killed barbarians beyond number, then collected all the booty
and captives and encamped close by awaiting the Emperor's

arrival. Stypiota did the same when he reached Pœmanenum and returned to the Emperor, who himself arrived at Cedrea towards sunset. Immediately some soldiers came to him and said there were an immense number of barbarians in the small towns situated quite near of the once celebrated hero, Burtzes. Directly the Emperor had heard their report, he prepared for action. He instantly summoned a descendant of the famous Burtzes, Bardas by name, and George Lebunes, and a Scythian called Pitican in his native tongue, brought up the troops under them to a sufficiently strong force and dispatched them against the Turks, and gave them orders that when they got there they were to send out foragers to lay waste all the neighbouring villages, and then drive out all the natives from their homes and bring them to him. So these men at once started on the journey assigned them, but the Emperor, holding to his former purpose, hastened to reach Polybotum and thence hurry on as far as Iconium. With these intentions he was on the point of commencing his task when he received reliable information that the barbarians and the Sultan Soliman himself on hearing of his approach, had set fire to all the crops and plains in Asia, so that there was no sustenance at all for man or beast. Another incursion of barbarians from the higher countries was heralded too, and the rumour flew quickly throughout Asia. So he was afraid for one thing that during his march to Iconium his whole army might fall a prey to famine owing to the lack of food, and for another he thought with suspicion and vexation of the barbarians he was likely to find there. Accordingly he formed a plan which was both prudent and audacious, namely, to enquire of God, whether he ought to abide by his decision of advancing on Iconium, or direct his attack against the barbarians round Philomelium. He wrote these questions on two papers, placed them on the Holy Table and spent the whole night in offering hymns and lengthy intercessions to God. At dawn the priest went in and picking up one of the two papers placed on the Table, opened it in the presence of all and read out to the Emperor that he was commanded to take the road to Philomelium. So much then about the Emperor.

Now Bardas, the descendant of Burtzes, whilst following the road we have already mentioned, saw a strong body hastening to join Monolycus by crossing the bridge at Zompi, consequently he at once got under arms, engaged them in battle in the plain of Amorium and defeated them severely.

But other Turks coming from an easterly direction and hurrying to Monolycus fell upon Burtzes' encampment before he had returned and carried off all the beasts of burden that were there and the soldiers' baggage. As Burtzes was returning victorious and bringing much plunder with him, he met one of the Turks coming from the camp and learnt from him how the Turks had stolen everything in his encampment and gone off with all the booty, so he meditated what he had better do. Although he wished to pursue the Turks, who journey very swiftly, yet he could not do so, because the horses were worn out. So he renounced the pursuit and to prevent anything worse happening he proceeded at a slow pace and in orderly manner and at dawn reached the aforementioned towns of Burtzes and ejected all the inhabitants. Then he gathered up the captives, took with him all the provisions the barbarians had, and after resting himself and his wearied soldiers for a short time in a suitable spot he took the road leading to the Emperor as the sun rose. On the way he met another Turkish force, and began a fight which flared up into a serious battle. The Turks sustained the combat for a long time and then asked for the captives and the spoil that had been taken from them, and promised faithfully that if this request were granted, they would undertake not to attack the Romans again but would go home. Burtzes, however, would not yield to the barbarians' request, but continued the battle and fought bravely.

As the Turks had not tasted water at all during the fight on the previous day, they now took possession of the banks of the river, and quenched their burning thirsts and then returned to the fight in batches. For while one party continued the battle, the other tired-out party refreshed itself by drinking the water. Burtzes seeing the barbarians' consummate boldness and worried to death by their numbers, felt quite helpless, and so did not send one of the common soldiers to carry news of his straits to the Emperor, but the George Lebunes I have already mentioned. As Lebunes could see no path which was not held by a number of Turks, he threw himself recklessly into the midst of them, pushed his way through and got safely to the Emperor. When the latter heard the news about Burtzes and found out fairly accurately the number of Turks, he realized that Burtzes required a large number of reinforcements, so he speedily got under arms himself and ordered the army to do likewise. Then with the army drawn up in phalanxes he advanced

against the barbarians in good order. The front wing was
held by Prince [Michael], thc right by Bryennius, the left by
Gabras and the rear by Cecaumenus. As the Turks stood
awaiting them at a distance, Nicephorus, the Empress' nephew,
who was young and longing to fight, rode on ahead of the line
and taking with him a few more devotees of Ares, engaged the
first man who attacked him and received a wound in the knee,
but struck the man who wounded him in the chest with his
spear. And the Turk straightway fell from his horse and lay
speechless on the ground, and the others behind him on seeing
this at once turned their backs upon the Romans. The
Emperor received the brave young man with delight and
praised him highly and continued his march to Philomelium.
He passed the lake of the Forty Martyrs and the next day
occupied the place called Mesanacta, then moved on again
and took Philomelium by assault. Next he selected various
units from the whole army and placing them under brave
leaders dispatched them to villages situated round about
Iconium to despoil these and deliver the captives out of the
Turks' hands. Accordingly they scattered themselves over
the country like wild beasts, brought back the barbarians'
prisoners in droves to the Emperor and then returned with
the prisoners' baggage after freeing them all. And the inhabitants of those regions who were Romans followed them
of their own accord fleeing from servitude to the barbarians ;
there were women with babies, even men, and children, all
rushing to the Emperor as if to a place of refuge. He then
drew up his lines in the new formation with all the captives,
women and children enclosed in the centre, and returned
by the same road as he had come, and whatever places he
approached, he passed through with perfect safety. And had
you seen it, you would have said a living walled city was
walking, when the army was marching in the new formation
we have described.

V As he proceeded further, the barbarians did not shew
themselves, but Monolycus followed him and lay in wait
for the army with a large force on either side of the road.
While the Emperor was crossing the plain between Polybotum and the lake we just mentioned, a detachment of the
barbarian army, without baggage, all light-armed, bold men,
who had lain in wait for the army on both sides, suddenly
appeared to them from the heights. And the arch-satrap,
Monolycus, then saw this new formation for the first time.
He was an old man, very experienced in wars and military

aD

science, and when he beheld this new arrangement of the
army he was struck dumb with surprise and asked the name
of the general in command. He divined that the Emperor
Alexius and no other must be the leader of the army and that
new formation. And he wanted to attack, but did not dare ;
nevertheless he ordered them to raise the cry, ' to battle ! '
With the intention of giving the Romans the impression
of a large army, he told them to advance at the double, not
in close formation, but in separate detached groups, their
usual method, as we described above, hoping by the suddenness of their appearance and the trampling of the horses
to deafen and dismay the Roman forces. But the Emperor
rode before the line like a tower or pillar of fire or some divine
and heavenly vision, exhorting his men and bidding them
march on in the same formation and be of good cheer, and
added that it was not for his own safety that he had undertaken this toilsome business but for the honour and glory
of the Roman Empire, and moreover he was quite ready to
die on behalf of them all. All took courage at his words
and each kept his own place and went on marching at his
ease ; so much so that to the barbarians they did not even
appear to be moving. Throughout the whole of the day the
Turks kept attacking the Roman army without any success,
for they were unable to break it up either entirely or even
partially, so they ran back to the hills without accomplishing
anything and lighted a great many bonfires and howled all
through the night like wolves and occasionally made jeering
remarks at the Romans ; for there were some semi-barbarians
among them who spoke Greek. When day dawned Monolycus with the same intention ordered the Turks to do the
same as before. In the meantime Clitziasthlan[1] himself,
the Sultan, arrived, and when he saw the perfect order of the
army, he marvelled, but like a young man jeered at the old
man, Monolycus, for having deferred battle with the Emperor.
Monolycus replied, " I, because I am old or cowardly, have
put off a close engagement with him up to the present ;
but if you are so courageous, go yourself and have a try ;
the proof will lie in the result." Accordingly Clitziasthlan[1]
at once attacked the rear, ordered some other satraps to
attack the Emperor from the front, and yet others he bade
open the battle on either flank. Now the Cæsar Nicephorus'
Bryennius who held the right wing, noticed the battle in the
rear, and longed ardently to go to the assistance of the men

[1] *Should be* Melek,

at the back, but as he did not wish to prove his inexperience or his youth he restrained his raging anger against the barbarians and continued to march on in good order and the same formation. As the barbarians were fighting vigorously, the brother I held dearest, Andronicus Porphyrogenitus, who commanded the left wing, wheeled round and with his own troops made a fierce set upon the barbarians. He had just reached the most charming period of his life, in war he displayed prudent boldness, a quick hand, and abundant wisdom, and then prematurely he died, and when none would have expected it, he left us and vanished.

Oh, youth and physical beauty and your light leaps on horseback, where in the world have you gone ? my grief compels me to utter a lament over him ; the law of history, however, again restrains me. But it is wonderful that nowadays nobody is changed, as they say happened in former days, into a stone or bird or tree or some inanimate thing, changing his nature into such things under the force of great calamities ; whether it is all a fable or truth. For perhaps it were better to exchange one's nature for another that is non-sentient, than to possess such a vivid perception of evil. If this had been possible, the ills that have befallen me would very likely have turned me into stone.

VI When Nicephorus saw that the battle had become a hand-to-hand contest, he dreaded a defeat and therefore wheeled round with all his troops and hastened to their aid. Hereupon the barbarians turned their backs and with the Sultan Clitziasthlan himself they fled at full speed and hurried back to the hills. Many fell in the battle on that occasion, but more were captured ; and the survivors all scattered. The Sultan himself in desperate fear escaped with only his cupbearer and climbed up to a chapel built on a mountain top, round which very tall cypresses stood in rows, as he was hard pressed by three Scythians and the son of Uzas who were pursuing him ; there he turned off in another direction, and, as he was not known to his pursuers, he himself escaped, but the cupbearer was seized by the Scythians and offered to the Emperor as a great prize. The Emperor rejoiced at this signal victory and in having prevailed over his enemies, but was vexed that the Sultan himself had not fallen into their hands too and been captured, but was saved ' by the skin of his teeth,' as the proverb goes. Evening had now overtaken them so he encamped on the spot, and the barbarians who had survived again mounted to the hilltops,

lighted exceedingly many fires and barked the whole night long
at the Romans like dogs. But a certain Scythian deserted
from the Roman army and finding his way to the Sultan said,
" Do not think of fighting with the Emperor in the daytime ; for it will not be to your advantage. But since the
plain is not very large, he has had the tents pitched very
close together, so let your light archers go down to the foot
of the hills and all night long discharge showers of darts upon
them, and they will inflict no trifling damage on the Roman
army." Upon this a semi-barbarian escaped without the
Turks noticing and ran to the Emperor and related to him
what the Scythian had come and suggested to the Sultan
and explained to him clearly all that they were planning
against the Roman army. On hearing this the Emperor
formed the army into two divisions and ordered one half to
keep watch inside the camp and keep sober, and the other
half to arm themselves and leave the camp and go to meet the
barbarians who were coming and engage them in battle.
And throughout the night the barbarians surrounded the army
and made many sallies round about the foot of the hills, and
discharged showers of arrows against the army ; but the
Romans acting on the Emperor's advice protected themselves
without breaking the line. When day dawned, they marched
on in the same formation and again placed the booty and
all the baggage and the prisoners with the women and children
in the centre of the formation, and journeyed to Ampus. And
there a serious and terrible battle awaited them.

For the Sultan had again collected his forces and now
encircled the army and attacked it from every side ; yet
he did not manage to break through the close ranks of the
Romans at any point, but as though he had attacked walls
of adamant he had to retire without accomplishing anything.
Therefore all through that night in vexation of spirit and
despair he took counsel with Monolycus and the rest of the
satraps, and when the light of day appeared he sued the
Emperor for terms of peace, as all the satraps thought this
the best thing to do. The Emperor did not reject, but
received, their petition and immediately gave the order for
the sounding of the recall, but ordered that the men should
keep quiet and halt as they were, and not get off their horses
or unload the baggage from the sumpter beasts, but halt
protected by shield, helmet and spear as they had been
throughout the whole journey. This order was given by the
Emperor for no other reason but this, that, if confusion

arose, the line might perhaps be broken and in that case all
could easily be captured. For he feared the host of Turks
which he saw was very great, and was afraid they might
attack the Roman army from all sides. Later he halted in a
suitable spot and with all his kin and a goodly number of
soldiers on either side he stood in front of them with his
relations and connections to left and right and close to them
a select band of soldiery, all mail-clad, and the fiery gleam
that shone from their weapons illuminated the air more than
the rays of the sun. And meanwhile the Sultan had approached with all his subject satraps, at the head of whom
came Monolycus, as he surpassed all the Turks in Asia in age,
experience and courage, and the Sultan met the Emperor
in the plain between Augustopolis and Acronium. When
the satraps espied the Emperor from a distance they got off
their horses and offered the obeisance usually made to Kings.
The Sultan several times attempted to dismount, but the
Emperor would not allow it, the other however jumped
down quickly and kissed the Emperor's foot, who gave him his
hand and begged him to mount one of the noblemen's horses.
When he had mounted and was riding close to the Emperor's
side, the latter suddenly took off the cloak he was wearing
and threw it round the Sultan's shoulders. After a short
silence he made known to him all he had decided upon,
saying, " If you are willing to submit to the Roman Empire
and cease your onslaughts on the Christians, you shall
enjoy favours and honour and live at peace for the rest of
your life in the countries assigned you, where you formerly
had your dwellings before Romanus Diogenes took over the
reins of government and suffered that terrible defeat when
he unfortunately joined battle with the Sultan and was
captured by him. Therefore you ought to choose peace in
preference to war, and keep your hands off the boundaries
of the Roman Empire, and be content with your own. And
if you listen to my words, who am giving you wise counsel,
you will never repent, but even partake of many privileges;
if you do not, then be assured that I shall be the destroyer
of your race." The Sultan and his satraps readily agreed
to these terms and said, " We should not have come here
of our own accord, if we had not elected to embrace peace
with your Majesty." After these speeches he dismissed
them to the tents allotted to them, promising to ratify the
treaty the next day. On the morrow the Emperor again
interviewed the Sultan called Saisan and after completing

the treaty with him in the usual manner, made him a present
of a very large sum of money and after giving his satraps
gifts too he sent them away well satisfied. In the interval
the Emperor had heard that the Sultan's bastard brother,
Masut, was aiming at the sovereignty and had plotted
Saisan's assassination . . . since some satraps had
got round him, as nearly always happens. So the Emperor
advised him to wait a little until he found out more details
of the plot, and then through knowing what had happened,
he would go away forewarned. But the Sultan disregarded the
Emperor's advice and with full confidence in himself adhered
to his decision. Now the Emperor did not wish to appear to
have forcibly detained the Sultan who had come to him of
his own will, and thus incur censure, so he yielded to the barbarian's decision, saying, "It would be wiser to wait a little
while ; but as your mind is set on going, you must do ' the
next best thing ' as they say, take a sufficient number of
mail-clad Roman soldiers from us who will conduct you
safely as far as Iconium." But the barbarian would not even
consent to this, for these barbarians are ever arrogant in
mind and imagine that they even overtop the clouds. Accordingly he took leave of the Emperor and after receiving
a liberal gift of money, started on his homeward way. But a
dream came to him at night, not a deceptive one, nor sent
by Zeus, nor did it incite the barbarian to battle, as the sweet
poem says, ' in appearance like the son of Neleus,' but it
predicted the truth to the barbarian. For he dreamt that
while he was breakfasting swarms of mice encompassed him,
and while he was eating they snatched the bread out of
his hands ; and, as he was disdainful of them and tried to
drive them away, they suddenly changed into lions and overpowered him. On waking he told his dream to the Emperor's
soldier who was accompanying him and enquired what it
meant. The man interpreted the mice and lions of the dream
as enemies, and yet the Sultan would not believe but pushed
on his journey hurriedly and without taking precautions.
He had indeed sent scouts ahead to look round and see
whether any enemies had come out foraging. The scouts
met Masut already approaching with a large army and after
conversing with him, they agreed to his designs upon Saisan,
and returned and assured the latter that they had not seen
anyone. Saisan believed their report and was journeying on
unconcernedly when the barbarian forces of Masut met him.
Running out from the ranks a man called Gazes, the son of

the satrap Asan Catuch, whom Saisan had killed some time before, struck him with his spear. Saisan turned round quickly and snatched the spear from Gazes' hands, saying, " I did not know that even women bear spears against us now," and then he fled taking the road back to the Emperor. But he was checked by Pucheas, who had long ago joined Masut's party though pretending to be Saisan's friend, and now came forward and suggested a better plan. But in reality he was [laying] snares and digging a pit for him, he advised him not to return to the Emperor, but to turn aside a little from the road and enter Tyragium, a small town situated very near Philomelium. Saisan, the fool, followed Pucheas' advice and on reaching Tyragium was received pleasantly by the Roman inhabitants who knew the Emperor's goodwill towards him. Soon the barbarians arrived and Masut encircled the walls and got ready for a siege. Then Saisan looked down from the walls and violently upbraided his fellow-barbarians, saying that the Roman forces with the Emperor were close at hand, and if they did not desist from fighting, they would suffer the worst. And the Romans inside resisted the Turks bravely. Pucheas who now shed his disguise and openly revealed the wolf hidden under his skin, came down from the walls after promising Saisan to encourage the inhabitants to make a bolder resistance, but really he threatened them, advising them to submit and open their gates to the Turks, if they did not wish to fall victims to the barbarians for many forces were already on their way from Chorosan itself. And they, partly through fear of the multitude of barbarians, and partly because they were persuaded by Pucheas' advice, granted the Turks entry. The latter seized the Sultan Saisan and put out his eyes, and as they had not got the instrument used for this purpose, the candelabrum given to Saisan by the Emperor served as the instrument. On this occasion the vessel of light could be seen as the begetter of darkness and obscurity. But he could still see a little ray of light, and confided this to his nurse and also to his wife when he was led back and arrived in Iconium. By some means this fact came even to the ears of Masut and deeply vexed the barbarian's soul, and overcome with rage he ordered Elegmus (one of the high-born satraps) to strangle him with a bow-string. To this sad end came the Sultan Saisan through his imprudence in not listening to the Emperor's suggestion. But the Emperor continued his journey to the capital, and kept his army in the same perfect order all the way.

VII Anyone hearing the word 'line of battle' and 'phalanx' or 'captives' and 'booty' or again 'general' and 'captains,' will think he is hearing about the things which every historian and poet mentions in his writings. But this battle-formation was new and seemed very strange to everybody and was such as had never been seen before or handed down to posterity by any historian. For while advancing along the road to Iconium, the army marched in regular order and moved forward in time to the music of a flute. And if you had seen the whole phalanx you would have said it was remaining motionless when in motion and when halting that it was moving. For thanks to the close formation of the shields and the men standing in serried lines it looked like the immovable mountains, and when it changed its route it moved like a very great beast, for the whole phalanx walked and turned as if directed by one mind. But after it had reached Philomelium and rescued men on all sides from the hand of the barbarians, as we have related before somewhere, and enclosed all the captives and the women too and the children and the booty in the centre it marched slowly on its return and moved forward leisurely, as it were, and at an ant's pace. Moreover since many of the women were with child and many of the men afflicted with disease, whenever a woman's time for bringing forth came, a trumpet was sounded at a nod from the Emperor and made all the men stop and the whole army halted on the instant. And when he knew the child was born, a different call, not the usual one, but provocative of motion, was sounded and stirred them all up to continue the journey. And if anyone died, the same procedure took place, and the Emperor would be at the side of the dying man, and the priests were summoned to sing the hymns for the dying and administer the sacraments to the dying. And after the rites for the dead had been duly performed and not until the dead had been put in the earth and buried, was the army allowed to move even a step. And when it was the Emperor's time for lunch he invited the men and women who were labouring under illness or old-age and placed the greater part of the victuals before them and invited those who lunched with him to do the same. And the meal was like a complete banquet of the gods for there were no instruments, not even flutes or drums or any disturbing music at all. In this way he made himself a source

of supply to such persons and when he reached Damalis
(it was the evening), he did not wish to make a brilliant
entry into the city, nor did he allow any regal pomp or
theatrical preparations but reserved the crossing for the
next day, as indeed was necessary. But he himself embarked
on a small galley at once about lighting-up time and reached
the palace. On the morrow he was fully occupied in caring
for the captives and guests. The children who had lost their
parents and were afflicted with the bitter evil of orphanhood
he distributed among his relations and others who, as he knew,
led a well-conducted life, or sent them to the abbots of the
holy monasteries with orders to bring them up, not as slaves,
but as free children and allow them a thorough education
and instruction in the Holy Writings. Some he also admitted
into the orphanage which he had established himself and
which he had converted more or less into a school for those
anxious to learn, and told the governors of it to give these
orphans a good general education. For in the quarters near
the Acropolis, where the mouth of the sea widens, he had
discovered a very large church, dedicated to the great apostle
Paul, and here he built up a second city inside the Queen of
Cities. For as this church was on the highest spot in the
city it stood out like a citadel. And the new city was laid
out in a certain number of stades (someone may remember
how many) both in length and breadth ; and all round in a
circle were a number of houses, dwellings for the poor and—
which shews even more his humane nature—residences for
mutilated men. Here you could see them coming along
singly, either blind, or lame, or with some other defect. You
would have called it Solomon's porch on seeing it full of men
maimed either in their limbs or in their whole bodies. This
ring of houses is two-storied and semi-detached, for some of
these maimed men and women live up above twixt earth and
sky, while others creep along below on the ground-floor.
As for its size, anyone who wants to visit them would begin
in the morning and only complete the round in the evening.
Such is this city and such are its inhabitants. They have no
plots of ground or vineyards or any of those things over which
we imagine men spend their time, but each man and woman,
just like Job, dwells in the house built for him and automatically receives everything for his food and shelter from the
imperial hand.

The strangest point is that these indigent persons, just
as if they were lords with large estates and rich reserves,

have as stewards and organisers of their life the Emperor himself and the Emperor's friends working diligently on their behalf. For wherever there was a farm in a good situation, granted it was easily accessible, he gave it to these brethren, so that wine flows down for them in rivers, and bread and all the things men eat with bread. And those who eat are beyond counting. And I say, audaciously perhaps, that the Emperor's work can be compared with my Saviour's miracle, I mean the feeding of the seven, and five, thousand. But on that occasion five thousand were filled with five loaves as it was God who worked the miracle, whilst on this the work of humanity results from the divine command; again in the former case there was a miracle and here an Emperor's bounty provides his brethren with sustenance. I myself have seen an old woman tended by a young one and a blind man led by the hand by one who saw, and a man without feet have feet, though not his own but another's, and a man without hands using other men's hands, and babies nursed by other mothers, and paralytics waited upon by strong men. Thus the number of those who were nourished was double, for half were those who were ministered unto, and the other half were the ministers. The Emperor was unable to say to the paralytic, " Rise up and walk! " or to bid the blind to see, and him who had no feet to walk. This was only in the power of the Only begotten Son, who for our sakes became man and lived this life here below for the sake of men. But what was possible, that the Emperor did; he gave servants to every maimed man and the same care to the halt as to the healthy. So that anybody who wishes to understand this new city which my father had built from the foundations, would see that the city was fourfold, or rather multifold, for there were people below, people above and people waiting on the two lots of them. But who could estimate the number of those who were fed daily, or the daily expense, or the care bestowed on each individual ? for I attribute to him the things that lasted after him. For he assigned to them benefits from land and sea, and he provided them with as much relief from pain as possible. One of the most prominent men acts as guardian of this populous city, and its name is the Orphanage. And it is called the Orphanage because of the Emperor's kindness to orphans and to men retired from service . . . and the name which came from his care for orphans, held its ground. For all these things there are judicial courts and accounts are demanded from those who administer the poor

men's money ; and Golden Bulls allotting inalienable rights
to the persons who are maintained.   A large and important
body of clergy was selected for the church of the great preacher
Paul and there was also lavish expenditure on lights.   And
in that church you would notice the choir singing antiphonally,
for following Solomon's example he appointed male and female
singers to the church.   He also carefully arranged the work
of the deaconesses, and took a great deal of trouble about
the Iberian nuns domiciled there, who when they first migrated
to Constantinople used to beg from door to door ; but my
father's solicitude built for them too a large convent and
supplied them with food and fitting garments.

Now the famous Alexander of Macedonia may boast of his
town Alexandria in Egypt, of Bucephale in Media and of
Lysimachia in Ethiopia.   But the Emperor Alexius would
not be as proud of the towns raised by him, of which we know
he built a number in all parts, as he is of this one.

On entering you would find the sanctuaries and monasteries
to your left ; and on the right of the large sanctuary stood the
grammar-school for orphans collected from every race, in
which a master presided and the boys stood round him,
some puzzled over grammatical questions, and others writing
what are called grammatical analyses.   There could be seen
a Latin being trained, and a Scythian studying Greek, and a
Roman handling Greek texts and an illiterate Greek speaking
Greek correctly.   And Alexius' interest in a training in logic
was just as great.   But the art of grammatical parsing was an
invention of younger men of our generation.   I pass over the
Styliani and those called Lombards, and all who employed
themselves collecting names of every kind, and the Attici
and the members of the ecclesiastical college of our great
church, whose names I omit.   But now the study of these
lofty matters and of the poets and historians and the wisdom
to be gained from them do not receive even secondary attention ; but the absorbing occupation is the game of draughts
and other unlawful things.   I say this because I am grieved
at the absolute neglect of general education and it makes me
glow with anger because I myself spent so much time over
the same things.   And when I was released from that childish
teaching and betook myself to the study of rhetoric and
touched on philosophy and in between these sciences turned
to the poets and historians, by means of these I polished the
roughness of my speech, then with the aid of rhetoric I felt
that the highly complex complications of grammatical parsing

were to be condemned. I had to add these few words, not as being outside the subject, but as a corollary to my argument.

VIII After this, in the course of the years of his reign, a very great cloud of heretics arose, and the nature of their heresy was new and hitherto quite unknown to the church. For two very evil and worthless doctrines which had been known in former times, now coalesced ; the impiety, as it might be called, of the Manichæans, which we also call the Paulician heresy, and the shamelessness of the Massalians. This was the doctrine of the Bogomils compounded of the Massalians and the Manichæans. And probably it existed even before my father's time, but in secret ; for the sect of the Bogomils is very clever in aping virtue. And you would not find any long-haired worldling belonging to the Bogomils, for their wickedness was hidden under the cloak and cowl. A Bogomil looks gloomy and is covered up to the nose and walks with a stoop and mutters, but within he is an uncontrollable wolf. And this most pernicious race, which was like a snake hiding in a hole, my father lured and brought out to the light by chanting mysterious spells. For now that he had rid himself of much of his anxiety about the East and the West he turned his attention to more spiritual matters. For in all things he was superior to other men ; in teaching he surpassed those whose profession was teaching ; in battles and strategy he excelled those who were admired for their exploits. By this time the fame of the Bogomils had spread everywhere. (For Basil, a monk, was very wily in handling the impiety of the Bogomils ; he had twelve disciples whom he called ' apostles,' and also dragged about with him some female disciples, wretched women of loose habits and thoroughly bad, and he disseminated his wickedness everywhere.) This evil attacked many souls like fire, and the Emperor's soul could not brook it, so he began investigating the heresy. He had some of the Bogomils brought to the palace and all proclaimed a certain Basil as the teacher and chief representative of the Bogomilian heresy. Of these, one Diblatius was kept in prison, and as he would not confess when questioned, he was subjected to torture and then informed against the man called Basil, and the disciples he had chosen. Accordingly the Emperor entrusted several men with the search for him. And Satanael's arch-satrap, Basil, was brought to light, in monk's habit, with a withered countenance, clean shaven and tall of stature. The Emperor, wishing to elicit his inmost thoughts by compulsion under the disguise of

persuasion, at once invited the man on some righteous
pretext. And he even rose from his chair to greet him, and
made him sit by him and share his table, and threw out his
whole fishing-line and fixed various baits on the hooks for
this voracious whale to devour. And he made this monk,
who was so many-sided in wickedness, swallow all the poison
he offered him by pretending that he wished to become his
disciple, and not he only, but probably his brother, the Sebastocrator Isaac, also; he pretended too to value all the words he
spoke as if they came from a divine voice and to defer to him
in all things, provided only that the villain Basil would
effect his soul's salvation. "Most reverend father," he would
say (for the Emperor rubbed sweets on the rim of the cup
so that this demoniac should vomit forth his black thoughts),
"I admire thee for thy virtue, and beseech thee to teach me
the new doctrines thy Reverence has introduced, as those of
our Churches are practically worthless and do not bring
anybody to virtue." But the monk at first put on airs and
he, that was really an ass, dragged about the lion's skin with
him everywhere and shied at the Emperor's words, and yet
was puffed up with his praises, for the Emperor even had him
at his table. And in all this the Emperor's cousin [?] the
Sebastocrator, aided and abetted him in the play; and
finally Basil spued out the dogmas of his heresy. And how
was this done? A curtain divided the women's apartments
from the room where the two Emperors sat with the wretch
who blurted out and openly declared all he had in his soul;
whilst a secretary sitting on the inner side of the curtain committed his words to writing. And the nonsense-monger
seemed to be the teacher while the Emperor pretended to be
the pupil, and the secretary wrote down his doctrines. And
that man, stricken of God, spun together all that horrible
stuff and did not shun any abominable dogma, but even
despised our theology and misrepresented all our ecclesiastical
administration. And as for the churches, woe is me! he
called our sacred churches the temples of devils, and our
consecration of the body and blood of our one and greatest
High Priest and Victim he considered and condemned as
worthless. And what followed? the Emperor threw off
his disguise and drew the curtain aside; and the whole senate
was gathered together and the military contingent mustered,
and the elders of the church were present too. The episcopal
throne of the Queen of Cities was at that time occupied by
that most blessed of patriarchs, Lord Nicholas, the Gram-

marian. Then the execrable doctrines were read out, and proof was impossible to attack. And the defendant did not deny anything, but immediately bared his head and proceeded to counter-demonstrations and professed himself willing to undergo fire, scourging and a thousand deaths. For these erring Bogomils believe that they can bear any suffering without feeling pain, as the angels forsooth will pluck them out of the fire. And although all . . . and reproached him for his impiety, even those whom he had involved in his own ruin, he remained the same Basil, an inflexible and very brave Bogomil. And although he was threatened with burning and other tortures he clung fast to his demon and embraced his Satanael. After he was consigned to prison the Emperor frequently sent for him and frequently exhorted him to forswear his impiety, but all the Emperor's exhortations left him unchanged. But we must not pass over in silence the miracle which happened to him. Before the Emperor had begun to take severe measures against him, after his confession of impiety he would occasionally retire to a little house which had recently been prepared for him situated fairly close to the royal palace. It was evening and the stars above were shining in the clear air, and the moon was lighting up that evening, following the Synod. When the monk entered his cell about midnight, stones were automatically thrown, like hail, against his cell, and yet no hand threw them, nor was there any man to be seen stoning this devil's abbot. It was probably a burst of anger of Satanael's attendant demons who were enraged and annoyed because he had betrayed their [secrets?] to the Emperor and roused a fierce persecution against their heresy. A man called Parasceviotes who had been appointed guard over that infatuated old man to prevent his having intercourse with others and infecting them with his mischief, swore most solemnly that he had heard the clatter of the stones as they were thrown on the ground and on the tiles, and that he had seen the stones coming in successive showers but had not caught a glimpse anywhere of anyone throwing the stones. This throwing of stones was followed by a sudden earthquake which had shaken the ground, and the tiles of the roof had rattled. However Parasceviotes, as he asserted, was quite unafraid before he suspected it was the work of demons, but when he noticed that the stones seemed to be poured down like rain from above and that the old heresiarch had slunk inside and had shut himself in, he attributed

the work to demons and was not able to . . . whatever
was happening.

IX Let this be sufficient about that miracle. I wished
to expound the whole heresy of the Bogomils, but ' modesty
prevents me,' as the beautiful Sappho says somewhere, for
though a historian, I am a woman and the most honourable
of the Porphyrogeniti and Alexius' eldest scion, and what is
the talk of the vulgar had better be passed over in silence.
I am desirous of writing so as to set forth a full account of the
Bogomilian heresy ; but I will pass it over, as I do not wish
to defile my tongue. And those who wish to understand
the whole heresy of the Bogomils I will refer to the book
entitled *Dogmatic Panoply*, which was compiled by my father's
order. For there was a monk called Zygabenus, known to my
mistress, my maternal grandmother, and to all the members
of the priestly roll, who had pursued his grammatical studies
very far, was not unversed in rhetoric, and was the best
authority on ecclesiastical dogma ; the Emperor sent for
him and commissioned him to expound all the heresies, each
separately, and to append to each the holy Fathers' refutations
of it ; and amongst them too the heresy of the Bogomils,
exactly as that impious Basil had interpreted it. The Emperor
named this book the *Dogmatic Panoply*, and that name the
books have retained even to the present day. But now my
story must return to Basil's death.

The Emperor had summoned Basil's disciples and fellow-
mystics from all over the world, especially the so-called
twelve disciples and made trial of their opinions, and found
that they were openly Basil's followers. For the evil had
gone deep even into very great houses and had affected a very
large number. Consequently he condemned those aliens to
be burnt, the leader of the chorus and the chorus too. When
the Bogomils who had been discovered, were assembled, some
clung to their heresy, while others recanted absolutely and
resisted their accusers strongly and expressed their abhorrence
of the Bogomilian heresy. The Emperor was not inclined
to believe them, and to prevent many a Christian being
confounded with the Bogomils as being a Bogomil, and a
Bogomil escaping as a Christian, he invented a new device
for revealing clearly those who were really Christians.
Accordingly the next day he took his seat on the imperial
throne and many of the senate and the holy Synod were present
and a chosen few of the monks who were learned men. Then
all the Bogomils accused of heresy were placed together in

the centre and the Emperor commanded each to be examined again. Some confessed to being Bogomils and adhered stoutly to their heresy, while others denied it absolutely and called themselves Christians and when accused by others did not yield an inch, so he glowered at them and said, "To-day two pyres shall be lighted and on one of them a cross shall be fixed in the ground itself. Then you shall all be given your choice and those who are ready to die to-day for their Christian faith, can separate themselves from the others and walk to the pyre with the cross, while those who cling to the Bogomilian heresy shall be thrown on the other. For it is better that even Christians should die, than live to be persecuted as Bogomils and offend the consciences of many. Go now and let each one of you choose his station." With this verdict against the Bogomils the Emperor pretended to have closed the matter. They were at once taken and led away and a large crowd had gathered and stood round about them. Then pyres were lighted, ' seven times as large as they were wont to be,' as the hymn-writer says, in the place called Tzycanisterin[1]; the flames rose to the heavens, and the cross stood above the one ; each of the condemned was given his choice to walk to which of the two pyres he wished, as all were destined to be burnt. Seeing that there was no escape, the orthodox among them walked to the pyre with the cross, ready really to suffer martyrdom ; whereas the godless ones who clung to their abominable heresy turned to the other. And they were all on the point of being thrown on the pyres at the same time and the bystanders all grieved for the Christians who were now to be burnt, and were very wroth against the Emperor, for they were ignorant of his plan. But an order from the Emperor came just in time to prevent the executioners carrying out their duties. Having in this way obtained certain proof of those who were really Bogomils he released the Christians, who had been falsely accused, with many admonitions. The others he recommitted to prison, but had the impious Basil's apostles separated from the rest. And these he sent for daily, and taught some himself, exhorting them earnestly to abandon their hideous religion, and for the others he ordered some picked men of the hierarchy to come every day and teach them the orthodox faith and advise them to relinquish the Bogomilian heresy. And some of them did change for the better and were released

---

[1] — The palace polo-grounds.

from confinement, but others were kept in prison and died in
their heresy, but were amply supplied with food and clothing.

X However all the members of the holy synod and the
chief monks, as well as the patriarch of that time, Nicholas,
decreed that Basil who was the heresiarch and quite un-
repentant, deserved to be burnt. The Emperor was of the
same opinion and after conversing with him several times
and recognizing that the man was mischievous and would
not abandon his heresy, he finally had an immense pyre
built in the Hippodrome. A very large trench was dug and
a quantity of wood, all tall trees piled up together, made the
structure look like a mountain. When the pile was lighted,
a great crowd slowly collected on the floor and steps of the
circus in eager expectation of what was to happen. On
the opposite side a cross was fixed and the impious man was
given a choice, for if he dreaded the fire and changed his
mind, and walked to the cross, then he should be delivered
from burning. A number of heretics were there watching
their leader Basil. He shewed himself contemptuous of all
punishment and threats, and while he was still at a distance
from the fire he began to laugh and talk marvels, saying that
angels would snatch him from the middle of the fire, and he
proceeded to chant these words of David's, ' It shall not come
nigh thee; only with thine eyes shalt thou behold.' But
when the crowd stood aside and allowed him to have a free
view of that terrifying sight, the burning pyre (for even at a
good distance he could feel the fire, and saw the flames rising
high and as it were thundering and shooting out sparks of
fire which rose to the top of the stone obelisk which stands in
the centre of the Hippodrome), then the bold fellow seemed
to flinch from the fire and be disturbed. For as if wholly
desperate, he constantly turned away his eyes and clapped
his hands and beat his thigh. And yet in spite of being thus
affected by the mere sight he was adamant. For the fire
did not soften his iron will, nor did the messages sent by the
Emperor subdue him. For either great madness had seized
him under the present stress of misfortunes and he had lost
his mind and had no power to decide about what was advantageous ; or, as seems more likely, the devil that possessed his
soul had steeped it in the deepest darkness. So there stood
that abominable Basil, unmoved by any threat or fear, and
gaped now at the fire and now at the bystanders. And all
thought him quite mad for he did not rush to the pyre nor
did he draw back, but stood fixed and immovable on the

spot he had first taken up. Now many tales were going round and his marvellous talk was bandied about on every tongue, so the executioners were afraid that the demons protecting Basil might perhaps, by God's permission, work some wonderful new miracle, and the wretch be seen snatched unharmed from the middle of the mighty fire and transported to some very frequented place. In that case the second state would be worse than the first, so they decided to make an experiment. For, while he was talking marvels and boasting that he would be seen unharmed in the middle of the fire, they took his cloak and said, " Now let us see whether the fire will touch your garments," and they threw it right into the middle of the pyre. But Basil was so uplifted by the demon that was deluding him that he said, " Look at my cloak floating up to the sky ! " Then they ' recognizing the web from the edge,' took him and pushed him, clothes, shoes and all, into the middle of the pyre. And the flames, as if deeply enraged against him, ate the impious man up, without any odour arising or even a fresh appearance of smoke, only one thin smoky line could be seen in the midst of the flames. For even the elements are excited against the impious ; whereas, to speak truthfully, they spare those beloved of God, just as once upon a time in Babylon the fire retreated from those young men who were dear to God, and enclosed them like a golden chamber. In this case the men who lifted up the accursed Basil had scarcely placed him on the pyre before the flames seemed to dart forward to snatch hold of him. Then the people looking on clamoured loudly and demanded that all the rest who belonged to Basil's pernicious sect should be thrown into the fire as well, but the Emperor did not allow it but ordered them to be confined in the porches and verandahs of the largest palace. After this the concourse was dismissed. Later, the godless ones were transferred to another very strong prison into which they were cast and after pining away for a long time died in their impiety. This was the last and crowning act of the Emperor's long labours and successes and it was an innovation of startling boldness.

And I think that men who lived then and associated with him must even now be marvelling at what was done then and think it was not real, and it must seem a dream and mere vision to them. For ever since the time when shortly after Diogenes' accession the barbarians first overstepped the boundaries of the Roman Empire and he at first start, as they say, made his disastrous expedition against them, from that time right on to my father's reign the barbarian power was never checked, but swords and spears were whetted against the Christians and there were battles, wars and massacres. Cities were wiped out, countries were laid waste, and the whole Roman territory was defiled with the blood of Christians. For some perished miserably by darts or spears, while others were driven from their homes and led away captive to the cities of Persia. And dread seized them all and they hurried to hide themselves from the dangers that threatened, in the caves and groves and mountains and hills. Among these some lamented aloud over the ills which their friends who had been taken away to Persia were suffering ; the few others who still survived in the Roman lands were sighing deeply, and lamenting, one for a son, another for a daughter ; or weeping for a brother or a nephew cut off before his time, and shedding bitter tears like women. In fact there was no condition of life free from tears and groans. Of the Emperors not one except a few, I mean Tzimisces and the Emperor Basil, before my father's time ever dared touch the land of Asia at all, even with their toes.

XI But why am I writing of these things ? for I notice that I have turned off from the high-road. The subject of history I have imposed upon myself necessitates a double duty, both to narrate and to lament the events that befell the Emperor, that is to say, to narrate his achievements on the one hand and on the other to compose a monody on the events which have wrung my heart. With these I would range his death and the destruction of all earthly fortune. But indeed I remember some words of my father's which disparaged history-writing, but incited one to elegies and lamentations. For I often heard him, and once I even heard him checking the Empress, my mother, when she ordered wise men to write a history, and thereby hand down to posterity his labours and all his conflicts and trials, saying they had better lament over him and deplore his misfortunes.

A year and a half had not passed after my father's return from his expedition before a second terrible illness fell upon him, and wove the noose of death for him, or to speak the truth, the downfall and destruction of everything. But since the magnitude of my subject demands it, and as I was very dear to my father and mother from the cradle, I am going to transgress the laws of history and relate, little as I wish to do so, my father's death.

A race-meeting had taken place and in consequence of a violent wind which was blowing at the time, the rheumatics had ebbed, as it were, and retreated from his extremities and fixed themselves in one of his shoulders. The majority of the physicians did not appreciate the danger to us which this threatened. But Callicles Nicholas (for so he was styled), was a foreteller to us of our fearful ills and said he was very afraid that, as the rheumatics had retreated from the extremities and attacked another part, they would cause the danger to the sick man to become incurable. But we could not believe him because we did not wish to. And not one of the doctors at that time, except Callicles, urged the cleansing of his system by purgatives. And he was not accustomed to taking these purgatives, in fact he was quite unaccustomed to drinking medicine. And so the majority of the doctors and above all Pantechnes Michael absolutely forbade any purging. But Callicles foresaw the future and said to them most emphatically, " Now the matter has left the extremities and settled in the shoulder and throat ; afterwards, if it is not evacuated by purgatives, it will flow into one of the principal members or into the heart itself, and cause irremediable mischief." For I was there myself by order of my mistress to adjudge the physicians' arguments, and I heard all they said and for my part agreed with Callicles' proposals. However the vote of the majority prevailed. Then at length the pain after exerting its sway over the imperial body for the usual number of days died away and the invalid recovered his health. Six months had not passed before a deadly sickness took hold of him, caused probably by his deep despondency over daily business and the mass of public duties. And I often heard him speaking about it to my mother, and, as it were, accusing it to her. " What in the world is this disease which has attacked my breathing ? for I should like to take a deep, full breath and get rid of this trouble worrying my heart. I have tried to do it repeatedly, but cannot manage to lift even a particle of the weight that is oppressing me. For the rest it is as if a very heavy stone were lying on my heart which cuts my breathing when I sigh, and I cannot understand the reason of it nor what has brought this suffering upon me. And I will tell you something else too, dearest soul, partner of my afflictions and thoughts, a fit of gaping often attacks me and when I am inhaling my breath gets caught and causes me very great pain. If you know what this new illness of mine is, please

speak out." When the Empress listened to him and heard
what he suffered she seemed to be suffering from the same
disease herself and her breathing too was caught by asthma,
so deeply affected was she by the Emperor's words. She
frequently sent for the more skilled physicians and compelled
them to enquire closely into the nature of the disease, and
asked to be taught the immediate and the indirect cause of
it. They placed their hands on his arteries and acknowledged
that they found in every movement of the arteries proof of
multifold irregularities, but they were quite unable to discover the cause. They knew too that the Emperor's diet
was not rich, but exceedingly moderate and plain like that
of athletes and soldiers and such as to prevent the rise of
humours due to too rich a diet. Consequently they referred
his difficulty in breathing to some other cause, and said that
the immediate cause of his illness was nothing but his intense
application to business and his continual and numerous
worries, by which his heart got inflamed, and drew all that
was superfluous out of the rest of the body. After this the
dreadful disease which had seized the Emperor gave him no
respite whatever, but throttled him like a noose. And the
disease made so much progress daily that it no longer came on
at intervals, but continuously and incessantly, and the
Emperor was unable to lie on either side and had not the
strength to draw a breath without making a violent effort.
Then every physician was summoned and the Emperor's
illness was the subject of their discussion. They were divided
in their opinions and at discord, and each one diagnosed it
differently and tried to apply the treatment according with
his diagnosis. But, however that was, the Emperor was in a
very bad state ; for not even for a moment could he draw
breath freely. He was obliged to sit upright to breathe at
all ; and if by chance he lay on his back or on one side, alas !
for the consequent suffocation. For he was unable to draw
in or out even a tiny drift of the outer air by the channels
for expiration and inspiration. And, whenever sleep pitied
him and overpowered him, then also he was liable to suffocation ; so that at all times whether sleeping or awake, the
danger of strangulation hung over him. As he was not
given purgatives they had recourse to phlebotomy, and they
made an incision at the elbow ; however, he derived no
benefit from it, but breathed with just the same difficulty as
before and there was always the danger that by breathing
so little he would expire under our hands. But his condition

grew easier after he had been given an antidote of pepper. And in our delight we did not know how to shew our joy, but we offered up prayers of thanksgiving to God. However, it was all a delusion, for on the third or fourth day the same fits of suffocation and the same difficulties with the lungs attacked the Emperor again. I wonder whether he was not made worse by that draught, for it spread the humours without getting a hold over them, and drove them into the cavities of the arteries and aggravated his illness. From that time on we could not find any way of making him lie down comfortably, for the disease had reached its height. And the Emperor would pass the night from evening to dawn without getting any sleep, nor could he easily take nourishment nor any of the things that might have helped him. I have often, or rather continuously, seen my mother spending a sleepless night with the Emperor, sitting behind him on the bed and supporting him in her arms and relieving his breathing somewhat. And verily the tears she shed were more abundant than the waters of the Nile. The care she bestowed on him by day and night, and the work she did while nursing him and continually changing his position, and devising all kinds of changes in the bedding, these cannot be described. But by no means at all was he able to get any relief. For the illness followed, or rather accompanied the Emperor like a noose, and never left off strangling him. As no remedy could be found for the disease, the Emperor moved to the part of the palace which looked to the South. For during this oppression he found a little refreshment in being moved, and the Empress contrived that he should have it continually, for she had legs fitted at the head and foot of the Emperor's couch and then ordered men to lift him and carry him, and there were relays of men for this work. After this he was removed from the large palace to Mangana. But even when this had been done, it did not contribute to the Emperor's recovery. When the Empress saw that the disease was gaining ground and she quite despaired of any human help, she made still more fervent intercessions to God on his behalf, and had numbers of candles lighted in every sanctuary and continuous and endless hymns sung, and largess distributed to the dwellers in every land and on every sea. And all the monks who dwelt on mountains or in caves or led their solitary life elsewhere she stirred up to making lengthy supplications. And all those who were sick or confined in prison and worn out with suffering she made very rich by donations and invited

them to offer prayers for the Emperor. But when the
Emperor's abdomen had swollen and become very prominent,
and his feet had swollen too and fever mastered his imperial
body, then the doctors had recourse to cautery and thought
little of the fever. But all treatment was useless and vain,
nor did the cauterization help, but his digestive and respira-
tory organs remained in the same bad state. And now as if
from some other source the rheumatics introduced themselves
into the uvula and the palate, as the medical fraternity term
it, and his gums became inflamed and his larynx congested
and his tongue swollen; consequently the ducts, through
which nourishment had to pass, were narrowed and closed
up at their extremities and the terrible evil of starvation
loomed before us. And yet, God knows, I occupied myself
diligently with the preparation of his food and brought it
to him daily with my own hands and tried to make it all
easy to swallow. All remedies applied for healing the inflamed tumours seemed . . . and all our efforts and those
of the physicians were vain. Eleven days had gone by since
the final stage of the disease attacked him, rose to its height
and threatened danger . . . his condition became worse
and diarrhœa supervened. Thus one ill upon another was
heaped upon us at that time. And now neither the disciples
of Asclepius nor we who nursed the Emperor knew which way
to look, nor . . . but all things pointed to the end.
For the future all our outlook was in confusion and tempest-
tossed, our normal course of life was disturbed, and fear and
danger hovered together over our heads. Yet even amidst
these imminent dangers, the Empress retained her brave
spirit, and during this crisis she shewed her courage most,
for she curbed her passionate grief and stood like a conqueror
in the Olympic games wrestling against those terribly cruel
pains. For she was wounded in soul and anguished in heart
at seeing the Emperor in such a state. But she pulled herself
together and remained firm in face of these sufferings, and,
though she was mortally wounded and pierced to the marrow
with grief, nevertheless she bore up. And yet her tears fell
in floods and the beauty of her face became withered, and her
soul seemed suspended in her nostrils. It was the fifteenth
of August and the Thursday of the week during which the
death of our Immaculate Lady, the Mother of God, is celebrated. In the morning some of the Asclepiadæ had anointed
the Emperor's head, for so it seemed right to them, and then
they went away home, not idly nor because of any pressing

necessity, but because they knew that danger was closely impending over the Emperor. His principal physicians were three, the excellent Nicholas Callicles, and the second, Michael Pantechnes, who got his surname from his family and the . . . the eunuch Michael. As for the Empress, the whole band of relations crowded round her and compelled her to take food . . . she had not had any sleep . . . but had watched several successive nights . . . nursing the Emperor . . . she obeyed. But when the last fainting fit attacked the Emperor . . . she expecting the . . . threw herself down on the [floor] and kept on [lamenting] and beating her breast and bemoaning the ills that had befallen her, and wished to pour forth her life on the spot, but could not. Then, although he was dying, and pain was overwhelming him, the Emperor proved himself stronger than [suffering and] death, as it were, and was distressed about the Empress, and tried with one of his daughters to subdue her excessive anguish. This was the third one, the Porphyrogenita Eudocia. For Mary, acting like another Mary, though not sitting at his feet then, as the other did on that occasion, but up by his head, was busy giving him water to drink from a big goblet, not from a cup, so that drinking might not be too difficult for him, as his palate was inflamed and his tongue too and his larynx, and she wanted to refresh him. Then he addressed some firm and manly counsels to the Empress, which were his last ones. " Why do you abandon yourself in this way to your grief for my death, and compel us to anticipate the end which is hastening towards us ? why do you not think of yourself and your future difficulties, instead of giving yourself up entirely to the flood of grief that has overwhelmed you ? " This he said to her, but it only tore open the Empress' wounds of sorrow the more. I myself tried every shift, and by God who knows all, I swear to the friends still living and to the men who will read this history later, that I was in no wise better than a madman, for I had become wholly absorbed in my grief. At that time indeed I despised philosophy and learning for I was wholly occupied with my father and in service for him. At one moment I watched the movements of his pulse and studied his respiration, then at another I would turn to my mother and cheer her up as much as possible. But . . . the regions were quite incurable . . . the Emperor could not recover from his last faint and the Empress's soul was hastening to depart at the same time as the Emperor's. Thus

was I placed . . . and in very truth in the words of the Psalm-
ist, "The pains of death encompassed" us at that hour.
And then I felt I was losing my senses . . . for I
had grown mad and did not know [what would become of me]
and whither I should turn, when I looked at the Empress
sunk in the sea of her troubles, and the Emperor, with his
continual faints, drawing near to the end of his life. But he
managed to recover from his second faint, as my dearest sister
Mary sprinkled cold water and essence of roses on him, and he
ordered her to do the same for the Empress. Soon he fell into
his third faint . . . and a change of place for the imperial couch
seemed advisable . . . on the part of those busied about his
body, and we carried the Emperor on his couch to another
part of the five-storied building, in the hope that he might
breathe fresher air and recover from his faint. For that room
looked to the North and there were no houses . . . to the doors.

Now the Emperor's successor had already gone away
secretly to the house set apart for him, seeing the Emperor's
. . . and hastened his going and hurried to the great palace.
The city at that time . . . was disturbed, but not entirely
. . . But the Empress said, "Let everything go to destruction " . . . and wailed "the diadem and the kingdom and
the power and every Empire and thrones and principalities,
and let us start the dirge." And I joined in her wailing,
forgetting all else, and mourned with her and . . . they tore
their hair with shrill lamentations. But we restored her to
her senses. For the Emperor was at his last gasp and,
as the saying is, was 'letting his soul break loose.' On the
ground at his head the Empress had thrown herself still
dressed . . . and with her red shoes and . . . she was
wounded and did not know how [to still] the burning sorrow
of her heart. Some of the Asclepiadæ came back again and
after waiting a little, felt the Emperor's pulse . . . the
beating of his arteries . . . all the same they dissembled
about the fatal moment and held out fair hopes which were
not justified. But they did this with a definite purpose
for they thought that, when life departed from the Emperor's
body, the Empress would breathe her last too. But the
intelligent Empress did not know whether to believe or
disbelieve them. She believed because she had long known
them as skilled men, but she felt she must disbelieve them
because she saw that the Emperor's life stood on the razor's
edge. So standing on the balance, as it were, she often looked
steadfastly at me and waited for my oracular decision as she

had been wont to do at other critical moments. And she waited for the prophecy I should give. And Mary, my mistress and dearest of my sisters, the ornament of our race, the constant woman, the stronghold of every virtue, stood between the Emperor and Empress, near his hand, and sometimes prevented her looking straight at the Emperor. But I again put my right hand on his wrist and watched the movement of his pulse, and . . . her putting her hands to her face . . . the veil. For in the situation she was in she intended to change her imperial dress, but I stopped her, whenever I noticed a little strength . . . in the pulse. But I was mistaken . . . for what seemed to me . . . was not strength but since the great . . . of breathing . . . the working of the artery and of the lung was interrupted. Then I let go the Emperor's hand and . . . to the Empress . . . I again applied [my hand] to his wrist . . . asphyxia. She often signed to me as she wanted me to tell her the state of his pulse. But when . . . I touched it again and I recognized that all his strength was giving way and that the pulse in the arteries had finally stopped, then I bowed my head and, exhausted and fainting I looked down to the ground, said nothing, but clasped my hands over my face and stepped back and wept. The Empress understood what that meant and in absolute despair uttered a sudden loud, far-reaching shriek. How can I possibly picture the disaster which overtook the whole world ? or how deplore my own condition ? the Empress took off her royal veil and caught hold of a knife and cut off all her hair close to the skin and threw off the red shoes from her feet and demanded ordinary black sandals. And when she wanted to change her purple dress for a black garment, no dress could be found at hand, But the third of my sisters had garments suitable for the time and occasion, as she had already experienced the ills of widowhood, so the Empress took them and dressed herself and put on a plain dark veil on her head. And at this moment the Emperor resigned his holy soul to God, and my sun went down. . . . Persons who were addicted to emotion sang dirges, beat their breasts and raised their voices to heaven in shrill laments . . . weeping for their benefactor who had . . . all things to them. But even to this day I am doubtful whether I am alive and writing this and recounting the Emperor's death, and I put my hands to my eyes and wonder whether the events I am relating now are not a dream, or if not a dream, whether it is not a delusion, and madness on my part, some strange and monstrous fancy.

For, as he has gone, why am I still numbered among the living and . . . or why did I not resign my soul too or expire directly he had expired and die without feeling ? or, if that was not to be my fate, why did I not throw myself down from some high and lofty place or cast myself into the waves of the sea ? I have recorded my life with its great misfortunes. But, as is said in the tragedy ' there is no ill or God-sent calamity whose weight I could not bear.' For verily God has made me the repository of many sorrows. I have lost the shining light of the world, the great Alexius ; and verily his soul was master over his suffering body. Another very great light has been extinguished too, or rather that brightly shining moon, the great achievement and pride of the East and the West, the Empress Irene. And yet we live and breathe ! One ill has followed upon another and hurricanes have beaten down upon us and we have been forced to see the climax of our troubles, the death of the Cæsar, and we have been reserved for such terrible catastrophes. For some days the ill prevailed and skill failed and I let myself sink into an ocean of despondency and amidst it all I only grieved that my soul still lingered in my body. And, it seems likely, that if I had not been adamantine, or fashioned of some other such substance . . . and distracted from my real self, I should have perished at once ; but now I live and have died a thousand deaths. We hear from some the wonderful story of Niobe . . . changed into stone by grief . . . then even after the change which transformed her into an insensitive substance her sufferings were immortal even in that insensitive substance. But I in truth am more unfortunate than she was, because after these very great and supreme misfortunes I am still alive and shall still feel others. It would have been better to be turned to senseless stone . . . and to have remained with tears flowing . . . without any feeling for sufferings . . . than to endure such ills ; and that intolerable troubles in the palace should be stirred up against me by men is more wretched than even Niobe's sufferings . . . the evils having proceeded so far . . . ceased. After the death of the imperial pair the loss of the Cæsar and my consequent grief would have been sufficient for the contrition of my soul and body ; but now like rivers flowing down from high mountains . . . the rivers of ills . . . into one torrent which is inundating my house. But now my history must be concluded, for if I were to describe sad events any longer I might become bitter.

INDEX

DATE DUE

OCT 2 1993			
			PRINTED IN U.S.A.